Bargaining for National Security

Studies in International Relations

Charles W. Kegley, Jr., and Donald J. Puchala,
Series Editors

BARGAINING FOR NATIONAL SECURITY:

The Postwar Disarmament Negotiations

by LLOYD JENSEN

UNIVERSITY OF SOUTH CAROLINA PRESS

Published in Columbia, South Carolina, by the
University of South Carolina Press

Manufactured in the United States of America

Library of Congress Cataloging-in-Publication Data

Jensen, Lloyd.
    Bargaining for national security: the postwar disarmament negotiations / by Lloyd
Jensen.
        p. cu. — (Studies in international relations)
    Bibliography: p.
    Includes index.
    ISBN 0-87249-529-9
    1. Nuclear arms control—United States. 2. Nuclear arms control—Soviet Union.
3. United States—Foreign relations—Soviet Union. 4. Soviet Union—Foreign relations—United States. 5. United States—National security. 6. Soviet Union—National
security.
    I. Title. II. Series: Studies in international relations (Columbia, S.C.)
JX1974.7.J445 1988   87-25054
327.1'74'0973—dc19   CIP

To my brothers

*Gene, Jay, Boyd, and Eldon and
in memory of my sister Beverly.
May their worlds be peaceful
and secure.*

Contents

Contents   vii

Tables

Acknowledgments

My debts in producing this study are many. I would like to thank Sage Publishers for permission to publish parts of two previous articles, revised portions of which can be found in chapter 3: "Negotiating Strategic Arms Control, 1969–79," *Journal of Conflict Resolution* 28 (September 1984): 535–59 and "Soviet-American Bargaining Behavior in the Postwar Disarmament Negotiations," *Journal of Conflict Resolution* 7 (September 1963): 522–41. Parts of chapter 5 have been drawn from my previously published book, *Return from the Nuclear Brink: National Interest and the Nuclear Nonproliferation Treaty* (Lexington, Mass.: D. C. Heath, 1974) and brief sections of chapters 6 and 8 were previously included in "SALT on the Shelf: Problems and Prospects," *Parameters: Journal of the U.S. Army War College* 10 (December 1980): 57–64.

Support for part of the research on the book was provided by Temple University in the form of a study leave during the academic year 1982–83. Stephen Saetz and Jongduck Park served as able research assistants. The project could not have been completed without the excellent word-processing skills of Gloria Basmajian.

Several colleagues have read portions of the manuscript and have been generous in providing useful advice. These include James Bennett, Daniel Druckman, Bernard Mennis, and Lynn H. Miller. My wife Jane has again taken time away from her own professional activities to serve as both loving critic and editor. Needless to say, I am grateful to all, but none need share the blame for any of the limitations found herein.

Bargaining for National Security

1

The Search for
National Security

The advent of the nuclear age brought with it increased concern about
national security as well as human survival. Since the first atomic
bomb was exploded over Hiroshima on August 6, 1945, advances in
nuclear technology and delivery systems have only served to enhance
the potential dangers. Whereas almost 100,000 people lost their lives
on the fateful day in Hiroshima, nuclear weapons currently threaten
the lives of hundreds of millions. The nuclear revolution has resulted
in the development of bombs measured in megatons (millions of tons
of TNT equivalent). The Hiroshima bomb, estimated at about 13 kilotons, is a mere toy compared to contemporary thermonuclear
devices—one of which was detonated by the Soviet Union and measured more than 50 megatons. In terms of TNT equivalence, such a
device is about four thousand times the size of the Hiroshima bomb.
Nuclear weapons of this size, however, make little military sense, for
they tend only to dig deeper holes. Several bombs in the low megatonnage range spread over an area are likely to be more efficient and can
be delivered by intercontinental ballistic missiles.

Not only has there been a revolution in the destructiveness of nuclear
warheads, but the means for delivering those warheads have improved
substantially in terms of capacity, speed, and accuracy. Since nuclear
weapons have been reduced in size over the years, more destructive payloads can be carried in each delivery system. The bombs dropped on
Hiroshima and Nagasaki were of such a size and weight that only one
atomic weapon could be carried in a bomber. Today that same destructive capability can be transported in an attaché case. The miniaturization
of nuclear bombs became particularly significant as the world entered
the missle age, for missles have a more limited carrying capacity than
bombers.

Missiles have also substantially reduced the delivery time required in transporting nuclear warheads to their destination. A thirty-minute warning time is all that is available for an intercontinental ballistic missile (ICBM) traveling between the Soviet Union and the United States. This time is cut to fifteen minutes or less with the submarine-launched ballistic missile (SLBM) or intermediate-range ballistic missile (IRBM).

Also contributing to the nuclear weapons threat is the increased accuracy of missiles. Whereas early missiles might be accurate only within several miles, both sides now have ICBMs capable of hitting within about three hundred feet of target. This pinpoint accuracy not only guarantees maximum destructiveness but also makes ICBM silos highly vulnerable to attack even when these silos are hardened with reinforced concrete.

As the technology race proceeds unabated, there is increasing concern with the potential destructiveness of nuclear war. Reflective of this concern is the growth of an extensive nuclear freeze movement and the publication of a number of treatises pointing out the dangers involved. Among the most influential of these is Jonathan Schell's *The Fate of the Earth*, which calls attention not only to the immediate death and destruction that could result from nuclear war but also to the long-term harm resulting from the destruction of ozone layers, lingering radiation, genetic damage affecting future generations, and agricultural and ecological damage.[1] Carl Sagan and other eminent scientists have estimated that only 500 to 2,000 nuclear warheads would be required to induce a climatic catastrophe.[2] The explosions from these weapons would create what they called a nuclear winter by shutting off sunlight for a considerable period of time. Nuclear war could indeed produce a world in which the living would envy the dead.

At the same time that the United States and the Soviet Union seemed to be marching toward Armageddon in what appeared to be an almost unrestrained arms race, the two were energetically involved in negotiations designed to restrain that race. Dozens of proposals have been made during hundreds of meetings in what sometimes seems to have been an almost futile effort to constrain various weapons systems. There have, of course, been some achievements along the way such as the successful negotiation of the Limited Test Ban Treaty in 1963, the Nuclear Nonproliferation Treaty in 1968, the SALT I and SALT II Treaties during the 1970s, along with a host of other less noteworthy agreements which will be examined in this study. But, on the whole, it must be said that the United States and the Soviet Union have chosen to rely principally upon military deterrence in their attempts to provide for their national security.

Before turning our attention to the long and tortuous course of U.S.-Soviet bargaining in the postwar disarmament negotiations, which is the subject of this study, it might be well to examine the role that nuclear deterrence can and has played in providing whatever security the world has enjoyed since World War II. It will be argued, however, that arms control negotiations can be useful in enhancing the stability of nuclear deterrence and should therefore be given serious consideration in the search for national security even though the achievements to date have not been overwhelming.

SECURITY THROUGH DETERRENCE

While nuclear weapons threaten the survival of the earth, they may have also provided a certain level of international stability by virtue of their deterrent value. The nuclear age has witnessed one of the longest periods of peace in European history. Advocates of nuclear deterrence argue that this phenomenon can be attributed to the existence of a deterrent system that has made war between the two superpowers unthinkable. In the past, other destructive weapons systems have been viewed as playing a similar role. For example, the airplane, because of its perceived deterrent value and the initial lack of any defense against it, was believed by some political leaders to make war in the future unlikely.

Establishing a causal link between the existence of nuclear weapons and the deterrence of war is not a simple matter. In order to prove that deterrence has been effective, it is necessary to demonstrate that the opposing power had the intention of attacking but failed to do so only because of the existence of nuclear weapons. Though a state may retreat in a confrontation, the retreat may be attibuted to factors other than the nuclear deterrent, such as a recognition that the possible gain is not worth other negative repercussions like adverse world opinion, loss of support of allies, or perhaps even internal opposition.

In examining Soviet behavior in the postwar world, there is reason to doubt whether it has been U.S. nuclear superiority that has deterred the Soviet Union from being more aggressive than it might have been. The fact of the matter is that the Soviet Union engaged in greater risk-taking behavior vis-à-vis the West before the Soviets achieved nuclear parity with the United States.[3] The Soviet Union pursued an adventurous foreign policy during the Stalin period despite the fact that the United States enjoyed an atomic monoply until 1949 and considerable military superiority for many years thereafter. In many respects, Nikita Khrushchev was more erratic and willing to take risks than his successor, Leonid

Brezhnev, yet the balance of military forces was more favorable to the Soviet Union during Brezhnev's tenure. A Brookings Institution study revealed that the Soviet Union engaged more frequently in "coercive action" in the late 1960s than in the mid-1970s, although it was only in the latter period that Soviet strategic nuclear strength had begun to approach that of the United States.[4]

Despite a strategic balance that has become more favorable to Moscow, an analysis of 215 postwar incidents in which the United States used or threatened the use of force revealed that the outcomes have actually been more favorable to the United States when U.S. military superiority has been less extreme. Short-term outcomes were found to be positive for the United States in its confrontations with the USSR in only 43 percent of the cases when the strategic balance was 100 to 1 or greater in favor of the United States, but this figure increased to 92 percent when the ratio of superiority decreased to less than 10 to 1.[5]

Even the events during the 1962 Cuban missile crisis, which is often used to illustrate the efficacy of nuclear deterrence, fail to prove that Khrushchev backed down primarily because of U.S. nuclear superiority. His willingness to concede had perhaps more to do with the asymmetry of interests between the two superpowers. Cuba and the missiles were peripheral issues for the Soviet Union but central to American concerns. Had the national interests of the two parties been more equivalent, the results may well have been different.

While it might be argued that nuclear deterrence has been effective in reducing the frequency of war in Europe, there is still reason for being wary about relying upon the balance of nuclear terror for world peace since that balance is a delicate one at best. A number of factors threaten the stability of the nuclear deterrent system, particularly those factors that might lead to an accidental nuclear war. The number of false warnings about an imminent Soviet missile attack has been substantial. One study noted at least 147 false indications during an eighteen-month period.[6] In one instance during June 1980, American forces were on nuclear alert for six minutes because of a computer error created by the malfunction of a circuit chip worth 46 cents. Accidental war might also arise because of psychological or physical problems among those who have charge of the nuclear deterrent. A House subcommittee reported that in 1977, a typical year, 1,219 American military personnel with some form of access to or responsibility for nuclear weapons were removed from duty because of mental disturbances, 265 for alcoholism, and 1,365 for drug abuse.[7] Political leaders themselves have not been immune from psychological breakdown, and the intense pressures resulting from international crises and fear serve only to increase the dangers of nuclear hostilities.

In addition to the possibility of nuclear war erupting by accident, there is also the danger of such a war arising by miscalculation. If one side or the other believes a nuclear strike is imminent, there would be considerable pressure to deliver the first blow. Such pressures would be particularly acute whenever one's retaliatory capability is felt to be vulnerable.

The threat of miscalculation is enhanced by virtue of the rapid pace of technology. The fear that the other side may be close to a scientific breakthrough is likely to cause particularly anxious moments. Most threatening would be a system capable of intercepting the bulk of the incoming missiles, thus signaling the end of deterrence. Since the incentives would be high to assure that the adversary never attain such a position, a preemptive strike would have to be seriously considered by the state fearing that it was about to lose the technological race for an effective strategic defense shield.

Miscalculation may result from concern about the viability of command and control structures in the nuclear age. John Steinbrunner has estimated that 50 to 100 nuclear weapons could disrupt the central nervous system of the U.S. command structure and a similar number could probably disable the Soviet Union.[8] In October 1981 President Reagan announced a $20 billion effort to improve command and control structures—a task he viewed as having higher priority than building new weapons systems.

The danger of nuclear weapons spreading to other nations and perhaps even falling into the hands of terrorist groups adds yet another threat to the stability of the nuclear deterrent system. Not only does increasing the number of nuclear powers increase the statistical probability that one of them might unleash a nuclear war but the new nuclear weapons state is perhaps more likely to use its recently gained nuclear capability than are existing nuclear powers. Any new nuclear weapons state is likely to have a less protected nuclear weapons capability since the costs of protecting offensive weapons may be prohibitively expensive for a state that has had to spend so much of its limited resources to develop its nuclear capability. In making the sacrifice to build a nuclear weapons capability, the state has also undoubtedly neglected its conventional capability, giving that state little option but to use its nuclear weapons in the event of war. Finally, since many of the potential nuclear powers are confronted with problems of internal political instability, it would require a very strong leader to resist domestic pressures for using the ultimate weapon in a serious conflict situation if such a weapon were available.

Given the many factors affecting the stability of the nuclear deterrent, several suggestions have been made for reducing the threat of a possible breakdown. Chief among these are actions designed to reduce the dangers of war by accident or miscalculation. Efforts have been made to minimize the danger of unauthorized use of nuclear weapons by centralizing command and control functions. In the United States the president is the only person empowered to initiate a nuclear strike, although there are contingencies in case the president is incapacitated. At every step in the decision to use nuclear weapons at least two individuals are made reponsible for setting in motion a nuclear strike under the so-called two key system. This procedure has been designed to reduce the danger of someone in the chain of command going berserk and initiating a nuclear attack. It might be noted that the system does not actually involve "two keys," for this would create the possibility of one of those involved overpowering the other and initiating a nuclear strike. Instead, each participant has critical information that is usable only if coordinated with the information available to the other.

If a nuclear bomb is accidentally dropped or a missle unleashed by accident or unauthorized action, it would become critical that the decision makers be able to communicate promptly and effectively with each other in order to reduce the possibility of an all-out nuclear war. To aid such communication, the two superpowers agreed in 1963 to establish a "hot line" between Washington and Moscow. Initially a cable was constructed between the two countries, but, with the development of satellite communication systems, the old cable system was replaced with a direct satellite communication link in accordance with an agreement reached by the two parties in 1971. Although one might have visions of the hot line's enabling the leaders of each state to be in direct telephone communication with each other, the current hot line actually uses teletype capability. In July 1984 agreement was reached between the United States and the Soviet Union to replace the twenty-year-old teleprinter capable of producing only sixty words per minute with modern machinery able to send nearly instantaneous exchanges of block messages and maps. To date the hot-line system has been used sparingly, most notably at the time of the 1967 Arab-Israeli war and again during the Afghanistan crisis in 1979.

Because of the danger of war arising by accident, it is desirable to delay a retaliatory response as long as possible in order to be certain that a nuclear reponse is justified. This can be done most effectively by creating what defense planners call an invulnerable retaliatory capability. Such a capability can be achieved by utilizing mobile vehicles, as in the case of submarines; dispersing existing retaliatory capabilities to make it more difficult to eliminate those capabilities; or by hardening the weapons which, in the case of missiles, involves placing them in underground silos with a thick cover made of reinforced concrete in order to assure survivability from all but the most direct hit.

Not only will the development of an invulnerable retaliatory capability reduce incentives for launching on warning because of the fear that one's retaliatory force and command centers will not survive a first strike, but such a capability assures the stability of deterrence by guaranteeing to the would-be attacker that a first strike will not be effective because of the assured destructive capability of the potential victim.

Finally, arms control and disarmament measures themselves may contribute to deterrent stability. Violence and the threat of voilence can be reduced by cutting the number and quality of weapons available to each party, particularly if the affected weapons include those that threaten the stability of deterrence.

ARMS CONTROL AND DETERRENCE

The relationship between arms control and deterrence is a complex one involving more than opposite approaches to the search for national security. Indeed, each approach may bolster the other. Deterrence is vital to arms control, for whatever agreement is reached, the remaining weapons on each side, along with the potential of accelerating the arms race, can serve to minimize the threat of violation of an arms control agreement. Even if the arms agreement involves reducing arms to the level necessary for internal defense, as envisioned in the general and complete disarmament proposals, deterrent force would still be required, perhaps in the form of a United Nations police force.

It has also been suggested that a deterrent arms buildup is necessary to produce ''bargaining chips'' that can be used to induce the other side to accept an arms control or disarmament agreement. This argument became the primary selling-point used by the Reagan administration for the development and production of the MX missile and its deployment in existing Minuteman missile silos. Since the MX basing-system in stationary silos made little sense from the perspective of the administration's concern about ICBM vulnerability, the bargaining chip argument perhaps provided the only rationale for proceeding. It should be noted that this argument has been used to justify almost every new weapons system. To the extent that bargaining chips have been ineffective in facilitating the reaching of arms control agreements, they have only helped to fuel the arms race. As will be shown subsequently, the latter seems more often to have been the case.

Arms control can contribute to the stability of deterrence by regulating or reducing any weapon that threatens to destabilize the system. The two kinds of weapons systems of most interest in this regard are those weapons capable of a first strike and those weapons or devices that threaten to provide a highly reliable defense against the other side's deterrent capability. Some defense analysts have asserted that the large land-based missiles of the Soviet Union with their ability to carry huge and multiple warheads represent a serious threat to the American ICBM. In May 1983 the U.S. Air Force estimated that by 1989 the Soviet Union could have so many accurate nuclear warheads that as little as one percent of the U.S. land-based missile force might survive "a well-executed Soviet first strike."[9]

Similarly, the MX missile, due to its great accuracy and heavy payload, is regarded by some as having first-strike potential and therefore would be highly threatening and provocative to the Soviet Union. If the primary mission of a missile is one of retaliation, such capabilities are not required, and small, mobile missiles as proposed in April 1983 by President Reagan's Commission on Strategic Forces make more sense from the standpoint of deterrence, particularly since mobile missiles are less vulnerable to a Soviet first strike.

Arms control agreements may be used to slow down the modernization of weapons systems, thereby enhancing the stability of deterrence. The fear that the other side might develop the ultimate defensive or offensive weapon fuels the arms race and creates pressures for a preventive strike if the balance is seen as slipping too far in the other side's favor. Past arms agreements, although not terribly successful, have sought to reduce such fears by placing restrictions on the testing of new weapons systems and by imposing limits on the size and power of any replacement delivery systems.

Arms control can be an important adjunct to military planning itself since quantitative arms agreements can lend predictability to the arms competition. In the absence of such quantitative constraints "force planners would be more inclined to base their weapons development and deployment decisions on worst case projections of the adversary's force. Therefore, numerical constraints can obviate some pressures for arms races and decrease costs associated with force acquisition and deployment."[10]

Finally, it has been argued that arms control negotiations are useful for deterrent stability even if agreement is not reached, for the debates themselves serve as useful seminars enabling each side to communicate its concerns on strategic issues. Since both sides have a vested interest in the stability of nuclear deterrence, both are likely to listen, or ought to listen, carefully to the presentation of the other side. During times of crises it is particularly useful to have a forum available where each might be able to reassure the other. Recent proposals for the creation of U.S.-Soviet, jointly manned crises control centers reflect this concern.

While there is compatibility between arms control and deterrence as approaches to national security, there are some obvious conflicts. Chief among these is the arms control objective of verification and the deterrent objective of creating an invulnerable retaliatory capability. Mobile basing-systems assure the greatest invulnerability, but mobile weapons are difficult to count if one wants to verify that arms control celings are not being violated. This conflict explains in large measure the difficulties in determining how to base the MX missile as over thirty basing-plans have been proposed at one time or another. In order to meet the verification requirements of the SALT II Treaty, the Carter administration settled upon a ''racetrack'' system that would allow verification of 200 MX missiles as they moved in open trenches between 4,800 protective covers. This was not only a costly plan but also a plan that ran into considerable political trouble in Utah and Nevada because of the extensive land area required for such a basing-system. After toying with other possible basing-plans, the Reagan administration eventually chose to emplace a scaled-down number of MX missiles in fixed silos, only to reverse itself in 1987 by proposing that MX be positioned on train cars.

A second incompatibility between arms control and a stable deterrent system arises from the role played by satellite observation. The same satellites that are so vital for verifying compliance with arms control agreements are equally available for finding targets for a disarming counterforce attack, thus threatening the stability of deterrence.

Third, certain unilateral arms control efforts designed to reduce the danger of nuclear war, or at least to minimize the damage from such a war, may actually destabilize deterrence. This is especially the case with respect to the hardening of command and control centers to lessen the danger of decapitation and the building of shelters to protect civilians from nuclear fallout. Such actions may be viewed by the adversary as provocative indications of plans to initiate a first strike, which in turn create pressures for preemption.

Finally, some of the incompatibility between arms control and deterrence derives from the fact that individual policy makers tend to concentrate upon one approach to national security while neglecting the other.

This is particularly true in the United States where the arms-controllers are found primarily in the State Department or the Arms Control and Disarmament Agency while the Defense Department focuses more upon deterrent strategies. In the Soviet Union the role of the military in arms control negotiations has been much more pronounced, which may facilitate a more coherent policy in the search for national security.

WHY NEGOTIATE?

The paucity of arms control agreements reached as a result of meetings numbering into the thousands might raise some question as to why disarmament negotiations have been so pervasive in the postwar world. For an answer to this question one has to make an examination of other motivations for entering into arms control negotiations beyond the narrow objective of reaching an agreement.

One of the major side benefits of negotiating arms control has been the use of such negotiations for propagandistic purposes. Disarmament negotiations are particularly useful for such purposes since virtually no one wants war and everybody wants peace. The tendency to use propaganda themes in disarmament negotiations can be seen from the results of a content analysis of statements made by the United States and the Soviet Union during the pre-1961 debates as summarized in table 1.1.[11] As might be expected, the objectives of peace and security were described as primary goals for both parties. By combining the eight themes coded for each side into a single index, it was found that the resulting propaganda scores for the United States and the Soviet Union moved in the same direction in 18 of 21 rounds of negotiations, producing an overall positive correlation of .56 ($p < .01$). A similar reciprocity was found with respect to the use of hostile themes such as those accusing the other side of lying, bargaining in bad faith, and cheating. In the latter instance the correlation between the hostility scores of the United States and the Soviet Union in the pre-1961 negotiations was .43 ($p < .01$).

A second objective of disarmament negotiations has been to divide the opposition. The Soviet Union has been particularly prone toward presenting proposals specifically designed to appeal to one part of the NATO alliance at the expense of the remaining members. During the 1950s it sought to separate France from NATO by supporting French proposals for banning missiles; also, during the same period, Soviet efforts were directed toward encouraging the Federal Republic of Germany to disassociate itself from NATO with offers of military disen-

Table 1.1 Propaganda Themes Used for
Explaining Disarmament Goals, 1945–60

Goal	USSR (%)	U.S. (%)
Peace	56*	48
Security	41	41
Prevent war	38	25
Tension reduction	35	23
Build confidence	25	20
Economic reasons	19	23
Prevent surprise attack	15	22
Reduce nuclear fallout	7	1

*Percentage based upon number of meetings in which the theme was raised. $N =$ 204 meetings for the Soviet Union and 153 for the United States.

Source: Lloyd Jensen, *The Postwar Disarmament Negotiations: A Study in U.S.-Soviet Bargaining Behavior*, pp. 244 and 246

gagement in central Europe, combined with promises for the reunification of Germany. The sixties saw Soviet nuclear nonproliferation proposals serving the same function. The SALT negotiations during the following decade led to further suspicions, particularly within the Western alliance, as the two superpowers dealt with strategic arms issues without the active participation of their respective allies. Further efforts to divide the West can be seen in threats issued by Soviet representatives during the disarmament negotiations as in the 1957 threat that "countries which have made their territory available to foreign bases will become the first targets for atom bombs." Similar threats have recently caused some concern in West European countries about the placing of cruise and Pershing II missiles on their territory.

Soviet proposals for banning the bomb, using savings from disarmament for economic development, creating nuclear free zones, and prohibiting the first use of nuclear weapons were all calculated to appeal to Third World nations. The primary purpose of such proposals seemed to be their propaganda value in attempting to portray the Soviet Union as pro-disarmament.

Since the Soviet bloc has been more monolithic than NATO, there has been little prospect for using the negotiations for dividing the Warsaw Pact nations. During the 1950s Polish interest in the military disengagement of central Europe might have been exploited more than it was by the United States, although the Soviet Union seemed to acquiesce to many of the proposals made by Polish Foreign Minister Adam Rapacki. A more promising split that the United States could have exploited was the division between the Soviet Union and Rumania over issues related to nuclear nonproliferation in the 1960s. By the time the United States became cognizant of Sino-Soviet differences on nuclear disarmament issues, the schism between the two communist powers was so deep that it hardly required further encouragement in the form of divisive disarmament proposals.

Proposals might also be designed to take advantage of divisions on disarmament issues among various groups within the adversary's nation. The Soviet Union has long sought to identify with the peace movement in various countries. It was perhaps most successful in this regard with its "ban the bomb" campaigns of the late forties and early fifties. Assertions have also been made that the Soviet Union has been encouraging nuclear freeze groups in the United States and Europe during the eighties. Similar encouragement, however, is not given to its own peace groups that question Soviet policies on disarmament.

A third objective of engaging in disarmament negotiations is to gain information concerning the military capabilities and intentions of the adversary. The disarmament proposals presented by each side provide important clues regarding the weapons systems in which the state has doubts. Many proposals, particularly those emanating from the West, would require extensive inspection of the territory of the adversary, thereby providing not only assurance of compliance with the disarmament scheme but also facilitating the collection of important information concerning the military capabilities and deployments of the other side. American proposals for open skies and for reducing the danger of surprise attack that were introduced in the late fifties are illustrative of proposals that fail to include any provisions for reducing or limiting weapons. These proposals led the Soviet Union to assert that the United States desired inspection without disarmament. With the advent of spy satellites, the need for reconnaissance flights and the exchange of military blueprints as provided in these proposals has ceased to exist.

Finally, an administration may enter negotiations for the primary purpose of reassuring its own domestic public. This appeared to be a major consideration for the Reagan administration, which had developed a hard-line reputation on defense issues. Public opinion polls, showing great concern about increased military spending and the threat of war, placed pressure upon the administration to engage in arms control negotiations. Of even greater moment were pressures emanating from the U.S. Congress demanding that the Reagan administration negotiate more seriously on arms control measures. In June 1983, for example, the House of Representatives approved continued work on the MX only after receiving written assurance from President Reagan that his administration would show greater flexibility in the upcoming disarmament negotiations.

Whatever the motivations for engaging in discussions on disarmament, it is clear that success in such talks comes about only after long and arduous negotiation. Our concern in this book will be with the problems and progress made in Soviet-U.S. disarmament negotiations in the postwar period as we seek to obtain a better understanding of superpower bargaining behavior and the contributions that arms control may provide in the search for national security.

Chapters 2 and 3 will focus upon the setting and process of U.S.-Soviet arms control negotiations. Among the topics to be examined are the cultural and ideological factors affecting bargaining style and interests; the impact of domestic pressures and negotiating structure upon bargaining behavior; the role played by concessionary behavior; and the effect of international tension and bargaining chips upon negotiating behavior.

Leaving the more theoretical aspects of negotiating disarmament, the remaining chapters will focus upon four sets of substantive arms control negotiations followed by a concluding chapter. The four negotiations include the nuclear test ban talks, negotiations on the problem of nuclear proliferation, the strategic arms talks, and arms control negotiations during the Reagan administration. Some readers less experienced with the complex and often jargon-ridden terminology of arms control may find it helpful to begin with these substantive chapters prior to reading the more theoretical materials found in chapters 2 and 3.

2

The Bargaining Setting

The domestic and international setting in which disarmament negotiations occur has had an important impact upon the negotiating outcome. Relevant factors include not only the ideology and values with which the participants come to the negotiations but also the precise setting of the negotiations themselves. Differences in outcome may depend upon whether negotiations are conducted bilaterally or multilaterally, whether they are open or closed to the public, or whether high-level officials or low-level officials are involved.

Frequent references have been made to the extreme length to which states will go to negotiate the shape of a table or who is to enter a room first or who can talk to whom. These considerations merely underscore the complexity and sensitivity of negotiations in which values, precedence, and status all play as much a part as rational problem-solving. To add further to the complexity of international negotiation, some of the hardest bargaining actually occurs before the negotiators sit down at the table. It is first necessary to obtain a consensus among bureaucratic and political interests in the home state, and at the same time, satisfy both domestic and world public opinion. This chapter is concerned with the setting in which negotiations occur in an effort to understand why the United States and the Soviet Union have adopted the bargaining strategies and policies they have in the postwar disarmament negotiations.

CULTURAL AND IDEOLOGICAL INPUTS

Much has been written about the negotiating behavior of the Soviet Union and how such behavior varies from that of the United States. Since the two states have experienced distinct histories and developed

14

different values and ideologies, differences in their approaches to negotiation are to be expected.

Most Western experts on the Soviet Union agree that Soviet society is far more conscious of rank and hierarchy than is the case in Western societies. This characteristic has implications not only for the way negotiations are conducted but also for the substantive outcome. Usually only the chief of the Soviet negotiating team plays a role in the process with subordinates sitting in an advisory capacity. Initiatives at lower levels are virtually unheard of. There is also greater preoccupation with the rank equivalence of the negotiators as only heads of delegations speak to those at their level and so on down the line.

Concern about rank equivalence also carries over to the state level as the Soviet Union in recent years has pursued a policy designed to assert itself as an equal to the United States. This drive for equal status has often led the Soviets to prefer bilateral over multilateral negotiating bodies and solutions. The codification of that equality through SALT became one of the primary objectives of the Soviet Union as it reacted in a most hostile fashion to the slightest hint that it might not be viewed as the equal of the United States.

Soviet negotiators have an overriding fear of being criticized by higher authorities. Perhaps this is not surprising given a history in which diplomats were demoted and some even lost their lives or were deported during the Stalinist purges of the thirties. A common accusation was that the negotiator had made "unnecessary" concessions.[1] Fear of being accused of deviating from official positions has led to considerable rigidity and lack of flexibility at the bargaining table. According to a major participant, Soviet SALT negotiator Vladimir S. Semenov was "so apprehensive about deviating from instructions during negotiations that he spoke of official matters from notes in both informal and even in social meetings."[2] In Semenov's case, given his past experience, such behavior was perhaps to be expected. After the 1953 East German uprising, Lavrenti Pavlovich Beria had come close to ordering Semenov's execution. His "life was saved only because he was absent from Berlin when the order to return to Moscow was made."[3]

The sense of insecurity among Soviet negotiators has sometimes been so great that they would not report home what an opponent said. To do so would give the impression that they had been moved by the adversary or that they were weak or lacked zeal in carrying out instructions.[4] Such insecurities may also help explain the general failure of Soviet negotiators to take initiatives in arms control negotiations. On occasion they have even asked the United States to introduce a given proposal, as the

Soviet representative did during the Intermediate-range Nuclear Force (INF) talks in November 1983 when he asked Paul Nitze to propose warhead reductions in Europe from 572 to 0 for the United States. In return the Soviet Union would limit its warheads to 360, leading to a reduction of SS-20s to 120. Washington instructed Nitze to reject the proposal, but "in one of the more curious turns in the INF negotiations, the Soviets falsely informed foreign governments and the public that this proposal was authored by Ambassador Nitze."[5] Perhaps it was simply a case of a Soviet negotiator exceeding instructions, then desiring to deny all involvement.

The insecurity of the Soviet leadership has also resulted in suspicion of Western efforts to establish on-site verification systems. Concern about the intrusiveness of inspection systems on Soviet soil and the incumbent threat upon its national sovereignty has been a recurring theme throughout the postwar disarmament negotiations. Sensitivity about this issue has been only partially mollified by the development of satellite technology that makes national technical means of inspection feasible. At the same time, the Soviet Union has to be concerned less about possible U.S. evasions of an arms agreememt, since the openness of American society allows the Soviet Union to discover American violations even without on-site inspection.

While Soviet negotiators are viewed as less secure personally than their American counterparts, they also show themselves to be more patient in negotiations. This may be related to acceptance of an ideology that tells them that, in the end, communism will triumph. It may also be the result of certain cultural traits developed over a long history in which life has not always been easy. Dealing with a highly bureaucratized system, standing in lines for food and other goods, and daily confrontation with a variety of inefficiencies probably contribute to the patience shown by Soviet citizens. Former Strategic Arms Reduction Talks (START) negotiator Edward L. Rowny has noted that the difference in patience between Americans and Russians can be seen in the games that are popular in each country. "The Russians play chess; we play video games. They like the well-thought through results of step-by-step reasoning; we like the instant results of electronic machines."[6]

Patience enables the Soviet negotiator to repeat positions endlessly without feeling any compulsion to compromise until ordered to do so by his superior. According to Rowny, the United States probably made four or five proposals to every proposal of the Soviet Union during the SALT negotiations. Americans, on the other hand, are more result oriented.[7] Democratic values instill in Americans the need to compromise for the sake of reaching agreement. It is probably for this reason that the United States tables so many variants of its proposals.

Patience does not seem to extend to complacency about radical changes in U.S. arms control policy as Soviet leaders tend to be upset by sudden and drastic changes in American negotiating positions. The Soviet leadership, despite its revolutionary pretensions, is essentially conservative and shares a high level of risk-aversion.[8] This conservatism may in part help explain initial negative Soviet reactions to the Kennedy March 1963 initiative on the test ban issue and Soviet hostility toward President Carter's call for more extensive reductions in strategic arms in March 1977 after largely cosmetic levels had been agreed upon at Vladivostok.

Critics of U.S. negotiating behavior have suggested that as a result of the democratic approach of reaching a consensus on issues, the United States, in making its proposals, engages in considerable self-constraint by making compromises before presenting such proposals in international forums.[9] Fred Iklé has noted that Soviet representatives scarcely think of having a position of their own, whereas Western negotiators, accustomed to looking critically at the policies of their government, often play the role of mediator. He asks rhetorically: ''If American officials mediate between the United States and the Soviet position, while Russian officials defend the position of their government as final, who is left to defend the U.S. position?''[10]

Although the United States may generally be more concerned than the Soviet Union about the negotiability of its proposals, it has been also guilty of presenting nonnegotiable positions. Alexander Haig has admitted that two major proposals made while he was Secretary of State—the zero-option proposal presented in the Intermediate Nuclear Force Talks and the first U.S. proposal in START—were both nonnegotiable and perhaps should not have been tabled.[11]

Henry Kissinger has suggested yet other implications emanating from contrasting Soviet and American cultural traits that would seem to provide advantages to the Soviet Union in negotiations. Kissinger views Americans as basically pragmatic and empirically oriented, a trait that he suggests dooms the United States ''to an essentially reactive policy that improvises a counter to every Soviet move, while the Soviet emphasis on theory gives them the certainty to act, to maneuver, to run risks.''[12]

Marxist-Leninist thought may also have a subtle impact on Soviet arms control and armament policy in view of the belief in the inevitable conflict between capitalism and communism. The belief in perpetual conflict makes the goal of global stability less important in Soviet thinking than it is in the case of the United States. Unlike the United States, the Soviet Union has not been so preoccupied with the stability of the nuclear deterrent system as the primary objective of its arms control policy.

The utopianism found in Marxist thinking regarding the inevitable triumph of communism may also predispose Soviet leaders to assume that military instruments of power are unnecessary for their objectives. Ideologies compete for the minds of men and as such are less dependent upon military weapons. Soviet lack of success in the ideological struggle to date, however, should give them reason to pause about their ability to prevail in a disarmed world. Experience has undoubtedly taught the Soviet Union that military weapons are necessary not only to deter expansion by external capitalistic and imperialist forces, but also to retain its Soviet satellite empire.

THE DOMESTIC POLITICAL SETTING

The positions taken by states in negotiations may have as much to do with domestic political constraints and opportunities confronting decision makers as they do with the responsiveness of the other side or even the state's own ideological goals. Indeed, such factors as executive leadership capabilities, bureaucratic politics, congressional attitudes, and the general mood of the public may be the most important factors explaining negotiating behavior.

The most obvious difference in the domestic policy setting of the United States and the Soviet Union relates to the fact that one state is a pluralistic democracy whereas the other is a highly centralized authoritarian regime. A centralized political system would seem to enjoy a number of advantages when it comes to international negotiation. In the first place, it can speak with a more unified voice in those negotiations, thus making its threats and promises more credible. It need not worry about political interests organizing to force the decision makers to reverse positions, thereby embarrassing the state internationally or hampering its bargaining strategy.

Decisions may also be more rational in the sense that the decision makers in a centralized system are less subject to both internal and external pressures. The nonpluralist state does not have to contend with a peace movement that can force it to take positions that are not viewed as being in the national interests or to make compromises simply to show that it is serious about disarmament.

Since the USSR is more centrally organized, there is also less opportunity for the United States to exploit differences on national security issues within the Soviet political process. On the other hand, pluralistic societies, like the United States, provide a number of opportunities for outsiders to influence its political process. The Soviet Union has become particularly adept in lobbying the U.S. Congress on arms control issues. It has also been able to design its proposals in a way to exploit differences among various bureaucratic agencies in the United States. More recently, the Soviet Union has even attempted to influence the American public directly through the use of advertising in major American newspapers and frequent appearances on U.S. television news programs.

The Soviet Union ought to feel reassured on verification issues due to the fact that it is dealing with a pluralistic society like the United States. Violations of arms agreements are more difficult to cover up in a democratic society than in an authoritarian one. Because of this the Soviet Union has expressed far less concern about verification capabilities in negotiating arms control agreements and instead has been far more concerned about the threat of intrusive verification to its national sovereignty.

An authoritarian regime like the Soviet Union's may also be able to negotiate in a more flexible way or at least change its positions more frequently. To reach a policy consensus in a pluralistic society requires considerable bargaining between various governmental interests, and, because of the great energy expended in the process, it becomes very difficult to change a hard won consensus. A prominent American statesman once reportedly told the Europeans that "by the time the United States government was ready to negotiate a position it was often so firmly fixed because of internal negotiations and agreements that it had little give."[13]

This is not to suggest that the authoritarian state has all of the advantages in a bargaining situation. Pluralism enables greater input into the policy process and as such the system should be more effective in the search to solve problems related to national security and disarmament. Even though authoritarian regimes may show some flexibility by being able to change policies that come through the bureaucratic maze, they have demonstrated their own rigidities. Such regimes are filled with "yes men" unwilling to challenge existing policies because of concern about their professional positions. Since the days of Khrushchev there has been an emphasis placed upon collective decision making in the Kremlin. This in turn has led to a high level of risk-aversion and incrementalism in foreign-policy making. Decision making based upon consensus is emphasized in order not to interfere with any important elite interests. Controversial issues tend to be left off the agenda, and positions once taken are difficult to reopen for discussion.

Executive Leadership

The personalities and preferences of the top-level leadership have perhaps had the greatest impact upon bargaining strategies and outcomes related to arms control. Postwar leaders have varied considerably in the degree of interest that they have had in disarmament and arms control. Stalin, beleaguered as he was by the considerable devastation wrought upon the Soviet Union by World War II and having a desire to expand the Soviet empire, showed little interest in arms control. He belittled the impact of nuclear weapons, arguing that permanently operating factors such as morale, command, and the quality and quantity of conventional forces were more important.

Stalin's immediate successor, Georgi Malenkov, placed new priorities on improving mass consumption and economic conditions in the Soviet Union. Slowing military spending would be one of the most important moves to satisfy such interests. As a result, new initiatives were taken in the arms control negotiations as the USSR made some of its most significant concessions up to that point in proposals presented in the fall of 1954. These included acceptance of the notion of reducing arms in stages, agreement on continuous inspection, and a willingness to give higher priority to conventional arms reduction.

William Hyland has suggested that Nikita Khrushchev, who assumed power in 1955, was responsible more than any of the postwar leaders for making arms control a perpetual aspect of the East-West debate.[14] Ironically, the impression Khrushchev created of progress on arms control may have cost him the much needed support of the military, resulting in his downfall in October 1964. The primary success of Khrushchev in the arms control area was the Limited Test Ban Treaty. His commitment to general and complete disarmament, beginning with the first Soviet GCD proposal in 1959, must be viewed largely as a propaganda effort.

In assuming the role of first secretary of the Party in 1964, Leonid Brezhnev brought with him considerable experience in national security matters, having served as Central Committee secretary for the defense industry and the top coordinator of the Soviet space program from 1956 to 1960. Since the military was critical to his rise to power, it was hardly likely that he would have taken positions strongly opposed by military interests. On issues of strategic arms limitations, Brezhnev seems to have placed himself squarely in the middle of the pro and anti arms control group.[15] Nevertheless, it was during his long eighteen-year-tenure that the most important arms control agreements were negotiated, including both the SALT I and SALT II treaties, the Nuclear Non-proliferation Treaty, and several other important agreements.

The transition from Brezhnev to Yuri Andropov in November 1982 had minimal impact upon the Geneva negotiations. According to Soviet negotiator Yuli Kvitsinsky, Andropov had already been personally involved in formulating Soviet INF policy for many months before his accession to the top job.[16] As former head of the KGB, Andropov assumed a fairly hard line on arms control issues and, although ill during much of his fifteen-month tenure, was responsible for the Soviet Union's leaving the Geneva START and INF talks in December 1983. His primary preoccupation had been with domestic reform rather than international issues.

From the beginning Konstantin Chernenko was viewed as an interim appointment as head of the Communist party after Andropov's death in 1984. It was Chernenko, according to all accounts, who almost single-handedly pressed the resumption of arms control talks with the United States. These talks began shortly after his death in January 1985.[17] Andrei Gromyko, the foreign minister, and Marshal Nikolai Ogarkov, the Soviet chief of staff, took a harder line in the internal debates on the issue, leading ultimately to the dismissal of the latter.

Mikhail Gorbachev, who assumed the position of general secretary upon the death of Chernenko, was a protégé of Andropov but has appeared to take a more moderate position than his mentor on arms control issues. In 1985, Gorbachev took a number of arms control initiatives such as undertaking a moratorium on nuclear weapons testing, reducing the number of SS-20s stationed in Europe by 54, and proposing a 50 percent reduction in nuclear weapons. During the next two years he made a number of concessions covering virtually every weapons system and in the process agreed to stringent verification requirements.

The role played by American presidents in the arms control process has varied considerably. Harry S. Truman, as president following the end of World War II, oversaw a massive disarmament program in which the United States pressed for rapid military demobilization in order to bring the boys home. The Soviet Union failed to follow suit, and it was only a matter of months before the cold war began in earnest. Despite these international political difficulties, Truman apparently remained convinced that the United States should try to make progress both on arms control and political settlement at the same time, but little progress was made during his tenure in office.

Although Dwight Eisenhower, as a retired general of the Army, had extensive knowledge about strategic matters, his involvement in the arms control area seemed relatively limited as indeed was that of the United States government in general. The number of governmental personnel in the United States working full time on arms control issues was extremely small, numbering less than a dozen during the Eisenhower administration. So little analysis of disarmament issues had been conducted within the government that the administration was ill prepared for the Soviet acceptance of a number of U.S. positions in the November 1954 and May 1955 Soviet proposals. Although the administration had become increasingly less supportive of the Baruch Plan, in view of a growing concern about verifying Soviet compliance, it was taken aback by the Soviet response and chose in September of that year to "reserve" all of its past disarmament proposals.

The primary initiatives taken during the Eisenhower administration in the arms control area involved the 1953 Atoms for Peace proposals, which became the basis for the creation of the International Atomic Energy Agency (IAEA) and the Open Skies proposals presented in 1955, which were far less successful, having little to do with the basic problem of controlling weapons. Lack of American interest in the arms control area may have had as much to do with the powerful role played by John Foster Dulles as a secretary of state who believed that it was impossible to negotiate with the Russians. Based upon a content analysis of all available public pronouncements about the Soviet Union made by Dulles, Ole R. Holsti discovered that his subject had an unwavering view of the Soviet Union as an evil actor in the international system.[18] Dulles's belief system led him to perceive that the Soviet Union made concessions only when it found itself in a position of military inferiority. Rather than viewing Soviet concessions as motivated by the desire to reach agreement, which would suggest the utility of U.S. reciprocation, Secretary of State Dulles believed that further pressure should be applied to assure continuing concessions on the part of the Soviet Union. Dulles's hostility to negotiating agreements with the Soviet Union was underscored by his comment that "an agreement is a meeting of minds. And so far I do not know of any agreement that the Soviet Union had made which has reflected a real meeting of minds."[19]

The issue of arms control came to assume a larger role in the presidential agenda during the Kennedy administration. This was reflected in the creation of the Arms Control and Disarmament Agency in 1961, which substantially increased the U.S. bureaucratic effort in the arms control area. Although President Kennedy came into office on a campaign alleging neglect of U.S. national security interests and asking for increased military spending, he took a number of initiatives to restrain the spiraling arms race. Among the most important of these was the special attention he gave to the issue of a nuclear test ban. Numerous concessions were made by the United States in its March 1961 test ban proposals. The important role played by Kennedy in negotiating the Limited Test Ban Treaty signed in 1963 has been fully described by Glenn Seaborg from his special vantage point as chairman of the Atomic Energy Commission during Kennedy's tenure in office.[20] According to Seaborg, Kennedy wrote several letters on the subject to Nikita Khrushchev, participated in numerous U.S. meetings on the subject, and became directly involved in the development of instructions to the U.S. delegation. Given the active role played not only by Kennedy, but also by his counterpart Nikita Khrushchev, Seaborg concluded that had Kennedy lived out a second term, and had Khrushchev survived in office, "significant further steps in arms control, including a comprehensive test ban, would have ensued."[21] The important role played by Kennedy can also be seen in negotiations on the Outer Space Treaty, in which Kennedy continued to advocate banning nuclear weapons in outer space despite receiving a "unanimous recommendation of all interested agencies and departments *against* such a ban."[22]

President Lyndon B. Johnson lacked both interest and knowledge about complicated foreign policy issues such as arms control. According to one assessment, he tended to stay aloof from the bureaucratic bargaining that accompanied the preparation for SALT, preferring instead to receive the unanimous position of the government rather than be told about disagreements.[23] In the waning days of his presidency, he made a determined effort to begin bilateral negotiations with the Soviet Union on strategic arms control, but the effort floundered because of the Soviet invasion of Czechoslovakia in 1968. The primary arms control achievement of the Johnson era was the successful negotiation of the Nuclear Nonproliferation Treaty.

Richard M. Nixon assumed the presidency in 1969 with both more interest and experience in the foreign policy area than most of his predecessors. Having earned a reputation as a strong anti-Communist, he was probably in a better position to achieve U.S. arms control objectives than other postwar presidents. At least he was less constrained by negative conservative reactions within the United States given his anti-Communist credentials. Nixon was not initially disposed toward arms control agreements, feeling that the Soviets were demonstrating too much interest in the subject. Consequently, the administration's opening bid involved no specific proposals but instead demanded that U.S. support for strategic arms control be linked to political settlements in Vietnam and the Middle East. Despite the slow start, more arms control agreements were signed during the Nixon era than during any other period. These included the Interim Offensive Arms Agreement, the Anti-Ballistic Missile Treaty, the Biological Convention, the Seabed Treaty, agreements to reduce the risks of nuclear war and to improve the hot line, and the Threshold Test Ban Treaty.

Some of the arms control successes during the Nixon era must be partially attributed to the role played by Henry Kissinger, first as national security advisor and then as secretary of state. Kissinger came to the job with considerable knowledge of both diplomatic and strategic matters. At the same time, he did not share former Secretary of State Dulles's paranoid attitudes about the Soviet Union. A replication of Holsti's content analysis of Dulles's speeches revealed that, unlike Dulles, Kissinger's evaluation of the Soviet Union changed over time, becoming more positive when the Soviets began making more conciliatory moves.[24] Under such conditions, concessions can be expected to lead to a greater responsiveness to initiatives taken by the adversary.

President Ford's priority on assuming the presidency in 1974 was to pull the nation together after Watergate. Nevertheless, in November 1974 he successfully negotiated the Vladivostok Accord, which ultimately became the basis of the SALT II treaty. To aid him in this exercise, Ford relied heavily upon Henry Kissinger during the early months for advice on arms control policy. After Donald Rumsfeld, a former congressman and close friend, assumed the position of secretary of defense, the more conservative Rumsfeld and Fred Iklé of ACDA came to play important roles on arms control issues. As the 1976 presidential election year approached, the Ford administration took a decidedly conservative position on arms control issues and the prospects of good relations with the Soviet Union deteriorated. In an effort to win conservative support for the upcoming election, Ford even chose to excise the term *détente* from his vocabulary and to further distance himself from Kissinger.

President Jimmy Carter took an avid interest in arms control from the very beginning of his presidency. Given his training in engineering and his preoccupation with detail, he pored over mountains of information and conflicting views before making up his mind on arms control matters. Carter apparently felt strongly that nuclear arms could be reduced substantially, leading him to introduce in March 1977 a proposal for deep cuts rather than to accept the high levels of armaments established by the Vladivostok Accord. To a certain degree such a radical change in policy might have been related to the desire to place his own stamp on arms control policy, but it also is reflective of his firm belief that nuclear deterrence could work effectively at much lower levels of armament. He startled the Joint Chiefs of Staff by asking them what they would think about the feasibility of a nuclear deterrent based upon 200 ICBMs for each side. Although Carter was ultimately successful in negotiating the SALT II Treaty, which included largely cosmetic restrictions on strategic arms rather than deep reductions, this treaty became a casualty of the Soviet invasion of Afghanistan in December 1979 and of a growing conservative mood in the country.

In contrast to Carter, President Reagan came into office with an essentially hostile attitude toward arms agreements with the Soviet Union. He saw the SALT II Treaty as fatally flawed and felt that the Soviet Union was prone to lying and cheating. As a result, he and his advisors had little interest in resuming disarmament negotiations. Reagan was also the most inactive of recent presidents when it came to the matter of mastering the intricacies of arms control policies. Strobe Talbott has identified several major gaps in Reagan's knowledge of strategic arms control matters such as his belated discovery that the Soviet Union had most of its strategic offensive capabilities in land-based missiles.[25] Reagan confessed to a number of visitors that he had never understood what "this throw-weight business is all about." He was also reported to have suggested that the advantage of the SLBM over the ICBM is that the former can be recalled. And the list goes on.

Despite his lack of knowledge in the arms control area, President Reagan prided himself on his ability to negotiate with adversaries. Part of this confidence came from his experiences as head of the Screen Actors Guild, where he was confronted with a number of difficult issues requiring delicate negotiations. It was in that role and in his position as governor of California that Reagan developed the practice of opening with high demands, revealing as little of his own plan as possible, and ultimately making limited concessions when interested in reaching agreement.[26] However, often these concessions came almost too late, resulting in compromises that gave the president far from what he wanted and perhaps less than he might have obtained by being more forthright. The continuing problems he has had in obtaining funding for the full contingent of a 100 MX missiles is a case in point. Congress had seemed more amenable to funding twice the number during the Carter administration.

Bureaucratic Politics

Executives are influenced in the positions they take on arms control measures by a variety of bureaucratic actors, each of whom has its own interests to defend. The executive is dependent upon such bureaucracies for information, advice, the conduct of negotiations, and the implementation of policy once agreed upon. Governmental bureaucracies also often speak for much broader constituencies within the country, making it difficult for any executive to ignore the will of the bureaucracy.

In the arms control area, defense departments and foreign offices play the most prominent roles. The intelligence community likewise has an active interest not only in terms of making assessments about military capabilities and intentions but also in verifying agreements once reached. The Atomic Energy Commission found itself involved in the nuclear test ban issue and the Department of Energy, which assumed some of the AEC's power in 1977, continues to take an interest in nuclear issues. It might be expected that the Arms Control and Disarmament Agency (ACDA) would play the central role in formulating arms control policy, but such does not appear to be the case. In statutory terms ACDA is subservient to the State Department, which has its own bureaus dealing with arms control matters. A survey of 59 governmental arms control experts underscored the relatively low standing of the Arms Control Agency as only 15 percent of the respondents felt that ACDA had been the most important when asked "what federal agency has been the principal actor in arms control and disarmament in the field of strategic nuclear weaponry."[27] As table 2.1 shows, the percentage selecting ACDA was even less during the immediate post-1969 period when the National Security Council, under the direction of Henry Kissinger, assumed the preeminent position in the arms control area. The Kissinger era also revealed a drastic reduction in the perceived role of the Defense Department in the arms control area as only 24 percent of the respondents felt it to be the most important compared with 50 percent earlier.

The impact that the bureaucracy has had upon arms control policy appears to have varied depending upon the leadership assumed by the chief executive. Presidents Eisenhower and Johnson both stood aloof from the bureaucracy on arms control issues, letting the bureaucracy thrash out the issues until it could develop a unified position. As a result, Senator Hubert Humphrey complained that the United States was immobilized on disarmament issues during the Eisenhower administration because interdepartmental committees could make relevant decisions only if they were unanimous. In effect, each department had a veto over the State Department's role in the negotiations in the absence of active

Table 2.1 Bureaucratic Assessments of the Most Important Actor in Strategic
Arms Control ($N = 59$)

Time	ACDA (%)	Defense (%)	State (%)	NSC (%)	Total (%)
Pre-1969	27	50	23	0	100
Post-1969	8	24	19	49	100
Overall	15	34	20	31	100

Source: Paul Francis Walker, *The U.S. Arms Control and Disarmament Agency*, p. 159.

presidential participation.[28] These divisions meant that the United States delegation negotiating a test ban had to proceed on several occasions without instructions. Similarly, U.S. negotiator Frederick Eaton was not provided with instructions at the Ten Nation Disarmament Conference in 1960. Bureaucratic divisions during the Johnson years made it impossible for the United States to raise the issue of multiple independently targeted reentry vehicles (MIRVs), thus missing the opportunity to control this highly destabilizing weapons system while it was still possible to do so.

Kissinger and Nixon sought to keep a tighter rein on the bureaucracy by establishing the Verification Committee—an interagency group chaired by Kissinger to deal with SALT-related matters. Given such centralization of policy, few problems arose in developing a United States position on disarmament during SALT I. But part of this success may be attributed to the so-called building block approach in which several options were developed and agreed upon by the bureaucracy. These could then be combined in a variety of ways by the negotiators themselves, making it unnecessary to return the issue for further bureaucratic advice.

By 1973 disarmament policy was in disarray. According to Kissinger, since "the agencies could not agree on a position and the President was immobilized by Watergate, the instruction sent on May 3, 1973, was a mélange of every agency's preference."[29] After Gerald Ford assumed the presidency in 1974, Kissinger, who remained as secretary of state, had increasing difficulties in marshaling a united bureaucratic position on arms control issues. U. Alexis Johnson, who served as SALT negotiator from 1973 to 1977, has noted that he was without instructions a good portion of the time since Washington could not agree.[30] Similar disagreements forced Kissinger to take two proposals to Moscow in January 1976—one favored by the Pentagon and the other by Kissinger.

Ignoring a divided bureaucracy does not seem to be the solution as Kissinger discovered in the spring of 1971 when he informed Moscow that the SALT I agreement could be concluded without the inclusion of SLBMs. When he raised the issue with members of the Verification Panel, they unanimously rejected the idea, forcing Kissinger to renege on earlier promises to the Soviet Union.[31]

During the Carter administration, bureaucratic consensus was difficult to obtain because of the intense rivalry between Cyrus Vance as secretary of state and Zbigniew Brzezinski as national security advisor. Under Brzezinski's influence, U.S. arms control policy hardened in 1978 as a number of retractions were made on the issue of a comprehensive test ban. In late April 1978 Cyrus Vance resigned as secretary of state, ostensibly over his disapproval of the failed Iranian rescue mission. Disagreement on a number of other policy issues, including arms control policy, contributed to the resignation as well. The Department of Defense provided an important input into the process primarily because of the stature of Secretary of Defense Harold Brown, who came to the office with considerable arms control experience.

Strobe Talbott has summarized the process of arms-control decision making during the first Reagan administration as being one in which the "bureaucracy churned away furiously, bucking its disagreements upward to the White House. The President then acted less as a decisionmaker in producing policy than as a rather reluctant and uninformed arbiter. It was a process that produced constant squabbles, temporary truces, and permanent, institutionalized acrimony."[32]

The major bureaucratic struggle during Reagan's first term in office occurred not between senior players but rather between two junior players—Assistant Secretary of State Richard Burt and Assistant Secretary of Defense Richard Perle. The latter by and large was able to prevail not only because of his long involvement in arms control policy as advisor to Senator Henry Jackson but more importantly because his boss Caspar Weinberger, as a close friend of Ronald Reagan, carried more clout on defense and arms control issues than did the secretary of state. On arms control policy, Weinberger in turn deferred to his young associate.[33]

Even after the issues are resolved within the bureaucracy and a position taken, individual bureaucratic agencies often continue to lobby for their preferred positions. Access to the negotiating forum is obtained through the agencies own representatives at the negotiating table. Defense, State, ACDA, the CIA, and so forth will usually have their own personnel on the negotiating team, allowing each agency to try to influence the delegation directly. Ambassador Johnson has noted how the Joint Chiefs of Staff frequently tried to countermand the president and Kissinger by asking Johnson to do something different from what his instructions stated.[34]

The existence of a number of U.S. governmental agencies interested in national security issues has often led to a lack of coordination in policy making with agencies working at cross purposes and taking contradictory actions. Several instances have been noted by Duncan L. Clarke. For example, Secretary of Defense Robert McNamara ignored ACDA Director William Foster's letters requesting notification as to when the B-47s were to be decommissioned in order to exploit the initiative in the disarmament negotiations. ACDA learned of the decision to employ chemical defoliants in Vietnam only after a decision had been made. Furthermore, ACDA had no meaningful participation in the decision to employ the ABM despite its arms control implications.[35]

Much less is known about the bureaucratic struggles within the Soviet Union, but it seems clear that the Soviets are no more immune to such happenings than are their American counterparts. Although the Soviet government is usually seen by Western observers as highly centralized, making the bureaucratic struggle less of a problem in decision making, one authority has suggested that a major reason for the Soviet Union's wait-and-see attitude, resulting in a slow concessionary rate at the beginning of SALT I, was related to its desire to minimize policy differences internally.[36]

According to Paul Nitze, even Brezhnev withdrew positions he previously agreed to on grounds that the Politburo had not concurred.[37] When Brezhnev at the June 1974 Moscow Summit Conference indicated that he could not agree to a SALT treaty that would last more than ten years, his excuse was that the Soviet military would not allow him to do so. The contrast in decisional latitude between Nixon and Brezhnev at the 1974 summit was particularly striking as Brezhnev had to delay decisions until after consulting the Politburo whereas Nixon pushed ahead largely on his own and with the advice of Henry A. Kissinger.

The drafting of Soviet arms control proposals, particularly during the Brezhnev era, appears not to have been done within the foreign office but rather within the Politburo by a growing cadre of Brezhnev's assistants. At the same time, a defector who served as former chief of the Disarmament Section of the Institute of World Economics and International Relations has written:

> On the whole one can say that the entire decision making process with respect to the Soviet position on SALT is structured in such a

fashion as to give preponderant expression to the interests and objectives of the military industrial complex, which are limited only by the economic and technological capabilities of the USSR.[38]

The Role of the Military

Among the more salient bureaucratic groups affecting arms control policy is the military. As the experts on arms technology and the group most directly affected by decisions on arms control, it is inevitable that it would have an important voice on the subject, even in a society like the United States, which prides itself on civilian control of the military. Although the president serves as the commander in chief of the armed forces and civilian secretaries head the key positions in the Pentagon, the persuasive force of military personnel remains high.

The military enjoys a number of advantages that enable it to play an effective role in the bureaucratic struggle over arms control policy. Perhaps chief among these is expertise on military matters. It is the brave civilian who will seek to press a position on which much of the U.S. military is in opposition. Furthermore, many high level military officers have important connections on Capitol Hill as well as contacts with major industrial leaders. Military officers may also make their positions public, which, given the authoritative position they enjoy on security matters, are taken seriously by the general public and its opinion leaders. It is doubtful that any arms control measure could survive without general support from the military.

The evidence is overwhelming that the U.S. military played a significant role in the decision to support a limited test ban rather than a comprehensive one. A limited ban would allow continued testing, albeit underground. As a reward for Joint Chiefs of Staff approval of the Limited Test Ban Treaty in 1963, the budget for testing was increased to the extent that more tests actually occurred in a comparable period of time after the treaty went into effect than before its implementation.

Although the U.S. military is not inevitably hostile to arms control, it tends to be skeptical of the process, given its firm belief in the importance of weapons in providing for national security. From time to time the military has supported particular disarmament proposals in order to protect a preferred weapons system. Since military budgets are not unlimited, mutual restraints on one weapons system will allow the savings to be utilized on another weapons system. In 1970 the Department of Defense was pleading for a negotiated freeze on strategic weapons in the face of congressional efforts to reduce defense spending by 5–10 percent a year. The Joint Chiefs of Staff in the midseventies reversed their position, fearing a ban on mobile missiles would threaten funds for producing the B-1 bomber. According to Colin S. Gray, one underappreciated reason for the Joint Chiefs' solid support of the SALT II Treaty was related to the fact that President Carter had impressed on them that if SALT II failed, strategic spending would have to increase substantially, thus squeezing funds for other defense functions.[39]

Since each armed service has interests in different weapons systems, it is not at all uncommon to see one service branch enthusiastically supporting arms control measures affecting the weapons systems of another service while attempting to protect its own arsenal. Soviet artillerymen were vehemently opposed to missile development, since it was Khrushchev's interests in building such weapons that led to drastic cutbacks in Soviet arms forces in the early sixties. As a result, they were predisposed toward supporting the SALT process since missile cutbacks might result in more resources being provided for Soviet conventional forces. Differences were also seen among the three U.S. services in terms of how to handle cruise missiles in arms control negotiations. As long as air-launched cruise missiles were protected, the Air Force could care less about sea- and ground-launched cruise missiles. And, as might be expected, the Navy fought hard to keep sea-launched cruise missiles off the bargaining table, particularly since it had visions of arming such missiles with conventional warheads.

In many respects the military seems to have played a more important role in arms control policy in the Soviet Union than it has in the United States. Some believe this to be due largely to the close link that the Soviet Union makes between military strategy and arms control policy— a linkage that critics say the United States, much to its disadvantage, fails to make. Evidence of the extensive involvement of the Soviet military in arms control policy can be seen first of all in the heavy proportion of military officers on Soviet disarmament delegations. One-third of the Soviet SALT I delegation, for example, was composed of military personnel, and the second in command was a military officer. The pattern has continued with subsequent strategic arms talks.

Unlike the United States, where civilian analysts tend to dominate the strategic and arms control debate, strategic policy analysis in the Soviet Union is dominated by the military. The power of military representatives has been particularly strong because of their possession and control of military data and knowledge of military strategy. In fact, during SALT I, one of the military members of the Soviet delegation took aside his American counterpart and requested that the United States cease providing data on Soviet military capabilities in the negotiating sessions.[40] According to U. Alexis Johnson, even Foreign Minister Andrei Gromyko could not talk knowledgeably since SALT channels bypassed the Foreign Office. It was only after he became a Central Committee member that he was allowed to participate fully.[41]

Nikita Khrushchev assumed a fairly prominent role in decision making on military matters, taking a number of moves that were bitterly opposed by Soviet military leaders, such as his decision in 1960 to reduce conventional troop strength by one-third. Nevertheless, Khrushchev complained about how the Soviet military and scientists pressed him into resuming nuclear testing as he ultimately did in September 1961, following a three-year moratorium. In his memoirs, Khrushchev also noted that military decisions were sometimes taken not on a rational basis but rather to appease certain military officials as in the case of giving the admirals cruise ships, which they desired.[42]

Despite considerable opposition from the Soviet military, Khrushchev was able to get the Soviet Union to accept the Limited Test Ban Treaty in 1963. But his struggles with the military were far from over, for it was the military and its supporters who were instrumental in forcing him from office in 1964.

The military appears to have assumed a greater role in the making of national security policy beginning with the Brezhnev era (1964–82). Richard Burt has suggested that Brezhnev had to win military acquiescence to arms control with the United States by making certain guarantees concerning defense spending and the deployment of specific systems.[43] The increasing power of the military during the Brezhnev period was also reflected in the promotion of Marshal Andrei Grechko to full Politburo membership in 1973. The only previous high-ranking military officer to enjoy full Politburo rank in the postwar period was Marshal Georgi Zhukov, who held the position for a brief time in 1957. Moreover, all marshals, most generals, and a few colonel generals held full membership in the very important Central Committee of the Party.[44]

Both Brezhnev and his foreign minister, Andrei Gromyko, have noted how much of a struggle it has been to get the Soviet military to support arms control measures. Gromyko, for example, informed an insider, who subsequently defected to the United States, that he [Gromyko] "hoped to bring the Soviet armed forces command around to thinking in terms of limiting weaponry, not just acquiring more."[45] In explaining why he could not agree to a SALT II Treaty lasting more than ten years, Brezhnev noted that it was because the military would not let him. In June 1974 Brezhnev was forced to overrule his military advisors in order to obtain agreement on the notion of equal aggregates for ICBMs, SLBMs, and strategic bombers.[46] The concept of equal aggregates was vital to eventual agreement since it allowed each side to choose a strategic force posture most compatible with its own defense needs.

It has been reported that two generals sitting behind Brezhnev at the Vladivostok summit would slip him pieces of paper every time the discussion became concrete. According to Henry Kissinger, Anatoly Dobrynin approached Kissinger at the break "and asked whether we couldn't confine the meeting to three people on each side—which got rid of the two generals. So after that, whenever numbers came up, we would explore the numbers, and then he [Brezhnev] would take about a forty-five minute break, either to consult the two generals and, on at least two occasions, to consult Moscow."[47]

Even though the Soviet military, beginning with SALT I, has enjoyed a more important role in the arms control process, assessments generally suggest that they were not enthusiastic supporters of strategic arms control. During the SALT I period, the Soviet military press maintained an almost complete silence on the subject of SALT.[48] According to Dobrynin, the Soviet Ministry of Defense had little use for SALT and as a result placed its most unimaginative and unenterprising general on the SALT negotiating team with instructions to block any initiatives put forward by the Foreign Office, which was technically in charge. The military representative would refuse to seek new instructions even if asked to do so by the head of the delegation.[49]

The reasons for the Soviet military's eventual acquiescence to the SALT process may well have been similar to those noted for the American military. The strategic arms race was extremely costly, and if it could be slowed, the resulting savings could be used for more manpower and conventional arms. The Soviet military had been deeply disturbed by what it saw as Khrushchev's overemphasis upon missiles. From 1955 to 1961 Soviet armed forces were unilaterally cut from over five million to just over three million, and Khrushchev is reported to have said in 1957 that "fighter and bomber airplanes can now be put into museums."[50]

Despite the harder line generally taken by the Soviet military on arms control matters, U.S. negotiator Paul Nitze found them to be more businesslike and less polemical than their civilian counterparts. He suggested that Soviet military representatives seemed almost embarrassed by their civilian colleagues' flagrant distortions of facts and figures.[51] An important U.S. participant in the Intermediate Nuclear Force talks also was reported to have said off the record that the Soviet military was unwilling to walk out of the INF talks in November 1983, hoping instead to constrain U.S. deployments to a minimum, but the military was overruled.[52]

Finally, it should be noted that, just as in the case of the United States, the Soviet military is not a monolithic unit, and one will find within its ranks some who are more hostile toward arms control and some who are less so. The political leadership is able to curry the favor of some military representatives over others, depending upon the leadership's attitudes toward national security and arms control. The Soviet decision to make another effort at arms control in late 1984 was reflected in the decision to remove Marshal Nikolai Orgarkov as first deputy minister of defense and chief of the general staff. Orgarkov had been the most consistently alarmist in the period 1980–84 and several years before that had served as the number two man on the SALT negotiating team.[53] Similarly, General Secretary Gorbachev was hopeful of defusing military criticism of his arms control initiatives by dismissing Defense Minister Sergei Sokolov and one of his deputies under the pretext of their failure to protect Soviet airspace from incursion by a 19-year-old West German citizen who buzzed Red Square in May 1987, landing near the Kremlin in a single-engine Cessna.

Congressional Input

The United States Congress has become an increasingly important actor in the making of arms control policy. Perhaps the most obvious power that the Congress enjoys in the arms control area lies in the authority of the Senate to approve ratification of all treaties. It is incumbent upon any administration to know exactly where the Senate stands on a whole host of negotiable issues. Though it was never put to a vote, the SALT II Treaty was in obvious trouble when President Carter withdrew the Treaty in January 1980 on the pretext of the Soviet invasion of Afghanistan. The withdrawal may have been related to a recognition that the SALT II Treaty would have failed to obtain the necessary two-thirds vote in the Senate.

Earlier disarmament agreements had little trouble obtaining Senate support. The Limited Test Ban Treaty passed easily with a vote of 80 to 19; the Nuclear Nonproliferation Treaty had a margin of 83 to 15; the Biological Convention of 1972 was passed unanimously; and the ABM Treaty received Senate support by an 88 to 2 margin after only two hours debate.

The power of the Senate to confirm top-level disarmament negotiators also provides some leverage for influencing arms control policy—a type of leverage that has been used more frequently in recent years. President Carter had special problems obtaining the approval of the Senate for his first ACDA director, Paul Warnke, who was considered by many to be too liberal on the issue of arms control. To gain support for the appointment, the president had to promise several opposition senators that the Joint Chiefs of Staff would play an important role in the negotiations.[54] The Senate also scrutinized the credentials of Kenneth Adelman as many members were disappointed with the performance of the Reagan administration in the arms control area and feared that Adelman might take an even more anti-arms control position than his predecessor Eugene Rostow. Congressional suspicions about Adelman's and the administration's lack of interest in arms control were intensified when Rostow, a leading member of the Committee on the Present Danger and a confirmed hawk on arms control issues, asserted that he had been dismissed because of his "zealous" championing of flexibility in the arms control negotiation.[55]

Not content to play a role at the end of the process, Congress sought to influence arms control policy at an earlier point through the use of resolutions and amendments to legislation spelling out congressional attitudes on arms control issues. For example, in May 1963 the Senate communicated its position on a comprehensive test ban that was under negotiation when it passed a resolution raising grave reservations about the United States asking for only seven on-site inspections annually. An even more interventionist position was taken in 1972 when the Jackson amendment was passed as part of the approval of the SALT I agreements. According to this amendment, any future SALT agreement must not limit the United States to levels of intercontinental strategic forces inferior to those of the Soviet Union as the Interim Offensive Weapons Agreement was alleged to have done. The amendment also required that a vigorous research, development, and modernization program be pursued. In a similar vein, the Derwinski amendment to ACDA's 1978 authorization bill declared it to be the sense of Congress that adequate verification should be an indispensable part of any arms control agreement.

These examples of congressional intervention are representative of efforts by those suspicious of arms control to influence policy by guaranteeing equality and verifiability, but one can find many examples where Congress has attempted to force the administration to take a more favorable position on arms control. Concern about how weapons developments would affect progress on arms control led the United States Congress in 1975 to pass legislation requiring that the Pentagon develop an arms control impact statement for every new weapons system. According to a 1980 estimate, there is no direct evidence that any weapons system has been significantly altered or dropped owing to factors raised in such statements. In fact, in only one case did an impact statement play a part in a congressional decision and that was with respect to the August 1977 decision on funding for the enhanced radiation warhead for the lance missile.[56] Arms control impact statements have been criticized as straining interdepartmental relations; being burdensome, time consuming and costly; and giving Congress ammunition to scuttle administration programs.[57] Perhaps dissatisfied with the limited effectiveness of arms control impact statements, the House shifted the burden to the administration by passing a resolution on May 31, 1985, which prohibits the development of submarine-launched cruise missiles (SLCMs) until the president submits a report to Congress describing a verifiable method of distinguishing such a missile from conventional SLCMs.

Since the Reagan administration has been viewed as uninterested in, if not actively opposed to, any arms control agreement, congressional activity designed to influence the administration's arms control policy has accelerated. This was particularly the case in 1982, influenced in part by the popularity of the freeze movement both within the United States and in Europe. Only after considerable lobbying was the administration able to defeat efforts in the House calling for an immediate weapons freeze. Republican control of the Senate enabled the administration to keep a similar resolution from going beyond the committee level. Despite this defeat, Congress has been successful in expressing its concern about Reagan's policies on arms control in several resolutions and amendments to military procurement bills. For example, in 1983 the House passed a resolution withholding appropriations for testing anti-satellite (ASAT) weapons for a year as long as the Soviet Union conducted no such tests. But the most vivid illustration of congressional intrusion in the arms control area occurred when the House, in amending the 1987 defense authorization bill, voted to ban spending for the deployment of nuclear weapons in excess of the SALT II limits (which the president said he intended to abandon), agreed to a one-year ban on ASAT testing, imposed a one-year moratorium on U.S. nuclear tests if the Soviets would agree to a similar ban, and agreed to continue a ban on the production of chemical weapons.

Congressional amendments of this sort have also been designed to influence the Soviet Union in the arms control negotiations as in the case of a May 1983 House vote threatening to proceed with MX procurement if strategic missile negotiations do *not* resume. Since it was the Soviets who walked out of the START talks, it was hoped that such a maneuver would induce the Soviets to return to the table.

Perhaps the best example of collusion between Congress and the administration in formulating an arms control position occurred with respect to the build-down proposal of 1983. This proposal, which would have required the United States and the Soviet Union to dismantle two missiles for every new missile built, was cosponsored by 45 senators, including 28 Republicans. After the administration accepted the plan as part of its own proposals presented in Geneva, Senator Charles Percy noted that "this is the first time in the history of the congress and the executive branch that we have worked out jointly an arms control proposal in which we are truly united."[58] Some have suggested, however, that the build-down proposal was accepted by President Reagan not because it made sense in terms of arms control but rather because the administration wanted congressional support for a critical vote on the MX.[59] General Rowny was reported on his return to Geneva to have suggested to his Soviet counterpart "that the old START proposal was the real one and that build-down was an ornament to placate the Congress."[60]

Congress, disturbed about what was perceived as a cavalier attitude with respect to the dangers of nuclear proliferation on the part of the Reagan administration, made a number of moves designed to minimize the dangers. In 1982, Congress outlawed the use of plutonium for commercial power plants and further sought to restrict the availability of plutonium by cutting off funding for the Barnwell spent-fuel reprocessing plant and the Clinch River breeder reactor. During the following year, the House passed an amendment to the Export Administration Act that sought to close loopholes by requiring full-scope safeguards as a condition for nuclear exports. Both houses also passed nonbinding resolutions banning administration-approved nuclear transfers to India, Argentina, and South Africa.

Congressional hearings may also serve to influence an administration's arms control policy. In noting the grilling that administration officials received in a June 1974 hearing of the Senate Armed Services Committee, former Secretary of State Henry A. Kissinger said that "the victim of the assault was any negotiating flexibility on SALT II at the forthcoming Moscow summit. All members of the bureaucracy were put on notice of the grilling that would await them before the Armed Services Committee; their safest course was to stick rigidly to the least controversial options."[61]

Serious interference with an administration's arms control policy and personnel occurred in 1974 when the Arms Control and Disarmament Agency was purged. According to one authority, it was due to Senator Jackson's urging that ACDA was purged in favor of more conservative personnel and the role of SALT negotiator and ACDA director was split.[62] Similar congressional pressures and concern about getting a SALT II treaty through the U.S. Senate led to the dismissal of Paul Warnke as head of ACDA in 1978 and his replacement by George Seignious, a retired Army general.

As a result of the activist role assumed by Congress in the arms control area, recent administrations have brought select congressmen into the process. Although in the early sixties President Kennedy was careful to keep congressional leaders informed of U.S. positions in the test ban negotiations, it was not until 1977 that Congress became actively involved in the negotiation process itself. It was in that year that President Carter first appointed members of Congress to serve as advisors to the SALT delegation, and many have attended sessions in Geneva since then. In the Geneva umbrella talks that began in 1985 ten senators were designated as an observer group and a permanent Senate office was established. One or two senators were assigned to remain in Geneva during critical sessions.

Having congressmen directly involved in the process may enhance bipartisan cooperation as well as reduce the likelihood that the product will be challenged. Balanced against this is the concern that congressmen might leak sensitive position papers or that they might use the information gained for domestic political purposes.

Soviet representatives apparently have not been disturbed by the direct participation of congressmen in Geneva, recognizing the critical role the Congress plays in issues of military procurement and arms control. In fact, the Soviet embassy in Washington actively lobbies the U.S. Congress in the hope of obtaining a more favorable hearing of Soviet positions.

It should not be assumed that all such organizational interventions are undesirable. If one disagrees with an administration's stance on arms control, whether viewing it to be too conservative or too liberal, such interventions may be viewed in a positive light. Congressional pressures may aid an administration in its bargaining with the Soviet Union as in the case of the 1963 Senate resolution on the issue of on-site inspection. This resolution placed the Soviet Union on notice that it would have to raise the number of on-site inspections if it hoped to obtain a comprehensive test ban treaty. Similarly, the Jackson amendment spelled out U.S. expectations for SALT II and as such was viewed by some as a bargaining chip for the United States. The 1972 Joint Congressional Resolution that reserved the right of the United States to withdraw from the ABM Treaty if a permanent strategic agreement was not reached in five years placed similar pressures on the Soviet Union to be more forthcoming in SALT II.

Just as Congress has sought to manipulate and influence the administration on arms control policy, various administrations have sought to use arms control negotiations to influence Congress on military procurement issues. For example, the proposal made by Assistant Secretary of State Richard Burt not to deploy the MX in return for the Soviet elimination of the SS-18 was designed to facilitate the development of MX. Congress would not dare to end the program if it were an essential bargaining chip.[63] Similarly, the Strategic Defense Initiative (SDI), introduced by President Reagan in 1983, became more difficult to attack because it had been introduced as a bargaining chip.

Little need be said about the parliamentary role in arms control in the Soviet Union since its involvement is so insignificant. The Supreme Soviet, which serves as the Soviet parliamentary body, meets only a few days each year, largely to rubber stamp political decisions made in various party and governmental organizations. Perhaps as a reaction to frequent American appeals that various proposals would not be acceptable to the American public or Congress, Stalin at Yalta demanded a certain concession lest he be unable to explain matters to the Supreme Soviet, but such an assertion can hardly be taken seriously.[64]

THE NEGOTIATING STRUCTURE

Disarmament negotiations in the postwar world have come in a variety of sizes and shapes. They have ranged from the United Nations Disarmament Commission, comprised of the more than 150 members of the United Nations, to the Strategic Arms Limitations talks, consisting of only the United States and the Soviet Union. Sometimes these negotiations have been restricted to specific disarmament issues such as a nuclear test ban, while, at other times, any subject related to arms control or building confidence among states had been germane. They have also varied considerably in terms of the size and status of the delegations involved. A listing of the major postwar disarmament negotiating bodies can be found in table 2.2

Table 2.2 Major Negotiating Forums

Years	Forum
	United Nations
1946–52	Atomic Energy Commission
1947–52	Commission for Conventional Disarmament
1952–	Disarmament Commission
1978 & 82	Special Session on Disarmament
	Multilateral Geneva Negotiations
1962	Ten Nation Disarmament Committee
1962–69	Eighteen Nation Disarmament Committee
1969–78	Conference of the Committee on Disarmament
1979–	Conference on Disarmament
	Trilateral Negotiations
1958–62	Geneva Conference on the Discontinuance of Nuclear Weapon Tests
1977–81	Comprehensive Test Ban Negotiations
	Bilateral Negotiations
1969–79	Strategic Arms Limitation Talks (SALT)
1981–83	Strategic Arms Reduction Talks (START)
1981–83	Intermediate-range Nuclear Force Talks (INF)
1985–	Geneva Umbrella Talks
1977–78	Arms Control in the Indian Ocean
1977–79	Conventional Arms Transfer Talks
1977–79	Anti-Satellite Arms Control Talks
1977–	Nuclear Nonproliferation
1977–	Chemical and Radiological Weapons Negotiations (revived 1986)
	Multilateral European Negotiations
1973–	Mutual Balanced Force Reduction Talks
1984–	Conference on Confidence and Security Building Measures and Disarmament in Europe

The early postwar disarmament negotiations were conducted primarily under the auspices of the United Nations. It was for this reason that the structure of these negotiations followed that of the United Nations. Since the Charter gave prime responsibility for keeping the peace and security of the world to the members of the Security Council, these members assumed the primary role in negotiating arms control as two separate bodies were formed—the Atomic Energy Commission and the

Commission for Conventional Disarmament.[65] These two bodies were merged in 1952 with the creation of the U.N. Disarmament Commission (UNDC).

As the membership of the United Nations expanded, currently numbering more than three times its initial 1945 total, pressure for increasing the number of states participating in disarmament forums was exerted. The General Assembly began to hold extended debates on disarmament issues in its First Committee as well as in its own plenary sessions. Unlike the Security Council, both bodies included the total membership of the United Nations. Pressures were also exerted by the growing number of U.N. members to increase the size of the U.N. Disarmament Commission (UNDC), which became a committee composed of the entire U.N. membership in 1958. By 1965 the commission had become dormant, only to be revived in 1978 when it was reactivated by the first U.N. Special Session on Disarmament. The UNDC, except for those years in which a Special Session is held, now meets annually to discuss general issues of disarmament.

During the 1960s the primary locus of disarmament negotiations was transferred from the United Nations in New York to negotiating bodies headquartered in Geneva. This change of location was reflected first in the tripartite Geneva Conference on the Discontinuance of Nuclear Weapon Tests, which met from 1959 to 1962. During 1960 the Ten Nation Committee on Disarmament, equally divided between Eastern and Western nations, became the focus of negotiations. This short-lived committee was followed two years later by the Eighteen Nation Disarmament Committee (ENDC), which added eight neutral states. Reflective of the pressures to increase the size of negotiating bodies, the number of nations included in the ENDC and its successors increased to 26 in 1969, to 31 some six years later, and reached its current size of 40 states in 1979.[66] In 1984 this Geneva body became officially known as the Conference on Disarmament.

Because the United Nations Disarmament Conference and the various Geneva negotiating forums became so large as to be unwieldy, subcommittee meetings and other smaller negotiating bodies have been utilized, particularly whenever negotiations become serious. From 1954 to 1957 a subcommittee of the UNDC met for intensive discussions in London. During the period 1959–62 negotiations for a test ban were conducted in tripartite meetings consisting of the United States, the Soviet Union, and the United Kingdom. With the creation of the Eighteen Nation Disarmament Committee, these three states met as a subcommittee of the ENDC.

The Limited Test Ban Treaty was negotiated in an ad hoc meeting in Moscow during the summer of 1963.

Beginning in 1969, the most important disarmament negotiations were conducted bilaterally between the United States and the Soviet Union with the opening of the Strategic Arms Limitation Talks (SALT) in Helsinki. Subsequent SALT meetings were held in Geneva and Vienna, but by 1973 Geneva became the permanent site for strategic arms negotiations. The bilateral Strategic Arms Reduction Talks (START) and the Intermediate-range Nuclear Force Talks (INF) were initiated in 1981 only to be suspended in December 1983 as the Soviet Union made good its threat to walk out of the talks if NATO proceeded with its planned deployment of Pershing II and cruise missiles. It was two years before bilateral negotiations on strategic and intermediate-range nuclear arms were resumed under the aegis of the Geneva umbrella talks. Also included in these discussions was the issue of strategic defense systems, which began to concern the Soviet Union as a result of the Reagan administration's decision to pursue the Strategic Defense Initiative, popularly referred to as Star Wars.

A number of other bilateral negotiations were undertaken by the United States and the Soviet Union during the late seventies. These included negotiations on chemical weapons, conventional arms transfer, Indian Ocean arms limitations, and anti-satellite systems. During this period, the two superpowers met with the United Kingdom in an attempt to negotiate a comprehensive test ban treaty. None of these negotiations was resumed during the first Reagan administration, but in late 1984 the United States and the Soviet Union agreed to hold bilateral talks on non-proliferation issues every six months. In March 1986 bilateral talks were initiated on the issue of curbing chemical weapons.

The United States and the Soviet Union have also been involved in two multilateral negotiations dealing with problems of European armaments. In 1973 the Mutual Balanced Force Reductions (MBFR) talks, which included nineteen NATO and Warsaw Pact members, were begun in Vienna and have continued to the present, albeit with no results. In 1984 a different tack was taken in a conference that began in Stockholm among the thirty-five states who participated in the Conference on Security and Cooperation in Europe. The emphasis in these talks was on confidence-building measures in the hope that the participants might be able to agree upon activities and reassurances that could reduce the level of international tension and thus create an environment that would in turn facilitate movement toward disarmament.

Size of Negotiating Body

The experience of past disarmament negotiations seems to suggest that the number of states involved can make a difference both in terms of the character of the negotiations and the likelihood of success. States participating in larger negotiating bodies are more likely to engage in propaganda than those in smaller bodies. With large numbers of participants, it becomes more difficult to conduct the negotiations in secret, making both states and citizens throughout the world attractive targets of propagandistic appeals. When many of those states are less developed nations, there is considerable incentive for the more powerful states to attempt to generate goodwill by promising that any savings from their proposed disarmament schemes will be used for global economic development. The appealing themes of peace and security tend to be repeated often in such forums.

Evidence that disarmament negotiations involving more participants engage not only in more propaganda but also more verbal hostility was found in a content analysis of Soviet and American speeches before both types of bodies during the period 1954–57.[67] Table 2.3 summarizes the results based upon the frequency with which eight propaganda themes and seven hostility themes were raised by the United States and the Soviet Union in 63 meetings of the five-power London Disarmament Subcommittee and 32 meetings of the much larger U.N. Disarmament Commission and the First Committee of the General Assembly. In all instances both propaganda and hostility scores were higher in the two larger bodies than they were in the five-power meetings. The difference was least noticeable for the propaganda scores of the United States, which were 2.00 and 1.78, respectively. The Soviet Union, on the other hand, scored an average of 3.91 propaganda themes per meeting in speeches before the First Committee and the UNDC as contrasted with a score of only 2.30 during the Subcommittee meetings. The hostility scores in the larger bodies for both the United States and the Soviet Union were more than double those found in the Subcommittee sessions. Regardless of size, the data also show the Soviet Union to be more prone than the United States to use both propaganda and hostility during disarmament debates.

The larger size of a negotiating body is also likely to affect the process of reaching a consensus. More interests and values will have to be reflected and compromised when large numbers of states participate. The result will often consist of vague or watered-down agreements in order to accommodate the diversity of interests involved. Also, it can be

Table 2.3 Propaganda and Hostility in Large and Small Negotiating Bodies, 1954–57

Negotiating Body Propaganda Average*	U.S.	USSR	Total
First Committee & UNDC	2.00	3.91	3.01
Disarmament Subcommittee	1.78	2.30	2.05
Hostility Average**			
First Committee & UNDC	.79	1.25	1.05
Disarmamament Subcommittee	.29	.52	.41

*Propaganda themes: Economic savings; prevent wars; prevent surprise attack; strengthen peace; reduce tension; security; build confidence; stop nuclear fallout
**Hostility themes: Adversary is aggressive; evasive; lacks good faith; seeks military advantage; engages in propaganda; lies; is not flexible

anticipated that such negotiations will require more time to reach agreements as each interest seeks to be heard.

A number of devices have been utilized in an effort to minimize the negative aspects of large negotiating bodies and to make them more efficient. During the Eighteen Nation Disarmament Committee meetings the practice of having the United States and the Soviet Union serve as cochairmen proved to be an effective procedure, particularly in terms of negotiating the 1968 Nuclear Nonproliferation Treaty (NPT). Not only were the cochairmen able to direct the agenda and ultimately to focus attention upon the problem of nonproliferation, they found it possible to resolve many of their differences on a bilateral basis in meetings outside the ENDC. By cooperating as cochairmen, the United States and the Soviet Union were able to develop a joint draft treaty proposal that was ultimately adopted with minor input from other members.

The process was not without criticism as it led the nonnuclear weapons states to complain that the two superpowers had developed a condominium between themselves that had the effect of forcing an unequal treaty upon the nonnuclear weapons states. It was argued that the NPT would restrict the nuclear aspiration of nonnuclear states while doing nothing about existing nuclear weapons. The cochairmen approach was also a major factor in France's refusal to participate in the Geneva talks, and it was only after the procedure was abolished in 1979 with the creation of the successor Committee on Disarmament that France took its seat at the table. This forty-member body, which continues to meet in

Geneva under its new title, the Conference on Disarmament, now provides for a monthly rotation of chairmen among all members.

Another technique in helping a large negotiating body to proceed in a businesslike fashion has been the use of consensus-building rather than formal voting. As the Conference on Disarmament expanded in size, it gradually dispensed entirely with voting arrangements in favor of group consensus. Although such a procedure may lessen some friction as states move toward the adoption of resolutions upon which all can agree, the process has not been very productive in furthering an arms control regime. In fact, no arms control agreement has come from these multilateral Geneva meetings since the Convention on Environmental Modification was negotiated in 1977. It requires only a few critical states to undermine the whole process as indeed the United States and a handful of other states did with respect to the Law of the Seas Treaty, which was negotiated over the period 1974 to 1982 using a similar consensus-building process. Dissatisfied with the results, the Reagan administration demanded that the treaty, upon which almost all other states had agreed, be renegotiated.

The use of large multilateral negotiating bodies has necessitated the creation of working coalitions in what would otherwise be a chaotic negotiating environment. These coalitions have reflected the major ideological groupings in the world—East, West, and neutral. The Eighteen Nation Disarmament Committee included eight neutral states who took an active role in lobbying the East-West protagonists and in presenting proposals of their own. With the growth in size to forty members, the neutral group in the Geneva negotiating body now numbers twenty-one and continues to meet frequently to develop a common position. Often a spokesperson will be designated to speak in the plenary sessions on behalf of the entire group.

Another innovative technique developed in the Geneva Conference on Disarmament involves the use of ad hoc subsidiary bodies focusing on a specific issue area. Participants may join any group they wish, whether it be the group dealing with chemical weapons, comprehensive disarmament, a comprehensive nuclear test ban, or outer space. Under rule 32, nations outside of the group of forty may request the right to participate in these ad hoc sessions as more than twenty states have done.

The involvement of neutral states in the negotiations has been beneficial to the extent that it has not simply provided an incentive to increase the propaganda level of the negotiations. A participant in the debates on the nuclear test ban, for example, has argued that the memo submitted by the eight neutral nations in 1962 was a major factor prompting the

Soviet Union to accept the notion of two or three on-site inspections per year.[68] The holding of the SALT talks and the progress toward strategic arms control resulting from those talks were in no small measure related to the continuing pressures exerted upon the superpowers by the non-nuclear weapons states to reduce strategic capabilities. Indeed, it was these states that forced the inclusion of article 6 in the Nuclear Non-proliferation Treaty. Article 6 makes continued support for the treaty dependent upon progress toward controlling strategic weapons on the part of the nuclear weapons states.

In addition to the ability of third parties to exert pressure upon the primary disputants, in this case the United States and the Soviet Union, they can serve other functions that may facilitate the negotiating process. For example, they may play an important mediating role by making suggestions—suggestions that will be easier to accept if coming from a third party rather than the protagonist. In such cases concern about losing face or damaging one's bargaining reputation will be minimized.

Third parties may also be able to play an important role in disarmament by serving on inspection teams. This role is likely to be an important one if the two sides can reach agreement on the issue of on-site inspection. Neutral inspectors might be viewed as preferable to inspectors from the other nation or the latter's allies. The Soviet Union, always sensitive about intrusive verification procedures, was quick to respond positively to an offer made in 1986 by six nonaligned states to monitor a comprehensive test ban.[69]

A long-time student of international negotiation, Charles Iklé, has suggested that the addition of neutral participants to the Eighteen Nation Disarmament Committee made the Soviet negotiators use more reasonable arguments than in earlier conferences that lacked neutral participation.[70] The Soviet Union under such circumstances was interested in obtaining the approval of the neutral states, which it recognized would not be forthcoming if the Soviet Union assumed unreasonable positions.

For political reasons it might also be useful to include allied states in the negotiations. Considerable strains appeared in the NATO alliance as the United States and the Soviet Union negotiated strategic arms control. The European states were concerned that the United States might undermine European security interests in those negotiations. Similarly, Japan has been fearful that an agreement to limit the deployment of SS-20s in Europe might only lead to their redeployment in the Far East.

Although inclusion in the negotiations might help reassure allies, increased opportunities are provided for the opposition to attempt to divide the allies from each other. The national security interests of allies are often not consonant, providing a wedge for the opponent to introduce proposals that are known to be divisive. The Soviet Union in the late fifties sought to divide France from other NATO members by supporting the French interest in a ban on ballistic missiles. More than two decades later the Soviet Union was seeking to divide NATO over the issue of theater nuclear weapons—an issue made all the more sensitive because of the European anti-nuclear movement, which was gaining momentum in several countries. West European suspicions of the Federal Republic of Germany have also provided another area that could be exploited by the Soviet Union to divide the Western alliance system. On the other hand, U.S. efforts to divide the Warsaw Pact have been much less successful. Nevertheless, Rumania has shown considerable independence from Russia on national security issues, particularly on the question of nuclear proliferation. Like France, Rumania has refused to participate in the Mutal Balanced Force Reduction Talks. But the most surprising divergence came with respect to the issue of intermediate-range nuclear forces when Nicolae Ceausescu endorsed the original U.S. zero-option proposal.

The extent to which the United States has attempted to reassure its European allies on the issue of strategic arms control can be seen in Ambassador Gerard Smith's comment that during the more than two and a half years of the SALT I negotiations, the United States held some twenty-two briefings.[71] Nevertheless, European suspicions and fears have remained, gaining further momentum as the United States and the Soviet Union began to negotiate the issue of theater nuclear forces in Europe during the Intermediate-range Nuclear Force Talks in 1981.

The constraints that allied powers place upon negotiating positions are obvious, but the existence of allies has sometimes been used by the superpowers as an excuse for hard bargaining. The position of the Federal Republic of Germany was used to rationalize the U.S. refusal to modify its demand that all U.S. and USSR intermediate-range nuclear forces be removed from Europe. In fact, however, Chancellor Helmut Kohl favored more flexibility on the issue.[72] By obtaining allied support on a given U.S. disarmament position, one would expect that position to have greater impact upon the Soviet Union at the bargaining table than if the United States presented it separately. Allied bargaining strength in the Mutual Balanced Force Reduction Talks is strengthened by the fact that all NATO proposals are presented by the alliance rather than by individual nation-states as is the case in all other disarmament bodies.

Whether or not to include neutral or allied parties in negotiations is not so critical as involving the most relevant parties. Relevance will be dependent upon the issue under discussion. If there is interest in reducing nuclear weapons to a very low level, it is vital to include most, if not all, nuclear powers in the discussion and eventual agreement. The absence of France and China from many of the postwar negotiations would have been a serious problem had the superpowers been able to agree to significant reductions. Successful efforts to stop the spread of nuclear weapons will require the active participation of those with the technological and economic capability of producing such weapons—the so-called nuclear threshold states. Or if one wants to obtain a comprehensive agreement controlling nuclear or conventional weapons in Europe, it becomes necessary to include other NATO and Warsaw Pact nations. The initiation of the Mutual Balanced Force Reduction Talks in 1973 involving twelve NATO members and seven Warsaw Pact nations was a recognition of this reality. Pressure will continue to be exerted to include France and the United Kingdom in multilateral discussions related to intermediate-range nuclear force capabilities or at least to take their capabilities into account in any final treaty. Both the French and the British have considerable intermediate-range nuclear capability that the Soviet Union asserts requires compensation, for such capability threatens Soviet territory as much as any U.S. nuclear capability.

The parties affected by U.S.-Soviet arms control negotiations often go beyond the obvious ones. For example, an agreement between the United States and the Soviet Union on the demilitarization of the Indian Ocean could have serious security implications for Pakistan and perhaps even Iran, increasing their incentive for becoming nuclear weapons states. Many states concerned about the continued supply of fissionable material have a vested interest in the discussions and agreements reached by the London Supplier Group. Unnecessary anxiety was aroused in such states because of the secrecy involved in the London meetings from which recipient states were excluded.

Negotiating Teams

Not only does the number of nations involved affect the character and possibly even the outcome of the negotiations but the nature and authority of the negotiating teams themselves may have an important impact. Obviously the higher the negotiator is in the national decision-making process, the greater is his or her ability to commit the state. Modern communications have diminished the negotiating power of the diplomat in the field as the negotiator is carefully instructed on each move. Even the smallest detail must be checked with the home government before a delegation can commit the state. Failure to obtain higher political approval for a proposed move may even lead to an official reproach as in the case of the dismissal of Harold Stassen as U.S. disarmament negotiator in the fall of 1957 for exceeding instructions and the disapproval by both U.S. and Soviet governments of a tentative agreement on intermediate-range nuclear forces worked out in the summer of 1982 by their respective Geneva representatives Paul Nitze and Yuli Kvitsinsky.

Negotiations at the chief executive or foreign minister level have certain advantages over lower-level negotiations. They communicate serious intentions on the part of the negotiators, for top-level decision makers are unwilling to commit their personal prestige unless agreement seems within reach. Higher-level officials can also commit their state more readily, adding to the credibility of the positions taken and the likelihood that the agreement will not be rejected subsequently. Such negotiations are likely to progress more rapidly and flexibly because of the greater ability of leaders to commit the state without relying upon instructions for every move.

Although certain advantages may accrue to higher-level negotiations, the utilization of such negotiations is not without its costs. The knowledge of the high-level official may be fairly limited when it comes to complex arms control issues. Criticism has been leveled against both Henry Kissinger and Richard Nixon for some of the positions they took at the Moscow summit conference in 1972 in their frantic attempt to complete the negotiation of the SALT I agreements. Even more serious were events which occurred at the Reykjavik summit in October 1986 when President Reagan, in private meetings with Mikhail Gorbachev and without input from the Joint Chiefs of Staff, came close to committing the United States to positions that many in the United States and Europe regarded as disastrous from the perspective of Western security interests. Only at the last moment did the deal fail as a result of the Soviet position on the Strategic Defense Initiative.

Flexibility in negotiation may also be reduced to the extent that foreign ministers and chiefs of state insist upon extensive involvement in the details of negotiation. A major problem during Kissinger's tenure, first as national security advisor and then as secretary of state, revolved around his insistence that many minor matters be cleared personally with him. The ability of the United States to respond in a timely manner was particularly undermined during Kissinger's tenure as secretary of state at which time he undertook not only to run the State Department but to engage in shuttle diplomacy in the Middle East. Kissinger's other preoccupations may have been a contributing factor in the slow progress made toward the negotiation of the SALT II agreement while he was in office.

A Kissinger strategy that was subjected to even more criticism was his utilization of two-track diplomacy in which many of the most significant moves by the United States and the Soviet Union were made in sessions between Kissinger and the Soviet Ambassador to the United States, Anatoly Dobrynin. These negotiations were undertaken without the knowledge of the chief U.S. negotiator at the SALT talks, Gerard Smith. His Soviet counterpart in these talks, on the other hand, was kept informed of these developments.

Although there was greater coordination between Washington and the Geneva delegation during the Carter period, higher-level foreign minister meetings as well as private contacts with Dobrynin in Washington frequently upstaged the SALT talks. Many of the most critical concessions were made in talks between Soviet Foreign Minister Andrei Gromyko and Cyrus Vance, the U.S. secretary of state.Gromyko also had a number of direct meetings with President Carter on SALT-related matters.

High-level U.S.-Soviet meetings during the Reagan administration have been few in number. It was not until into his second term as president that Ronald Reagan finally met his Soviet counterpart despite the fact that U.S.-Soviet summits had become almost regular affairs. Reagan's first meeting with Andrei Gromyko, the Soviet foreign minister, had occurred only a little over a year before that.

Reagan's first secretary of state, Alexander Haig, had planned to open back-channel negotiations with his counterpart Andrei Gromyko to discuss arms control issues, but Haig's premature departure from government in 1982 precluded such activities.[73] His successor George Shultz was initially reticent about such meetings, perhaps in part because of his relative lack of knowledge and experience in the arms control area. In the first Gromyko-Shultz meeting, which occurred in New York in September 1982 when Gromyko was attending the United Nations, the issue of arms control was hardly raised. The same can be said of their next meeting at the Conference on Security and Cooperation in Europe in Madrid in September 1983, which has been described as the "chilliest, most vituperative high-level Soviet-American session in decades."[74] The special interaction with Soviet Ambassador Dobrynin was largely halted as he was denied the parking privileges at the State Department that he had enjoyed since Kissinger's tenure there.

Although it is heads of state and foreign ministers who receive all the press attention, it is the chief negotiator and his or her team at the bargaining site who deserve much of the credit. Such negotiators sit through hundreds of meetings listening to endless repetition. On the whole, Soviet chief negotiators have had greater longevity and experience in arms control negotiations than their American counterparts. Following the pattern of longevity in office shown by Andrei Gromyko, who served as foreign minister for twenty-eight years, Yakov A. Malik, Vladimir Semenov, Semyon K. Tsarapkin, and Viktor P. Karpov served as key Soviet spokespersons on disarmament issues for more than a decade each. Soviet Ambassador Anatoly F. Dobrynin, whose important role in the back-channel negotiations has been noted, held the position of Soviet ambassador to the United States for almost a quarter of a century before returning to Moscow in 1986 to assume a high-level Party post.

In contrast, virtually every major set of negotiations has seen a new U.S. disarmament chief, and several negotiations have had more than one head. Gerard C. Smith was replaced as chief U.S. negotiator after the successful negotiation of SALT I; Paul Warnke, as SALT negotiating chief under President Carter, was forced out after only two years in the job; and Paul Nitze and Edward L. Rowney did not return to their posts as head, respectively, of the INF and START talks when debates on these issues were resumed in 1985. Seldom have U.S. disarmament chiefs assumed their positions with much experience in arms control negotiations as illustrated by Frederick Osborn during UNAEC days and William C. Foster at the 1958 Surprise Attack Conference. More recently, President Reagan selected attorney Max Kampelman as overall chief of the Geneva negotiations that resumed in 1985, but Kampelman had little experience in disarmament negotiations, let alone international negotiations, save for his role in the Madrid Conference of the European Conference on Security and Cooperation in 1983.

The problem of continuity is not limited to the chief negotiators as the turnover at the staff level has also been extensive. Foreign service officers and military advisors generally have not been interested in a long tenure in the arms control area, for it does not enhance their careers. Two or three years appear to be the norm for service on disarmament staffs. The occasional purges of arms control specialists, resulting from concern that they may become too pro-arms control, have also taken their toll on ACDA. Not only were fourteen high-level ACDA officials fired after the signing of the SALT I agreements, but the purge was extended to one-third of the agency's personnel.

Any institution that turns over its membership that frequently is bound to lose institutional memory, making it necessary to begin each set of negotiations anew. Those individuals just beginning their roles as negotiators are bound to feel a sense of personal insecurity, particularly given the level of experience of their Soviet counterparts. To hide such insecurities, negotiators will often resort to excessive belligerency in their personal interactions, but this does not bode well for successful negotiation.

As new administrations have assumed power they have tended to distrust all that has happened before them, particularly when a change of party is involved. President Carter's disarmament advisors sought to disassociate themselves from the Kissinger era by proposing deep cuts in offensive capabilities, but, because of the hostile Soviet reaction to the proposals, they were forced to retreat to positions more similar to those of their predecessors. In the meantime, valuable time was lost in the negotiating process. Similarly, President Reagan campaigned in 1980 on the issue of an allegedly flawed SALT II Treaty only to announce subsequently that he would abide by the treaty if the Soviet Union would do the same.

Just as important as experience in assuring successful negotiation is the level of access which the negotiator enjoys with top-level decision makers. Arthur Goldberg has noted his advantages over his Soviet counterpart in negotiations on the Outer Space Treaty in 1967. In this negotiation Goldberg enjoyed direct access to the power centers whereas the Soviet representatives could only send a telegram to whomever was supervising the activity in the foreign office and who would in turn pass it up the Soviet hierarchy.[75] In the process, such messages as they move up the decision-making ladder can be grossly distorted from what was communicated in the first place by the negotiator in the field.

The earlier success of the Harriman mission to Moscow in 1963 to negotiate the Limited Test Ban Treaty was in no small measure related to the complete access that Harriman had with President Kennedy and to the latter's hour-by-hour monitoring of the situation. Most ACDA heads and chief negotiators have had very limited access to the president, often being forced to go through the secretary of state.

Part of the problem of access is related to the relatively low priority that is given to disarmament negotiations in both the United States and Soviet decision-making structures. That SALT was not the highest priority for the Soviet Union is suggested by the fact that on the eve of the opening of those negotiations, the Soviet Union replaced its chief negotiator because, as a deputy foreign minister, his services were needed in negotiations with China. On the other hand, the Soviet Union showed increased concern about arms control when in January

1987 it appointed Yuli M. Vorontsov, a deputy foreign minister, to be its chief negotiator.

How close a negotiating team is perceived to be with its home government will have important implications in terms of how credible that team will be regarded in the disarmament negotiations. The Soviet Union may be somewhat leery of a U.S. negotiating team which is considered by Washington and important members of Congress to be too inclined to compromise. After all, the Soviet Union was embarrassed by the fact that President Carter was unable to obtain Senate approval of the SALT II Treaty.

Relations between the negotiating team and the capital were perhaps least cordial during the SALT I period, leading ultimately to the extensive purge noted earlier. Part of the strain was related to the disdain with which both Nixon and Kissinger held bureaucrats. The fact that the SALT negotiators were not informed of higher-level negotiations led to considerable confusion in the negotiating process. Gerard C. Smith has chronicled a number of cases in which the SALT team was not only kept in complete ignorance of negotiations between Henry Kissinger and Anatoly Dobrynin but was also instructed to convey different messages to the Soviet Union than Kissinger was presenting. While Kissinger was telling the Soviets and the world that the Soviet proposals in September 1970 were negotiable, the SALT negotiators were under quite different instructions.[76]

This is not to say that the presentation of varying positions by different actors within the same nation is dysfunctional. Indeed, it may be illustrative of the frequently used bargaining strategy of tough cop/soft cop in which the person playing the soft cop attempts to befriend the target by being supportive while the tough cop is out of the room. General Rowny has noted that Soviet disarmament negotiators have often asked Western negotiators to ally with them against the Soviet military or the Kremlin, who was assuming a harder line. Henry Kissinger and Richard Nixon also were reported to have used the technique during various negotiations. William Safire has written that "sometimes Kissinger played the tough guy, sometimes Nixon did, so the bid they presented could not always be analyzed in terms of the next step."[77] Kissinger and Secretary of Defense James Schlesinger were also reported to have played a similar carrot and stick approach in bargaining with the Soviet Union.[78]

THE NEGOTIATING PROCESS

Given the many years of disarmament negotiation, certain norms have evolved regarding how negotiations are to be conducted—norms that if violated can set the negotiations back several months. One of these requires that major proposals be presented informally before being introduced in public sessions so as not to create any surprises and to allow the adversary time to respond. Such a process was used in both MBFR and SALT. Indeed, the Soviet Union's harsh reaction to the March 1977 SALT proposals calling for extensive strategic arms reductions may have been partially related to the fact that the U.S. administration presented the proposal publicly before showing it to Soviet representatives. Similarly, the United States showed strong disapproval in December 1985 when the Soviet Union published its proposals for a fifteen-year disarmament scheme prior to tabling them at Geneva.

Bilateral U.S.-Soviet negotiations have provided a useful balance between formal and informal meetings. Informal contacts between lower-level personnel have been particularly important with respect to feeling out the position of the other side and developing innovative solutions to problems. Suggestions can be made before they become written in stone through public presentation of the proposals in more formal meetings. This procedure allows retreat from untenable positions without sacrificing face.

Informal approaches have sometimes been made by individual delegates who have sought to break deadlocks. Jerome Weisner has noted his suggestion made to his counterpart Yevgeni K. Federov that one way for the test ban negotiations to get off dead center would be for Khrushchev to state to Kennedy that three or four inspections per year would be sufficient. The president might counter with seven or eight, which he did. This in turn might be compromised at five or so.[79] It has been reported that Soviet representatives have sometimes departed from the official line, even offering suggestions on how certain U.S. concessions might help them break through bureaucratic bottlenecks with the Soviet Union.[80] Numerous informal meetings have also occurred between low-level negotiators. Gerard Smith, for example, noted that he worked informally with his Soviet counterpart Vladimir Semenov for hundreds of hours during SALT I.[81]

There is a danger that the process may become too informal, for if each member of a negotiating team were allowed to go off on his own, confusion would result. It could become impossible for the other side to recognize just which position a state is taking. Suspicions might arise that trial balloons are being floated with individual participants solely for the purpose of gaining intelligence about the opponent's bargaining position. To correct the problem, centralized control may be established by requiring that every informal meeting be reported along with details of the discussion. In fact, in SALT I all such contacts had to be cleared in advance.[82]

Agencies in Washington and Moscow have generally been the ones that have pressed for more formal meetings in view of their desire to control the negotiations. They prefer such meetings, because they provide the verbatim negotiating record necessary to counter moves they believe not to be in the interest of the nation or their particular agency. The more that various bureaucratic agencies conflict over arms control policies, the more insistent such agencies will be upon formal record-keeping. Verbatim records are also important in order to clarify interpretations of positions when a state subsequently attempts to evaluate compliance with an arms control agreement. It was based upon such concerns that Ambassador Gerard Smith expressed amazement that a formal record of a number of White House discussions with the Soviet Union on SALT matters was never kept.[83]

Another norm followed in recent U.S.-Soviet bilateral negotiations is that of secrecy. Unlike the openness of multilateral negotiations with the published records of the proceedings, verbatim bilateral negotiations and proposals, beginning with the Strategic Arms Limitation Talks in 1969, remain secret. But during the Carter and Reagan administrations there has been an increasing tendency to make major proposals public. There are a number of advantages to secret negotiations, chief of which is the need to insulate the proceedings from international and domestic groups who may impede the process while delicate negotiations are under way. Congressmen as well as individual governmental agencies and foreign governments have not been immune to providing one-sided interpretations of moves being taken in disarmament negotiations, thus undercutting proposals before they have had a fair hearing.

Negotiations that are conducted in secret may make compromise easier. Public presentation of proposals may stiffen a state's position as it needs to publicly defend itself. Compromise becomes more difficult because of concern about losing face or bargaining reputation. Public awareness of positions also enables opponents to charge that one side is giving up more than the other side—for example, in the case of concessions on the number of on-site inspections for the proposed nuclear test ban in the early sixties. U.S. flexibility was undercut with the argument that it had given up more than the Soviet Union by reducing the number of annual inspections from twenty to six while the Soviet Union fluctuated only between zero and three. Overlooked in this case was the fact that verification capabilities by national technical means had improved considerably during the time involved.

The increased use of propaganda in public sessions also interferes with the progress of negotiations. Speeches tend to be much less businesslike as attempts are made to appeal to both domestic and international audiences. Evidence of this can be found in the content analysis noted earlier, which showed that U.S.-Soviet hostility and propaganda scores were somewhat lower in the closed London Disarmament Subcommittee meetings in 1954–57 than they were in corresponding meetings in larger, open forums debating disarmament at the same time.

It should be noted that secrecy does not eliminate political interference. Indeed, it may only accelerate such interference because of the suspicion that may arise over whether the negotiators are looking out for the national interest—suspicions that may be ameliorated by opening negotiations to public scrutiny. Allies and neutrals may be reassured by more openness so that they do not feel that their interests are being ignored or, worse, having their interests sacrificed for the sake of superpower agreement. The lack of information about on-going negotiations may result in fewer positive interventions in the negotiating process. The more that is known about the negotiating positions, the more outsiders may be able to suggest ways out of a given bottleneck. Public awareness can place pressure upon negotiators to resolve their differences. The ratification process may become easier if the public is made aware of the issues at stake. The educational value of disarmament negotiations should not be underestimated. It may even be that concessions presented publicly will be more acceptable to domestic publics than those that have the flavor of closed-door conspiracies. As Daniel Druckman writes " . . . the same compromise arrived at secretly may not look nearly so bad as if arrived at openly. . . ."[84]

CONCLUSION

Bargaining behavior between the United States and the Soviet Union in the postwar disarmament negotiations has been affected by a wide variety of domestic and international factors, beginning with the cultural and ideological traits that the two states bring with them to the bargaining table. The Soviet Union, given its insecurities, appears to be highly rank- and hierarchy-conscious, leading it to prefer negotiations in which equality is recognized in terms of both negotiators and states.

While Soviet negotiators suffer from considerable paranoia resulting in rigid bargaining behavior, they also show great patience, enabling them to outlast the opposition in the pursuit of their goals. This is particularly true in negotiations with a democratic state like the United States, which some analysts believe is willing to make concessions too readily in the belief that compromise is the way to get things done.

Many observers have noted that some of the most intense bargaining goes on within states rather than between states. On this score, the Soviet Union, with a more centralized decision-making process, is less threatened by bureaucratic struggles. Since divisions can be exploited by outsiders, the authoritarian state enjoys certain advantages in being able to manipulate external domestic groups. At the same time, while authoritarian states may be more flexible in shifting positions rapidly, they suffer from their own rigidities and a lack of creativity as a result of the fear of raising and exploring all options.

Positions assumed by the United States and the Soviet Union have in no small measure been related to the interest and persuasiveness of the top leadership. Kennedy and Carter were perhaps the most enthusiastic about arms control among postwar presidents, but Nixon with the assistance of Kissinger was among the most successful as he negotiated the SALT I agreements and ushered in an era of détente. Ronald Reagan and his advisors, on the other hand, have been the most hostile toward arms control, caring little if any agreements are reached. Most U.S.-Soviet arms agreements were signed during the long tenure of Brezhnev, although Khrushchev personally was probably more predisposed toward arms control. The most active Soviet leader in terms of taking arms control initiatives has been Mikhail Gorbachev. Whether these initiatives are designed to exploit a reluctant Reagan administration or are serious overtures toward arms control remains to be seen.

Despite high-level interest in arms control, the bureaucracy has shown itself capable of undermining the best-intentioned leaders. The military has generally been the most powerful bureaucracy to be reckoned with in both societies when it comes to arms control policy. Yet it would be an oversimplification to say that it has been the military that has been the primary obstacle to arms control. For example, the Senate, led by Senator Henry Jackson, sought to restrain the arms control policies of Nixon and Kissinger, which were viewed as giving up too much to the Soviet Union. During the Reagan administration, pressures from Congress have been directed toward pressing the administration to negotiate seriously with the Soviet Union on arms control.

Finally, it has been noted that the negotiating structure itself may affect bargaining styles and outcomes. Generally speaking, U.S.-Soviet negotiations have been more productive when conducted in bilateral and closed rather than in multilateral and open forums. The larger the size of the negotiating body, the more likely propaganda and hostility are used. This does not mean that larger forums, particularly those in which one or more states can play the role of a mediator, have not been useful. The United Kingdom played an important role in negotiating the test ban issue, and the neutral states in the various Geneva negotiating bodies have been influential in pressing for progress on disarmament and in suggesting plausible solutions to problems. States whose cooperation is essential for a given arms control regime to be effective should be included in the negotiating body. If one anticipates substantial nuclear arms reductions between the superpowers, it will be critical that France, the United Kingdom, and China participate.

Other important factors relating to the success of negotiations involve the composition of the negotiating teams and perhaps even more importantly their access to top-level decision makers in the home government. There is no substitute for skilled and knowledgeable diplomats capable of generating trust both at home and in the opposing camp. The Soviet Union may have some advantage in this respect over the United States because of the longevity of its disarmament negotiating teams. The United States replaces its teams frequently, often using members with little or no experience in the arms control area.

The probability of success is also related to the negotiating process itself. Generally speaking, informality and secrecy have proved more conducive to successful negotiations. But it may be that negotiators more interested in a successful outcome are more willing to utilize informal and closed meetings than those wanting such negotiations to fail. A more detailed examination of the role that compromise has played in the postwar disarmament negotiations will be provided in the next chapter.

3

Concessionary Behavior

Perhaps more than anything, effective bargaining requires a willingness to make concessions if the goal is to reach agreement. Since concessions provide a major indicator of the propensity of a nation to negotiate seriously on disarmament, they furnish a means for analyzing bargaining in the postwar disarmament negotiations.

The patterns of United States and Soviet concessionary behavior were examined in three major sets of negotiations in an effort to develop a better understanding of the progress and problems of bargaining for disarmament. These included efforts to negotiate more general disarmament agreements during the period 1945–60, the negotiations leading to the Limited Test Ban Treaty signed in 1963, and the Strategic Arms Limitation Talks (1969–79).

All available disarmament proposals and statements were carefully studied in an effort to identify substantive concessions and retractions to the position of the other side. These were readily identifiable for the pre-1960 disarmament negotiations and the Limited Test Ban negotiations since the debates and proposals have been published, usually in verbatim form. In the case of the SALT negotiations, it was necessary to rely more upon secondary sources, for the negotiations were conducted in secrecy. Despite these limitations, a fairly complete record of the most important moves are available to the researcher because of the many memoirs and articles published by the participants in the SALT negotiations, the diligence of many scholars and journalists as well as government documents and the record of congressional hearings conducted on the subject.[1] Since there are some discrepancies in these various sources with regard to the exact date of a move or its precise characteristics, preference was given to the assessments of participants over more distant observers whenever there seemed to be a conflict. Concessions and retractions for the three sets of negotiations can be found in appendix A. Since it would be misleading to measure a nation's propensity to compromise simply by counting the number of concessions and subtracting the number of retractions from previously held positions, an effort was made to weight the moves on a five-point scale. A magnitude of 5 indicates a very important concession and a 1 suggests a minimal concession. Retractions similarly were weighted from -1 to -5 with a -5 being the most serious retraction. In those cases where a concession was made conditional upon the acceptance of a retraction, the procedure used was to weight the two as if separate, then to calculate the difference.

As an aid to weighting the various concessions and retractions, the following rules were developed for both my use and that of independent coders:

1. Vague concessions should not be given as much weight as specific ones.
2. A clue to importance might be seen in whether the opposition accepts the concession, compromises, or rejects it.
3. A concession of principle is to be regarded as more important than a concession of number.
4. An earlier change in principle is more important than subsequent modifications.
5. In general, concessions on numbers will be ranked 1 to 3, and concessions in principle 3 to 5. Modifications of principle of minute proportions may rank 2.
6. The first commitment to a number may be viewed as a concession of medium to low magnitude, unless the number is much lower than expected.
7. A "concession" may go too far, making it a low-level concession at best, e.g., moving a disarmament measure from the third stage to the first stage, thus making both proposals equally unacceptable.[2]

CHARACTERISTICS OF CONCESSION-MAKING

As is apparent from the list of conciliatory moves in all three sets of negotiations, concessions far outnumbered retractions for both the United States and the Soviet Union. During the early postwar disarmament negotiations (1945–60), the Soviet Union made a total of 53 concessions and 16 retractions. For the United States, the scores were 27 and 4, respectively. The ratio of retractions to concessions was even lower during the SALT negotiations as some 113 concessions were compiled for the Soviet Union and 81 for the United States while the Soviet Union made 6 retractions and the United States 7. A steadily narrowing of differences has occurrred over time in the various sets of negotiations with the SALT negotiations proving to be the most productive in terms of the agreements reached.

Given the relative paucity of retractions during the negotiations, little support is found for the assertion made by Joseph Nogee and John Spanier that the Soviet Union tends to make concessionary proposals that include a number of "jokers," defined as provisions totally unacceptable to the United States.[3] An analysis of the early postwar disarmament negotiations, which were among the most propagandistic of all, suggests that the Soviet use of "new jokers" to offset concessions was minimal, for the majority of proposals involving concessions did not include retractions from a previous position. Of a total of 28 separate Soviet proposals involving changes important enough to merit a concession score, only 6 included retractions. The United States was somewhat less likely to make concessions contingent upon acceptance of undesired provisions as only 1 of its 20 conciliatory proposals included a retraction. Most retractions have been made apart from concessions and consequently may be regarded as the reason for rejecting concessions. Even when retractions were linked with concessions in the same proposal, the concessions usually predominated. For example, the six Soviet proposals containing both concessions and retractions showed a weighted concession score of 46 as contrasted to 23 for retractions, indicating an overall bridging of differences.

While not necessarily making a concession contingent upon the acceptance of a retraction, the SALT negotiations are replete with instances in which one party or the other specified exactly what was expected in return for a concession. In several cases such proposals would entail action on a totally unrelated weapons system. The Soviet Union, for example, proposed allowing the United States to retain its foreign bases if the United States would compensate the Soviet Union with higher ceilings for missile launchers (August 1970 and July 1973); the Soviet Union would drop its proposed ban on air-launched missiles if the United States would relinquish its proposed ban on land-mobile missiles (November 1974); and the USSR would accept U.S. ICBM fractionism rules if the latter would limit air-launched cruise missiles to twenty per bomber. The fourteen similarly linked concessions made by the United States included proposals to link control of the ABM to Soviet reductions of heavy missiles (August 1970) and to ceilings on the number of SLBMs (March 1972). The United States also sought specific compensation for allowing Soviet Backfire bombers to be excluded from the treaty (September 1975 and January 1976) and for the existence of heavier Soviet throw-weight (April 1974 and June 1974). But perhaps the most interesting proposed linkage was the January 1971 offer by the United States to help the Soviet Union modernize its economy if the Soviets would soften their SALT position.

The majority of concessions do not explicitly state what reciprocation is expected. Rather it is assumed that the other side will be forthcoming to the initiatives taken. In responding to a concession, a state may react in at least three ways: it may reject the concession because it does not go far enough; it may offer its own compromise without entirely accepting the position of the other side; or it may accept the concession in its entirety. The results show that out of 42 Soviet concessions made during the course of the Limited Test Ban talks, the United States agreed to 18 Soviet concessions without modification, rejected 5, and compromised with regard to 19 of them. The Soviet record was somewhat less impressive, for out of a total of 44 American concessions the Soviets accepted only 14, while rejecting 20 concessions without qualification. The remaining 10 concessions led to compromise proposals by the Soviet Union. Translating this into percentages, we find that the Soviets rejected unconditionally 45 percent of all United States concessions made during the Test Ban talks as contrasted with the United States rejection of only 12 percent of the Soviet concessions.

The tendency of the Soviet Union to reject U.S. concessions outright decreased during the SALT negotiations, suggesting a more businesslike atmosphere in those negotiations. Only 6 Soviet total rejections were found in response to the 81 U.S. concessions, as most concessions were either accepted or a compromise was subsequently negotiated on the issue. The United States, on the other hand, was coded as rejecting outright 11 of the 113 Soviet concessions. In fact, 4 of the 11 rejections were recorded during the first year of the SALT negotiations. Subsequently, the United States became somewhat more conciliatory in its bargaining behavior.

While these results would seem to suggest that the United States has been more conciliatory, the concession scores of the Soviet Union were somewhat higher than those of the United States in all three sets of negotiations. This situation may be explained by the tendency of the Soviet Union to begin a round of negotiations with a far more extreme bargaining position than it is willing to accept, later making concessions to demonstrate to world public opinion that it is negotiating seriously.

THE RECIPROCATION OF CONCESSIONS

To determine whether or not concessions were reciprocated, the weighted concession scores were calculated for each round of negotiation. Table 3.1 shows the results for twenty-two rounds of negotiation on general disarmament issues for the period 1945–60. Two major patterns of concession-making appear to predominate. First, there is the tendency for concessions to be reciprocated in the same round, for example, during the periods 1946 through 1948 and 1957 through 1960. The second pattern consists of a delay of one round before concessions are reciprocated, for example, 1949 through 1952. Since the sessions of the 1949–52 period were so abbreviated, given the intensity of U.S.-Soviet hostility at the time, there was simply inadequate opportunity for responding to the initiatives of the other side during the same round. However, whether concessions are reciprocated in the current round or in the subsequent one, it appears that the making of concessions plays a very important role in terms of inducing the opposition to be more conciliatory.

Table 3.1 Weighted Concession Scores in The Early Postwar Disarmament Negotiations

Date Ending	USSR	U.S.	Date Ending	USSR	U.S.
December 1946	12	8	May 1955	21	3
September 1947	17	11	October 1955	4	-14
October 1948	4	0	January 1956	0	0
July 1949	5	0	May 1956	4	8
November 1950	0	3	January 1957	6	0
December 1951	7	0	September 1957	11	5
August 1952	0	11	December 1957	0	0
April 1953	0	0	December 1958	-1	0
November 1953	0	0	November 1959	-6	0
July 1954	0	5	June 1960	17	10
October 1954	12	3	November 1960	-2	0

The year 1955 is more difficult to explain as the United States reacted to the high level of Soviet concessions by retracting its own previous positions. Perhaps the United States became skeptical of its own proposals simply because the Soviet Union was beginning to accept them. Only too often this has been the logic of cold war politics. Or perhaps the United States had made the concessions only on the assumption that the Soviet Union would not reciprocate, thereby providing a propaganda victory for the United States. The reversal of the U.S. position did serve to raise questions about whether the United States was serious about disarmament.

Despite what might appear to be bargaining in bad faith on the part of the United States, the moves and countermoves of the United States and the Soviet Union during this early period show considerable reciprocity. If one excludes the year 1955 from the calculations and takes into account the necessary delayed reactions during the 1949–52 negotiations, the correlation between the weighted concession scores of the two sides is .57, which is statistically significant at the .01 level.

Similar patterns of reciprocity were found in the test ban negotiations—at least during the first seven rounds as shown in table 3.2. By October 1960, 17 articles and the annex had been agreed upon for a comprehensive test ban with only three articles remaining to be negotiated. Nevertheless, it took almost three more years before a much more restricted Limited Test Ban Treaty was signed.

Table 3.2 Weighted Concession Scores in the Nuclear Test Ban Negotiations

Date Ending	USSR	U.S.	Date Ending	USSR	U.S.
December 1958	14	10	May 1961	-5	25
May 1959	27	22	September 1961	-13	10
August 1959	22	4	January 1962	1	-1
December 1959	6	0	June 1962	4	5
April 1960	9	14	September 1962	0	6
August 1960	2	10	January 1963	8	2
December 1960	0	4	July 1963	5	3

During the test ban negotiatons the two sides showed approach-avoidance bargaining behavior. The theory of approach-avoidance, which is usually applied to individual motivation, suggests that if one is ambivalent about a goal when he or she is at a distance from that goal, there is a tendency to approach; as the goal is within reach the tendency to avoid is greater. The result is a self-sustaining conflict at the point where approach and avoidance tendencies cross.[4] When applied to a bargaining situation, this theory would suggest that as long as the goal of agreement appears to be remote, concessions can be made at minimal cost. As agreement is approached, concessions become more costly, particularly if there are strong predispositions toward avoidance of agreement. When agreement is imminent, concessions are unlikely, and retractions become the basic mode of bargaining.

During the early phase of the test ban negotiations there was a tendency for the two nations to reciprocate concessions. In fact, the two weighted concession scores showed a positive correlation of .60 ($p < .01$) for the first seven rounds ending in December 1960. It was at the point, when agreement appeared imminent, that the tendency to avoid became pronounced as the Soviets made several retractions. In a final effort to reach agreement on a nuclear test ban, the Kennedy administration in March 1961 made a number of concessions that failed to affect Soviet bargaining behavior. Yet even these U.S. concessions are consistent with the approach-avoidance notion. Since agreement was no longer imminent, given the Soviet retractions, a state not serious about reaching a test ban agreement could make a number of "cheap" concessions that it knew were not likely to be accepted.

In view of the increasing recalcitrance of the Soviet Union on the test ban issue, it is remarkable that the United States was caught off guard by the Soviet resumption of testing in September 1961. The Soviets bargained vigorously during the early years of the test ban negotiations, scoring their first retraction in June 1960, but they failed to make any concessions during the year immediately preceding their resumption of testing. Mysteriously, Soviet disarmament proposals and speeches also paid less attention to the testing issue, perhaps in anticipation of Soviet plans to resume nuclear testing.

Few concessions were made in the post-September 1961 period as each side bargained from incompatible positions. As a starting point, the Soviets demanded a comprehensive test ban without controls, and the United States offered the option of a partial test ban without controls or a comprehensive one with controls. The United States no longer seemed willing to agree to a moratorium on testing that would depend upon Soviet good faith alone.

Despite the resumption of Soviet testing, discussions on test ban issues continued over the next two years until agreement was reached in the summer of 1963. The resumption of testing by the Soviets had seriously impaired the debates, and concessions came most grudgingly. The momentum of the earlier negotiations was never quite recaptured despite the divergence between the two which should have made concessions appear "cheap."

The fact that approach-avoidance tendencies were finally surmounted in 1963 may be attributed to several factors. Chief among these was the fact that a partial test ban applying to the environments of the atmosphere, outer space, and underwater would placate the major concerns of the United States and the Soviet Union. The United States would no longer need to fear possible evasion of the treaty, for scientific advances appeared to guarantee that national inspection systems would be capable of detecting any violation. Since national devices were adequate in all environments but underground, the Soviets did not need to feel threatened by an international inspection system capable of penetrating their relatively closed society. Both sides could continue testing under the treaty since it did not apply to underground testing.

Agreement was also spurred by pressures external to the major actors involved. World public opinion, despite the vagueness of the concept, was an apparent factor in reaching agreement. The dangers of radioactive fallout had been heavily publicized, and nations like India and Japan became intensively involved in the movement for a ban on atmospheric nuclear testing. The structure of the Eighteen Nation Disarmament Conference, representing as it did East, West, and neutrals, provided a useful framework for pressure as well as for serious negotiation. The primacy of the powers directly involved was epitomized in the utilization of subcommittee meetings composed of the United States, the Soviet Union, and the United Kingdom. Pressure could be exerted upon the three members of the subcommittee by the larger conference since the subcommittee was required to report its progress to the Eighteen Nation Conference. Arthur Lall, who represented India in these debates, argues that the eight neutral nations' memo presented in 1962 was "one of the factors" prompting the Soviet Union to accept two to three on-site inspections per year.[5] It also influenced the United States to accept the notion of an uncontrolled ban on outer space and underwater tests. These moves, though limited, had the effect of breaking through a serious deadlock in the negotiations.

A final factor in eventual agreement might be attributed to the momentum of concession-making. Given the earlier willingness to make concessions, considerable progress had been made in the test ban negotiations. As a result, expectations and hopes were raised among both domestic and foreign publics on the prospects of reaching agreement. Leaders in the United States and the Soviet Union may not have been very serious about agreement on a test ban except on their own terms. But they became in effect victims of their own earlier performance, creating an environment in which some kind of agreement had become essential due to public pressure and expectations. A limited test ban may have been the reasonable way out. It would represent some success but not impinge upon Soviet fears of an invasion of sovereignty. Nor would the United States need to fear Soviet evasion. In this sense, reciprocation of concessions may be viewed as an important forerunner of agreement even though the preference of the actors might have been avoidance of agreement.

In applying the same analysis to the Strategic Arms Limitation Talks, the evidence suggests a considerable degree of reciprocity within a given round of negotiations.[6] As can be seen by examining the data in table 3.3, the weighted concession scores of the two sides proceeded in the same direction in all but six of the twenty-three rounds. The product moment correlation for the two weighted concession scores is .49 ($p <$ .01).

Table 3.3 Weighted Concession Scores in the Strategic Arms Limitation Talks

Date Ending	USSR	U.S.	Date Ending	USSR	U.S.
December 1969	3	3	May 1975	-1	3
August 1970	10	14	August 1975	11	0
December 1970	20	0	January 1976	13	8
May 1971	18	14	July 1976	0	0
September 1971	12	1	December 1976	2	2
February 1972	14	2	May 1977	4	6
May 1972	18	11	December 1977	12	16
December 1972	6	1	April 1978	13	8
July 1973	7	12	August 1978	10	0
December 1973	-4	0	December 1978	27	8
July 1974	22	18	June 1979	18	10
November 1974	18	22			

The reciprocal concessions shown during the SALT negotiations in no small measure account for the success obtained, first with the successful negotiation of the SALT I agreements in 1972 and then the SALT II Treaty signed in 1979. Although, as in the case of the Limited Test Ban negotiations, there is evidence of settling for less comprehensive solutions, major reversals of the magnitude of the Soviet retractions in the test ban talks did not occur. The exception might have been with respect to the Carter proposals of March 1977, which sought to reduce substantially the offensive ceilings agreed upon at Vladivostok. The motivation for the U.S. proposals, however, seemed to be related to a concern to negotiate deeper reductions rather than to accept the cosmetic conclusions of the Vladivostok Accord, which would have entailed further arms buildup to reach the proposed ceilings.

Not only does there appear to be considerable responsiveness between states in a given round of negotiations, but negotiators appear to monitor the relative "size" of moves made by the other side in determining concession rates in the next round—a process Daniel Druckman has referred to as threshold/adjustment bargaining.[7] According to this notion, when a difference of a certain size (threshold) is found, an adjustment will be made toward the position of the other in order to achieve a synchronous pattern. To illustrate the concept, Druckman reanalyzed the test ban concession scores reported in table 3.2. Based upon rank order statistics, he found a $-.57$ ($p < .025$) lagged correlation between the difference in round n concession scores and the total amount of concessions in round $n + 1$. In other words, the larger the difference in the previous round, the less the overall propensity to compromise in the next round. Applying the same procedure to the concession scores in the SALT negotiations, however, produced an insignificant rank order correlation of .24, suggesting that the harder team may have softened its position in the subsequent round.

The above calculations, by looking at the total difference of concessions in n and relating that score to the total concession rate in $n + 1$, fail to take into account which state created the imbalance in concession scores and how each in turn reacted to that imbalance. To explore this aspect, U.S. and Soviet concession scores for each period during the test ban negotiations were ranked from a hard position in which concession rates were lower than those of the adversary to a soft position in which concessions were higher. A lagged rank order correlation of .66 ($p < .01$) was found between the U.S. ranked difference score and Soviet concessions while the lagged correlation between the Soviet difference score and U.S. concessions was an insignificant .01. The results suggest, in other words, that the Soviet Union increased its rate of concessions in response to a more hard-lined U.S. posture in the previous round, but no relationship was found between Soviet differential concession rates and U.S. concession scores.

Applying the same procedure to the SALT data also revealed different tendencies for each state. As in the case of the test ban results, Soviet lagged concession scores were found to be positively related to the harder U.S. position as measured by the difference in concession rates (.35, $p < .10$). The rank correlation between a harder Soviet position as measured by concession differences and U.S. concessions in the subsequent round was -.25 ($p =$ n.s.), suggesting that the United States made relatively fewer concessions in response to a Soviet imbalance in concession scores.

Richard J. Stoll and William McAndrew used the U.S. and Soviet SALT concession scores reported in this study to test a cooperative reciprocity and an inverse reciprocity model on the SALT I, SALT II, and Vladivostok data.[8] They discovered that in analyzing responsiveness to the behavior of the other side in the previous round that U.S.-Soviet interactions were characterized more often by cooperative reciprocity than by inverse reciprocity. However, in one negotiation for each side (Vladivostok for the Soviet Union, SALT II for the United States), the inverse reciprocity model provided the better fit of the two models.

Stoll and McAndrew also related the data to three other reciprocity models, the first of which tested reciprocity in terms of the direction of the concession scores, whether positive or negative; the second, referred to as the trend model, looked at reciprocation in terms of whether the opposition increased or decreased its concession score from the previous period; and the third, or comparative reciprocity model, involved comparing one's own score in the previous period with that of the other side in order to determine how to respond. The comparative reciprocity model provided the best fit for both the United States and the Soviet Union and was also the best model in three of the six runs using data from separate SALT negotiations. The trend model was superior in the three remaining cases. Collectively these studies illustrate the predominace of reciprocity in superpower bargaining behavior in the disarmament negotiations since similar results have been found using a variety of models and data sets. Less frequently is support for the hard-line strategies or inverse-reciprocity model obtained.

CONCESSION RATES

There is by no means unanimous consenus among observers that a party in a bargaining relationship should be quick to compromise, for such behavior rather than facilitating the reaching of agreement may actually postpone agreement. Making concessions too readily may only increase the level of aspiration of the adversary, leading the latter to increase its demands. These conclusions were derived from a number of experiments conducted by Siegel and Fouraker, who found that parties starting with hard positions and showing a reluctance to compromise generally fared better than those who pursued soft bargaining strategies.[9]

There is some evidence that the United States may have made concessions too readily during the early phase of various disarmament negotiations as can be seen in table 3.4. This predisposition was most striking in seven selected rounds in the negotiations from 1945 through 1960, including meetings of the Disarmament subcommittee, the Surprise Attack Conference, and the Ten-Nation Disarmament Conference.[10] By dividing each of these rounds chronologically into thirds, it was found that the United States made 82 percent of its weighted concession score in the *first* third of a round of negotiations. The Soviet Union, rather than reciprocating early in the round, made 75 percent of its concession score during the *final* third of the round.

Table 3.4 Percentage of Weighted Concessions Made during Each Third of the Negotiations

Negotiations	First Third	Second Third	Final Third
Seven Selected Rounds (1945–60)			
USSR	14	12	75
U.S.	82	14	5
SALT I (1969–72)			
USSR	14	40	46
U.S.	38	33	29
SALT II (Vladivostok, 1972–74)			
USSR	12	31	57
U.S.	7	25	68
SALT II (Carter Period, 1977–79)			
USSR	19	27	54
U.S.	46	17	38

Although not quite as extreme, the pattern continued during the Strategic Arms Limitation Talks. After dividing the SALT I negotiations into three ten-month periods, it was found that the Soviet Union made only 14 percent of its weighted concession score during the first ten months compared to the United States 38 percent. The figures for the final ten-month period were 46 percent and 29 percent, respectively. Similar results were found in the SALT II negotiations during the Carter period with almost half of the United States score being made during the first third of those negotiations compared with only 19 percent for the Soviet Union. Negotiations on the Vladivostok Accord, on the other hand, showed little difference between the two as the United States followed the Soviet pattern of making the bulk of its concessions during the final phase of the negotiations.

Participants in the SALT negotiations have noted the predisposition of the United States to make concessions somewhat more freely than the Soviet Union. U.S. SALT negotiator Gerard Smith, for example, asserted that the "Soviets do better at reacting than at proposing specific arms controls,"[11] and former Secretary of State Henry A. Kissinger claimed in reference to the SALT negotiations that he knew of "no instance in which a breakthrough did not result from an American initiation."[12]

There may be some risk in beginning negotiations with extreme positions since more extensive concessions eventually will be required to reach the point of mutually acceptable agreement. John Cross has argued that if a party unduly delays concessions while pursuing a strategy of bluffing, it faces the danger that it will eventually be compelled to make a large concession, assuming there is an interest in reaching agreement.[13] By this very act of concession, the party is communicating a weakness, or a fear of risk, that will inhibit concessions by the other side. Alternatively, sticking with an extreme position could easily doom the negotiations to failure. Either way a more moderate starting position would seem preferable from the perspective of negotiating mutually satisfactory agreements.

Of course, if there is little interest in reaching agreement, holding doggedly to an extreme opening position can make some sense. Such might have been the case with respect to the Reagan administration's unwillingness to move from the zero-zero option proposed at the Intermediate-range Nuclear Force talks. The administration continued to press a nonnegotiable formula requiring the Soviet Union to reduce *existing* intermediate-range missiles in return for *potential* American equivalents. Also omitted from the formula were French and British nuclear weapons as well as other U.S. forward-based nuclear weapons.

The fact that the Reagan administration began during the spring of 1983 to hint of possible compromise on the issue would seem to be due to a realistic recognition that the zero side of the equation might only affect U.S. intermediate-range forces. European governments, with their growing anti-nuclear movements, threatened to reject the emplacement of such weapons on West European soil, particularly if the United States continued to be recalcitrant on arms control issues.

The difficulty presented by opening with high bids, which then require high concession rates, might be minimized by beginning negotiations without specific proposals. Experimental research conducted by Daniel Druckman has revealed that representatives of opposing teams that met informally to discuss issues and were instructed not to take positions in these sessions were able to resolve a greater number of issues in a shorter period of time than those representatives who began with formal positions.[14] Just such an informal approach to initial negotiations was supported by Henry Kissinger in the SALT I talks. He proposed that the United States not table formal positions but instead pursue a strategy of presenting a series of alternatives for discussion. His suggestion that the Soviet Union do likewise was perhaps not necessary, for the history of Soviet bargaining behavior has generally been one of insisting that the United States present its cards first. The Kissinger strategy may have been counterproductive as in the case of the American presentation of alternative ABM proposals involving zero ABMs or ABM sites around the respective national capitals (NCA). When the Soviet Union soon opted for the NCA position, Kissinger was quick to point out that it had chosen the wrong option and it would therefore be necessary to choose again.

Given this experience, U.S. SALT I negotiator Gerard Smith has been particularly critical of beginning with vague, alternative proposals.[15] He asserts that negotiations are not seminars and that ony those positions the United States can live with should be presented. Philip E. Mosely, who has also had considerable experience negotiating with the Russians has suggested that "the technique of constantly trying out variant versions, which works well in the western style of negotiation, only confuses the Soviet representative, who suspects some new trick in each new variant and must subject each in turn to exhaustive interpretation."[16]

If the problem of opening with an extreme position is that eventual agreement will require making large concessions and increase the demands and expectations of the other side, what chance for success does a strategy of slicing concessions very thin and offering them over a long period of time have? Kissinger has been critical of such a strategy, which he has labeled the "salami" approach.[17] He suggests that the "method confers an illusory impression of toughness. Since neither side can know which slice of the salami is the final one, each is tempted to wait out the process and thus protract it further. Inevitably, pressure grows for what has absorbed so much time, energy, and commitment to succeed; this can easily carry the negotiations beyond prudent limits." An example of salami tactics occurred with the Carter administration's efforts to limit Soviet heavy missiles by proposing a ceiling of 150, 190, 220, 250, and finally 308 heavy missiles—the number of missiles the Soviets possessed at the time. All of these proposals were made during a six-month period in 1977 without any Soviet reciprocation on the same issue. Whether U.S. concessionary behavior in this instance made the Soviet Union more conciliatory on other issues cannot be ascertained for certain; but in the two months after U.S. acquiescence to 308 heavy Soviet missiles, the Soviet weighted concession score was higher than in any two-month period since the Vladivostok Accord of November 1974.

If the earlier concession scores of the United States are suggestive of a softer bargaining strategy by that nation, do they also mean that the agreements reached have favored the Soviet Union given the latter's more recalcitrant bargaining strategy? Making estimates of who wins in a bargaining situation is extremely difficult with respect to issues as complex as strategic arms control negotiations. There is little question that SALT I included a number of positive aspects from the American perspective, such as the cancellation of a costly ABM race that would have threatened the stability of nuclear deterrence. The five-year freeze on the number of ICBMs and SLBMs was beneficial inasmuch as it placed a cap on Soviet missile development for a period of time during which the United States had no plans to build any additional units of its own. An analysis of the SALT II Treaty revealed that an overwhelming number of its provisions were more compatible with the positions pressed by the United States than those taken by the Soviet Union. Of 28 provisions in SALT II, 22 were found to be more consonant with the position of one side or the other; and in 17 of the 22 cases, the provision seemed closer to the position of the United States with the remaining 5 favoring the Soviet Union.[18] Although the discrepancy may be partially due to the more extreme bargaining positions taken by the Soviet Union, the analysis does suggest that the United States did not fare badly in those negotiations despite its failure to open with extreme positions and its tendency to make concessions more readily early in the negotiations.

In evaluating who wins in a bargaining relationship it should also be noted that an agreement reached at an earlier point in the process may be more valuable than one obtained at a subsequent point. The Interim Strategic Offensive Arms freeze signed in May 1972 would have been more significant from the perspective of the United States had it been agreed upon several months earlier at a time in which the total number of missiles favored the United States. From this perspective, the firm position taken by the United States in 1970–71 might have worked against U.S. interests, for it only resulted in a less desirable agreement. It was known as early as December 1970 that the Soviet Union would agree to an ABM Treaty with limited sites as well as to a less formal agreement constraining offensive missiles, according to SALT negotiator Gerard Smith.[19] Similarly, Carter's March 1977 SALT proposals, which retreated from what had been agreed upon at Vladivostok, delayed the conclusion of the SALT II Treaty to a point at which negative forces began to make U.S. ratification more problematic. Among these were events in Africa, alleged Soviet troops in Cuba, the Soviet incursion into Afghanistan, and the approaching U.S. presidential election.

Concession rates are affected not only by opening bids and concessions made by the other side, but the establishment of real or imagined deadlines also seems to play a role. Notions of approach-avoidance bargaining behavior would seem to suggest that concession rates will be higher during the early phases of a negotiation, slowing as one nears agreement. Evidence from the SALT negotiations, on the other hand, suggests that deadlines can increase concession rates. Due to a deadline for signing the SALT I agreements at the Moscow Summit Conference in May 1972, the United States made 38 percent of its SALT I weighted concession score for the final year of negotiation in the last month. The corresponding figure for the Soviet Union was 30 percent. The attempt to meet a deadline also resulted in signed agreements containing a number of typographical errors and other mistakes that subsequently had to be corrected. The 1974 deadline for completing a SALT II treaty that was pressed by Kissinger in 1973 seems to have been productive in obtaining the Vladivostok Accord in November 1974 as the United States and the Soviet Union each made about one-third of their score during the final month. Specific deadlines were not established during the Carter period, and the same feverish concessionary behavior did not take place during the last month of the SALT II negotiations.

BARGAINING BY FORMULA

In an insightful article, I. William Zartman has rejected the concession-convergence notion of bargaining behavior, suggesting instead that "negotiation is a matter of finding the proper formula and implementing detail."[20] Mutual concession-making occurs, if at all, with regard to detail instead of with respect to developing basic formulae. Interviews with fifty ambassadorial-level diplomats at the United Nations revealed that they tend to pay minimal attention to the number of concessions made by the other side. Instead, concessions were viewed largely as symbolic moves made most often toward the end when agreement was in sight and it was believed that the other side was likely to accept the package being offered.

Similar assessments of the bargaining process were discovered by Gilbert R. Winham in his interviews with participants in the Kennedy round of trade negotiations (1964–67).[21] The interviewees showed minimal awareness of the concessions made by other participants and were unable to agree on when breakthroughs occurred or whether concessions were even made. In complex negotiations of this sort, responses seemed to be related more to whether or not a state was predisposed toward a liberal trade policy than to the specific behavior of the other negotiators.

It may be that Zartman's and Winham's real or implied rejection of the concession-convergence model is related to the fact that interviews with negotiators rather than an analysis of moves taken by the negotiators served as their primary data base. Participants in negotiations are habitually reluctant to admit that the other side makes any significant concessions, whereas an analysis of U.S.-Soviet behavior in the SALT talks and other postwar disarmament negotiations appears to negate such views. It should also be noted that Zartman and Winham were dealing with a multilateral bargaining situation rather than a bilateral one as in the case of the SALT talks, and it is more difficult in multilateral negotiations to identify specific concessions. This is not to suggest that the notion of behaving according to or seeking a valid formula is an inaccurate one but rather that both concessions and the discovery of major formulae are vital to successful negotiation.

The SALT talks are filled with illustrations of the development of major formulations that became the basis for futher negotiation and compromise. One of the most important of these principles was the decision to count each weapon in the triad as a unit and to allow each side, within certain ranges, to establish its own mix of forces. Equally important was the formula that all verification for an offensive arms agreement would be by national technical means. A similar breakthrough was achieved in May 1977 when the United States and the Soviet Union agreed upon a three-tiered formula for SALT II involving a three-year protocol, a treaty to expire in 1985, and a joint statement for follow-on negotiations.

To the extent that the search for a formula is the first priority, many commentators have alluded to the Soviet tendency of seeking agreement in principle prior to spelling out the details. Gerard Smith has noted how the United States tabled detailed positions in SALT I while the Soviet Union favored general formulations.[22] To counter this strategy it became U.S. policy not to react in principle until it knew the details.

INTERNATIONAL TENSION AND CONCESSIONARY BEHAVIOR

The conciliatory behavior of the other side is not the only factor that helps to explain concessionary behavior. Many writers and statesmen have called attention to the role that international tension and political differences play in affecting concession rates and the prospects of successfully negotiating arms control agreements. Opinions on the subject vary from those who argue that arms create international tension and thus must be tackled first to those who suggest that arms reductions are impossible as long as international political tensions exist. While accepting the circularity of the problem, Inis L. Claude, Jr., suggests that "there are strong indications that the elimination of war is more dependent upon intervention into the vicious circle at the points of political conflict than at the point of military technology."[23] J. David Singer, on the other hand, argues that arms races have a dynamism of their own and as long as there are armaments, political tensions will persist. Therefore the only way to deal with the armaments problem is to "disarm-by-disarming."[24]

Those supporting the primacy of political settlement and tension reduction as the first step toward peace usually argue that armaments are only symptomatic of underlying political difficulties. This view was expressed succinctly by Hans J. Morgenthau in testimony before the Senate Subcommittee on Disarmament a number of years ago when he suggested that "if we can imagine for a moment that all the outstanding political issues were settled, nobody need worry about the fact that nations have arms because there would be no incentive, no issue for which those nations might want to use those arms."[25]

In support of the argument that political settlements are essential to the reaching of agreements on arms control, advocates usually call attention to the Rush-Bagot Treaty between the United States and Canada, which demilitarized the Great Lakes in 1817, and the Washington Naval conference of 1922, which placed a limit on tonnage among the major naval powers. The success of both of these arms limitation measures, according to this view, was due to the prior or concurrent resolution of other controversies.[26]

During the early postwar disarmament negotiations it was clear that the United States and the Soviet Union took decidedly different views on the priority to be given to political settlement or arms reduction. A content analysis of U.S. statements in the pre-1961 disarmament debates showed that out of 26 references on the subject 92 percent held that political settlement and/or tension reduction *must accompany* arms reduction, while the remaining two references went further by insisting that political settlement must actually *precede* disarmament. No examples were found in the debates in which the United States was willing to admit that extensive arms reduction might precede political settlement and tension reduction. This contrasts sharply with the attitude of the Soviet negotiators who verbalized the opinion in 25 out of 28 instances or 91 percent of the time that political settlement and/or tension reduction need neither precede nor accompany disarmament. In only three instances did the Soviet negotiators even admit the possibility that they might accompany each other.[27]

It was not until the Soviet proposals of May 10, 1955, that the Soviet Union officially admitted the intricate relationship between political settlement, tension, and disarmament. In these proposals the Soviets were most conciliatory toward the Western position, but after discussing the problems created by tension and political differences, their prescription was still one of extensive disarmament regardless of what actions are taken in the political arena.

Since those early postwar disarmament negotiations, the positions of the two sides on the political settlement issue have remained somewhat the same, with the United States emphasizing the need for achieving political settlements first. However, during the Vietnam War Brezhnev and other Soviet spokespersons frequently argued that no arms control agreement would be possible as long as that war continued.[28] As the war became more violent, Moscow suggested that the Southeast Asian conflict made arms control talks all the more urgent.[29] In contrast to the expectations of many, the Soviet Union agreed to go ahead with the scheduled May 1972 summit, during which the SALT I agreements were signed, despite the fact that just days before the United States had damaged Soviet ships by mining Haiphong Harbor and had escalated the bombing of North Vietnam. Nevertheless, General Secretary Mikhail Gorbachev demonstrated in April 1986 that the Soviets could use the linkage argument just as well as the United States when he noted that: "when one sees these things in an international context, the crusade against Libya and also the persistence in nuclear tests and the threats against Nicaragua cannot be seen in isolation. The American administration must be aware that Soviet-American relations cannot be developed independently of how the U.S. behaves in the international arena."[30]

Although the United States, following the death of Secretary of State John Foster Dulles, had become less insistent that progress on arms control be linked with the settlement of political disputes, President Nixon revived the linkage concept in the initial stages of the SALT negotiations, hoping to place pressure upon the Soviet Union to help resolve conflicts in the Middle East and Vietnam. The strategy was soon dropped as it became apparent that progress on either front would be impossible as long as the United States insisted upon linking arms control and political settlements. President Gerald Ford renewed the strategy of linkage when he refused to follow up on the Vladivostok Accord as a result of Soviet actions in Angola in 1975–76.

The Carter administration initially rejected the notion of linking political settlements with arms control policy, only to begin a gradual shift of policy in 1978 at a time in which National Security Advisor Zbigniew Brzezinski was assuming a more influential role in foreign policy matters. In a March 1, 1978, speech, Brzezinski explicitly used the notion of linkage for the first time during the Carter period when he complained that Soviet and Cuban activities in the Horn of Africa would inevitably complicate SALT.[31] Subsequently, the Shaba incident in Zaire, the alleged Soviet brigade in Cuba, and the Soviet invasion of Afghanistan were all linked by the Carter administration to its arms control policy. With respect to the Cuban brigade issue, Brzezinski writes in his memoirs that Secretary of State Cyrus Vance's tough policy on the Cuban brigade issue may have been directed more toward domestic opinion than toward the Soviet Union. He notes that Vance publicly "assumed an extremely tough stance, whereas privately he [Vance] moved gradually toward a softer position. . . . Presumably he felt that a tough public posture would protect SALT."[32] Brzezinski makes it clear that he bitterly opposed Vance on this issue, and, by and large for the remaining period of the Carter presidency, the administration assumed a much harder line on arms control issues.

The Reagan administration, which was generally suspicious of Soviet intentions, emphasized that its positions on arms control would be contingent upon Soviet good behavior in other areas. In January 1982, Secretary of State Alexander Haig informed the Soviet Union that as a result of Soviet behavior in Poland the United States would not agree to set a date for the beginning of the START talks. The delay in developing the initial arms control positions of the administration, however, probably had as much to do with internal divisions within the administration as it did with the international climate. Alleged Soviet use of chemical warfare in Southeast Asia and Afghanistan and Soviet military action and aid to Afghanistan, Africa, Central America, and the Middle East were used to justify U.S. reticence on arms control. Nevertheless, Secretary of State George Shultz noted in November 1984 that the downing of Korean Airline 007 did not involve linkage, for the president decided to send the negotiators back to the bargaining table despite the incident.[33]

There is little doubt that deteriorating relations between the United States and the Soviet Union have affected the postwar disarmament negotiations adversely. The beginning of the SALT talks was delayed because of the Soviet invasion into Czechoslovakia in 1968, and the SALT II Treaty was shelved by President Carter as a direct result of the 1979 Soviet incursion into Afghanistan. At the same time, arms control negotiations have continued and substantive results have been achieved during periods of considerable tension. Soviet concessions leading to agreement on the Limited Test Ban Treaty came on the heels of the Cuban missile crisis. Disarmament negotiations continued during the Suez and Hungarian crises of 1956; the conflict in Cambodia and Vietnam in the early seventies was insufficient for derailing the SALT talks; and arms control negotiations have continued during the eighties even though President Reagan was referring to the Soviet Union as the "evil empire."

Efforts were made to determine whether or not there were any statistical relationships between concessionary behavior and measures of international tension, but, for the most part, little of significance was discovered because of a lack of linearity between the two variables. In an earlier study of the pre-1961 negotiations, it was discovered that periods of both high and low tension, as measured by polls asking about public expectations of war, were generally unproductive periods of concession-making.[34] Concessions tended not be made during periods of high tension such as the Korean War. At the same time, rounds of negotiation when tension levels were at their lowest, as measured by public expectations of war, such as during the period 1958–59, were accompanied by low concession levels. Most concessions tended to be made during the moderately low tension levels of the midfifties, except for the aberration noted earlier when the United States reserved its past disarmament positions in September 1955. Too much tension may lead to distrust of the other side, and too little tension may reduce incentives to negotiate seriously.

Further evidence that some tension between the United States and the Soviet Union may facilitate more serious negotiations is found by relating conflict events data collected by the Conflict and Peace Data Bank at the University of Maryland to concession scores aggregated on an annual basis during the SALT negotiations.[35] The rank order correlation between Soviet conflict behavior was a positive .40, suggesting that the United States was prone toward making concessions during more conflictual periods. The correlation between U.S. conflict scores and Soviet concessions during SALT was a more moderate, but still positive, .22. It should be noted that both correlations were not statistically significant possibly because of the curvilinear effect of tension levels upon bargaining behavior.

A similar pattern was found when using yet another indicator of tension based upon responses to U.S. public opinion polls in which the respondent was asked whether too much or too little was being spent for defense.[36] The assumption was made that the more respondents indicating that too little was being spent, the greater the international tension. The rank order correlation between this measure of international tension and SALT concessionary behavior was .24 for the United States and .28 for the Soviet Union—in both cases positive but statistically insignificant.

Research by P. Terrence Hopmann, relating measures of international tension to the test ban negotiations, on the other hand, found a negative relationship between international tension and conciliatory behavior in disarmament negotiations.[37] Event data, measuring both external conflictual and cooperative behavior between the United States, Great Britian, and the Soviet Union, were related to their internal behavior within the Limited Test Ban Negotiations, and it was discovered that greater external conflict tended to result in more negative responses within the negotiations and vice versa for all three participants. However, U.S. negotiators seemed to be affected more than Soviet negotiators by events outside the conference.

Part of the explanation for the difference in findings between these studies, which suggest that external tension has only a negative impact on negotiations, and our own may be related to the fact that the Hopmann studies measured internal bargaining by including not only concessions and retractions but also statements such as promises, indications of verbal agreement, acknowledgement of the contributions of others, and threats. Since such statements are more spontaneous and require less bureaucratic input than do concessions, they are more likely to reflect the climate of external relations between the states at any point in time. Proposals, which were used for measuring concessions, tend to be more rationally calculated on the basis of perceived national interest. It should also be noted that the Hopmann studies covered a more limited time period involving only a year-and-a-half span of the Limited Test Ban negotiations.

To the extent that there is a linkage between international tension and arms control negotiations, some have viewed that linkage to be one in which arms control negotiations cause increased international tension. David E. Lilienthal, for example, argued that nuclear disarmament discussions on the diplomatic level added directly to international tension and hostility.[38] Robin Ranger has written that "the extension of detente through arms limitation via the NPT helped the Soviets to invade Czechoslovakia without a significant cost in terms of their relationship with the United States."[39] Still others have worried that arms control negotiations tend to lull a state into a false sense of security with the state's inviting aggression by not being adequately vigilant or by neglecting its national defense capabilities.

It has even been suggested that success in the arms area may facilitate success in other areas. Gerard Smith notes that Henry Kissinger, in reflecting upon an important Soviet initiative, wondered aloud whether "the Soviets might have been more tractable during the recent Middle East crisis if we had accepted that proposal and reached an ABM treaty."[40] Barry M. Blechman has suggested that progress in arms control talks facilitates success in other areas. He writes: "As U.S.-Soviet relations deteriorated, the Soviets pressed harder across the range of negotiations, adopting increasingly conciliatory positions and raising expectations in several."[41]

BARGAINING CHIPS AND CONCESSIONARY BEHAVIOR

In addition to international tension levels, the military balance between states appears to affect their bargaining behavior in disarmament negotiations. One of the most persistent themes in bargaining theory is the need to negotiate from strength. With respect to disarmament negotiations this notion has usually been expressed in terms of bargaining chips. In an excellent study relating the concept to recent arms talks, Robert J. Einhorn has noted a number of instances where bargaining chips seemed to have worked.[42] These include U.S. efforts to bolster its ABM system in the early seventies to induce the Soviet Union to agree to an ABM Treaty; the U.S. threat to build cruise missiles that ulimately allowed the United States to trade away limited restrictions on cruise missiles in return for important restraints on Soviet strategic power in SALT II; the threatened and subsequent deployment of intermediate-range nuclear missiles that induced the Soviet Union to talk seriously about restraints on its comparable weapons; and the U.S. threat to resume ASAT testing and development in 1985, which led to a Soviet moratorium on ASAT tests.

At the same time, there have been instances where such chips have not facilitated concessions from the other side such as in the case of multiple independently targeted reentry vehicles (MIRVs), the development of which only led to a destabilizing arms race. The cruise missile has similarly been viewed by some as a failed chip since its deployment only created a weapons system in which there had been little bureaucratic interest as well as a system that not only threatened deterrent stability but also introduced considerable verification problems. Despite President Reagan's monumental defense buildup, often premised on the notion of developing bargaining chips to deal with the Soviet Union, his administration may well become the first U.S. administration in years not to achieve a significant strategic nuclear arms control agreement.

In an effort to determine if there were any pattern between military buildup and concessionary behavior in the disarmament negotiations, data were collected on annual changes of military expenditures in the United States and the Soviet Union. When relating annual changes in military expenditures, adjusted for inflationary effects, to changes in the concessionary behavior of the United States and the Soviet Union in the early postwar negotiations and the SALT negotiations, no significant patterns were discovered. The Spearman rank correlation between changes in Soviet military spending and U.S. concessionary behavior during the pre-1961 negotiations was the only one found to be positive, but only slightly so at .08. Soviet concessionary reactions to U.S. military spending changes during this period showed a rank correlation of only -.12. In contrast to the bargaining chip hypotheses, increases in military spending seemed not to be productive of concessionary behavior on the part of the other side during the SALT negotiations and in fact were slightly negative for both the United States and the Soviet Union.

A partial explanation for the failure to find a good fit between efforts to create additional bargaining chips by increased military spending and changes in concessionary behavior is related to the fact that a state that feels confident in its military power has little incentive to negotiate, whereas a state feeling insecure about its military capabilities, as shown by efforts to increase them, may be fearful of negotiating seriously, believing itself to be in an inferior bargaining position.[43] Consequently neither party will have the incentive to make concessions under such conditions. It is for this reason that positions closer to military parity are more conducive to concession-making and the reaching of agreement on arms control. The SALT I agreements probably would have been impossible but for the fact that the Soviet Union finally was approaching strategic parity with the United States.

Increased military spending may also fail to relate systematically to concessionary behavior since estimates of such spending have often been inaccurate. Recent CIA estimates now suggest that the annual growth in Soviet military spending has been 2 percent or less since 1976—far lower than figures supplied by the Reagan administration to justify its huge defense buildup.[44] Moreover, Soviet growth in defense spending may have been as much directed against China as it was against the United States. Such increases should therefore have minimal impact on U.S. perceptions of the threat if viewed accurately. American increases in military spending over the years, on the other hand, can be partially attributed to the greater costs of troops as the United States moved to an all-volunteer army. Changes in defense spending may also fail to send the appropriate signal since the purpose of such increases or decreases may be seen by the adversary as having been motivated by internal factors such as stimulating the economy or reducing taxes rather than being motivated by external factors.

Individual weapons systems may be more relevant than aggregate military buildups when it comes to analyzing the bargaining chip argument. Robert Einhorn concludes in this regard that the more effective bargaining chips have been high tech items which he notes led to Soviet proposals for banning tests on ASAT, nuclear weapons, anti-submarine weapons, and strategic defense systems—weapons systems in which the Soviets felt they would be unable to compete effectively. The Soviet Union seemed less concerned about the MX and Trident missile systems, the B-1 bomber, and upgraded command, control, and communication systems.[45]

Virtually every U.S. weapons system built in recent years has been justified on the grounds that it would provide a bargaining chip with the Soviet Union in arms control negotiations. The evidence as to whether or not they have been effective is not always clear. The U.S. decision to press on with the Safeguard ABM system in the early seventies was probably not necessary to achieve agreement on the ABM, for the Soviet Union was demonstrating little interest in continuing its own system at the time as it stopped work on the Moscow Galosh system with only 64 missiles in place. Unilateral constraint on the part of the United States probably would have been sufficient for stopping worldwide ABM development, thus saving the several billion dollars that were spent on U.S. ABM systems now in mothballs. Both sides apparently had concluded that the costs of building an ABM system were out of proportion with the value of these systems.

Other weapons systems sold largely as bargaining chips such as the MIRVed missile and the cruise missile rather than facilitating the reduction of weapons actually led to the acceleration of the arms race. The fact of the matter is that it is difficult to cash in such bargaining chips, particularly after the weapons have been tested, and virtually impossible once they have been deployed.

It is possible that a weapons system might provide some bargaining leverage even if there is little intention to barter it away. This seemed to have been the belief of the Scowcroft Committee, which recommended in 1983 that the United States build 100 MX missiles to be deployed in existing silos. In testimony on Capitol Hill, Brent Scowcroft argued that the deployment of MX would convince the Soviets "that their big missiles in silos are wasting assets."[46] According to this view, the MX would decrease Soviet incentives to hold on to their large MIRVed ICBMs. A more likely Soviet response would simply be to rely more upon mobile missiles in which the Soviet Union has certain advantages over the United States since it is confronted with fewer domestic constraints that might interfere with preferred basing systems and enjoys a larger geographical area in which to deploy such weapons.

Despite such arguments favoring deployment, many in Congress have been dubious and have consequently been slow to provide the administration with the full complement of MX missiles it has proposed. After all, the Soviet response to MX deployment may be the habitual one of simply increasing the number of its own land-based missiles. It has already demonstrated its ability to prevail over the United States in the quantitative missile race. Making the MX a bargaining chip may have been more effective in inducing Congress to fund the MX program than it has been in pressuring the Soviet Union to compromise on arms control. Because the MX concentrates so much power on a single missile and enjoys deadly accuracy, it is an especially attractive target and as such may only contribute to destabilizing the nuclear deterrent system. Consequently, the bargaining chip argument may be the only plausible rationale for producing the system. Despite such a limited justification, the bargaining chip argument can be a persuasive one since no congressman wants to be accused of thwarting the prospects for disarmament by not being willing to build what many believe to be an effective bargaining chip.

The Strategic Defense Initiative (SDI) has obviously been important in inducing the Soviet Union to the bargaining table following its 1983 walkout, but whether it will be an effective bargaining chip in facilitating the reduction of armaments remains to be seen. President Reagan is adamant that SDI not be considered a bargaining chip, despite pressures from some both in and outside the administration to trade the system for a reduction in Soviet offensive arms. Unless such a deal is struck, the more likly outcome will be an accelerated offensive and defensive arms race as will be argued in chapter 7.

Only too often bargaining chip calculations have affected weapons choices, resulting in choices that conflict with rational strategic considerations. According to R. James Woosely, the basic reason that the administration reversed the 1977 decision of Secretary of Defense David Packer by accelerating production of the Trident submarine instead of the Trident I missile "was to spend more money faster so they could convince the Russians, or themselves, or somebody that they had resolve."[47] Similarly, Kissinger forced the cruise missile upon a reluctant military in order that the United States might have additional leverage in SALT II. Whether or not the system was needed or would contribute to the stability of deterrence was not considered at the time.

Not only does the bargaining chip argument sometimes lead to the development of unneeded or militarily less desirable weapons systems, it may also delay the withdrawl of obsolete and redundant weapons. The U.S. Titan missile and the Soviet SS-4 and SS-5 missiles remained in service many years beyond their effectiveness. Keeping obsolete systems in service may add unnecessarily to the military burden, given the operational costs involved. It therefore seems quite probable that the negative consequences of bargaining chips may outweigh any positive benefits. Rather than easing the arms burden for a state, such chips are just as likely to speed the arms race.

CONCLUSION

This chapter has examined U.S.-Soviet bargaining behavior in three sets of negotiations consisting of the early postwar disarmament negotiations (1945–60), the test ban negotiations (1959–63), and the SALT talks (1969–79). According to a considerable amount of experimental and actual negotiations, there is a tendency to reciprocate concessions within the same round of negotiations. Failure to reciprocate, creating an imbalance in concession scores, often leads to reduced concessions in the next round. Nevertheless, data from both the test ban and SALT negotiations showed a positive rank correlation between lagged Soviet concession scores and an American imbalance in concession scores, suggesting that a hard-line strategy may be productive in obtaining concessions in the next round. Although not significant, the relationship was in the opposite direction when applied to the United States, as lower relative Soviet concession rates led to a reduced U.S. concession score in the next period.

Whereas the state beginning negotiations with an extreme position may expect to gain more from the negotiations, the evidence from SALT does not support this conclusion. An extreme position will require higher levels of concessions subsequently if agreement is desired. The probability that the other side will expect to receive even more concessions may only increase. If both sides adopt extreme positions, the probability of agreement will be reduced considerably.

In all three sets of negotiations the United States tended to make a far higher percentage of its concessions in the earlier phase of the negotiations than did the Soviet Union. This initial soft bargaining posture seems not to have been detrimental to the U.S. interests. The Limited Test Ban Treaty was clearly in the interest of both states, and an examination of the SALT I and SALT II treaties reveals a number of provisions more compatible with the American position than the Soviet one. In evaluating the utility of concessionary behavior, one should recognize that to the extent that the refusal to compromise leads to a delayed agreement, such a refusal may work to a state's disadvantage. This is particularly true of negotiations for a weapons freeze wherein delay may only allow the other side to gain proportionally in military strength as the Soviet Union was allowed to do during the protracted process leading to SALT I.

Concessionary behavior also appears to be affected by the level of international tension and relative military strength. Although no strong linear patterns were found between these two variables and concessionary behavior, certain patterns are nevertheless identifiable. Low tension levels appear to breed complacency, thus providing little incentive to do something about the armaments problem, whereas too much tension tends to create distrust that is hardly compatible with making the concessions necessary to reach agreement. Similarly, military bargaining chips have often been unproductive in facilitating concession-making behavior. The more common response has been one of duplicating the arms achievements of the other side rather than negotiating arms constraints.

In the following four chapters, we will explore how the United States and the Soviet Union have bargained in four major sets of negotiations—the test ban negotiations, negotiations on nuclear nonproliferation, the SALT negotiations, and negotiations during the Reagan era. This will provide us with an opportunity to examine in detail the major obstacles confronting the search for national security through the arms control approach as well as to evaluate the prospects and factors that might facilitate successful negotiation.

4

The Nuclear Test Ban Negotiations

The difficulties of achieving comprehensive solutions to the problems presented by nuclear and conventional armaments had become obvious during the early period of the postwar disarmament negotiations. Whenever negotiations became more serious, there was a tendency to restrict discussion to partial and achievable measures. One such area involved negotiations for a ban on nuclear testing that resulted in the first significant arms control agreement reached in the postwar period—the Limited Test Ban Treaty (LTBT), which was opened for signature in 1963. Efforts to extend this treaty to a comprehensive test ban agreement have proved futile despite hundreds of hours of negotiation since that time, although a Threshold Test Ban Treaty in 1974 and the Peaceful Nuclear Explosions Treaty of 1976 added further restrictions to testing.

Placing limits on the testing of weapons has been viewed as one of the most important moves that can be taken to stop or slow the development of a weapons system. Few decision makers are likely to rely upon a weapon that has not been adequately tested; and, hence, they will not move to the production stage without such testing. Moreover, restrictions on testing can limit the potential power of a weapons system, making it more difficult to increase the accuracy of the destructive capability of the weapon. Finally, limits on testing have often been pressed by states that already have a given weapons system as a way of preventing other states from joining the select company of nuclear weapon states.

Not only may restrictions on testing nip weapons development in the bud, such restrictions also provide the decided advantage of being more verifiable than restrictions on the production, possession, or use of weapons. Once a state has adequately tested a given weapons system, uncertainty arises about whether the state has proceeded to the production stage. Once produced, a weapons system, particularly one as small as a nuclear warhead, becomes virtually impossible to detect.

EARLY SKIRMISHING

Interest in a nuclear test ban goes back to the mid-1950s as growing public concern was raised about the dangers of nuclear fallout. With the United States entering the thermonuclear age in 1952 and the Soviet Union following suit the next year, there was increased anxiety about the health hazards of nuclear fallout. No longer was one dealing with atomic weapons that could be measured in the low kiloton range, but now such weapons were measured by the megaton with a corresponding increase in radioactive fallout. A fifteen-megaton bomb exploded by the United States in the Bikini Atolls on March 1, 1954, sprinkled radioactive fallout on Marshall Islanders, and a few days later, the Japanese fishing boat, the *Lucky Dragon*, docked with 23 irradiated fishermen aboard, one of whom subsequently died. The public outcry against further atmospheric testing intensified as Prime Minister Jawaharlal Nehru of India called for a separate and immediate nuclear test ban. Support for such a ban was also provided by the pope, Albert Einstein, Albert Schweitzer, and a number of other notables throughout the world.

The Soviet Union was the first to respond in a positive way to such appeals as Nikita Khrushchev announced on February 14, 1955, that "we [the Soviets] are willing to accept certain partial steps—for example, to discontinue the thermonuclear weapons tests."[1] As part of its dramatic policy shift shown in its May 10, 1955, proposals, the Soviet Union suggested ending nuclear tests at the very beginning of the first stage of its comprehensive disarmament plan. The United States response was one of opposition, for it argued that any ban on nuclear testing must be made a part of a comprehensive, safeguarded disarmament agreement. At best, the United States was willing to consider nuclear test restrictions during the second stage of the disarmament process, and a complete ban on testing would not come until the third stage, according to its April 1956 proposals.

The Soviet Union continued to press for a separate ban on nuclear testing in a number of proposals tabled before the onset of the Geneva talks, whereas the United States remained adamantly against such a separation. A U.S. proposal in May 1957 provided that a test ban be linked to a cut-off in the production of nuclear weapons and, in a letter sent to Soviet Premier Bulganin in December, President Eisenhower added agreement on limiting other weapons and providing assurances against surprise attack to the list of conditions for agreeing to a test suspension.

The essentially negative position taken by the United States on the issue of a nuclear test ban during this period reflected deep divisions within the government. Aside from the general reservation that such a ban would interfere with scientific progress, concern was expressed about restrictions that would impede specific weapons programs. Nuclear weapons had become a central part of U.S. military doctrine with the introduction in 1954 of the New Look strategy, which emphasized the threat of massive retaliation should the Soviet Union seek to extend its power in the world. Given the importance assigned to nuclear weapons, some believed that continued testing was necessary to ascertain the effectiveness of existing weapons.

Several new weapons systems were also believed to require testing. As part of its nuclear strategy in the mid-1950s, the United States had decided to emphasize small tactical nuclear weapons that required continued testing to miniaturize nuclear warheads. Smaller weapons would be able to reduce collateral damage and could be used in the battlefield, thus reducing the number of troops needed to balance Soviet conventional superiority. The downsizing of nuclear warheads was also necessary as the world entered the missile age since the throw-weight of such delivery systems was severely limited, particularly when compared to the bomber, which had been the primary vehicle used previously. In addition, the United States was beginning research on an anti-ballistic missile system with its Nike-Zeus system, which would use nuclear warheads to destroy incoming warheads. There was also interest in developing a neutron bomb, which would produce intense radiation but minimize structural damage. But perhaps the scientific dream that raised the most interest among those opposed to a test ban was the possibility of developing a "clean bomb." Apparently, Edward Teller's promise that a thermonuclear bomb that would be 96 percent free of fallout could be developed in four-five years led President Eisenhower to back away from his decision to support a nuclear test suspension in June 1957.[2]

Although Eisenhower and a number of military officials were primarily interested in a clean bomb as a way of reducing collateral damage in nuclear war, thus making such weapons more useful in battle, it was hoped such a device could be used for peaceful explosions involving huge earthmoving efforts such as those required for building harbors, canals, and so forth.

The United States was also constrained during that early period by opposition to a test ban from its allies, Britain and France. It was not until 1957 that the British tested their first thermonuclear device; and, of course, France had yet to test any nuclear devices since its first test did not occur until February 1960.

Still others were concerned that a test ban might diminish support for increasing military budgets or that it might generate additional pressure for disarmament. Henry A. Kissinger, writing in *Foreign Affairs* on the eve of the Geneva Conference on the Discontinuance of Nuclear Weapons Tests in 1958, expressed the fear that such a ban would be the first step in an increased campaign to outlaw nuclear weapons altogether;[3] and the head of the U.S. Atomic Energy Commission, Lewis F. Strauss, argued that such a ban would lead to public complacency, making it difficult to get defense budgets passed by Congress.[4]

Whatever the motivation for the American reticence, the Soviet Union was able to capture the moral high ground as it intensified its advocacy of an immediate test ban. In June 1957 it proposed a two- to three-year moratorium on testing that would be separate from other disarmament measures. The Soviets sweetened the offer by suggesting for the first time that they would be willing to accept on-site inspection. With these important concessions, public support for a test ban was intensified. Nobel laureate Linus Pauling submitted a petition with the signatures of thousands of scientists calling for a nuclear test ban, and a number of religious leaders, including Billy Graham and the pope, were calling for unilateral suspensions of testing to force the Soviet Union to follow suit. American public support for such a ban was also intensifying. The Gallup polls, for example, showed an increase in support for such a ban from 20 percent in April 1954 to 63 percent in 1957.

President Eisenhower responded to these pressures in a June press conference by proposing a ten-month suspension of nuclear tests. Such a limited time was roundly criticized on the grounds that it was meaningless, for it usually took that long to prepare for a new test series. Secretary of State John Foster Dulles supported such a suspension since it would be short enough not to risk the dislocation of scientific personnel should the ban fail to be extended, and it would also provide time to make headway in terms of putting an inspection system into place and to make certain that verification procedures would be adequate.

The pressure intensified the following year when the Soviet Union announced that it was unilaterally suspending all atmospheric testing on March 31 and would continue to adhere to such a ban as long as the United States and its allies refrained from testing. This offer came, however, just after the Soviet Union had completed a long series of nuclear tests and was therefore hoping to stop the United States from conducting similar tests. When the United States announced its own moratorium to begin on October 31, 1958, it likewise was just concluding its most intensive series of tests in history. The United Kingdom, initially hostile to the proposed U.S. test moratorium, agreed to accept it after moving up its own testing program to August 1958 rather than waiting until late fall as initially planned. The pattern of conducting a series of nuclear tests then immediately calling for a test suspension by all parties continued to be used on several subsequent occasions prior to the negotiation of the Limited Test Ban Treaty.

The Soviets' March 31, 1958, moratorium placed considerable political pressure on the United States to respond to the Soviet initiative in some way. The United States, concerned about being upstaged on the test ban issue, proposed in a letter from President Eisenhower dated April 8 that technical discussions be opened to determine the feasibility of an effective verification system. Khrushchev objected to the idea of technical talks, suggesting that agreement on the principle of a test ban must be reached before technical talks on verification could begin. Much to the surprise of the United States, the Soviet Union relented on May 9 by accepting the idea of technical expert talks. Soviet interest in a test ban was apparently much greater than that of the United States at the time, for not only would such a ban prevent the United States from duplicating the recent Soviet test series, but a general test ban could help resolve the problem of nuclear proliferation as the Soviet Union began to worry about the nuclear aspirations of the Federal Republic of Germany and the People's Republic of China. Since the Soviet Union did not share the U.S. interest in developing tactical nuclear weapons, it was less concerned about keeping the testing option open for that reason. Furthermore, the Soviets had considerable interest in slowing the arms race because of the economic costs involved and the need to bolster their domestic economy.

The Conference of Experts, consisting of scientists from the United States, the USSR, and several of their respective allies, met during the summer of 1958 to discuss the verification requirements for a nuclear test ban. The conference proved to be an interesting experiment in international bargaining, as it was composed of academically oriented scientists rather than seasoned diplomats. The American scientists were somewhat at a disadvantage, not only because they lacked the level of diplomatic experience of their Soviet counterparts, but they also failed to receive diplomatic instructions. This was partially due to the failure of Washington to agree upon a negotiating position. It was also probably related to the fact that Washington viewed the negotiations as a scientific exploration of the problems and prospects of verifying a nuclear test ban, not the final word on verification. The Soviet Union saw the negotiations as a process for reaching political decisions on how much verification would be necessary.

In agreeing to the Experts Conference, Khrushchev had proposed an unrealistic demand that the Experts' Report be completed within thirty days after negotiations begin—a tactic often used by the Soviet Union to place pressure upon the United States to reach agreement or be blamed for the failure. President Eisenhower responded by calling for a report within sixty days or as soon as possible thereafter.

The negotiations proved to be quite hectic with sessions often going late into the evenings. These negotiations, as well as subsequent ones dealing with the verification issue, were somewhat impeded by the fact that both sides were reticent about exposing their prized methods of detection. As a result, candid discussion on the requirements and capabilities of verification was often exceedingly difficult. Eventually the scientists were able to agree upon an inspection system that would include some 180 land-based control posts. It was believed that this number would be sufficient to detect underground explosions as low as 5 kilotons in size. The experts also recommended four technical measures for detecting nuclear testing: acoustical waves, electromagnetic waves, radioactive debris, and seismic signals.

The State Department was somewhat displeased that the Experts' Report had agreed upon a single set of control sites rather than leaving the issue for further negotiation. After initial hesitation, President Eisenhower agreed on August 22, 1958, to accept the report as the basis for further negotiation. The Soviet Union in the subsequent Geneva negotiations continued to raise the report to support various positions that it took on the test ban issue.

NEGOTIATING THE LIMITED TEST BAN TREATY

During the nearly five years it took to negotiate the Limited Test Ban Treaty, the positions taken on test ban issues by the two superpowers varied considerably. The United States began the negotiations in the fall of 1958 by insisting that a test ban agreement be linked to progress on other measures of disarmament, particularly a nuclear weapons production cut-off. On January 19, 1959, the United States announced that it would no longer insist upon such a linkage. Apparently, the Defense Department and the Atomic Energy Commission had softened their positions on the issue, perhaps believing that agreement on a test ban treaty was unlikely anyway. It was not until the Reagan administration came into power in 1981 that the United States reversed itself by insisting that a comprehensive test ban agreement be linked to other measures of disarmament.

In June 1961 the Soviet Union began to insist upon linkage as it sought to make the issue of a nuclear test ban conditional upon agreement on general and complete disarmament. The Soviet negotiator, Semyon Tsarapkin, in supporting the shift in policy, argued that the situation had changed in the last two or three years and that a test ban agreement would no longer be very useful. Instead, a verified ban would only provide intelligence gathering in the absence of disarmament.

When the Soviet Union broke the three-year moratorium on nuclear testing on August 31, 1961, yet another form of linkage was suggested when Khrushchev announced that the Soviet Union had resumed testing only to shock the allies into beginning negotiations on Berlin and other German issues. He also repeated the notion that a test ban should be linked to disarmament and hypothesized that the resumption of testing might induce the West to negotiate more seriously about disarmament.

On the eve of the final Moscow negotiations in the summer of 1963, which produced the Limited Test Ban Treaty, Khrushchev was insisting that a test ban be linked to a nonaggression pact between the Warsaw Pact and NATO nations—a proposal that had long been on the Soviet agenda but was equally objectionable to the West. Only after the Soviets dropped this linkage was it possible to conclude the Limited Test Ban Treaty.

Several factors have influenced decisions to link a nuclear test ban with other issues. The early insistence by the United States that a test ban be linked to broader disarmament issues was partially motivated by the desire to retain the moral high ground and to counter the propaganda advantages derived by the Soviet Union's position in calling for an immediate end to nuclear testing. Similarly, the Soviet Union's argument that it had resumed testing in August 1961 only to force the West to negotiate on more meaningful disarmament measures was an effort to minimize the global hostility created by its resumption of atmospheric testing.

Linkage has also been pressed by some as a device to assure that given negotiations are doomed to failure. By making a cut-off in the production of nuclear weapons a condition for supporting a nuclear test ban in the late fifties, the United States was guaranteeing that such an agreement would not be negotiated. The Soviet Union would hardly accept such a proposal at a time when its nuclear stocks were far inferior to those of the United States.

Proposals for linking a test ban to broader disarmament measures may also be motivated by the perception that the other side is more interested than oneself in a nuclear test ban and consequently may pay a price to obtain it. But in this case neither the United States nor the Soviet Union was that interested in a test ban. The exception might have been for brief moments when one party or the other felt itself ahead and wanted to lock in the advantage. The interest shown in a test ban agreement was probably more related to the pressures exerted by an aroused public concerned about the dangers of atmospheric testing.

Linkage may even be supported by those concerned with reaching more significant agreements, believing that measures such as a test ban are largely cosmetic and do little to control the threat of nuclear weapons. If the linkage does not hold some attraction for the adversary, such an approach will do little to further the cause of disarmament. Instead, it might be preferable, as some disarmament proponents have suggested, that agreement on small issues such as a test ban be reached in order to build the trust that is necessary for obtaining agreement on more controversial issues or to gain experience and reassurance regarding verification.

Positions also changed over time regarding whether a test ban should be comprehensive or partial. The Soviet Union up to the present time has generally favored a comprehensive test ban that would include weapons testing in all environments—atmospheric, outer space, underwater, and underground. The United States has often opposed a comprehensive solution largely on the basis that tests in certain environments, particularly those conducted underground, could not be adequately verified. Thus any restrictions should be limited to those explosions that would be verifiable.

The United States was the first to offer the possibility of a partial test ban agreement when Eisenhower proposed in a letter to Khrushchev, dated April 13, 1959, that the United States would support a comprehensive test ban only if the Soviet Union would change its position with respect to procedures for on-site inspection, eliminate its veto requirement, and enter into early discussion of procedures for detecting high altitude testing. If the Soviet Union were unwilling to make such changes, the president proposed that a first step be taken by suspending atmospheric tests up to 50 kilometers while political and technical problems were being resolved.

The Soviet Union rejected the partial approach suggested by Eisenhower, perhaps in the belief that it would benefit the United States more than the Soviet Union. It was assumed that the United States would have more to gain from testing in the nonrestricted environments since the United States had a greater interest in tactical nuclear weapons than did the Soviet Union and such tests are most suitable for testing underground.

With the recognition that some tests would not be readily verifiable with existing means of verification or that the verification procedures required would be so onerous as to be unacceptable to sovereign nations, the United States and the Soviet Union eventually agreed that the more difficult tests to detect could be restricted through the process of an unverified moratorium, at least in the short run. The two states differed, however, in how long that moratorium could last while the parties sought to improve verification procedures and to negotiate a comprehensive test ban treaty. The Soviet Union insisted upon a four- to five-year moratorium, whereas the United States wanted it limited to one to two years.

Verification

As in so many arms control negotiations, verification became the major obstacle to agreement. The ability of the Geneva Experts Conference to reach a consensus on the verification requirements for a nuclear test ban agreement suggested that perhaps these negotiations would not be as vituperative as earlier disarmament negotiations. Yet despite the fact that both the United States and the Soviet Union ultimately accepted the Experts' Report as the basis for the test ban talks beginning in October 1958, verification issues continued to plague the negotiations.

As in the case of negotiations for a comprehensive plan of disarmament, the United States continued to place far more emphasis upon verification procedures than did the Soviet Union. Under early U.S. plans the international control organ would have been required to be "installed and working effectively" prior to the institution of the nuclear test ban.

The priorities of the Soviet Union were just the opposite as it sought to obtain an agreement on the principle of a test ban prior to discussing control procedures. It was not until November 1958 that the Soviet Union accepted a control system as an integral part of the test ban agreement. Prior to that time it had insisted upon a separate protocol dealing with the control system.

A partial explanation for the alleged failure of the Experts Conference to evaluate verification capabilities accurately may have been related to a general lack of data on the problems involved in the detection of underground tests. Most nuclear tests after all had been conducted above ground prior to 1958. With the flurry of tests that began just prior to the opening of the Geneva Conference on the Discontinuance of Nuclear Weapons Tests, the United States was able to collect new data that led to a reassessment of verification capabilities. The U.S. series, Hardtack II, revealed that the minimum yield for safely detecting an underground test using the Geneva Experts' formula was 20 kilotons rather than the 5 kilotons previously estimated. Although a 20-kiloton level would have assured the detectability of virtually any test above the size of the Hiroshima bomb, many experts felt this was insufficient.[5] In presenting the evidence for the Hardtack II series in January 1959, the United States argued that the restoration of the 5-kiloton level would require 10 times as many on-site inspections annually or a control network of some 500 stations.[6] The Soviet Union rejected this contention, arguing that the United States was basing its conclusions on a single shot, the 5-kiloton Logan test.

Although the Hardtack II results led the United States to assert that the Geneva Experts' assessments were inadequate, a more serious attack on the Geneva system resulted when the United States raised the possibility of decoupling underground nuclear explosions in order that such tests would not register so high on seismological instruments and might even escape detection altogether. The idea of decoupling, which was introduced by Albert Latter in 1959, suggested the possibility of digging a large hole underground in which a nuclear device could be exploded. The large cavity in effect would lessen the shock to the surrounding earth and thus be less detectable. In fact, Latter's suggestion that the decoupling effect could be as high as 300 would have meant "that a 100 kiloton explosion would not even be detected and located by the experts control system."[7]

U.S. scientists were clearly divided on Latter's decoupling theory. Many felt that to dig a large enough hole to muffle a nuclear explosion would be a difficult and costly task. To do so without being detected, as would be required if one wanted to test surreptitiously, would be a virtual impossibility. To dispose of the excavated materials would be a huge undertaking.

The theory of decoupling was applied in the Cowboy series of experiments (December 1959–March 1960), which used data extracted from chemical explosions to suggest a decoupling factor of 120. Soviet scientists referred to experiments that showed a decoupling factor of only 2, but U.S. scientists were able to demonstrate fallacies in the calculations. Whatever the proper assessment, the argument of decoupling assumed a less significant role in subsequent debates on a comprehensive test ban.

In seeking to ascertain the number of on-site inspections required, the United States wanted that number to be determined on a scientific basis rather than based upon a political compromise as proposed by the Soviet Union. The United States preferred a sliding scale in which the number of on-site inspections would be related to the number of suspicious events during any given year. Prime Minister Harold Macmillan supported the notion of an annual quota for inspections in his effort to get the United States and the Soviet Union to compromise on the issue.

In May 1959, the United States accepted the idea of an annual quota for on-site inspections as long as a Soviet veto would not be applicable. Debate over the next few years revolved around the question of how many on-site inspections would be allowed annually. The United States began by demanding twenty such inspections per year, whereas the Soviet Union was willing to accept three at most. In May 1961, the United States accepted a sliding scale for on-site inspections on Soviet territory that would range from twelve to twenty per year. Subsequent moves resulted in further reductions so that on the eve of agreeing to the Limited Test Ban Treaty in 1963 the United States was insisting upon only six such inspections annually. At the same time, the Soviet Union was proposing a limit of only two or three, reversing a position it had held for several months that would have denied any on-site inspections on Soviet territory.

Despite all of the energy exerted in debating the issue of on-site inspection and control posts, Swedish scientists, among others, raised questions as to whether such procedures could be effective even if allowed. Congressional hearings on the Limited Test Ban Treaty revealed that the digging of just one hole to find radioactive debris as uncontestable evidence of a test explosion would take as much as fifty-five days after an explosion occurs.[8] The costs of an effective system also raised questions as even the more limited Experts' proposals for a control system would have cost into the billions.

In April 1962 the eight nonaligned states in the Eighteen Nation Disarmament Committee sought to simplify verification requirements by proposing that the inspection system be based upon existing national networks of observation posts. After all, over 7,800 seismological stations already in existence throughout the world would be able to monitor underground explosions. Research was also demonstrating that many nuclear explosions could be distinguished from earthquakes because of the differences between the two in the initial shock waves.[9]

When evaluating the costs and complexities of the test ban verification system, it should be remembered that the number of control posts and on-site inspections being discussed was related to a ban that would cover only the larger underground tests. Concerned about the problems of detecting low-yield underground tests, the United States in February 1960 proposed placing the threshold on underground explosions at 4.75 on the Richter scale. It was estimated that any test above the size of that exploded at Hiroshima would register at least 4.75 or better. A month later the United States agreed to the notion of a unilateral moratorium on tests below the 4.75 threshold while negotiations and research would continue in an effort to reduce that threshold, leading ultimately to the abolition of all underground testing. The Soviet Union was quick to accept the 4.75 threshold level with a moratorium on testing below that level but insisted the proposed Experts' Report provided sufficient verification capabilities for all tests, both above and below the threshold. In August 1961, the United States indicated a willingness to eliminate the 4.75 threshold entirely if the Soviet Union would agree to increasing the number of control posts and on-site inspections. This overture, however, became the victim of the Soviet Union's resumption of nuclear testing announced a day or so after the U.S. proposal was tabled.

The fact that the United States was beginning to be more conciliatory on verification issues, following the hard line it had taken in the years 1959–62, was related in large measure to the significant progress that was being made in research to improve verification procedures. Initially, such efforts were insignificant, raising questions about the United States' seriousness about a nuclear test ban. Prior to 1960 the United States had spent only a total of 20 million dollars on the problem of nuclear test detection—an insignificant amount considering how seriously the United States took the verification issue in the debates.[10]

Beginning in 1960, research into the problems of verification was considerably bolstered with the establishment of the VELA program. During FY 1960 and 1961, over $50 million had been appropriated for the program with $59 million designated for FY 1962 alone. On the basis of research conducted under these programs, it was discovered that the sensitivity of seismographic equipment could be increased by a factor of five or ten by placing the equipment in deep holes rather than at the surface. Research also indicated that the number of shallow earthquakes in the Soviet Union was far fewer than had been previously thought, reducing the number of suspicious events requiring investigations. It was further discovered that underground explosions conducted in alluvium produced deep cavities that would be detectable from the air.[11] This discovery was significant since such tests were the most difficult to detect with seismological equipment. Increasing the number of control posts and placing them closer to areas where earthquake activity occurs would also increase detection prospects. The development of tamper-proof detection systems or "black boxes" also improved the prospects of verification with limited damage to Soviet sensitivities about national sovereignty. In December 1962, Premier Nikita Khrushchev agreed that three such stations could be placed upon Soviet territory.

Progress on detection techniques was such that the United States felt it could make a number of concessions on verification procedures to be used. For example, President Kennedy announced on August 27, 1962, that a substantial reduction could be made in the number of control posts required and, more importantly, from the perspective of Soviet sensitivity to its sovereign rights, these posts could be manned by Soviet nationals with international supervision.

By 1963, improvements in verification procedures led to estimates that stations located outside the territory of the USSR would be just as effective in detecting Soviet underground tests as the verification system proposed in the 1958 Experts' Reports.[12] As noted earlier, the Experts insisted that a number of control posts be situated on Soviet territory as well as externally located. Because of these improvements it was reported that President Kennedy and Prime Minister Macmillan, during talks in Bermuda in 1962, regretted that the United States had made so much of the possibility of clandestine underground testing.

Although most of the attention in the nuclear test ban negotiations was given to the problems of detecting underground nuclear explosions, verification of testing in other environments was not without controversy. Concern about possible evasion of high-altitude testing restrictions led President Eisenhower on May 5, 1959, to make continued U.S. participation in the negotiations dependent upon an early discussion of the problems involved. As a result, Technical Group I was formed at the Geneva Conference to evaluate verification requirements for a high-altitude test ban. During these talks, the Soviet Union accepted all but one of the eleven verification procedures proposed, several of which would take advantage of the then developing technologies of outer space satellites. In its final report, Technical Group I recommended the placement into orbit of 5 or 6 large satellites able to detect radiation from nuclear explosions in space.[13] Progress was such that the United States representative in Geneva admitted in the spring of 1962 that larger nuclear explosions could be detected by national verification means. He also pointed out that detection capabilities were considerable with respect to outer-space and underwater testing, but doubts remained on the ability to detect underground tests.[14]

Despite this optimism the fact remains that the VELA system launched in 1970 was not completely reliable. A White House panel was unable to reach an airtight conclusion on whether South Africa had exploded a nuclear device over the Atlantic Ocean in 1979.[15] The Defense Intelligence Agency claimed there had been a nuclear explosion, but others were not so certain.

The Moratorium on Testing

The fact that a test ban agreement could be negotiated at all is in no small measure related to the unilateral moratorium on further nuclear testing that both sides had accepted by the fall of 1958 and continued to adhere to until the Soviet Union resumed testing on September 1, 1961. Once into the moratorium, pressure was exerted upon both parties not to be the first to break it. Indeed, each side had pledged that it would not resume testing until the other side did. The Soviet Union persisted in honoring its unilateral moratorium after the French exploded their first atomic bomb in February 1960 despite the fact that it had made continued adherence to the ban contingent upon observance by *all* Western states.

The United States was the first to blink on the moratorium as the Eisenhower administration was pressed by various domestic interests to renew testing, given the slow progress of the talks. Among those taking such a stand was Nelson Rockefeller, who was preparing for a run for the presidency in 1960, John A. McCone, the chairman of the Atomic Energy Commission, and Senator Clinton P. Anderson, the chairman of the Joint Committee on Atomic Energy. On August 26, 1959, President Eisenhower announced that the U.S. moratorium would be extended to the end of the year. In so doing, he was merely extending it two months beyond the initial one-year moratorium that was to have expired on October 30th. In agreeing to such a limited extension, Eisenhower was communicating his frustration that more progress had not been made on negotiating a test ban. He was unwilling to support the British position that the moratorium should continue as long as negotiations were in progress. On December 29, 1959, President Eisenhower went a step further by announcing that the United States considered itself free to resume nuclear weapons testing but added that it would ''not resume nuclear testing without announcing our intention in advance of any resumption.''[16] The chief British negotiator, Sir Michael Wright, has criticized this position by suggesting that it created the worst of all possible worlds. The United States would lose whatever security benefits might be gained by resuming testing and, at the same time, would be subjected to world criticism, allowing the Soviet Union "to claim that the West was the first to speak of resuming."[17]

Despite the announcement that it no longer felt itself bound by the moratorium on nuclear testing, the United States made no immediate effort to prepare test sites, nor did it provide any budgetary allocations for nuclear testing. The Atomic Energy Commission finally declared on March 16, 1960, that it would prepare for underground tests in New Mexico in 1961 and Dwight Eisenhower, after leaving the presidency, noted that he would have resumed nuclear testing following the 1960 presidential election had Richard Nixon won.[18]

During this period, the Soviet Union continued to give assurances that it would live up to the moratorium. On August 11, 1959, Premier Khrushchev pledged not to be the first to resume nuclear testing. He continued to reassure the United States on this score by promising President Kennedy as late as the Vienna summit in June 1961 that the Soviet Union would not resume nuclear testing until the United States did. In making the promise, it may well have been that the Soviet Union had anticipated that the United States would be the first to break the moratorium. Support for such a viewpoint could be found in the changing climate of opinion on the subject in the United States. The Joint Chiefs of Staff in February 1961 had asked for a resumption of testing if agreement were not reached on a test ban within sixty days, and Gallup polls were showing a 2 to 1 majority favoring the unilateral resumption of testing by the United States.

The Kennedy administration appeared to be more predisposed than the previous administration toward reaching agreement on a nuclear test ban treaty as reflected in the substantial number of concessions it made in the March 21, 1961, proposals. The Soviet Union was not responsive to the U.S. overture, perhaps because it had already made the decision to resume nuclear testing.

When the Soviet Union resumed testing on September 1, 1961, the immediate U.S. response was an offer to ban all atmospheric testing, but the Soviets were given only a week to react. Since the Soviet Union had just begun its largest test series ever, involving a total of fifty atmospheric tests within a period of sixty days, the response, as might be expected, was *nyet*. As a result, the United States resumed its own testing on September 15, albeit underground. The following month, Prime Minister Macmillan sought President Kennedy's agreement for a two-month moratorium on atmospheric testing, but Kennedy rejected the proposal. According to some insiders, the reason for this decision was premised on the belief that the Soviet Union would be more inclined to negotiate an end to the arms race once it realized that the West would not stand idle and let the Soviet Union benefit militarily without a response.[19]

Despite the importance of extended moratoria for creating the appropriate environment for negotiating a test ban, it has been argued that the effect of breaking any such moratorium is decidedly against a democracy. It would be virtually impossible for a democracy to break a test ban as abruptly as the Soviet Union did, for the time and effort required for preparing nuclear weapons tests would undoubtedly be leaked in the democratic society. Also democratic states appear to be more concerned about the impact of adverse domestic and international opinion than do their more authoritarian counterparts. Because of this disadvantage and disappointment with the turn of events, President Kennedy declared in an address to the nation on March 2, 1962, that "we know enough now about broken negotiations, secret preparations and the advantage gained from a long test series never to offer again an uninspected moratorium."[20]

Such reservations did not prevent President Kennedy from announcing in his American University commencement address on June 10, 1963, that "the United States does not propose to conduct nuclear tests in the atmosphere so long as other states do not do so. We will not be the first to resume."[21] This statement, along with other conciliatory gestures made in the speech, set the tone in making it possible to conclude negotiations on the Limited Test Ban Treaty 55 days later. Premier Nikita Khrushchev is reported to have told U.S. negotiator Averell Harriman that the American University speech was the "best speech by any President since Roosevelt."[22]

The United States decision to initiate another uninspected moratorium, despite having been caught off guard by the Soviet resumption of nuclear testing in September 1961, was made as a result of the feeling that the Soviet Union had not gained that much militarily. According to data reported by the U.S. Atomic Energy Commission, the United States made up for the Soviet encroachment by exploding more than twice as many weapons as the Soviet Union during the two years following the Soviet resumption of testing.[23]

The Third Party Role

The success of the negotiations resulting in signing the Limited Test Ban Treaty in the summer of 1963 was also partially due to the role played by third parties. The United Kingdom lobbied the United States vigorously on occasion in an effort to get the latter to be more responsive to Soviet concessions on test ban issues. Rather than serving simply as a negotiating partner to the United States, the British often sought active mediation between the superpowers.

The British position on the test ban issue, however, was initially hostile. This was particularly true prior to its first hydrogen bomb test in 1957 after which the United Kingdom became an eager advocate of a test ban agreement. The British government had greater domestic pressures affecting its arms control policies than did the United States, given the strong anti-nuclear attitudes of large segments of the British population. Sensitivity to those public attitudes was heightened in 1959–60 due to the fact that Prime Minister Harold Macmillan was coming up for reelection. The British also had more to fear from nuclear weapons in the late fifties and early sixties than did the Americans since the number of intercontinental-range ballistic missiles capable of hitting U.S. soil was extremely limited at the time. Consequently, Britain, at closer range, was more of a nuclear hostage to the Soviet Union than was the United States.

In his role as mediator between the superpowers, Macmillan visited Moscow in February 1959 at which time he sought to break an impasse on the inspection issue by proposing a quota system for on-site inspection. Efforts to press the United States to be more forthcoming can be seen in Macmillan's last-minute flight to the United States in the spring of 1960 to lobby for U.S. acceptance of the principle of an annual quota for on-site inspections. Apparently, this particular trip was not completely necessary for the United States was already becoming more conciliatory on the issue. The CIA head, Allen Dulles, and others had concluded that the United States was ahead in nuclear technology and therefore could lock in the U.S. advantage by becoming more responsive to Soviet positions for the sake of agreement.[24]

After Kennedy assumed the presidency, Macmillan continued to press the testing issue, trying first at the Nassau December 1961 meeting to dissuade Kennedy from resuming atmospheric testing. In March 1963 it was Macmillan who wrote Kennedy suggesting that he meet directly with Khrushchev on the issue of arms control. Although rejecting Macmillan's suggestion for a summit meeting, the president did agree to the idea of a high-level conference, and on June 8 the Soviet premier accepted, setting the stage for the negotiation of the LTBT in Moscow.[25]

Other third party pressures for a nuclear test ban came from the nonaligned countries in the Eighteen Nation Disarmament Committee. Among the more significant initiatives taken by these eight states was a memo dated April 16, 1962, which sought to provide a compromise on verification issues. The memo called for an inspection system based primarily upon existing national observation posts. By using the 7,800 existing meteorological and geological land stations, the need for creating new control posts, particularly on Soviet territory, would be largely negated. It was also largely pressure from the eight neutral states in 1962 that caused the Soviet Union to accept the notion of two to three on-site inspections per year.

Although the Limited Test Ban Treaty was negotiated primarily during tripartite negotiations involving the United States, the Soviet Union, and the United Kingdom, the treaty itself was opened to signature by all states. By 1987, the LTBT had become one of the most universally accepted arms control agreements with around 120 signatories. With the exception of France and the People's Republic of China, virtually all important states are members. Furthermore, no state has exercised the rather easy requirements for withdrawal, which involves only a three-month notice.

EVALUATING THE LIMITED TEST BAN TREATY

Any evaluation of the Limited Test Ban Treaty, which was signed in Moscow on August 5, 1963, must be mixed. As the first significant arms control agreement in the postwar world, it represented somewhat of a breakthrough. The treaty symbolized a period of improved relations between the United States and the Soviet Union, and it was hoped that the LTBT would provide the beginning of a series of more significant arms control agreements. The nearly universal adherence to the treaty raised some hope that the problem of nuclear spread would be minimized since so many threshold nuclear states were included among the signatories. India, having ratified the LTBT, was forced to test underground as it did in 1974 or violate the treaty. In conducting its one underground test, India took great pains to assert that the test was a "peaceful nuclear explosion."

The treaty helped minimize a potential health hazard by eliminating the dangers of nuclear fallout from atmospheric explosions. This was not an insignificant achievement, for research had indicated serious health hazards, particularly since strontium 90 threatened to damage uncounted numbers of children because of contamination of milk supplies. The 1958 atmospheric tests alone were expected to double the amount of this dangerous chemical in the soil by 1960, and the areas most at risk would be in the northern hemisphere.[26]

Secretary of Defense Robert McNamara supported the Limited Test Ban Treaty because he believed it would freeze U.S. nuclear superiority.[27] It was felt that the extra costs imposed by underground testing would dilute limited Soviet military resources. Even more important, a partial test ban would impede Soviet development of an ABM system that could be more effectively tested in the atmosphere than underground. It was also believed that since the Soviet Union preferred larger nuclear devices than did the United States, the former would be at a disadvantage, for underground testing is not as desirable a testing environment for the very large nuclear device.

On the negative side of the ledger, the treaty did not stop nuclear testing, in fact, such testing increased significantly after the treaty was opened for signature, albeit underground. Data in table 4.1 comparing the number of nuclear tests for the five nuclear powers reveal that more tests per year were conducted after the treaty was signed in 1963 than before it was opened for signature. The number was especially high for the United States. Soviet testing accelerated somewhat in 1978, while U.S. tests have remained somewhat stable since 1975. British testing virtually ceased after 1963, making a comeback after Margaret Thatcher assumed power in 1979. France and China have not ratified the LTBT and have engaged in active testing programs that included atmospheric tests until 1974 for France and until 1980 for China. It remains to be seen whether the current lull in Chinese testing that began in 1985 will continue.

A partial explanation for the increase in testing by the United States is related to the fact that the Joint Chiefs of Staff were able to obtain agreement from the president to increase the number of tests if the chiefs would agree to support the Limited Test Ban Treaty. Without their support, it would have been difficult, if not impossible, to obtain Senate approval for ratification of the treaty. Perhaps it can be assumed that the Soviet military received similar concessions for they also had initially been extremely hostile to the treaty.

Had the LTBT provided for an inspection system, it might have been judged more successful in contributing to the control of the U.S.-Soviet arms race. For many proponents of arms control, the precedence of establishing an inspection system on Soviet territory at times seemed to be more important than the objective of stopping further nuclear testing. It might even be argued that arms control advocates, preoccupied with establishing the precedence of on-site inspection, played into the hands of those who sought to use verification concerns to defeat all efforts to obtain a comprehensive test ban. It was perhaps a case where demanding the best was the enemy of the good. The Soviet Union after all was willing to accept limited on-site inspection and unmanned seismic stations in

Table 4.1 Known Nuclear Test Explosions

Time Period	U.S.	USSR	Britain	France	China
July 1945–Aug. 1963	331	166	23	8	0
Aug.-Dec., 1963	14	0	0	1	0
1964	29	6	1	3	1
1965	29	9	1	4	1
1966	40	15	0	6	3
1967	29	16	0	3	2
1968	39	13	0	5	1
1969	29	15	0	0	2
1970	33	13	0	8	1
1971	15	20	0	5	1
1972	15	22	0	3	2
1973	12	14	0	5	1
1974	12	20	1	7	1
1975	17	15	0	2	1
1976	15	17	1	4	4
1977	12	18	0	6	1
1978	16	27	2	8	3
1979	15	29	1	9	0
1980	14	21	3	13	1
1981	16	21	1	12	0
1982	18	31	1	6	0
1983	17	27	1	7	2
1984	17	27	2	8	2
1985	15	8	1	8	0
1986	14	0	1	8	0
Total	813	570*	40	149	30

*The Stockholm International Peace Research Institute and the Swedish National Defense Research Institute reported 18 additional Soviet tests between 1956 and 1958. Sixteen more tests were reported by the French Ministry of Defense between 1963 and 1977.

Source: Based upon data from Natural Resources Defense Council as reported in Michael R. Gordon, "The Arms Race Shows No Signs of Slowing Down," *New York Times*, March 23, 1986, p. E3. Robert S. Norris of the NRDC kindly supplied the figures for 1986.

1963—procedures that would have provided considerable assurance against evasion for all but the smallest underground nuclear devices.

Whether the Limited Test Ban Treaty has been instrumental in stopping the spread of nuclear weapons to other states is uncertain. The treaty allows its signatories to test nuclear devices as long as the tests are conducted underground as was India's nuclear explosion in 1974. The added cost of testing underground cannot be considered a sufficient deterrent to any state that is determined to develop nuclear weapons. Moreover, testing itself may not be essential for the development of primitive nuclear devices. Since 1945 every state that has tried to detonate an atomic bomb has succeeded on the first attempt, at least as far as publically available information shows.[28]

It has also been suggested that the Limited Test Ban Treaty did a disservice to the cause of disarmament by taking the issue of nuclear testing off the front pages of newspapers and television. After the test ban was put into effect, there was less need for the public to be concerned about the environmental hazards of testing. By going underground, the dangers had been reduced considerably. The incentive for extending the test ban was somewhat diminished, particularly since the main selling point for stopping nuclear testing had been the danger of nuclear fallout. The LTBT may also have dissipated the public and political forces favoring disarmament in general, for testing was to become a less visible symbol of the dangers of nuclear war.

THE THRESHOLD TEST BAN TREATY

The fact that more than a decade elapsed before the United States and the Soviet Union could agree upon further restrictions on nuclear testing provides some evidence of just how the Limited Test Ban Treaty had taken away the momentum for restricting nuclear testing. The Threshold Test Ban Treaty (TTBT), signed by the United States and the Soviet Union at the 1974 Moscow summit, did little to restrict U.S.-Soviet testing since the threshold at 150 kilotons was placed so high. Tests above that level were unnecessary, for extrapolations can be made from smaller tests that allow accurate design judgments to be made for more powerful nuclear devices. Besides, the larger devices are more likely to vent, threatening health hazards, and if the resulting radiation drifts beyond national borders, there would be a violation of the Limited Test Ban Treaty.

Although little pressure for restricting underground nuclear testing came from U.S. and Soviet domestic interests, third parties had begun to make the issue of a comprehensive test ban the central arms control issue. Interest in extending the test ban was particularly intensified during the debates on the Nuclear Nonproliferation Treaty during the sixties. A number of nonnuclear weapon states felt that they were being discriminated against by being asked to give up the nuclear weapons option while the existing nuclear weapon states could continue to expand their nuclear armaments. A comprehensive test ban came to be viewed as one of the most important first steps that the superpowers could take to show that they too were serious about restricting nuclear weapons. Also, unlike the NPT, such a treaty would place equal obligations upon both nuclear and nonnuclear weapon states.

To support their case, the nonnuclear weapon states called attention to the Preamble of the Limited Test Ban Treaty, which obligated the parties to continue negotiations in an effort to end all nuclear weapons tests. These states also referred to article 6 of the Nuclear Nonproliferation Treaty, which demanded that progress be made on controlling the arms race by the superpowers. The SALT I agreements were regarded by these states as largely cosmetic since they did not reduce existing weapons systems.

It was the Soviet Union that sought to keep alive the issue of a comprehensive nuclear test ban, perhaps recognizing the propaganda value of doing so. Often, for example, the issue of a comprehensive test ban treaty would be at the top of the list of priorities that the Soviet Union presented in agenda debates before the Eighteen Nation Disarmament Conference in Geneva.

In February 1974, the Soviet Union began another offensive in favor of a comprehensive test ban treaty. Rebuffed by the United States, which believed that testing was necessary to improve its nuclear arsenal and regarded a comprehensive agreement as nonverifiable, the Soviet Union suggested the possibility of establishing a quota that would allow so many tests annually. When this too was rejected, Brezhnev proposed during Henry Kissinger's visit to Moscow in March 1974 that a "threshold" limit be placed upon underground tests. Kissinger was willing to discuss this proposal since the Soviet Union was more dependent upon high-yield weapons than the United States, and these would be the sorts of tests that would be disallowed under a threshold test ban.[29]

During subsequent expert discussions in Moscow, the United States was concerned to keep the threshold high. In particular, Kissinger was afraid that a low threshold would alienate France and particularly China by placing extraordinary global pressure upon them to desist from their weapons testing programs. As a result, he pressed for a 200-kiloton threshold, but eventually compromised on a 150-kiloton level.

Unlike the Limited Test Ban Treaty, which took years to negotiate, the Threshold Test Ban Treaty was completed in a matter of weeks. The final details were finished at the Moscow summit meeting toward the end of June. Also, in contrast to the LTBT, this treaty was negotiated and signed only by the United States and the Soviet Union.

Political objectives rather than arms control objectives seem to have provided the primary impetus for this treaty. Chief among these was the desire to produce a U.S.-Soviet agreement that could be signed at the Moscow summit in June–July, 1974. President Nixon was under great pressure to have an international political success in view of the Watergate scandal, which resulted in his resignation only weeks after his return from the summit.

The TTBT also may have been viewed as a sop to the nonnuclear weapon states which were to meet the following year in the First Review Conference on the operation of the Nuclear Nonproliferation Treaty. The failure of the superpowers to comply with article 6 calling for progress toward arms control was certain to be high on the agenda. At least, the superpowers might argue that the Threshold Treaty was a step in that direction.

The United States might have viewed the effort as a way of reducing the advantages that the Soviet Union gained from propagandizing in support of a comprehensive test ban agreement. Just as the LTBT served to lessen the intensity of the cry for a ban on nuclear testing, the Threshold Test Ban Treaty might diminish pressure for a ban on all tests.

Since the TTBT provides only a partial ban, it has some of the weaknesses of the Limited Test Ban Treaty. The chief limitation is that underground nuclear testing is still allowed. A threshold of 150 kilotons has to be regarded as quite trivial, particularly since most U.S. weapons tests have been below 10–15 kilotons, with many less then 2 kilotons. Seismic data show a similar pattern for the Soviet Union. Just as in the case of the earlier treaty, Defense Department support for the Threshold Test Ban was held hostage to agreement to accelerate testing and $100 million appropriation was used for this purpose.

The acceleration of testing, even above the 150 kiloton level, was made possible by virtue of the fact that the TTBT was not to go into effect until March 31, 1976. The basic reason for this delay was to allow time for the negotiators to agree upon how peaceful nuclear explosives were to be handled. The United States was concerned that such explosions could be used to provide information that could be invaluable for military purposes. After all, there is little, if any, difference in the mechanisms for peaceful or warlike nuclear explosions. Both can wreak considerable damage.

PEACEFUL NUCLEAR EXPLOSIVES

Concern has been expressed by both the United States and the Soviet Union about the need to allow peaceful nuclear explosions that, unless exempted, would violate the test ban agreements. Article 1 of the LTBT prohibits nuclear explosions that cause "radioactive debris to be present outside the territorial limits of the State under whose jurisdiction or control such explosion is conducted." Even without such legal restrictions, radioactivity would have to be reduced to a minimum or the consequences might mean considerable damage to the environment as well as a real threat to life. As a result, enthusiasm for peaceful nuclear explosions has had its ups and downs over the years depending upon the degree of optimism concerning the prospects of developing relatively radioactive-free nuclear explosions.

The hypothetical benefits of peaceful nuclear explosions have long been recognized and include the use of such explosions for mineral extraction and the building of storage facilities, harbors, canals, highways, and landslide dams. Research has also suggested the possible use of nuclear explosions for distilling seawater, separating isotopes, generating thermal power from the heat inside the earth, and even for producing hydroelectric power by creating land depressions into which seawater can flow.[30]

The drafters of the LTBT were aware of the treaty's restrictions upon the use of nuclear explosives for peaceful purposes. In fact, it was because of this concern that the number required to amend the Limited Test Ban Treaty was changed during the negotiations from two-thirds to a majority for the explicit purpose of facilitating a future amendment allowing peaceful nuclear explosions near the surface.[31] Few treaties can claim such undemanding amendment requirements. President Kennedy, in a letter designed to gain Senate support for the Limited Test Ban Treaty, promised the Senate leadership that the "United States will diligently pursue the development of nuclear explosives for peaceful purposes by underground tests within the terms of the treaty, and as and when such developments make possible constructive uses of atmospheric nuclear explosions for peaceful purposes, the United States will seek international agreement under the treaty to permit such explosions."[32]

At the time of the signing of the Limited Test Ban Treaty, U.S. optimism about the utility of peaceful nuclear explosions was in decline. Because of the perception that there would not be a positive payoff for peaceful nuclear explosions (PNEs) for some time, Averell Harriman, in negotiating the Limited Test Ban Treaty for the United States, sought to relinquish the peaceful nuclear explosions option in return for Moscow's agreement to include a withdrawal clause in the treaty. The interest in research on peaceful nuclear explosives, dubbed Project Plowshare, continued to lose support, and by 1978 the plowshare program had disappeared entirely from the budget.

Soviet interest in peaceful nuclear explosions proceeded in the opposite direction. In 1959, Seyom Tsarapkin, the Soviet delegate to the Geneva Conference on the Discontinuance of Nuclear Weapon Tests, objected vehemently to allowing nuclear explosions for peaceful purposes. He regarded such explosions as fraught with harmful consequences for humanity as well as a stimulus to the nuclear arms race.[33] The fact of the matter is that a peaceful nuclear explosive cannot be distinguished from one that could be used to kill people.

In the seventies, it was the Soviet Union which was interested in allowing peaceful nuclear explosions as it began to envision huge earth-moving projects that would perhaps be feasible physically and monetarily only if nuclear explosives were used. Among these were proposals for diverting rivers and building harbors. Given such interests, the Soviet Union has tested a hundred or so PNEs since the late 1960s, whereas the United States has not tested any since 1973.[34]

It was against this background that the Peaceful Nuclear Explosion negotiations began in Moscow in October 1974. Six rounds were held over the next 18 months, resulting in an agreement in April 1976. With its mammoth earth-moving projects in mind, the Soviet Union wanted to allow peaceful explosives as high as 400 kilotons and expressed interest in having as many as 20 simultaneous explosions of bombs with a total yield of 3 megatons.[35] A compromise was reached in the final treaty, which limits simultaneous explosions to 1.5 megatons.

For the first time in any arms control agreement, the Peaceful Nuclear Explosions Treaty provides for on-site inspection on Soviet and U.S. soil as observers from the other side are permitted anytime several peaceful devices total over 150 kilotons. By agreement, they may even be allowed when the explosion is expected to be in the 100-150 kiloton range. The PNE Treaty also enables these observers to place instruments down into the hole where the nuclear device is emplaced in order to get a more accurate reading. As part of the verification procedure, extensive amounts of information must be provided about *all* PNEs of any yield, before and after the explosion.

Following the successful negotiation of the Peaceful Nuclear Explosions Treaty, both the PNET and the Threshold Test Ban Treaty were submitted to the U.S. Senate for consideration. Although in 1974 the TTBT had been politely received, albeit with no great enthusiasm, by

1976 the picture had changed. The détente of the Nixon era was over with President Gerald Ford even excising the term *détente* from his campaign rhetoric. An American presidential election year was hardly the time for pressing a controversial arms control agreement with the Soviet Union. Even the traditional supporters of arms control agreements failed to be supportive and instead criticized the high thresholds that were established by the treaties. Rather than being the precursor to a more comprehensive test ban, these treaties were viewed largely as the death knell for such an agreement. When Carter assumed the presidency in 1977, the two nuclear testing treaties remained on the shelve because of the new administration's interest in negotiating a comprehensive test ban.

The failure to ratify the TTBT and the PNET, while at the same time living up to the obligations imposed by the treaties, has had some serious disadvantages from the perspective of U.S.-Soviet security interests. Chief among these is the opportunity to obtain more information about the testing programs of the adversary. The Threshold Test Ban Treaty, for example, provides for the exchange of geological and geophysical information and for the exchange of data on two previous tests so that the seismometers used in the verification process can be calibrated. It would also require that the parties identify their test sites and that they agree not to conduct tests elsewhere. As already pointed out, the Peaceful Nuclear Explosions Treaty provides for on-site inspection which would help establish the precedent and experience for this type of verification on Soviet soil. Only by gaining experience with such procedures can their weaknesses be recognized and the means for improvements be realized.

CARTER AND THE TEST BAN ISSUE

During the first two years of the Carter presidency considerable progress was made on the issues dividing the United States and the Soviet Union with regard to a comprehensive test ban treaty. In his first letter to Leonid Brezhnev, which was written within days of the presidential inauguration, President Jimmy Carter urged that negotiations for a comprehensive test ban be undertaken. The initial Soviet response was positive as the Soviet Union agreed to voluntary on-site inspection in March 1977. Tripartite negotiations, which included the United Kingdom, were inaugurated in June of that year and lasted until November 1980. Early in these negotiations, the Soviet Union made a number of concessions to the U.S. position, including a willingness to accept a moratorium on peaceful nuclear explosions (later clarified as a three-year moratorium, but with prospects for renewal). The Soviets also accepted the U.S. proposal for a treaty of indefinite duration. But most importantly the Soviet Union was no longer insisting as it had in 1975 that all nuclear weapon powers be included in a comprehensive test ban; such a requirement would have doomed the treaty to failure, given the attitudes of France and China on the issue.

While initially enthusiastic about a comprehensive test ban, the Carter administration began backing off from some of its own proposals, partially because of a divided administration in which Zbigniew Brzezinski, the national security advisor, James Schlesinger, the secretary of energy, and the Joint Chiefs of Staff were all opposed to such a ban. In fact, Brzezinski has written in his memoirs that he went along with internal and external discussions on the issue simply because President Carter badly wanted a comprehensive test ban, whereas he felt that both a SALT and a comprehensive test ban treaty would overload the legislative system. Brzezinski was willing to go along with his commander in chief only if some testing were allowed.[36]

The first of several retractions occurred in May 1978, when the United States retreated from its proposal for a comprehensive ban of unlimited duration. The United States now wanted a treaty limited to five years. The Soviet Union accepted the U.S. change. In September, the United States, because of internal pressure to allow at least some testing, proposed permitting small nuclear "experiments." It was difficult, however, for the administration to define exactly what threshold would be used for the permitted tests. At the same time, the Carter administration again changed its position with regard to the issue of duration, proposing that the treaty be limited to three years. More serious, however, was the demand that after three years the treaty be renegotiated and ratified rather than merely extended if no one disapproved.

Retractions also occurred in 1979 as the United States position hardened even further. For example, the United States demanded that the seismographs to be positioned on Soviet territory be manufactured in the United States and that real-time satellite readings be provided from the seismic stations. U.S. negotiators were also under instructions not to accept the preambular hortatory language found in earlier treaties that called for ambitious disarmament goals.

The United Kingdom began to assume a harder position in 1979 as well. Great Britain, in view of its smaller geographical area, began to balk at the number of unmanned stations that would be placed upon its territory. While the United States was able to get Britain to change its position on this issue, other differences led Brezhnev and Carter to agree at the June 1979 Moscow summit conference that they would go ahead with a comprehensive test ban without Britain if necessary.

Despite these retractions, considerable progress had been made toward a comprehensive test ban treaty when the trilateral negotiations were recessed in November 1980. According to what had been agreed, the ban would rely upon automatic national seismic detection stations on the territory of the three powers: ten each for the two superpowers and a lesser number for the United Kingdom. Voluntary on-site inspection would be utilized, based upon challenges and responses. If the parties failed to agree, the argument could be taken to the United Nations Security Council. A consensus had further developed that there would be a moratorium on peaceful explosions, during which time further studies would be conducted on ways to allow such explosions without providing military advantages.[37]

REAGAN AND THE TEST BAN ISSUE

The Reagan administration came into power with a generally hostile attitude toward arms control. During the presidential campaign, Ronald Reagan had declared the SALT II Treaty to be "fatally flawed," and he was no more supportive of the test ban agreements. The new administration made no effort to revive the trilateral talks on a comprehensive test ban treaty that had recessed in November 1980. It also demanded that the Threshold Test Ban Treaty and the Peaceful Nuclear Explosion Treaty be renegotiated before ratification would be considered. The primary concern has been the verifiability of the treaties as violations of the Threshold Treaty have become part of the litany of alleged Soviet violations of various arms agreements. President Reagan in his February 1985 report to Congress on Soviet arms control violations noted that a number of Soviet tests "constitute a likely violation of legal obligations under the Threshold Test Ban Treaty. . . ."[38] The Soviet Union has also accused the United States of repeated instances of exceeding the 150-kiloton limit.

Soviet compliance with the 1963 Limited Test Ban Treaty has likewise been challenged by the Reagan administration, which has called attention to the fact that radioactive fallout from underground tests has drifted beyond Soviet borders in violation of the treaty. Richard Perle complained of almost 200 such instances in the last 23 years, but prior to the Reagan era these alleged violations were not challenged. At least 100 U.S. tests since 1964 have also released radioactive gases, but since the Nevada test site is not as close to the national border as those of the

Soviet Union, the Limited Test Ban Treaty, for the most part, was not violated.[39]

Concerned about such violations, the Reagan administration proposed in February 1983 that formal talks be undertaken to develop on-site verification procedures for the Threshold Test Ban Treaty, which does not include any such provisions. Those negotiating the treaty had believed on-site inspection was unnecessary to obtain a better reading of the magnitude of underground explosions. The administration's proposal would have required that American experts be able to observe the placement of sensitive sensors in any Soviet testing cavity where the detonation is expected to be in excess of 75 kilotons. Even prominent Republicans were upset with the harsh stance on verification taken by the Reagan administration. Senator Charles Percy, while chairman of the Senate Foreign Relations Committee, threatened to hold up the nomination of Kenneth Adelman as chief of the Arms Control and Disarmament Agency if he did not get action on the Threshold Test Ban Treaty.[40]

By proposing the renegotiation of two existing test ban treaties, the administration hoped to divert attention from the issue of a comprehensive test ban. In this way, it could claim to be interested in a comprehensive ban if such a ban could be made verifiable. It could also expect the Soviet Union to reject any effort to renegotiate the existing treaties, given the latter's interest in a comprehensive test ban treaty. Such a treaty in turn would render the Threshold Test Ban Treaty and the Peaceful Nuclear Explosions Treaty superfluous.

In the summer of 1983 the Reagan administration admitted for the first time that its refusal to engage in negotiations for a comprehensive nuclear test ban was related to a desire to continue underground nuclear tests for national security reasons. In a written response to the House Appropriations Committee, the Arms Control and Disarmament Agency noted: "While a CTB continues to be a long-term U.S. objective, nuclear tests are specifically required for the development, modernization and certification of warheads, the maintenance of stockpile reliability and the evaluation of nuclear weapons effects."[41] Among the administration's proposals for a substantial military buildup was a plan to build seventeen thousand new nuclear warheads over a period of six years. Continued testing was viewed as essential to the program. A more critical objection to negotiating a total ban came as a result of the decision in March 1983 to pursue the Strategic Defense Initiative, which would entail a space-based defense system. Although many of the defensive weapons envisioned in this program would involve conventional components, one of the key defensive systems required development of an X-ray laser powered by a small nuclear explosion. The first of such experiments was conducted December 28, 1985, under the code name Goldstone.

The United States, in opposing even to negotiate on a comprehensive test ban, found itself at some variance with most of its allies and virtually isolated on the issue globally. In December 1982 it was the only state to vote against a UN resolution requiring that all nuclear testing be outlawed; the resolution carried, 111 to 1, with 35 abstentions. Two years earlier only the United Kingdom joined the United States in voting against a UN resolution calling for multilateral negotiations on a comprehensive test ban.

There would seem to be a number of advantages for supporting a comprehensive test ban, not the least of which is that such a ban would be more in line with the overwhelming demand of other states. Some twenty resolutions calling for the prohibition of nuclear testing have been adopted by the UN General Assembly during the period 1975–84. The average vote on these resolutions was 121 states in favor.[42] Many states in ratifying the Nuclear Nonproliferation Treaty explicitly referred to the need to make further progress on a comprehensive test ban and other disarmament measures as a condition for their continued adherence to the treaty. During the three Review Conferences that have been held on the Nuclear Nonproliferation Treaty to date, the issue of a comprehensive test ban has been the disarmament measure most frequently mentioned.

A second advantage of a comprehensive test ban lies in its ability to restrict the qualitative arms race. The failure to limit Soviet testing allows the Soviets to make improvements on the weight to yield ratio of nuclear weapons. With their advantage in terms of throw-weight, further refinements in the size of Soviet nuclear warheads will only allow Soviet missiles to carry considerably more destructive payloads. It has also been suggested that a test ban might inhibit Soviet ability to field a cruise missile force as efficient and as sophisticated as that of the United States. The problem is that with each month's delay in negotiating such a ban, the Soviet Union may catch up with the United States in terms of weapons design.

Third, a comprehensive test ban would remove the major loophole in existing test ban treaties, which allows underground testing to continue. India, in exploding its underground nuclear device in 1974, used such a loophole as it asserted that it was merely developing a peaceful nuclear device. For a test ban to aid in stopping the further spread of nuclear testing, it needs to be comprehensive. For some states, lacking unpopulated territories, conducting underground is the only place they can test anyway, given the hazards of radioactive fallout.

Fourth, some of the verification difficulties in determining compliance with a high threshold such as that allowed in the TTBT can be minimized by a treaty that bars all tests. It is more difficult to ascertain the precise yield of an underground test than it is to determine whether or not an event occurred at all. Of course, the problem remains that some of the very smallest of nuclear explosions may not be detected, as will be discussed subsequently. But the question remains whether or not tests of such low magnitude provide any important military advantages. According to Leslie Gelb, experts generally agree that cheating at very low levels of one kiloton to five kilotons would not allow the development of new strategic weapons.[43]

How valid then is the position of the Reagan administration that the 1974 and 1976 treaties and the proposed comprehensive test ban treaty are not in the national security interests of the United States? As noted earlier, the first reservation raised by the administration for not ratifying the two treaties or engaging in comprehensive test ban talks was related to the alleged nonverifiability of nuclear testing programs. However, considerable progress has been made over the years in improving detection capabilities. At present, it is difficult to find any scientists, including even those opposed to a ban on underground testing, who will not admit that, with a few seismic stations on Soviet territory, it is possible to detect any explosion above 10 kilotons. In fact, respected seismologists Lynn R. Sykes and Jack F. Evernden have asserted that with fifteen such stations, strategically placed, the only explosions "with a significant likelihood of escaping detection" would be those of less than one kiloton.[44] This assessment would apply to decoupled explosions from underground cavities as well.

A number of procedures have been developed to help distinguish earthquakes from nuclear explosions, including instruments capable of pinpointing where an event occurs and at what depth. Because of the costs and difficulties of digging deep holes to explode weapons without the other side detecting the excavation, any event deeper than fifteen kilometers is most certainly an earthquake. Also, the first waves of earthquakes and nuclear explosions, as measured by seismological equipment, are quite distinct.

Verification potential has also been improved by the October 1985 offer by India, Argentina, Greece, Mexico, Sweden, and Tanzania to monitor a comprehensive ban on underground tests with seismic devices on their own soil and to implant devices near nuclear test sites in the Soviet Union and the United States.[45]

Since the probability of detection is relatively high and since it requires several such tests to feel completely confident with a new nuclear weapon, it is unlikely that a state would want to take much of a risk of being caught. States presumably sign treaties because they perceive that doing so is in their national interest, and they do not want to give other states an excuse for withdrawing from a treaty. The gains to be derived by exploding a few, very small nuclear devices would seem to be hardly worth the risk of discovery.

Verification becomes problematic if one is attempting to establish whether or not a state is violating a high threshold such as that established by the Threshold Test Ban Treaty. Determining whether the United States or the Soviet Union has surpassed the 150-kiloton limit is difficult, particularly as these two states attempt to push the limits. As pointed out earlier, the Soviet Union has been accused of surpassing the 150-kiloton limit on more than fourteen occasions. Recent assessments made by scientists selected by the Department of Defense, however, indicate that the estimates of the magnitude of such explosions should be reduced by at least 20 percent. The primary reason for recommending such a reduction is related to the fact that the Nevada test site is more geologically active than the Soviet test sites making seismic waves emanating from the latter somewhat stronger for a given explosive magnitude. If such a reduction were made, most, if not all, of the Soviet tests could be regarded as complying with the Threshold Test Ban Treaty.[46] In April 1986 the Central Intelligence Agency decided to adjust its mathematical multiplier downward by 20 percent, but the administration was quick to argue that a number of Soviet tests would still have been in violation.[47]

That the inadequacy of verification capabilities was not really the major reservation to a comprehensive test ban on the part of the Reagan administration is suggested by the fact that little was being spent to improve seismic research and no interdepartmental review was undertaken for two years despite improvements in verification capabilities.[48] Even if a foolproof inspection system were feasible, it is unlikely that the administration would support a comprehensive test ban in view of its belief that continued testing is necessary to U.S. national security interests. As noted earlier, a number of tests are viewed as necessary for modernizing the American nuclear force. Several of the newer delivery systems, however, already have available warheads as in the case of the cruise, the MX, and the Midgetman missiles; the Trident can use existing MK 12A warheads. Although a comprehensive test ban might interfere with the development of the Trident II missile, the X-ray laser, and smaller yield warheads, each of these particular systems has been criticized because of its probable effects on the stability of the nuclear deterrent system. The Trident II has been viewed as a first strike weapon due to its hard-kill capability, and concern has been expressed about reducing the yield of nuclear weapons that will make their use more probable. Finally, many scientists have opposed the development of the X-ray laser for reasons that will be examined in chapter 7.

In the past, continued testing has been seen as necessary to improve the yield to weight ratios of nuclear warheads. According to Wolfgang Panofsky, director of the Stanford Linear Accelerator, however, the technological limits in this area have essentially been reached.[49] After all, given present efficiencies, it would not require much more than a small suitcase to transport a nuclear device with the destructive capacity of the Hiroshima bomb.

Nuclear testing has been viewed by the Reagan administration and some scientists as essential for ascertaining nuclear stockpile reliability. Nuclear weapons are fabricated from chemically active materials that deteriorate in unexpected and unpredictable ways, making periodic testing of stockpile weapons necessary. In an effort to make the case for the need for reliability testing, the Reagan administration released data in March 1986 showing that a large percentage of Polaris warheads would have failed during the 1960s because of deterioration and design problems, and similar instances were found during the 1970s with respect to Poseidon and Minuteman warheads.[50] However, it is not clear that test explosions are necessary to discover such problems as several respected scientists have argued that most such testing is done by disassembling and reassembling a warhead's parts. They note that all of the components can be tested one by one just as is done in building the weapon initially.[51]

The former director of the Los Alamos National Laboratory, Donald Kerr, has suggested, however, that the reason little proof testing has been done in the past is that stockpile and design problems are often corrected by adding an experiment to a test that is part of the continuing program. Such would be precluded in a comprehensive test ban, making direct proof tests more important, particularly since the expected lifetime of a stockpile is typically between fifteen and twenty-five years.[52]

Whether or not proof testing is necessary for assuring the reliability of stockpiled weapons largely boils down to how the weapons are designed. During Glenn Seaborg's tenure as head of the Atomic Energy

Commission (1961–71), nuclear weapons were designed on the assumption that a comprehensive test ban agreement would be negotiated. At some time after that period, design policy was changed so that more sophisticated and efficient designs were emphasized, thereby making reliability testing necessary.[53] By returning to a more simple design policy, it would be possible to remanufacture weapons that have been proof tested many years earlier.

Finally, even if a comprehensive test ban were to make the reliability of existing nuclear weapons questionable, Bruce Russett and Fred Chernoff have suggested that this might actually be a virtue rather than a liability. If both sides lost some of the certainty about whether their weapons would work "they might hesitate to launch an attack that could misfire. By this reasoning, deterrence is strengthened by any factor that contributes to a prospective attacker's lack of confidence that everything will work according to plan."[54] Such a view, however, is not universally accepted as seen by a 1986 letter from Deputy Secretary of Defense Frank J. Gaffney, Jr., to Congressman Ed Markey. According to Gaffney, the Russians would worry whether their arsenals were still in working order and might get edgier if reliability testing were disallowed.[55]

The latest rationale for continued testing was presented by George H. Miller of the Lawrence Livermore National Laboratory who argued in February 1987 that continued testing is necessary not so much to develop new weapons for the Strategic Defensive Initiative but rather to study the possible threat of the Soviet Union using X-ray lasers to defeat a space-based defense system. The purpose of continued testing, according to this view, would be to provide information critical for developing a counterdefensive system directed against the X-ray laser.[56]

Despite U.S. reservations about a separate comprehensive test ban treaty, political initiatives taken by the Soviet Union in 1985–86 have placed considerable pressure on the United States to respond more favorably to proposals for a comprehensive test ban. In August 1985 Gorbachev announced that the Soviet Union would institute a six-month unilateral ban on nuclear testing, which was subsequently extended to March 31, 1986. Gorbachev went even further on March 13, 1986, when he announced that the unilateral ban would remain in effect until the United States resumed its nuclear testing.

The United States response to the March initiative by Gorbachev was to conduct yet another underground test later that same month. But despite the U.S. resumption of underground testing, Gorbachev, on the heels of the Chernobyl nuclear disaster in May, extended the ban until August 6, the forty-first anniversary of the bombing of Hiroshima, subsequently making January 1, 1987, the date on which the Soviet Union's unilateral moratorium on testing would end. The Soviet moratorium remained in effect until the United States exploded its first underground test in February 1987, whereupon the Soviet Union, as promised, announced it was no longer bound by its nineteen-month unilateral moratorium. At the same time, the Soviets indicated they would resume the moratorium if the United States would stop its tests even though the latter had conducted twenty-six nuclear tests during the Soviet moratorium.

In late July 1986, the United States and the Soviet Union, partially in response to increasing domestic and international pressures favoring a comprehensive nuclear test ban, met for the first time on the test ban issue since President Reagan came into office. In agreeing to the meeting, Gorbachev indicated a willingness to consider President Reagan's four-year-old proposal to have specialists from both countries discuss better monitoring of underground nuclear testing. The Soviet Union also accepted the offer of the private U.S.-based Natural Resources Defense Council to set up sealed seismographic instruments at three sites in the Soviet Union and agreed in principle to a May 1986 U.S. Geological Survey proposal to establish an experimental network of up to eighteen seismic monitoring stations on Soviet territory.[57]

In view of the various Soviet concessions, it is doubtful that U.S. arguments that verification problems make it impossible to negotiate a comprehensive test ban treaty will be able to stem the growing tide of opinion favoring such a ban. Perhaps some temporizing might be done if the United States were to agree to ratify the Threshold Test Ban Treaty, which would be a positive, though limited, step. Such a move would at least meet the administration's interest in testing new devices as well as checking the reliability of existing stockpiles. At the same time, U.S. ratification would be viewed by arms-controllers as just another cosmetic move to give the illusion of progress.

CONCLUSION

A possible ban on nuclear testing has been a prominent issue on the arms control agenda since the late 1950s, particularly among those who saw it as a way to slow the spread of nuclear weapons to additional states. Primary concern was initially focused upon the possible health hazards of continued atmospheric testing, but once this problem was solved with the signing of the Limited Test Ban Treaty in 1963, which prohibited atmospheric testing, public interest in the test ban issue dissolved. But because testing underground was still allowed by the treaty, more tests were actually conducted before, rather than after, the signing of the treaty.

Efforts to negotiate a comprehensive test ban as envisioned by provisions in the LTBT have been largely unsuccessful. The 1974 Threshold Test Ban Treaty established a limit of 150 kilotons on all underground nuclear tests, but most of the tests conducted underground have been somewhat below that level since it is possible to extrapolate from smaller tests. The Peaceful Nuclear Explosions Treaty of 1976 provided procedures for exploding peaceful nuclear devices in order that such explosions would not be used as a ruse for testing. This treaty established for the first time the important precedent of on-site inspection on Soviet territory. The current lack of interest shown in peaceful nuclear explosives, however, has rendered that treaty relatively unimportant.

Neither the Threshold Test Ban Treaty nor the Peaceful Nuclear Explosions Treaty has been ratified. Upon assuming office, President Carter withdrew the two treaties from Senate consideration, hoping instead to negotiate a comprehensive test ban that would make the treaties superfluous. They remain unratified to date as the Reagan administration opposed further restrictions upon nuclear testing. Initially the reason given was that the treaties were not verifiable, but subsequently Reagan advisors have argued that nuclear testing is necessary as long as the world must rely upon nuclear deterrence for its security. The primary reason for desiring continued nuclear testing is related to a plan to produce some seventeen thousand new nuclear warheads and to keep open the option to test nuclear components to be used in the Strategic Defense Initiative. Many in the Reagan administration also believed testing to be necessary to determine the continuing reliability of existing nuclear stockpiles.

Despite the dismal prospects for a comprehensive test ban, a number of advantages might be gained if such an agreement could be negotiated. A comprehensive test ban would be popular with most other states in the world and may even be the price that will have to be paid to assure continued adherence to the Nuclear Nonproliferation Treaty. Additionally, such a ban could aid in restricting the qualitative arms race; close a critical loophole in present treaties; and reduce the difficulties of ascertaining whether a given underground explosion has surpassed some artificial threshold.

Improvements in verification procedures, Soviet acceptance of on-site inspection, the unilateral moratoriums on nuclear testing announced by the Soviet Union in 1985 and 1986, as well as congressional opinion have also exerted considerable pressure on the United States to resume negotiations on a comprehensive test ban treaty. But as long as the current administration or any subsequent one believes testing to be essential to develop new nuclear devices or to ascertain the reliability of existing ones, progress cannot be expected regardless of the advances in verification technology.

Thirty years of negotiating on the nuclear test ban issue have provided a number of lessons of relevance both to the problems of negotiating within governments and between governments. Since nuclear testing involves a highly technical area, scientists as well as the military have been able to play a particularly important role in the negotiations. It was conservative scientific opinion that was apparently critical in influencing President Eisenhower initially to oppose any test ban moratorium, and scientists at national testing laboratories were influential in leading President Carter to retract a number of concessions related to a comprehensive test ban. Promises have also had to be made to the military in both the United States and the Soviet Union to get them to acquiesce to the various treaties that have been negotiated, often allowing them to increase the amount of testing in return for their acceptance of various restraints upon the size and location of testing.

The positions taken by the United States and the Soviet Union on the issue of nuclear testing have also been affected by the pressures of other states in the international system. The nuclear testing issue has often been made the litmus test for U.S.-Soviet seriousness about arms control and disarmament. Nonaligned states pressed hard for a nuclear test ban during the negotiations that resulted in the Limited Test Ban Treaty in 1963. Britain's role as a participating mediator between the United States and the Soviet Union during these negotiations should also not be underestimated.

Public concern about the dangers of nuclear fallout provided additional pressure leading to the 1963 partial test ban. Once the danger was taken from the headlines, mass public concern about the nuclear test ban became minimal. Occasional public protests against continued underground testing have developed subsequently, but nothing to compare with the massive concern expressed during the late fifties and early sixties.

The desire to gain military advantages and to keep technological options open have also been important factors that help explain the positions taken by the United States and the Soviet Union in the test ban negotiations. A common feature of these negotiations has been the tendency of one side or the other to propose a ban on further testing following its own successful series of tests, apparently in an effort to lock in the technological advantages gained and to prevent the other side from doing the same. The desire to keep technological options open has been shown by the efforts of both sides to at least allow some testing to continue.

It is because of such technological uncertainties as well as concerns about the verifiability of a nuclear test ban that the United States and the Soviet Union have shown a tendency to engage in approach-avoidance bargaining behavior during the test ban negotiations. On at least two occasions the United States and the Soviet Union were close to agreement on a test ban treaty only to have one or the other party back off due to uncertainty about the implications of the treaty for its national security interests. Most of the provisions for a test ban treaty had been agreed to by both parties in 1960, but the Soviet Union subsequently began to make a number of retractions, culminating eventually in its decision to resume nuclear testing in September 1961. Similarly, the two had come close to agreement on a comprehensive test ban in 1978, only to find the Carter administration backing away with a number of retractions from its previous position. The pressures are such that one can expect that the issue of a comprehensive nuclear test ban will remain on the agenda, but the ambivalences about the security implications will continue to impede a total ban.

5

Nonproliferation of Nuclear Weapons

Concern has been expressed from the beginning about the dangers of the proliferation of nuclear weapons. Early predictions about when the Soviet Union would join the nuclear club were generally far off the mark. President Truman, for example, is reported to have thought that the United States would be able to retain its nuclear monopoly for ten to twenty years, but it took the USSR only four years to duplicate the American feat.[1] The United Kingdom followed suit in 1952; France, in 1960; and China, in 1964.

During the sixties, predictions about the number of states likely to become nuclear weapon states generally measured in the dozens. President Kennedy in 1963 speculated that some twenty five countries would have nuclear capability by the mid-1970s.[2] Despite such dire predictions, only India with its 1974 underground test has been added to the list of five powers known to have tested a nuclear device.

This chapter explores the reasons for the concern about the spread of nuclear weapons and includes an analysis of the efforts to control such spread. The United States and the Soviet Union, as the largest nuclear power states, have assumed prominent roles in the unending struggle to stop the spread of nuclear weapons, often pursuing nonproliferation policies in concert with each other. As a result of such cooperation, one of the most significant arms control agreements of the postwar world was opened for signature in 1968—the Nuclear Nonproliferation Treaty. The nonproliferation regime has also been strengthened over the years by agreements regulating nuclear suppliers, a more active nonproliferation role played by the International Atomic Energy Agency, and the signing of a number of bilateral and regional restrictions upon nuclear spread.

125

THE EFFECT OF NUCLEAR SPREAD ON SECURITY

It has been commonplace to argue that the spread of nuclear weapons will add to the insecurity of all nations. As spread occurs, there are more chances for accidental war or war by miscalculation, increased probabilities of irresponsible or irrational leaders obtaining control of nuclear weapons, and increased opportunities for nuclear blackmail. Yet these arguments have often fallen upon deaf ears as national leaders assess the utility of nuclear weapons in terms of prestige, a larger voice in world and alliance affairs, and the opportunities to enhance security by controlling the nuclear strike option. There is also the fear that no nuclear weapon state would risk possible annihilation to protect the non-nuclear state from nuclear blackmail or massive conventional strikes, let alone a nuclear attack.

It may well be that in some instances the prophets of doom have exaggerated the destabilizing effects of nuclear spread and that a world of five nuclear powers, two of whom have overkill capabilities, is already sufficiently terrifying and dangerous. One study, for example, argues that dissemination has already occurred and that since the distribution of nuclear power is dangerously unequal, the acquisition of nuclear weapons by additional countries might help stabilize power relationships.[3] Kenneth N. Waltz likewise minimizes the dangers of nuclear spread as he argues that such spread to American allies has complicated Soviet calculations and consequently strengthened deterrence. He argues further that small nuclear forces can have a similar deterrent effect regionally. Nuclear weapons may even dampen regional arms races, for less military capability is needed if the primary objective is merely to deter a regional adversary. All that is required is the ability to inflict unacceptable damage.[4]

To a certain degree there may be a grain of truth in such views. If nuclear deterrence is largely a matter of being able to communicate the credibility of a probable nuclear retaliation to a first strike, then having nuclear capabilities in the hands of the potential attack victim should be more credible than relying upon the nuclear force of an ally. Indeed, French President Charles DeGaulle's major concern with the United States was that the latter would not risk nuclear war in case Western Europe was struck massively with conventional force. Having a small nuclear force in the territory of the potential victim and controlled by that victim so that it need not rely entirely upon the superpower to initiate the nuclear strike is viewed as one way of making certain that nuclear weapons will be used if they are believed necessary for defense. By having this triggering potential, it is hoped that the nuclear threat will be made more credible and hence able to deter the threatened attack.

A crucial aspect in evaluating the relative dangers inherent in nuclear spread relates to whether or not such spread is limited to responsible leadership. It is perhaps erroneous to assume that small powers desiring nuclear status are the only ones that are likely to behave irresponsibly, yet there might be something to the notion that the smaller, developing state has less to lose and will therefore be less constrained in its use of nuclear weapons. Pressures of internal instability with which many of these states appear to be plagued might also tend to induce rash international behavior to redirect internal frustration. But even assuming that irresponsibility is as likely to arise in any political system, whether developed or underdeveloped, it is a statistical fact that the more national decision-making units having control over nuclear weapons, the greater are the chances that one of them might behave in an irrational and irresponsible fashion.

Even the most mature and responsible leadership, as long as it has nuclear weapon capability, is going to be tempted to use that capability if it becomes engaged in a war of attrition or possible defeat. A most humane leader can sometimes be convinced of the utility of using nuclear weapons if confronted with the dangers of certain defeat or if such an option would appear to reduce unacceptable levels of bloodshed among one's own citizens. It should be remembered that it was the United States that was the first and fortunately thus far the only state to use nuclear weapons, apparently with little concern for the moral issues involved.

As nuclear weapons spread to less wealthy nations, protection against accidental firings is likely to be deemphasized. The smaller nuclear power, having sacrificed extensively to develop a nuclear capability in the first place, simply cannot afford the luxury of multiple protection for its nuclear striking power. It will be less likely to contribute the necessary funding to develop an invulnerable retaliatory capability through the hardening of underground silos or through mobility by using train cars or naval vessels. As a result, any such striking force will be ''soft'' and hence provocative since the state with unprotected missiles can hardly afford the luxury of delayed response. Dangers of war by miscalculation and hasty reaction to nuclear accidents are increased under such circumstances.

EARLY PROPOSALS FOR PREVENTING NUCLEAR SPREAD

The effort to negotiate a nuclear nonproliferation treaty in the midsixties was by no means the first time that the issue of stopping the spread of nuclear weapons has been raised in disarmament negotiations. In a sense, the history of the negotiations since World War II has been very much motivated by the desire to prevent additional nations from obtaining nuclear weapons. Among the many proposals that have been made for slowing the spread of nuclear weapons have been those for a nuclear production ban, nuclear test bans, nontransfer agreements, nuclear free zones, plus a variety of measures to make independent nuclear capability less necessary as far as nonnuclear states are concerned.

The earliest postwar proposals sought to tackle the problem of nuclear spread by prohibiting the further production and possession of nuclear weapons by all national governments. The Baruch Plan, introduced in 1946 by the United States, would have placed nuclear weapons and technology under the control of the International Atomic Development Authority. The Gromyko Plan, presented by the Soviet Union as an alternative to the Baruch Plan, called for immediate destruction of all nuclear weapons that were then a monopoly of the United States. As a nonnuclear power, the Soviet Union felt it could not allow its security to be determined by an international control organ certain to be dominated by the West. Security could not be guaranteed until the Soviets also acquired nuclear weapons. Prior to that they could only hope that the West would not violate the agreement.

When it became clear that the Baruch Plan had little chance for success, the United States began to emphasize Atoms for Peace in 1953. These proposals would have diverted some fissionable materials to peaceful purposes, but the proposals had little relevance for nonproliferation and disarmament in general because of their limited scope. The Atoms for Peace proposals emphasized the positive aspects of nuclear energy in terms of its advantages for economic development. Both superpowers began courting developing nations with optimistic promises concerning the future of atomic energy for peaceful purposes. The current threat of nuclear proliferation is in no small measure attributable to the competition between the United States and the Soviet Union in providing nuclear reactors and information on the peaceful atom to Third World countries during the mid-1950s.[5]

Apparently in developing the Atoms for Peace program, little attention was given in the United States to the arms control implications of providing fissionable materials and nuclear technology to nonnuclear weapon states. The U.S. Atomic Energy Commission, for example, was informed of the proposal only after the fact. Soviet Foreign Minister V. M. Molotov recognized the potential dangers when he asked Secretary of State John Foster Dulles what in the world the United States had in mind in proposing to allow stockpiles of weapons grade material to spring up all over the world.[6] Despite reservations, the Soviet Union could not allow the United States to be the sole beneficiary of the good-will of developing countries, which had been sold on the economic miracles of peaceful nuclear energy.

The Atoms for Peace proposals became the basis of the International Atomic Energy Agency, which was established in 1957 to deal with peaceful nuclear activities and to serve as a clearing house for the exchange of peaceful fissionable materials and technology under international control. From the perspective of reducing the dangers of nuclear proliferation, the most important function of IAEA was its inspection obligations designed to assure fissionable materials would not be used for weapons purposes. The IAEA was somewhat slow in assuming such responsibilities in part because of the hostility toward verification demonstrated by the Soviet Union and other states. It was 1961 before the safeguards system was instituted. Even then its inspection activities were limited to smaller reactors, because agreement to include reactors with outputs above 100 megawatts-thermal was not reached until 1964. States would be subject to safeguards only if they received assistance from the IAEA or if they requested safeguards. Consequently, significant amounts of fissionable materials were not covered. As late as 1966 Sterling Cole, the first director general of the IAEA, noted that "not a single nuclear power plant capable of producing by-product weapon material has come under Agency control" except for psychological gestures or demonstration and test purposes.[7]

Other direct forerunners of the nonproliferation proposals are found in the various plans calling for "atom free zones," which were a prominent feature of the disarmament debates in the midfifties. Most such plans for denuclearization of a region have dealt primarily with central Europe, Africa, and Latin America; but proposals have also been made involving the Balkans, the Adriatic and Mediterranean areas, the Middle East, Scandinavia, and Asia and the Pacific. The Soviet Union began hinting of the possible denuclearization of central Europe as early as 1956, but the most fully developed plans were presented by the Polish foreign minister Adam Rapacki on October 2, 1957. The Rapacki Plan would have provided for a ban on the production and possession of nuclear weapons in both East and West Germany as well as in Czechoslovakia and Poland. A modification of the plan in November 1958 would have covered the reduction of conventional weapons in the area as well—a stance designed to appeal to the NATO membership, which had long been concerned about Soviet conventional superiority in Central Europe.

The official U.S. position taken on these proposals was highly negative, not only because of concern over the lack of inspection and enforcement procedures, but also because of the fear that the implementation of such proposals would force the Federal Republic of Germany out of the Western alliance system. Chancellor Konrad Adenauer of the Federal Republic was opposed to considering any such proposals and the United States deferred to him on the issue.

Although nuclear free zone proposals continued to be made, it was not until 1967 that success was obtained with the signing of the Treaty of Tlatelolco which provided for a nuclear free zone in Latin America. Some twenty-two states now embrace this agreement which prohibits both the production and transfer of nuclear weapons into the region. In July of 1964 the Organization of African Unity declared its readiness to undertake a nuclear nondissemination treaty for the continent of Africa but has yet to follow through on such a treaty. In 1986 thirteen South Pacific nations, including Australia and New Zealand, signed the South Pacific Nuclear Free Zone Treaty. The treaty participants asked the five nuclear weapons states to ratify protocols which would forbid nuclear testing in the area as well as prohibit states from using or threatening to use nuclear weapons in the region. Despite the fact that the protocols would not interfere with ongoing activities such as the passage of nuclear warships, the Reagan administration rebuffed the treaty as did France, which wanted to be able to continue testing in the area. Both China and the Soviet Union, on the other hand, agreed to sign the protocols.

Pressure for a more global nonproliferation agreement began to develop with the 1958 Irish draft U.N. resolution, which called for the creation of a committee to study the dangers of nuclear dissemination. This resolution was not brought to a vote. The Irish government was back the following year with a similar resolution, which was passed unanimously except for thirteen abstentions. Two additional resolutions sponsored by the Irish delegation were adopted in 1960 and 1961.

Despite the considerable support rallied behind the notion of nonproliferation as evidenced by the General Assembly votes, the Ten Nation Disarmament Committee and its successor in 1962, the Eighteen Nation Disarmament Committee, failed to discuss the issue for several years. Instead, general and complete disarmament (GCD) became the main topic of debate with the Soviet Union presenting such a plan in 1959 and the United States tabling its first general and complete disarmament plan during the following year. Both proposals for GCD provided for the nonproliferation of nuclear weapons during the first stage of the proposed three-stage plan.

Support favoring a nonproliferation treaty developed briefly when President John F. Kennedy asked Ambassador Averell Harriman to raise the issue of nonproliferation at the 1963 Moscow meetings in which the Limited Test Ban Treaty was negotiated. Khrushchev, however, refused to discuss the issue of China and proliferation while the United States did not want to press the issue given West German and French anxieties.[8]

In a unilateral move with some implications for the proliferation problem, President Johnson announced in April 1964 that the United States would reduce the production of U-235 (weapons-grade uranium) by 40 percent and plutonium production by 20 percent over a four-year period. Premier Khrushchev responded by announcing that the USSR would not proceed with the construction of two large nuclear reactors intended for the production of plutonium. Although such actions promised to reduce the total supply of fissionable materials, the significance of these moves as a precursor of nuclear arms reduction was minimal. The cutbacks after all were primarily a response to extensive nuclear stockpiles on both sides. Nevertheless, the initiative demonstrated the possibilities of unilateral and reciprocal constraints upon armaments.

THE NUCLEAR NONPROLIFERATION TREATY

Impetus for a broadly based nuclear nonproliferation treaty was provided by nearly unanimous resolutions passed in 1965 in both the General Assembly and the United Nations Disarmament Commission, calling for the Eighteen Nation Disarmament Committee to give priority to negotiating such a treaty. Progress was slow primarily because of differences between the United States and the Soviet Union on the issue of the Multilateral Force (MLF). In 1964 the United States had proposed the creation of MLF, which would have provided for some twenty-five surface ships loaded with nuclear weapons to be placed under NATO control. These ships would be manned by citizens of at least three NATO countries, each of which would have a veto over the use of those weapons. The Soviet Union was particularly concerned that the Federal Republic of Germany, which was to play a central role in MLF, would thus be able to get its finger on the nuclear trigger.

The Soviet Union's initial proposal for a nonproliferation treaty presented in September 1965 contained several provisions that not only would have prevented MLF but would have made allied nuclear consultation extremely difficult, if not impossible.[9] According to former U.S. Arms Control and Disarmament Agency Director William C. Foster, the Soviet plan was so broad that it would even deny consultation between

NATO allies in preparation for their defense against possible nuclear attack.[10]

Whereas the Soviet proposal sought to restrict nuclear sharing in any form, the United States attempted to legalize such a process by arguing its legitimacy on the basis of individual or collective self-defense. In a draft treaty tabled at the Eighteen Nation Disarmament Conference on August 17, 1965,[11] the United States proposed restricting only the number of decision makers having control over the use of nuclear weapons. Since, under the multilateral force proposals being debated at the time, the United States would retain a veto over the use of nuclear weapons, it was argued that there would be no increase in the number of decision-making units with control over the use of nuclear weapons.

After the United States decided in the fall of 1966 not to press the issue of a multilateral force, some progress in the arms talks was achieved. The United States and the Soviet Union began to cooperate in their search for solutions to prevent the spread of nuclear weapons. Their cooperation on the issue was such that the nonnuclear weapon states began to accuse them of forming a condominium against those states not having nuclear weapons.

In August 1967 the United States and the Soviet Union, as cochairpersons of the Eighteen Nation Disarmament Committee, tabled identical texts of a draft Nonproliferation Treaty. These drafts were essentially complete except for provisions related to verification, which were added in January 1968. Although other states were able to discuss the draft treaties presented by the two superpowers, it was clear that such states could do little to change the basic content. Despite the many reservations expressed by nonnuclear weapon states in ENDC meetings and subsequently in General Assembly discussions on the proposed treaty, the final document essentially followed the draft outlines provided in 1967 by the superpowers.

Perhaps the most fundamental change between the jointly sponsored 1967 Draft Treaty and the Final Treaty was the insertion of article VI, which obligated the nuclear weapon states to pursue negotiations for nuclear arms reductions. The nonnuclear weapon states were particularly disturbed that the NPT did nothing to restrain what they referred to as vertical disarmament on the part of the nuclear weapon states while restricting horizontal nuclear proliferation among states. If nonnuclear weapon states were to forego the nuclear option, they wanted the existing nuclear powers to at least begin to reduce their nuclear arsenals. Further differences had to do with changing the duration of the treaty, which would be limited to twenty-five years rather than unlimited as previously proposed. Review conferences would be held every five years, allowing the nonnuclear states to monitor whether the superpowers were living up to their obligation to do something about existing nuclear weapons.

The heart of the Nuclear Nonproliferation Treaty, which was opened for signature on July 1, 1968, is found in its first two articles. The first article provides that each nuclear weapon state not transfer nuclear explosives or otherwise assist a nonnuclear weapon state in developing such weapons. Article II places obligations on the nonnuclear weapon state not to receive or manufacture nuclear explosive devices. The third article, dealing with verification, requires that states party to the treaty individually or collectively negotiate safeguards agreements with the IAEA. Articles IV and V were designed to reassure nonnuclear weapon states that they would be able to enjoy the peaceful uses of nuclear energy and nuclear explosions without discrimination. Nuclear weapon states are obligated under these articles to provide not only technological assistance but also material assistance to nonnuclear weapon states.

Having successfully negotiated the Nonproliferation Treaty, the United States and the Soviet Union were confronted with a number of problems in helping to assure a viable nonproliferation regime. The fact that so many states continued to have serious reservations about the treaty, as shown by the debates as well as the reservations that many states attached after signing the treaty, did not augur well for the goal of preventing the spread of nuclear weapons. A content analysis of the 1968 General Assembly debate on the NPT revealed that 62 percent of the eighty-seven speakers raised questions about the security implications of the treaty. Another 44 percent thought the measure should be linked to broader disarmament while 41 percent expressed concern about how the treaty might affect the peaceful uses of energy.[12]

Many speakers expressed concern that the treaty would not obtain universal support, for a number of states made it clear that they had no intention of ratifying the NPT. Among these were the nuclear weapon states, China and France, although the latter announced that it would behave as if it were a member. More significantly, a number of so-called nuclear threshold states with the technological and economic capability of eventually producing nuclear weapons held out on ratification. In fact, as late as January 1987, almost two decades after the treaty was opened for signature, states like India, Pakistan, Brazil, Argentina, South Africa, and Israel were still refusing to ratify the NPT. Even among the nuclear threshold states that have ratified the treaty, a number of reservations are attached to their signatures. This is particularly disquieting since the requirements for withdrawing from the treaty are so undemanding. All that is required is three months advance notice by the state desiring to relinquish its obligations. The long list of reservations makes it questionable whether the treaty will be renewed when it expires in 1995.

THE SAFEGUARDS SYSTEM

The implementation of the Nonproliferation Treaty required that safeguards agreements be negotiated with the International Atomic Energy Agency, which was to serve as the primary organization verifying compliance with the treaty. Considerable delay occurred in completing these safeguards agreements as the majority of states involved failed to meet the required eighteen-month to two-year deadline. Such delays in applying safeguards raised questions about the possibility that fissionable materials might have been stockpiled during the five years and possibly longer between the time that the NPT was opened for signature and the time in which most safeguards were put into operation.

Even with the IAEA safeguards system in place a number of reservations have been raised about its efficacy in guaranteeing that fissionable materials will not be diverted to weapons purposes. Among the complaints leveled against safeguard procedures are the lack of real-time monitoring of plant operations; the refusal of certain states to accept inspectors of particular nationalities; the lack of money for an expansion of the numbers of inspectors; and the need for an increase in remote monitoring equipment commensurate with expanded global numbers of plants and throughput of materials.[13] In testimony before the Senate Foreign Relations Committee in 1981 a former inspector argued that IAEA inspectors have limited or no access to certain kinds of materials; are occasionally denied access to areas they are required to inspect; are rarely able to make "surprise" visits; and are overwhelmed by reporting or analysis backlogs.[14] The IAEA admitted that same year that it was unable to carry out full safeguards functions in Pakistan and India.[15] It was the fear of just such safeguards deficiencies that led Israel to attack the Iraqi Osirak research reactor in 1981, despite the fact that the facility was under IAEA inspection.

In attempting to evaluate the effectiveness of the IAEA safeguards system, it should be remembered that even national and corporate control systems do not have a perfect record in accounting for fissionable materials used in nuclear facilities. A Department of Energy audit for an eight-month period in 1980–81 revealed that 55.6 pounds of plutonium could not be accounted for—enough material for a half dozen bombs. In 1977 another federal study found that a cumulative total of more than 8,000 pounds of highly enriched uranium and plutonium had disappeared since the beginning of the nuclear era.[16]

With the development of the fast breeder reactor, the dangers of illegal diversion are likely to be compounded because of the capability of these reactors to produce more fissionable materials than they consume. It is anticipated that a breeder reactor will be able to produce two plutonium-239 nuclei for every one that is burned, which means that the reactor will be able to double its plutonium stock over the period of a decade. Unless effective controls can be established forcing the return of this excess plutonium to the control agency, substantial numbers of bombs could be produced by states that are not yet members of the nuclear club. The difficulty of safeguarding global plutonium supplies, which had more than doubled during the period 1975–80, has been underscored by Victor Gilensky, a member of the Nuclear Regulatory Commission. In a speech at MIT, Gilensky concluded that "separated plutonium is not safeguardable by any means now available to us—we cannot count on warning in time to head off an illicit weapons effort."[17]

The question naturally arises as to how much potential diversion can be allowed with states still feeling secure. Since existing nuclear weapon stockpiles have grown to such proportions and threaten to grow substantially more, it would seem that any evasion of the IAEA system would not be as destabilizing on a global basis as it might have been in an earlier day. Proliferation within a particular conflict region might be quite another matter. At any rate, support or nonsupport of the NPT revolves around the problem of balancing risks. Reservations concerning the effectiveness of any inspection system need to be balanced against the perceived dangers inherent in the failure to put a disarmament measure into operation. Support for an effective inspection and control system also needs to be balanced against the fears that the inspection system will be too onerous in terms of both costs and threats to sovereignty.

Considerable controversy has raged over the question of where to apply IAEA controls. The treaty was viewed as creating a considerable imbalance of obligations as far as the nuclear and nonnuclear states were concerned. Inspection was to be applied only to current nonnuclear states, but the United States and the United Kingdom agreed in December 1967 to have similar controls placed upon all of their peaceful nuclear activities. In February 1983 the Soviet Union announced that it would place some of its peaceful nuclear power plants under IAEA safeguards, and China unexpectedly followed suit in September 1985. Since

France earlier had indicated that it would allow similar inspections of its plants and would act as if it were a member of the treaty, all five nuclear weapon states now accept safeguards applied to some of their peaceful nuclear facilities. Although such actions helped to redress some of the imbalance, the nuclear weapon states are still free to designate which plants are to be considered peaceful ones and which ones are outside the control system.

The Indian representative in viewing the efforts to control peaceful nuclear activities while disregarding warlike nuclear activities suggested that it was "like an attempt to maintain law and order in a society by placing all its law abiding citizens in custody while leaving its law-breaking elements free to roam the streets."[18] Arguments raised against gun control laws in the United States have been strikingly similar.

In addition to the controversy over whether or not to exempt the nuclear weapon states from the inspection system, debates arose over the issue of which nuclear activities should be inspected in order to guarantee that the nonnuclear state was complying with the treaty. Some states preferred that controls be established only at crucial points in the nuclear fuel cycle and that even these controls should be as automated as possible. Other states believed that controls should be applied to the entire fuel cycle including uranium enrichment plants, reactors, fabrication plants, and reprocessing plants.[19]

SECURITY ASSURANCES

In an effort to generate support for the Nonproliferation Treaty, the Soviet Union and the United States sought to reassure those states that were hesitant to support the treaty that their security interests would be taken into account. The treaty itself did little to satisfy the security concerns of the nonnuclear weapon states as the United States and others believed that security guarantees should be negotiated separately from the treaty. A major reason for this strategy was the recognition that it would take considerable time to negotiate such an agreement. No blank article was left as was the case with article III concerning safeguards in the 1967 United States and Russian NPT proposals, presumably because of the contention that the United Nations provided a basic formula for peace and security or at least as much of an obligation as the United States and the Soviet Union were willing to accept.

The preferred security guarantee sought by the nonnuclear states was a negative one in which the nuclear weapon states would agree not to use nuclear weapons against nonnuclear weapon states. More than half of those states showing concern about the security issue suggested a nuclear-use ban as a desirable option. Whereas the United States has been skeptical of such guarantees because of the lack of enforcement procedures, the Soviet Union has frequently favored use bans throughout the history of the postwar disarmament negotiations. In 1966 the Soviet Union expressed its support for such a guarantee within the framework of a treaty to halt nuclear spread but subsequently supported the U.S. position of deferring the issue.

During the debates on the treaty, the United Arab Republic proposed an amendment incorporating the Soviet proposal that nuclear weapon states would not undertake to ''use or threaten to use nuclear weapons against any non-nuclear weapon state party to this Treaty which has no nuclear weapons on its territory.'' This would have meant that a state like the Federal Republic of Germany, albeit a nonnuclear weapon power, would not be protected by the security guarantees since United States nuclear warheads are stationed on its soil.

The debates on the security guarantees indicated a number of serious reservations concerning the use of the United Nations as the protector of security interests. Although the UN resolution providing such guarantees was passed by a vote of 10 to 0, the five states that abstained (Algeria, Brazil, India, France, and Pakistan) made it clear that they were most disillusioned with the resolution. Nations both within the Security Council and outside of it viewed the resolution as inadequate because of the veto and the fact that not all of the permanent members of the Council were expected to sign the treaty. India was also critical of the fact that the resolution and the individual guarantees offered by the United States, the United Kingdom, and the Soviet Union were contingent upon a state's signing the NPT. This the Indians regarded as actually against the spirit of the UN Charter, which was designed to apply to all members and even to nonmembers if there is a threat to world peace.

Several states would have preferred that Security Council guarantees be written directly into the treaty. Perhaps part of the motivation for keeping the treaty and the guarantees separate was related to the desire to get agreement on the NPT first. It would then be possible to resolve the issue of security guarantees—an issue that was recognized from the beginning as a sensitive one that might preclude any chance of agreements. Reservations were also raised concerning the meaning of the word *aggression* as used in the UN resolution. Would the guarantee apply to the threat of aggression or to protection from conventional attack? Furthermore, if assistance were required, it was not at all clear how much and what kind would be provided.

Should the Security Council fail to act on behalf of the victim of aggression as has often been the case as a result of the use of the veto, both the Security Council resolution and the guarantees of the three nuclear weapon states provide the right of individual and collective self-defense in accordance with article 51 of the United Nations Charter. This article, however, fails to protect a state against nuclear blackmail since an attack need actually have occurred. A state must also be a part of an alliance system before it can feel reasonably confident that article 51 of the UN Charter will be activated on its behalf. Yet even members of alliance systems might have some concern for their security in view of the flagrant violation of Czech sovereignty by the Soviet Union in August 1968. The Czechoslovakian crisis raised questions in the minds of many of the representatives of the nonnuclear states regarding the extent to which nuclear weapon states could be trusted either in terms of desisting from attack or defending the victim in the event of armed aggressioin. As a result, the crisis was used by a number of states to justify their procrastination in signing and ratifying the treaty.

Because of the continuing pressure from nonnuclear weapon states, the United States, the United Kingdon, and the Soviet Union added additional guarantees during the UN Special Session on Disarmament in 1978 when they agreed not to use nuclear weapons against any state that had renounced the acquisition of such weapons. The Soviet Union excepted any state that had nuclear weapons on its soil, and the United States indicated that the nonnuclear weapon state must not be engaged in an armed attack or be allied with a nuclear weapon state. The Russian formula was directed against states like the Federal Republic of Germany while the U.S. position made it clear that the West might use nuclear weapons against a Warsaw Pact state if an attack came from the East. In 1982 Brezhnev went a step further in the Second UN Special Session on Disarmament when he announced that the USSR "assumes an obligation not to be the first to use nuclear weapons." He added that "in the formulation of its policy, the Soviet Union will naturally take into account how the other nuclear Powers act. . . ."[20]

With respect to positive guarantees, representatives from the United Kingdom and Canada argued during the NPT debates that stronger security assurances could not be given except under military alliance with nuclear powers. The general reluctance in the United States to provide even limited security guarantees beyond current alliance commitments to nonnuclear states was demonstrated most vividly by the fact that almost a third of the United States Senate voted for the Ervin amendment, which would have made Senate approval contingent upon the understanding that no commitments to defend smaller nations from nuclear aggression be undertaken.[21] Even though the proposed amendment was defeated, such moves were hardly likely to inspire confidence in what were already regarded as totally inadequate security guarantees by many nonnuclear states.

The Nixon Doctrine, which stressed that Asian states must take greater responsibility for their own defense and cannot expect the United States to intervene on a massive scale on their behalf, reduced confidence in alliances with the United States. Japan and Australia were particularly concerned about the seeming withdrawal of the United States from Asia and were shocked by the failure of their ally even to consult them concerning changing U.S.-Chinese relations. Additional questions about the reliability of the United States as an ally arose with the collapse of South Vietnam in 1975 and the fall of the Shah of Iran in 1979. President Reagan raised similar sensitivities among West European allies when he claimed that it would be possible to keep a nuclear war on the European continent limited to a tactical exchange.[22]

Despite uncertainties about alliances, it might still be assumed that states belonging to formal alliances would be less likely to be concerned about receiving security guarantees or some other form of assurance than those that do not have such protection. Since presumably allies of nuclear powers are more apt to enjoy the protection of the nuclear umbrella, one would expect that they would be less concerned about giving up the nuclear option and less insistent about obtaining formal guarantees from the nuclear powers. Thus it was possible for the Australian delegate to suggest calmly that "if States become parties to the treaty and if they are subsequently threatened, their recourse would be to seek support by a larger Power or combination of Powers."[23] On the other hand, the nonaligned state cannot be as certain of such support, hence the very real concern about security guarantees. The content analysis of the final General Assembly debate noted above found that 90 percent of the thirty nonaligned states participating in the debates expressed reservations about security guarantees, whereas only 51 percent of the fifty-seven nominally aligned states raised the question of security. A chi-square test indicated this relationship to be significant at the .001 level. Similar support suggesting that nonaligned states were more likely to be concerned about the treaty than aligned states was found as 78 percent of the nonaligned states ($N = 40$) indicated general dissatisfaction with the treaty either verbally or by voting against it or abstaining during the Assembly debates as constrasted to only 30 percent of the nominally aligned ($N = 61; p < .001$).[24]

THE PEACEFUL ATOM

Since nuclear energy can be used for both weapons or peaceful purposes, a number of states raised questions about how the Nuclear Nonproliferation Treaty might affect the use of the peaceful atom. Several states were particularly interested in the possible negative effect of the treaty upon the competitive position of nuclear energy as a fuel source. Among questions posed were the following: Will international safeguards make such fuels noncompetitive? Will adequate fissionable supplies be guaranteed at a reasonable price? Will the nuclear powers share nuclear technology or would they assume an exploitive monopolistic position? These questions seemed to take on even greater urgency with the 1973 OPEC oil embargo and the subsequent spiralling of oil prices.

Attitudes about the competitive position of nuclear energy have fluctuated over the years with considerable optimism being shown during the midfifties as a result of the publicity surrounding the Atoms for Peace program. There followed a period of considerable pessimism as the nuclear weapon states were slow to convert their nuclear stocks to peaceful purposes, and experts were beginning to conclude that nuclear power was not competitive with other energy sources. Studies presented at the Third and Fourth International Conferences on the Peaceful Uses of Atomic Energy in 1964 were somewhat more optimistic since it was discovered that fissionable materials had a longer life than expected.[25] New technologies such as breeder reactors and the development of the less expensive centrifuge process for enriching uranium added to the optimism. The sharply increasing prices of oil during the seventies meant that nuclear energy might become more competitive.

Counterbalanced against these optimistic assessments were increasing reservations about the environmental hazards of nuclear energy, which reached a peak with the Three Mile Island nuclear accident in 1979. The Soviet nuclear reactor accident at Chernobyl in 1986 served only to heighten anxiety about the peaceful uses of nuclear energy. At the same time, increasing construction costs and long delays in building nuclear reactors further contributed to the pessimism. The hopeful assessments about nuclear energy suffered an additional blow when the United States, during the Carter administration, decided not to proceed with the Clinch River breeder reactor while attempting to discourage other states from developing similar facilities on the grounds that such reactors would contribute to the proliferation problem. Breeder technology had seemed so promising because it would produce more plutonium than it would consume. Although this would contribute to enlarging the fuel supply and providing less expensive nuclear energy, it would also increase the danger of plutonium being diverted to weapons purposes.

The effect of the treaty on the use of nuclear explosions for large earth-moving projects was also cited as an issue of concern by more than a quarter of the participants during the 1968 General Assembly debates on the Nonproliferation Treaty. The language of the treaty is most restrictive on this issue because of the fact that it is impossible to distinguish a peaceful nuclear explosion from a nuclear weapon explosion as discussed in the previous chapter. The superpowers sought to retain control over the technology of peaceful explosions while guaranteeing that they would share that technology with nonnuclear weapon states under international supervision. Accordingly, article V of the NPT requires that the potential benefits from any peaceful applications of nuclear explosives be made available under international control and at the lowest possible cost to nonnuclear weapon states that are party to the treaty.

As indicated in the previous chapter, assessments of the potential of peaceful nuclear explosions have fluctuated over the years. In the late 1950s the Soviet Union wanted to prohibit all nuclear explosions, peaceful or otherwise, whereas the United States had an active peaceful explosions research program underway with its Plowshare program. U.S. interest in peaceful nuclear explosions began to decline in the midsixties, so much so that by 1978 the Plowshare program had disappeared entirely from the federal budget.[26]

While U.S. interest was declining, the Soviet leadership began to show greater optimism about the potential of nuclear explosions for large earth-moving projects. During the Peaceful Nuclear Explosions Treaty negotiations in the midseventies, the Soviets asserted that they would like to conduct peaceful explosions as high as 400 kilotons in clusters up to 3 megatons. At the top of the Soviet list was a project that would divert the waters of at least one northbound river into the southbound Volga.[27]

Despite these fluctuations in optimism about the peaceful uses of nuclear energy, many states still believe in its potential and, as a result, continue to oppose any aspect of the NPT which they fear will interfere with the peaceful atom. The treaty has not yet provided the signatories with the anticipated advantages of the peaceful atom, and, according to one assessment, "non-parties could be argued to have had the bulk of the help offered in this area."[28] The preference shown to nonsignatories has occurred largely as a result of the desire on the part of the nuclear weapon states to appease those states that are viewed as the most likely proliferators. Such a policy, however, is likely to erode existing support for the treaty.

In addition to attempting to reassure nonnuclear weapon states about economic and security concerns, both the United States and the Soviet Union have from time to time exerted direct pressure upon various states in an effort to reduce the danger of proliferation. Such pressure was used against Euratom in 1967 as the U.S. Atomic Energy Commission indicated that restrictions would be placed on the American export of fissionable materials if Euratom did not comply with the IAEA regarding reexport.[29] Veiled threats were also made to India in President Johnson's Food for Peace message to Congress delivered on February 2, 1967, wherein the president suggested that those states that spend vitally needed resources on "unnecessary military equipment" can no longer take food supplies for granted.[30] However, India refused to sign the treaty. The reported demand made by a former U.S. assistant secretary of defense that Israel sign the NPT in return for the shipment of Phantom jets was likewise unsuccessful.[31]

Pressure of this sort decreased considerably, for the Nixon administration assumed a much more ambivalent posture on the question of nuclear spread, leading the Japanese to question whether the United States cared any longer about limiting the number of nuclear powers.[32] This seeming lack of concern about the proliferation problem was perhaps partially related to a preoccupation with other issues such as Vietnam as well as the desire not to antagonize U.S. allies. At any rate, the failure of the Nixon administration to press the nonproliferation issue partially explains why it took almost two years before the Nuclear Nonproliferation Treaty came into effect with the required forty ratifications in addition to those of the United States, the Soviet Union, and the United Kingdom.

It took the Indian underground nuclear explosion in 1974 to force the Nixon administration to realize that it should be more sensitive about the dangers of nuclear proliferation. It was at that time that the U.S. Atomic Energy Commission, in an effort to reduce weapons-grade fissionable materials, announced that it would accept no new contracts for the enrichment of natural uranium. Anxiety about the further spread of fissionable materials to other regions led the United States in 1974 to invite the Soviet Union, Britian, West Germany, France, Japan, and Canada to discuss the prospects of creating a Nuclear Supplier Group that would regulate the shipment of fissionable materials. In 1978 the Supplier Group, which had increased in size to some fifteen states, agreed upon guidelines that required that certain nuclear technology, equipment, and material could be transferred only if the recipient nation agreed to apply IAEA safeguards to the item supplied and would use such materials only for peaceful purposes.

Fear of nuclear proliferation was intensified in 1975 when France and the Federal Republic of Germany decided to sell important components of the nuclear fuel cycle to several threshold states that had refused to ratify the Nuclear Nonproliferation Treaty. Germany agreed to provide Brazil with enrichment services and facilities while France planned to supply Pakistan and South Korea with plutonium reprocessing plants capable of producing weapons grade materials. Under pressure from the United States, France decided in 1978 not to provide the components needed to complete the plutonium reprocessing plant it was helping Pakistan build.[33] Similar pressures against West Germany by the Carter administration may help explain the German announcement in June 1977 that it was establishing a formal ban on any future export of nuclear reprocessing technology.[34] Germany, however, did not renounce its nuclear arrangement with Brazil, and Pakistan, having lost the assistance of France, decided to construct a uranium enrichment plant of its own by relying upon overseas purchases of parts and technology from commercial suppliers. Direct pressures upon the threshold states themselves, enabled the United States to persuade South Korea and Taiwan not to proceed with their respective plans for constructing reprocessing plants.

While the Soviets had a more cavalier attitude about the dangers of proliferation during the early postwar years than did the United States, the Soviets soon changed their position. As early as 1960 ''the Soviet Union pressed for the strictest possible safeguards on nuclear exports, while the U.S. government favored looser controls.''[35] It was also at the insistence of the Soviet Union that strict safeguards were applied to the nuclear programs of the East European satellites. The IAEA safeguards system for East Germany, for example, has been regarded as a model safeguards agreement. By 1967 the Soviet Union was endorsing IAEA inspection for all nonnuclear weapon states.[36]

The Soviet Union has generally sought to influence the proliferation policies of other states by utilizing less publicized techniques as it did in pressuring India to accede to safeguards in exchange for heavy water supplies.[37] Similarly, the Soviets delayed nuclear plant construction in Cuba until an IAEA safeguard agreement was negotiated in 1980.[38] In 1977 the Soviet Union alerted the United States to the fact that South Africa was preparing a nuclear test site. After confirming the information, the United States successfully pressed South Africa to desist from its nuclear plans.[39]

The Soviet Union held a long series of ad hoc negotiations with the United States on the subject of nuclear proliferation beginning in 1977. These talks were resumed in December 1982 with the Reagan administration. Although the START and INF talks fell victim to the U.S. deployment of intermediate-range nuclear forces in Europe the following year, talks on nonproliferation continued to be held.

THE NONPROLIFERATION POLICIES
OF CARTER AND REAGAN

In evaluating possible approaches to controlling the proliferation of nuclear weapons, the contrasting approaches of the Carter and Reagan administrations are instructive. For the Carter administration the problem of proliferation was essentially a technical one in which an effort was made to establish international control over the entire nuclear fuel supply. The Reagan administration, on the other hand, saw the problem as a political one in which the effort should be one of guaranteeing a nuclear fuel supply in order to discourage nonnuclear weapon states from developing their own fuel cycles that would not be under U.S. or international control.

The Carter administration, unlike its predecessor, supported congressional efforts to pass the Nuclear Nonproliferation Act (NNPA) in 1978. Going beyond previous U.S. policy, the NNPA mandates that two years after passage any recipient of U.S. nuclear exports has to apply comprehensive safeguards to the entire fuel cycle whether or not that state is a member of the Nuclear Nonproliferation Treaty. This required that existing bilateral supply agreements be renegotiated, placing considerable strain on U.S. relations with various states that were disturbed by the breaking of contractual relationships.

If all supplier states had followed the United States lead, the danger of proliferation could have been reduced. But, with the exception of Canada, few states established such requirements. This worked to the benefit of other nuclear suppliers as recipients preferred the less onerous safeguard requirements. France, for example, replaced the United States as a supplier of fissionable materials to India since the latter was unwilling to accept the new American safeguard demands. Although the Reagan administration opposed certain aspects of the Nuclear Nonproliferation Act, it has chosen not to amend the act for fear that the debate over the issue would further reduce confidence in the constancy of the United States as a supplier nation.[40]

The Carter administration believed in treating all nonnuclear weapon states alike as far as nuclear controls were concerned, whereas the Reagan administration proposed making distinctions that would give preferential treatment to the advanced industrial states and those states that were not regarded as likely proliferators. Since plutonium production was seen as a major problem with respect to the dangers of nuclear proliferation, Carter proposed denying plutonium reprocessing plants to both domestic and international commercial interests. The Carter decisions to cancel the breeder reactor and to close the Barnwell reprocessing plant were reflective of the administration's desire to create a nuclear technology less dependent upon plutonium as the fuel source. The Reagan policy was based on a willingness to provide reprocessed plutonium, but not the reprocessing facilities, to nonnuclear weapon states. Reliance on this approach would help ensure that production facilities would remain under U.S. control. It was felt that a restrictive policy would only force nonnuclear weapon states to build their own reprocessing facilities.

The Carter administration attempted to educate other states about the dangers of a plutonium-based fuel cycle as it pressed for a 1978 conference referred to as the International Fuel Cycle Evaluation (INFCE). It was hoped that a general dialogue involving some 66 supplier and consumer states would aid in developing a consensus in support of an effective nonproliferation regime—an objective that the United States, given its declining influence, could not achieve alone. After three years of discussion, most states remained unpersuaded on the issue of the dangers of plutonium reprocessing and showed more concern about the problems and uncertainties of supply than about proliferation dangers. The environmental hazards of plutonium storage and the proliferation potential of enriched uranium, which is used in some reactors, were viewed by the INFCE as more serious problems.[41] The Reagan administration remained unconvinced about the dangers of plutonium as it reactivated the Clinch River breeder reactor, recommissioned the Barnwell reprocessing plant, and substantially increased the production of plutonium.

It was the policy of the Carter administration to exert strong pressure upon other states in order to discourage them from exporting sensitive nuclear technology and material to nonnuclear weapon states. As a result, the administration assumed an active role in pressing the Suppliers Group to adopt a trigger list of items that would be subject to international control. The Reagan administration was more concerned about the possible negative reactions of allies and others who would be disturbed by such restrictions. Accordingly, it sought to modify the trigger list through bilateral negotiation. Reagan was also interested in minimizing certain restrictions in order to aid the U.S. nuclear industry, which was suffering a severe economic decline in view of numerous slowdowns and cutbacks of nuclear reactor orders throughout the world, and particularly within the United States itself. Billions of dollars in potential nuclear exports were at stake, which would only go to foreign competitors if restrictions were not removed. In support of more relaxed controls, the Reagan administration argued that with the increased mastery of nuclear technology throughout the world, the ability of any one country to control proliferation had diminished considerably.[42]

As part of its strong nonproliferation policy, the Carter administration complied with the requirements of the Glenn-Symington amendment to the 1961 Foreign Assistance Act when in early 1979 it cut off all aid to Pakistan. According to this amendment, both economic and military aid are to be denied any country that delivers or receives enriched or reprocessing technology without full safeguards. It had become obvious by that time that Pakistan was intent upon developing the bomb as it continued to reject verification over critical nuclear facilities and materials. In contrast, the Reagan administration in 1981, as part of its effort to bolster security in the Persian Gulf, asked for a waiver of the amendment and subsequently instituted a five-year program of economic and military aid to Pakistan.[43] Four years later, President Reagan sought a similar exception to the Glenn-Symington amendment with regard to nuclear exports to Argentina, but the House Committee on Foreign Affairs rejected the request.[44]

There is evidence that President Reagan may have become somewhat more sensitive to the dangers of proliferation. For example, the president warned Pakistan in a letter dated September 12, 1985, that Pakistan risked losing American military assistance if it continued its nuclear weapons development program.[45] However, this did not stop the president from asserting in November 1986 that Pakistan "does not possess a nuclear explosive device"—a proclamation that was necessary in order to continue the $600 million economic and military assistance program to Pakistan. This assertion was made despite a Defense Intelligence Agency report that Pakistan detonated a high explosive device in September as part of its continuing efforts to build an implosion-type nuclear weapon.[46]

Denial of military assistance to a country may have a negative impact upon the goal of discouraging nuclear proliferation in view of what has been called the "dove's dilemma." It is argued that providing a state with the military assistance that the state deems essential for its national security will actually have the effect of making the state less likely to seek the nuclear option. This was the rationale used by the Reagan administration in providing conventional arms aid to Pakistan. To the extent that such conventional armaments are used only for deterrence and defense, such use can also be seen as contributing to peace and security in the region. But conventional arms aid can also lead to regional arms races as experience with arms aid to South Asia has demonstrated over the years.

Despite its strong stance against nuclear proliferation and a 298 to 98 House vote disapproving the action, the Carter administration persisted in a 1980 plan to send nuclear fuel shipments to India. In undermining its own anti-proliferation policy, the administration showed that it was more concerned about the threat of the Soviet Union to South Asia, following the 1979 Afghanistan invasion, than it was about the dangers of proliferation.

Both economic and security interests led the Reagan administration to negotiate a thirty-year nuclear assistance pact with the People's Republic of China, which was signed by the president during his trip to China in April 1984. Objections were raised to this pact by virtue of the cavalier attitude assumed by China about the proliferation problem. Prior to the 1980s China even hinted that further spread of nuclear weapons would be useful in undermining imperialism. The danger of Chinese re-exports of nuclear technology and fuels to other potential proliferators concerned many experts, particularly since reports suggested that China had provided inadequately safeguarded nuclear assistance, to such potential proliferators as Pakistan, Iran, Brazil, South Africa, and Argentina.

The Reagan administration delayed submitting the U.S.-China nuclear assistance pact to Congress as required by law. More than a year was spent trying to obtain greater security assurances from China, assurances it was reluctant to provide. Since China decided to join the IAEA and to accept agency safeguards over its nuclear export program, some, but not all, congressional opposition was overcome. Despite lobbying by influential senators on both the right and the left, Congress was unable to muster the necessary votes to defeat the agreement, and it automatically went into effect in January 1986. The potential $25 billion return for the U.S. nuclear industry was apparently too much of an incentive to ignore.

CONCLUSION

The experience of the United States and the Soviet Union in negotiating nuclear nonproliferation has shown that even when the two superpowers agree on an arms control issue, they are not always able to obtain the support of other states. Part of the problem in generating a consensus on nonproliferation policy is related to the fact that states of different sizes and technologies have varying economic, political, and security interests. All cannot agree that proliferation to additional states, particularly to themselves, is destabilizing. Furthermore, to the extent that atomic energy promises economic benefits, many states are unwilling to accept a nonproliferation regime that might interfere with the peaceful atom.

The United States and the Soviet Union were ultimately successful in negotiating the Nuclear Nonproliferation Treaty in 1968 that, even though it now has more adherents than any other arms control agreement, may not remain viable in the long run in light of the many reservations appended by the signatories as well as the refusal of several nuclear threshold states to join. Criticism of the treaty has been extensive at the three review conferences held thus far, and the viability of the treaty beyond its expiration date of 1995 must remain in doubt.

Subsequent efforts have been made by both the United States and the Soviet Union to strengthen the nonproliferation regime, including the exertion of pressure upon states to ratify the NPT, the development, in concert with other members of the Nuclear Supplier Group, of a trigger list of nuclear materials and technology requiring safeguards, and efforts to strengthen the International Atomic Energy Agency, which applies safeguards for the NPT.

Of the postwar governments, the Carter administration adopted the most stringent nonproliferation policy. Believing that plutonium presented the greatest danger to proliferation, the administration sought to reduce global dependence upon such fuel. Among its actions were efforts to encourage the development of nuclear reactors that would not require plutonium, efforts to restrict the reprocessing of spent fuel rods, and an attempt to stop the development of breeder reactors that have the capability of producing more plutonium than they consume. The Reagan administration reversed these policies and went a step further with its decision to distinguish in its nuclear supply effort those states it believed to be likely proliferators from those which were not so regarded. The Carter policy had been one of applying similar restrictions to both.

The debate on how best to achieve the objective of a nonproliferation regime continues. Some see the solution as one of restricting nuclear technology and materials whereas others favor allowing states to develop their own nuclear facilities but under international safeguards. By refusing as a supplier to cooperate, the danger is that a nonnuclear state may choose to use both legal and illegal means to develop its own nuclear capability for which there would then be no control. Furthermore, the new nuclear state may exacerbate the proliferation problem by becoming nuclear suppliers themselves.

Though answers are by no means easy, the problem is such that even during periods in which arms talks on other issues have been disrupted and relations seriously strained between the United States and the Soviet Union, the two superpowers have continued their periodic meetings to deal with the issue of proliferation. Such cooperation has not been without its costs as other states accuse the superpowers of exploiting the atom not only for military purposes but also for economic gains.

Perhaps the clearest lesson to be learned from the many debates on the subject of nuclear proliferation is that the positions that states take on issues that have decided military, political, and economic implications will be dictated by what they perceive to be their national interests. Unlike so many other areas of arms control, this is an area where the objectives of the United States and the Soviet Union coincide, often in opposition to the interests of the nonnuclear weapons states. As long as this identity of interests between the United States and USSR is recognized, progress can be made in controlling the spread of nuclear weapons, but when one or the other or both seek to exploit the situation for temporary economic or political gain, the results can be disastrous as when both states during the 1950s sought to gain the favor of the developing world by exaggerated claims about the potential of peaceful nuclear energy.

Domestically, the nuclear power industry has taken an avid interest in the proliferation issue. Possible international restraints on nuclear energy facilities tend to be resisted by the nuclear industry as do constraints on the export of nuclear technology, fuel, and components. At stake are billions of dollars in sales and construction contracts. Whereas the American public appears much less concerned about the proliferation problem than they do about nuclear testing in the atmosphere, their elected representatives in recent years have been quite active on the issue. In 1978 Congress passed the Nuclear Nonproliferation Act, which sought ever greater restrictions on nuclear sharing with nonnuclear weapon states. Congress has also fought with various U.S. presidents in an effort to restrain activities that threatened the nonproliferation regime, opposing President Carter on the shipment of nuclear fuels to India in 1980 and President Reagan in his attempts to build a breeder reactor and to place greater reliance upon plutonium production.

The political advantage of generating goodwill by providing nuclear assistance to other countries versus the security concerns of the military and intelligence agencies over such acts has often pitted foreign offices against the military and other security agencies. For the most part the Soviet Union has been more resistant to nuclear sharing than the United States, but this may be partially due to the primacy that the Soviet military enjoys in the arms control area.

The Strategic Arms Limitation Talks

Although the atomic explosions at Hiroshima and Nagasaki in 1945 were generally welcomed in the allied countries as a way of saving lives and ending the war, it was soon clear that these weapons could also threaten the future of the world. Many experts on the subject were aware that the secrets of the bomb would not remain a monopoly of the United States for long and that efforts to control these highly destructive strategic weapons should begin as soon as possible.

PRE-SALT NEGOTIATIONS

When the United Nations Atomic Energy Commission began its deliberations on June 14, 1946, the United States tabled its first strategic arms control plan in the postwar period—the so-called Baruch Plan named after the head of the U.S. delegation Bernard Baruch. The plan provided for complete control of atomic weapons development from the mining of fissionable materials to the production of the completed weapon itself. The plan remained the cornerstone of United States strategic disarmament policy until the fall of 1955, when a reservation was placed upon all past U.S. disarmament proposals.

It has been suggested that the Baruch Plan was a generous offer to the Soviet Union since the United States, as the only nuclear weapons state at the time, was demonstrating a willingness to turn over all nuclear weapons and their development to an international control organization. The proposal for a variety of reasons was not seen by the Soviet Union to be within its national security interest. First, acceptance of the plan would foreclose the possibility of the Soviet Union's ever developing its own nuclear capability, while, at the same time, forcing it to accept the fact that the United States had unlocked the secret to the atomic bomb

151

and could just as easily withdraw the nuclear facilities from international control. Second, since the control organ would be subject to the supervision and direction of the United Nations, the Soviets would be placed in the position of a permanent minority on all decisions related to the operation of the control organ. At the time, the Soviets could count on only about five votes in the United Nations General Assembly in contrast to about forty-five for the United States. Soviet interest would not be protected by the right of veto—a procedure that was explicitly eliminated under the Baruch proposals. Third, the nuclear facilities themselves would be located geographically at positions closer to the territory of the United States and its allies than to the Soviet Union, making it easier for the former state to commandeer those facilities should the United States perceive such action to be within its national interest.[1]

These factors, combined with a distrust of the United States dating back to U.S. efforts to reverse the outcome of the Bolshevik revolution as well as American hostility toward communist ideology, led the Soviet Union to counter with a simplistic proposal of its own that called for the abolition of all nuclear weapons within a period of three months. The plan, named after the Soviet representative Andrei Gromyko, failed to include provisions for verification and enforcement, providing only that the parties to the convention would, within six months, pass legislation requiring severe penalties for violations.

Given the extreme positions taken by the two protagonists, it was inevitable that little progress would be made on the issue of nuclear disarmament. The Soviet Union, for the reasons noted, was hardly in a serious negotiating mood prior to exploding its own nuclear device in August 1949, several years earlier than many U.S. nuclear experts predicted. With the entry of the Soviet Union into the nuclear club, another issue came to complicate the search for nuclear disarmament—concern about the past Soviet nuclear production. By the early fifties, American scientists and politicans were beginning to ask how one would be able to determine the number of nuclear weapons in Soviet stockpiles. Concealing such weapons would be a relatively simple matter, according to most scientists. Robert J. Oppenheimer, the father of the atomic bomb, had asserted, for example, that the only way that one could verify whether or not a nuclear bomb was hidden in a wooden box would be to use a screwdriver.[2] To locate any nuclear weapons that the Soviet Union would choose to hide was a virtual impossibility, particularly since the Soviets refused to allow on-site inspection. After August 1953 the threat of past nuclear production took on a more ominous tone as the Soviet Union exploded its first hydrogen bomb only nine months after the United States entered the thermonuclear age.

Since the problem of past nuclear production was such a serious one in the minds of American decision makers, the United States nuclear policy in 1953 began to emphasize "Atoms for Peace." As outlined in a speech to the United Nations on December 8, 1953, President Eisenhower proposed a program to develop the peaceful use of atomic energy. The plan called for joint contributions of fissionable materials from both American and Soviet stockpiles to an International Atomic Energy Agency. The plan, however, was not a disarmament program, for the amounts to be diverted were expected to be small. In some respects the emphasis upon the peaceful atom served only to exacerbate the spread of nuclear weapons as pointed out in the preceding chapter. At the same time, these proposals provided the basis of the International Atomic Energy Agency, potentially the most important agency for guaranteeing the peaceful use of atomic energy as far as nonnuclear weapon states are concerned.

The diversion from nuclear disarmament policy reflected the growing disenchantment of United States decision makers with the Baruch Plan. Although the plan remained American policy until 1955, statements were increasingly being made to the effect that the United States would continue to support the plan only until a better one could be devised.

Due to the growing disenchantment of the United States with its own nuclear disarmament proposals, the Soviet Union in late 1954 and particularly in its May 1955 proposals accepted a number of suggestions being made by the West with respect to the control of both conventional and nuclear weapons. These included acceptance of the notion of dealing with the control and reduction of weapons in stages, the elimination of the requirement of a use ban as a precondition for nuclear disarmament, and the creation of ground inspection control posts. On September 19, 1955, the Soviet Union went so far as to agree that it would consider aerial inspection in the final stage of the disarmament scheme. But the concession came too late, for the United States had only a few days earlier placed a reservation upon its own disarmament proposals, including the Baruch Plan.

Just as the growth of technology led to a severalfold increase in the destructiveness of nuclear weapons within the span of a few years, the technological revolution also affected the means of delivering those weapons. Bombers were developed that had intercontinental range, but perhaps even more critical from the strategic standpoint was the development of missiles.

Although Hitler had used V-2 rockets against Britain in World War II, the development of long-range missiles was fairly slow in coming. There was the recognition prior to the development of the hydrogen bomb that long-range missiles would be unable to carry the heavy payload of nuclear weapons. After all, the bomb dropped on Nagasaki, quite appropriately dubbed the "fat man," weighed some ten thousand pounds and measured sixty inches in diameter yet yielded only fourteen kilotons of destructive power.[3] Subsequent refinements have meant that similar amounts of destructive power can be packed into an attaché case. Nor did the United States anticipate the Soviet Union's rush to develop intercontinental missiles capable of carrying nuclear warheads. In October 1948 the Joint Chiefs of Staff estimated that it would be 1977 before the Soviet Union would have such a capability.[4] As it happened, the Soviet Union was able to launch its first intercontinental ballistic missile (ICBM) two decades earlier than the time predicted. That the Soviet Union was able to catch the United States by surprise was related to the fact that the Soviets started their program in 1946 and continued it to completion, whereas the United States did not initiate a serious and persistent program until 1954.[5]

While rockets and missiles were still under development, there were few references in formal U.S. and Soviet disarmament statements and proposals to controlling these weapons. In one of the few early comments regarding the issue, the Soviet delegate on June 8, 1954, informed the Disarmament Subcommittee meeting in London that rocket weapons should not be forgotten; President Eisenhower in a letter to Soviet Prime Minister Bulganin dated August 4, 1956, noted that he favored "elimination of the growing threat of nuclear weapons and new means of delivery."[6] Although the Soviet Union, prior to the launching of Sputnik, indicated a willingness to regulate missiles and rockets, its stance became tougher in 1958 as it sought to extract an agreement to liquidate foreign military bases and to prohibit nuclear weapons as the price for even discussing limits on missiles and space vehicles.[7] The United States, which was behind in the missile race at the time, proposed after Sputnik to place limits upon the production, but not the testing, of missiles in an effort to forestall all-out Soviet deployment of such weapons. The Soviet Union was particularly critical of these proposals since they dealt only with the control of ICBMs not other means of delivery such as intermediate-range ballistic missiles (IRBMs) and bombers in which the United States had the advantage given its overseas bases and substantial number of bombers.

Rather than deal with the basic problem of the production and possession of nuclear missiles, attention in 1958 was directed toward the issue of banning nuclear weapons from outer space. The Soviet Union again sought to link such a ban with its concern to abolish all foreign bases but was unsuccessful in this effort.[8] The linkage was later dropped, leading to the successful negotiation of the Outer Space Treaty which was opened for signature in 1967.

Reflective of the general retreat from nuclear disarmament in United States arms control policy was the increased concern expressed about the dangers of surprise attack, particularly on the part of United States negotiators. Sophisticated delivery systems served only to enhance such a danger. Although the United States was successful in getting the Soviet Union and its allies to the bargaining table to discuss the issue in November 1958, the resulting Surprise Attack Conference was a complete disaster. The two sides failed to communicate in these debates as the West spoke largely in favor of inspection and control procedures to reduce the dangers of surprise attack, whereas the Soviet Union and its allies argued that the only way to reduce such dangers would be through nuclear disarmament.

The effort to negotiate seriously about the control of strategic weapons suffered its greatest setback in the fall of 1959 when the Soviet Union introduced its first plan for general and complete disarmament (GCD).[9] Designed as it was to abolish all conventional and nuclear weapons in the short period of four years, the presentation of the plan could hardly be regarded as any more than a propaganda ploy on the part of the Soviet Union. Assertions that states could retain those weapons necessary to their internal security and the liberalizing of the four-year deadline hardly made these proposals any more palatable or realistic. Nevertheless, in order not to lose the propaganda battle, the United States was forced to respond in kind as it, along with its allies, introduced its first general and complete disarmament proposal in March 1960. Unlike the Soviet plan, no explicit deadlines for reducing weapons to a level consistent with internal security were included. The Western plan called for a number of actions to be taken as rapidly as possible such as the prohibition of weapons of mass destruction in space, international observance of missile launchings, and cessation of the production of fissionable materials for weapons purposes. Reduction of existing weapons was simply cited as an ultimate goal, and a number of joint U.S.-Soviet studies were proposed for seeking to obtain such an objective.

When the Kennedy administration came into power in 1961, more serious attention was given to the issue of arms control and disarmament. The Arms Control and Disarmament Agency was created, greatly expanding the number of government personnel working on these issues. New initiatives were undertaken with respect to efforts to control strategic weapons. Most significant of these was the McCloy-Zorin talks, which produced an agreed statement of principles dated September 20, 1961.[10] The statement reaffirmed the commitment of the two sides to general and complete disarmament; but, as desired by the United States, the required reductions would be completed in stages. Sufficient verification that all requirements of a given stage had been met would have to be assured before progressing to the next phase of reductions.

Modifications continued to be made in the GCD proposals by both sides over the next three years. In April 1962 the United States matched the specificity of Soviet proposals for GCD by presenting a treaty outline that called for the completion of general and complete disarmament in three stages over a period of nine years. For its part, the Soviet Union began to hint of greater flexibility in its proposed four-year schedule for GCD.

That the Soviet Union was using its GCD proposals for propaganda purposes and perhaps to split the Western alliance system is evidenced by its September 1962 proposals. These would place a ban on the production and possession of missiles in the first stage rather than delaying complete abolition to the third stage as provided in the initial Soviet plan for general and complete disarmament. In so doing, the Soviets were complying with the preference of France to give the highest priority to controlling missile development and production. The reversal in staging may also have been related to changing Soviet perceptions of the military balance. When presenting its first GCD proposal, the Soviet Union thought itself to be ahead in the missile race and wanted to retain that advantage as long as possible by delaying the abolition of nuclear missiles to the last stage. By 1962, it was clear that the United States was in the superior position, making the abolition of missiles in the first stage a highly desirable option from the Soviet perspective.

A slight concession was made to the U.S. position in September 1963 when the Soviet Union conceded that a "nuclear umbrella" for the two superpowers could remain into the third stage of general and complete disarmament. But the proposed umbrella would consist only of ICBMs, not SLBMs in which the United States had a considerable qualitative and quantitative advantage.

Although the last formal proposals for general and complete disarmament were made in 1964, references to the goal have continued to be made from time to time during the disarmament negotiations. Whenever the negotiations have taken a more serious tone, they have tended to focus upon partial measures of disarmament such as a nuclear test ban or nuclear nonproliferation.

The control of strategic weapons also was introduced as one of several options of partial arms control measures. In January 1964, for example, the United States proposed a verified freeze on the character and numbers of strategic nuclear offensive and defensive vehicles. The proposal was quickly rejected by the Soviets not only because of the verification provisions but also because of the fact that the Soviet Union was far behind the United States in terms of both the quantity and quality of missiles. The Soviet leaders responded to this gap by sending missiles to Cuba in the fall of 1962 in a desperate effort to obtain short-term security.

In January 1964 the United States presented yet another one-sided proposal when it suggested scrappping medium-range bombers. The plan would have removed some 80 percent or more of the total Soviet air fleet capable of delivering nuclear weapons, but it would merely have phased out the B-47—a bomber that the United States was planning to replace with the B-52.

It was also in January that the United States proposed halting the production of fissionable materials, taking advantage of the fact that its nuclear stockpile was substantially larger than that of the Soviet Union. Three months later these proposals were made more concrete when President Johnson unilaterally announced that the United States would close one separation plant and reduce the production of fissionable materials. The move led to private negotiations between the United States, the Soviet Union, and the United Kingdom during which unilateral pledges were made to reduce the production of fissionable materials. In these pledges the United States agreed to cut its production of U-235 by 40 percent over a period of four years and plutonium production by 20 percent. The Soviet Union promised similar substantial reductions and agreed not to proceed with the construction of two large atomic reactors which had been planned.

Subsequent unilateral reductions of delivery vehicles by the United States seem not to have had the same results in terms of stemming Soviet delivery capabilities. On April 26, 1965, Adlai Stevenson announced to the United Nations that by mid-1966 the United States would have inactivated or destroyed more than 2000 B-47s, it would have reduced the number of B-52s, and it would forego the construction of some Minutemen missiles that had been planned.[11] A month later Secretary of Defense Robert McNamara indicated that at least half of the existing B-52s would be phased out by 1970.[12] Former American arms negotiator

William C. Foster expressed concern over the failure of such announcements to be linked with demands that the Soviet Union make similar reductions.[13]

Concern about controlling strategic weapons was considerably heightened by the progress being made on the anti-ballistic missile (ABM). Although the United States had begun ABM development with its Nike-Zeus system in the mid-1950s, the Soviet Union surpassed the United States in the early 1960s, first with the installation of the Tallinn system around the Estonian capital and then with the Galosh system encircling Moscow. As early as 1963 Soviet leaders were boasting about having solved the missile defense problem. Such bravado was particularly disconcerting for, if true, an effective Soviet ABM system could neutralize the United States nuclear deterrent.

Instead of responding to Soviet ABM developments in kind, Secretary of Defense Robert McNamara chose to emphasize a buildup in offensive capability. Of greatest significance was the decision to proceed with the development of the multiple independently targeted reentry vehicle (MIRV). It was reasoned at the time that an accelerated competition for anti-ballistic missiles would be particularly destabilizing since such competition would increase the incentives for the state falling behind to initiate a preemptive nuclear strike before an effective ABM system could be put into place by the other state. What is critical is not whether such a system could be built but rather whether one or both parties felt that it could be built.

In December 1966 the United States responded to the ABM threat by calling for U.S.-Soviet talks limited to the question of defensive missile systems. As might be expected, the Soviet Union responded in January 1967 by insisting that the proposed talks also include offensive weapons rather than be limited to the ABM, in which it felt superior.

Positions on ABM controls gradually changed, for by late 1967 most United States intelligence analysts agreed that the Tallinn system had no ABM capability and could not be easily upgraded.[14] The Soviets themselves became less enthusiastic about the Galosh system, and they decided in the same year, largely because of the system's relatively poor performance, to curtail by one-third the originally planned 96 ABM missile system around Moscow.[15]

Pressures began to mount in the United States to develop an ABM system to replace the then defunct Nike-Zeus system. Acquiescing to these pressures for fear of the electoral consequences, Secretary of Defense McNamara announced the creation of the Sentinel ABM system on September 18, 1967. In his announcement McNamara took special pains to reassure the Soviet Union that the system was not meant to be one capable of defending against a massive nuclear missile strike. Instead, it would be designed to defend only against a limited strike involving either the accidental firing of a few missiles or a launch from China or some other country lacking sophisticated nuclear missile delivery systems.

The sensitivity of the Soviet Union to United States ABM developments is further illustrated by the June 27, 1968, announcement made by Andrei Gromyko that the Soviet Union was ready to begin negotiations on strategic arms limitations. It was not entirely by coincidence that this statement was made three days after the United States Senate defeated an amendment that would have denied funds for the deployment of the Sentinel ABM system.

President Johnson, vilified for his role in Vietnam and concerned about his image in history, was particularly interested in holding talks on strategic arms limitation at the highest level before retiring from the presidency in January 1969. As a result, a summit meeting to discuss these issues was scheduled for September 30, 1968. Soon after an agreement to hold the summit talks was reached, the entire effort fell victim to the Soviet invasion of Czechoslovakia on August 21, and the SALT effort was delayed until the arrival of the Nixon administration.

THE STRATEGIC ARMS TALKS

It was not until November 17, 1969, that the Strategic Arms Limitation Talks got underway in Helsinki, Finland. The delay of several months was due to the desire of a new administration to have sufficient time to develop its disarmament policy—a process that requires intensive discussion and debate within the government as well as between allies. In addition, President Nixon believed that the Soviet Union was more interested in the SALT talks than the United States. This impression was conveyed by Foreign Minister Gromyko who, on the very day of the inauguration, invited the Nixon administration to hold such talks as soon as possible. Given such perceptions, the new administration was determined that the Soviets would pay a price, and that price was the controversial linkage policy that demanded that settlement on a wide variety of political disputes such as Vietnam and the Middle East would have to be reached first. Unfortunately, the willingness of the Soviet Union to make such trade-offs was found not be great, for some elements in the Soviet Union appeared to be interested in the talks only as a way of dividing the West. Ultimately, the United States was forced to drop its linkage requirements and to negotiate limitations on arms on their own merits.

Ten years and hundreds of meetings were spent negotiating strategic arms control during the SALT period. Although the results have not been overly impressive, several agreements related to the control of nuclear weapons were reached. These included two SALT agreements signed by Richard Nixon and Leonid Brezhnev in May 1972. The first involved a five-year interim offensive arms agreement that froze United States and Soviet ICBM and SLBM levels as of July 1972. The second and more significant was an Anti-Ballistic Missile Treaty that limited each side to two ABM sites, one around its capital and the other to protect one ICBM missile site. A year later this agreement was modified so that each side would be allowed to retain only one site located either around its capital or at a missile site. The United States subsequently chose to place its ABM site situated in North Dakota into mothballs, and the Soviet Union has not extended its Galosh ABM system around Moscow to the levels allowed in the revised agreement. The SALT process also produced agreement in 1971 on measures to reduce the danger of accidental nuclear war as well as an agreement on improvements in the hot line between Moscow and Washington, making use of the latest satellite technology. In 1973 the two states also signed an agreement on procedures for preventing nuclear war. The SALT process culminated in 1979 with the signing of the SALT II Treaty, which called for some reduction in nuclear delivery systems, but this treaty was never ratified, having been withdrawn from Senate consideration by President Jimmy Carter following the Soviet incursion into Afghanistan in December 1979.

Defensive Weapons Control

In any arms control negotiation one of the most complex issues is that of which weapons should be covered. Such was certainly true of the strategic arms talk. Of particular concern in the early phases of the SALT negotiations was the issue of offensive vs. defensive weapons. The linkage between the two is a very real one affecting the stability of the nuclear deterrent itself. Failure to control the development of the antiballistic missile system, for example, might stimulate an offensive missile race in the effort to assure each state of its ability to penetrate the defenses of the other. The threat of the adversary's producing an effective ABM system became the main rationale for developing the MIRV system. By releasing independently targeted missiles a short time before hitting their target, the MIRV would make it far more difficult for any ABM system to intercept incoming missiles. Not only would there be the danger of an offensive arms race, involving both MIRVed and unMIRVed weapons systems, there could be the costly threat of a defensive arms race as well.

Traditionally, the Soviet Union has been more defense-minded than the United States, spending a ratio of about 3 to 1 for defense compared to 1 to 1 for the United States.[16] Such an approach is to be expected for a state that has suffered numerous military invasions in the past, culminating in the loss of some 20 million lives during World War II. The United States, on the other hand, has never been subject to such an invasion. Despite preoccupation with defense, the Soviet Union became concerned about the ABM developments of the United States and the possible neutralization of its own offensive capability. Gradually the Soviet Union began to revise its position, which held that the ABM was an instrument of peace since its purpose was defensive, not offensive. By the time the SALT talks had begun, control of the ABM had become a Soviet priority.

It was not until the second round of SALT I, which began in Vienna in March 1970, that the United States presented its first ABM proposals. It offered the Soviet Union the option of either zero ABMs or one site to protect the national command authorities (NCA) in Moscow and Washington. In making this proposal, the United States was hopeful of inducing the Soviet Union to accept various alternative offensive arms limits that were made at the same time. Not only did the alternative ABM proposals fail to provide a sufficient incentive for the Soviet Union to agree to offensive weapons control, but the Soviet Union also selected the least desirable ABM option, from the American perspective, when it quickly accepted the national command authorities proposal over the zero option. Whereas NCA would have satisfied U.S. Defense Department interests in continuing research and development efforts on the ABM, it was soon recognized that it would be difficult politically for Congress and the administration to build an ABM site limited to Washington. Such might be perceived in the American hinterland as a selfish effort on the part of the politicians to save their own skins while caring little about the rest of the country. As a result, the United States began to back away from its own proposals by asking for an imbalance in ABM sites favoring itself. Kissinger sought to deflect the embarrassment of the United States' rejecting its own proposals after they had been accepted by the Soviet Union by joking that the Soviets had simply chosen the wrong option and would have to choose again. Subsequently, the

United States retreated from the zero option when it proposed in March 1971 that the United States be given four ABM sites around various missile fields while allowing the Soviet Union to retain only its Galosh system around Moscow. Later, the United States proposed a 3 to 1 then a 2 to 1 ratio favoring itself before agreeing in March 1972 to two ABM sites each. The last proposal, however, was made conditional upon Soviet acceptance of limits on submarine-launched ballistic missiles. Although the Soviet Union agreed to an SLBM freeze in April, it refused to accept U.S. proposals for a special clause in the ABM Treaty that would allow withdrawal if a more complete offensive weapons limitation agreement was not reached within five years.[17] Ultimately, the United States had to be content with a unilateral threat of withdrawal if progress was not made on strategic arms limitations. The ABM Treaty in article XI required only that active negotiations be continued on the subject.

The final treaty signed between Nixon and Brezhnev on May 26, 1972, met the Soviet objective of equality and more importantly, from the Soviet perspective, it required that one site must be around the capital; both could not be used to protect missiles as the United States preferred. Although research and development on the ABM could continue under the treaty, each party agreed not to develop, test, or deploy ABM systems or components that were sea-based, space-based, or mobile land-based. The ABM Treaty also prohibited MIRVed and rapid reload ABM capabilities and, according to Agreed Statement D appended to the treaty, future exotic ABM systems were to be subject to discussion and possible amendment.

Offensive Weapons Control

Soviet views on the control of offensive weapons fluctuated considerably during the SALT negotiations. They had rejected out of hand American proposals made in the mid-sixties for a nuclear weapons freeze since a freeze at that time would have placed them in a position of permanent inferiority. As the seventies approached, the strategic weapons gap was beginning to close. Whereas its growing offensive nuclear weapons capabilities encouraged the Soviet Union to think more seriously about strategic arms control and particularly about the possibilities of a freeze, the fact that the United States was not adding to its ICBM stockpiles after reaching the number of 1054 such vehicles in 1967 meant that the U.S. had limited leverage in inducing the Soviet Union to accept an offensive weapons agreement. The United States hoped that Soviet interest in an ABM agreement would be a sufficient inducement for the

Soviet Union to accept an offensive weapons agreement; and, as a result, the United States throughout SALT I rejected the Soviet preference for an ABM Treaty only.

Despite the stabilization of U.S. missile numbers, the offensive arms race continued. The United States conducted its first MIRV tests in August 1968. Since MIRV was the only ongoing American offensive missile system in the early days of SALT, it would have been necessary to place that system on the negotiating table if any progress toward arms control was to be achieved. The United States was reluctant to do so; and when it finally introduced the possibility of MIRV controls, President Nixon insisted that any agreement on the issue must include on-site inspection—a requirement that would guarantee that the proposal would be rejected. Also, the Soviets were not interested in pressing the MIRV issue since it was not until 1973 that they tested their first MIRV vehicles, some five years after the United States. Soviet reticence to deal with this issue is reminiscent of their abrupt rejection of the Baruch Plan at a time in which they did not have the atomic bomb.

Forward-Based Systems

Controversy also revolved around the issue of what constitutes a strategic weapon. The United States regards its triad of weapons—the ICBM, SLBM, and long-range bombers—as strategic weapons. Shorter-range missiles and bombers stationed overseas are not considered part of the strategic capability of the United States even though many such weapons are capable of delivering nuclear warheads to Soviet territory. While the nuclear forces of the United Kingdom and France, which are not inconsiderable, were viewed by the Soviets as a strategic threat to their territory, such weapons have not been calculated as part of the U.S.-Soviet strategic balance. The Soviets, throughout SALT raised the issue of these forward-based systems, demanding their abolition or some compensation in terms of being allowed additional strategic weapons.

Proposals to ban forward-based systems go back to Soviet suggestions for banning all foreign bases. Since the Soviets had few such bases and, until Cuba, none in close proximity to U.S. territory, the United States had little incentive for accepting such proposals. As the range of delivery systems increased with the development of the ICBM, foreign bases became less important to American defense, leading the United States by the mid-sixties to remove its intermediate-range missiles (Thor and Jupiter) from Western European territory. Nevertheless, in an effort to show support for Europe, thousands of U.S. nuclear warheads remain in Europe, some of which could be used on strategic missions.

The United States persisted in its efforts to keep forward-based systems out of the SALT talks. The Soviets were just as insistent that they be included. Occasionally, the latter would hint at compromise on the issue if there was adequate compensation. In August 1970, for example, the Soviet Union proposed that it be allowed higher ceilings of ICBMs and SLBMs than the United States. By the following May, the Soviets had tacitly dropped the FBS issue when they agreed to support an interim offensive missile freeze plus an ABM Treaty. At the same time, they issued a warning against possible increases in British and French nuclear forces. In a unilateral statement made at the signing of the Interim Offensive Arms Agreement in May 1972, the Soviets indicated that if the United States, the United Kingdom, and France collectively exceeded the freeze levels on submarines and SLBMs, the Soviet Union would increase its own numerical limits.

During the SALT II talks the Soviet Union in July 1973 requested additional missile launchers to compensate not only for FBS but also for the Chinese nuclear threat, which the Soviets perceived to be primarily directed toward them. Two months later they were asking for the withdrawal of all nuclear forces from abroad. This demand would have affected thousands of nuclear warheads for the United States while having little or no effect upon the Soviet capabilities. In February 1974 the Soviet Union hinted that it might drop its insistence on counting FBS when and if all other issues are resolved. At the November 1974 Vladivostok meetings, during which agreement was reached on equal aggregates of 2,400 strategic delivery systems, the Soviet Union officially dropped its insistence upon including FBS in the strategic calculation. Less than two months later it was again asking some compensation for FBS. Although no action was taken on FBS in the SALT II Treaty, the United States and the Soviet Union signed a joint statement of principles that would allow either party in subsequent negotiations to raise any issue related to the further limitation of strategic arms. For the Soviet Union this meant forward-based sytems.

The Issue of Equivalence

A second major factor complicating negotiations on the control of strategic weapons has been that of determining the equivalence of weapons systems. The offensive force structures of the two sides are substantially different, influenced as they are by differing geopolitical requirements and disparities in weapons technology. Since the force structures of the two sides are highly asymmetrical, it is virtually impossible to obtain agreement upon comparable reductions in a given weapons system. For example, the Soviet Union has 70 percent of its strategic capability in the form of land-based ICBMs compared to 30 percent for the United States. Efforts to establish numerically comparable levels of missiles are impossible to achieve in a given category. The solution in SALT I was simply to freeze missile launchers at 1972 levels, giving the United States a total of 1,710 strategic missiles compared to the Soviet's 2,350.

The United States could justify its acceptance of lower levels of missiles by virtue of the fact that its ICBMs and SLBMs were more accurate. Under the 1972 Interim Agreement, the United States would be able to MIRV each missile, effectively increasing the number of strategically deliverable nuclear warheads severalfold. Soviet ability to catch up was limited, because it had not even tested the MIRV when the Interim Agreement was signed in 1972 while the United States had begun MIRV deployment two years earlier. Although the Soviet Union would eventually be able to emulate the United States as it has done on every other weapons system, the five-year period for the Interim Agreement was viewed as sufficient time for negotiating a follow-on comprehensive offensive weapons agreement to deal with the inequalities. Other factors such as the superior number of American long-range bombers, the existence of British and French nuclear capabilities, and U.S. forward-based systems meant that the imbalanced missile freeze was not necessarily to the disadvantage of the United States. In addition, the United States had not planned to add to its number of missiles during the five-year period anyway. Nevertheless, the Interim Agreement, limited as it was to strategic missiles, gave the appearance of providing the Soviet Union a strategic advantage over the United States. This alleged inequality led Senator Henry Jackson in the fall of 1972 to press through an amendment that required that any future agreements on strategic arms must be based upon equivalence. Asserting such a principle is far simpler than determining at what level of arms such equivalence is achieved.

During SALT II the formula developed for providing the appearance of equivalence was based on the notion of equal aggregates. Under this scheme a state could retain, within a range, its own preferred mix of ICBMs, SLBMs, and long-range bombers, each of which would count as one unit. At the Vladivostok summit meeting between Brezhnev and Ford in 1974, an overall aggregate of 2,400 vehicles was accepted by both parties. Ultimately this was to be reduced in the 1979 SALT II

Treaty to 2,250 each. SALT II also provided a sublimit of 1,200 MIRVed missile launchers of which 820 could be ICBMs. In addition, 120 heavy bombers could be loaded with air-launched cruise missiles, providing a total of 1,320 multi-warhead delivery vehicles.

While the concept of equal aggregates was an ingenious solution for dealing with diverse weapons systems, determining equivalence remains difficult at best. The meaningfulness of equal numbers is affected by the probable survivability of the various systems. In this regard, the United States has the advantage with its greater emphasis upon SLBMs rather than the more vulnerable land-based ICBMs. Its superior bomber force is also less vulnerable than the ICBM, which constitutes the bulk of Soviet strategic forces, since some bombers can be kept in the air all the time or can be in the air within minutes in case of a real or imagined attack.

Comparing relative numbers of SLBMs also may not provide an accurate assessment of relative strength, for the United States is able to have far more submarines on active duty at any one time. Because of the lack of overseas bases, it has been estimated that customarily the Soviet Union has only 11 percent of its SLBMs at sea in contrast to 50 percent for the United States.[18]

Other complications in ascertaining strategic equivalence relate to the performance capabilities of the weapons themselves. The Soviet Union has alway emphasized missiles capable of carrying heavier payloads. On the other hand, Soviet missiles have generally been less accurate and their nuclear warheads less compact than those of the United States. With the greater payload capability, the Soviet Union with its SS-18 is able to deliver nuclear warheads up to 25 megatons in size compared to about 5 megatons for the United States' largest missile. There was even some concern that the SS-18 might be able to carry as many as 30 MIRVed warheads, each with almost as much explosive power as the warheads placed on the U.S. Minuteman III, which has been fitted with only three MIRVs. The end result is a huge imbalance in missile throw-weight capability between the United States and the Soviet Union. One estimate provided by the Congressional Research Service in 1982 placed U.S. ICBM throw-weight at 2,220,330 pounds compared to 9,954,100 pounds for the Soviet Union.[19]

Despite the imbalance in nuclear missile throw-weight, the United States has had the advantage in terms of numbers of warheads. When the SALT II Treaty was signed in 1979 the United States had an estimated 9,200 strategic nuclear warheads compared to 5,000 for the Soviet Union.[20] This advantage was due not only to rapid progress in U.S.

MIRVing activities but also to the higher payload capability of bombers that constitute a substantially higher proportion of the U.S. nuclear deterrent system.

The air-launched cruise missile (ALCM) limits in the SALT II Treaty would also seem to provide advantages to the United States, whose technology in this area is superior to that of the Soviet Union. Whereas the SALT II Treaty limited MIRVing to fourteen warheads on SLBMs and ten on ICBMs, the treaty allows an average of twenty-eight cruise missiles on each bomber. Although the United States agreed to place no more than twenty cruise missiles on each B-52, which was designed to carry the cruise missile initially, similar limits will not apply to deployments of cruise missiles on other heavy bombers as long as the average limit of twenty-eight is not exceeded. SALT II left open the option of sea- and ground-launched cruise missiles, at least after the initial three-year term of the protocol, which would have expired December 31, 1981, had the treaty been ratified.

As one grapples with the issue of equivalence, the question arises as to whether or not it makes much difference what the precise numbers are given the huge nuclear weapons arsenals available to each side. Since both sides have overkill capabilities does it make any difference whether one has the capability of killing everyone once or dozens of times? The fact of the matter is that only about two hundred sites in the Soviet Union are useful targets for nuclear weapons. A single Trident submarine carries enough nuclear warheads to destroy virtually all of those targets. This is not to say that some redundancy in weapons systems is not desirable, nor does it mean that there are no psychological or political advantages to having superior numbers of weapons, particularly as related to less sophisticated publics and political leaders. But in an age of overwhelming overkill one has to question any drive toward nuclear superiority, as did Henry A. Kissinger on July 3, 1974, when he asked rhetorically: '' . . . what in the name of God is strategic superiority? What is the significance of it politically, militarily, operationally at these levels of numbers? What do you do with it?''[21]

Qualitative vs. Quantitative Limits

Perhaps the most important restraint that could be placed upon strategic weapons is that of limiting qualitative developments. Yet placing restrictions upon technological development is difficult not only because of the problems involved in verifying research and development but also because once a given weapons system is identifiable to outside observers, too many vested interests have come into existence, making a change in course difficult. There is also the concern of any state to be on the cutting edge of technology combined with a general unwillingness to accept technological constraints, particularly out of fear that the other side will not live up to similar obligations. Nevertheless, if qualitative controls are to be effective, they almost of necessity must be in place before a weapons system is fully tested.

No state is likely to produce or to rely upon weapons that have not been adequately tested. According to former Secretary of Defense Harold Brown, the number of tests required before a weapon can be considered reliable ranges between twenty and thirty.[22] Restrictions upon testing can therefore provide one of the best means for impeding technological development. Unfortunately, the point in which a test ban might have slowed strategic weapons development significantly has long passed as more and more sophisticated strategic weapons have entered the arsenals of the superpowers. The missile age might have been forestalled had restrictions been placed upon missile testing during the 1950s. The MIRV might have been stopped had the United States and the Soviet Union agreed to forego MIRV testing during the late sixties and early seventies. A number of experts were urging that the United States postpone its MIRV tests to determine whether a ban on such testing might be negotiable, but the Nixon administration chose to push ahead with the testing and production of the MIRV as a bargaining chip. The vulnerability that the United States feels at present with respect to the survivability of its ICBMs is related in no small measure to the fact that testing has been allowed to continue to the point that the Soviet Union now has ICBMs capable of hitting within a few hundred feet of target.

Despite the difficulties involved, there was some effort during the SALT negotiations to place qualitative constraints upon the development of weapons systems. The Interim Offensive Arms Agreement attempted to place certain limitations upon the modernization of ICBMs by disallowing "significantly increased" silo measurements. An agreed interpretation at the time placed these limits at 10–15 percent, limits believed to provide an adequate restraint upon substantial increases in missile size. With such restrictions on silo size, the U.S. negotiators hardly expected that the Soviet Union would be able to increase the volume of a missile by 50 percent as the Soviets did when they replaced the SS-11 with the SS-19. Such a fete was accomplished by more efficient use of silo space and better missile propellant. At the same time, Secretary of State Henry A. Kissinger was quick to point out that the current size of U.S. missile silos would allow the United States to emplace heavy missiles in existing silos and thus to move toward equality of throw-weight if it chose to do so.[23]

The Interim Agreement did not place any limit on the size of SLBMs or the size of the submarines carrying them. The United States was interested in producing the Trident submarine system, which would considerably increase the size and capability of both SLBMs and submarines. Since the agreement did not include restrictions on bombers, research and development, or the MIRVing of missiles, the United States would still be able to increase its offensive capability considerably.

The Anti-Ballistic Missile Treaty similarly pays more attention to quantitative restrictions than to qualitative ones. Research and development of ABM systems based upon new technologies such as lasers are not prohibited by the treaty. At most, the parties are only expected to discuss possible limitations upon future exotic ABM systems that might be developed.

The SALT II Treaty included some important limitations upon qualitative improvements not found in the Interim Agreement, which permitted almost unlimited modernization of missile forces. SALT II, prior to its expiration in 1985, would have permitted only one new ICBM missile system each for the United States and the Soviet Union. Limits were also placed upon how many reentry vehicles (RVs) could be emplaced upon each missile, allowing SLBMs to have up to fourteen independently targeted nuclear warheads and the ICBM to have as many as ten, the number designated for the MX missile. Such a restriction was viewed by many to represent a victory for the United States, particularly since it was believed that the giant Soviet SS-18 might be able to carry as many as thirty or so RVs.

The SALT II Treaty did little to limit the testing of weapons systems. Although the United States favored restrictions upon the number of missile tests that could be conducted, the final treaty required only that advance notice be given of certain tests. Additional restrictions were placed upon the testing of sea- and ground-based cruise missiles as well as mobile ICBMs only during the period covered by the protocol. Even had SALT II been ratified, it would not have impeded qualitative developments in those areas although some opponents of the treaty, interested in keeping all cruise and mobile missile options open, were fearful that the protocol provisions might be extended.

SALT II did provide an outright ban upon two weapons systems— fractional-orbital ballistic missiles (FOBs) and the emplacement of missiles on surface ships. The United States was particularly concerned about the Soviet development of a missile that would allow the Soviet Union to place a nuclear warhead into partial orbit (thereby not violating the 1967 Outer Space Treaty) and then direct the warhead to a U.S. target. Such a device would enable the Soviet Union to send a nuclear device the long way around the earth, striking the United States from the south. The Soviet Union, on the other hand, appeared the more anxious to restrict missiles from surface ships because of Soviet comparative weaknesses in that area.

Although efforts had been made to restrict the range of air-launched cruise missiles during the SALT II negotiations, the Soviet Union ultimately agreed not to impose any limits upon their range as Foreign Minister Gromyko conceded that the United States could send them around the earth if it wished. On the other hand, there was great concern about the range of the Soviet Backfire bomber, which some felt had intercontinental range and therefore should be included in the SALT limits. Although it was generally accepted that the Backfire could fly one-way suicidal missions against the United States, a return flight would require refueling in the air. Despite many reservations, the Backfire bomber was excluded from the SALT ceilings. The Soviet Union in a separate letter from Brezhnev indicated that it would not increase the capabilities of Backfire nor would it increase the production rates of the bomber beyond the current thirty per year.

The SALT process has done little to restrict the quantitative arms race, particularly since the MIRVing process allowed the superpowers to increase substantially the number of strategically deliverable nuclear warheads. In terms of numbers of missiles, the Interim Agreement was successful in establishing a freeze on the number of missile launchers, and the SALT II Treaty went further by placing limits that, for the first time, would require the reduction of offensive weapons systems. Under the SALT II ceilings, for example, the Soviet Union would have been required to dismantle a total of 250 missiles.

One of the possible consequences of any effort to establish quantitative limits on weapons systems is that such limits might only stimulate a qualitative arms race—the kind of arms buildup which the United States has generally emphasized. The Soviet Union, on the other hand, traditionally has concentrated upon increasing its quantity of arms to make up for the lack of technological equality. Older weapons frequently have not been retired as new ones come on line, leaving the Soviet Union with many antiquated, less effective liquid-fuelled missiles. The SALT I agreements by allowing modernization of existing weapons forced dismantlement of the old weapon as each new unit came on line. Such a change in the direction of the arms race may not be entirely beneficial, for qualitative arms races are generally more expensive than quantitative ones. Qualitative arms races may also be more destablizing because of the fear that the other side might achieve a major scientific breakthrough which could undermine the deterrent threat.

Verification

Perhaps no issue has impeded progress toward strategic arms control more than that of concern about verification. In a world filled with suspicion how can anyone trust the other side to live up to its end of the bargain? The problem of verification was highlighted during the 1930s when Nazi Germany proved itself effective in evading the arms control limitations established by the victorious powers in the Versailles treaty. Verification became a central issue during the debate over the Baruch Plan as Bernard Baruch insisted that the veto not be allowed for fear of its being used by the Soviet Union to evade the inspection and control provision of the plan.

Generally speaking, it has been the United States which has been the most preoccupied with the effectiveness of inspection and verification procedures. In the 1950s this concern was often phrased in terms of the need to establish foolproof inspection systems to guarantee that the other side not cheat. The Soviet Union, on the other hand, has been highly sensitive to the possibility that verification procedures would interfere with its closed system by allowing alien ideas to penetrate Soviet society. Soviet leaders believed that Western disarmament plans amounted to little more than an effort to penetrate Soviet territorial sovereignty, having minimal effect upon reducing armament levels. Such concern may well have been justified in the midfifties when the United States proposed its "open skies" scheme, which the Soviet Union regarded as intrusive inspection without corresponding arms reduction.

The Soviet Union, having earlier presented proposals that precluded any inspection, accepted the notion of establishing ground control posts on Soviet and American territory in May 1955 and four months later agreed to aerial inspection in the final stage of disarmament. Soviet officials were reported in 1974 to have been willing to consider on-site inspection for monitoring a proposed chemical weapons treaty, allowing inspectors to visit predetermined locations to ascertain treaty compliance.[24] The first U.S.-Soviet arms treaty providing on-site inspection is the 1976 Peaceful Nuclear Explosions Treaty. This treaty, along with its companion Threshold Test Ban Treaty, has yet to be ratified by the

United States, and the Reagan administration has indicated that it will not support ratification until verification procedures are strengthened in the two treaties. The Soviet Union, on the whole, has been more willing to accept elaborate verification procedures whenever more extensive reductions have been involved. Soviet general and complete disarmament proposals generally included provisions for on-site inspection, ground control posts, and aerial inspection.

At the same time that a rapidly changing technological environment has complicated the control of strategic weapons, that same technology has begun to provide instruments capable of detecting possible arms control violations from outside the country. Photography from satellites is now able to identify something as small as a basketball from hundreds of miles in the air. Satellite electronic devices can detect huge metallic objects like missiles that are placed underground. Supplemented with other sophisticated monitoring devices utilizing ground radar posts and aerial flights near the border, a state is able not only to identify every missile launcher that the other side possesses but to go a long way in ascertaining many of the missile's qualitative characteristics as well.

The techniques used to monitor an arms control agreement that do not intrude upon the territory of another state have come to be referred to as national technical means (NTM). A critical turning point in SALT I occurred when the CIA certified the ability of national technical means to verify the arms control restrictions under negotiation. In June 1973, the United States went a step further by accepting the notion that even the qualitative limits under consideration in SALT II would be verified only by national technical means. For its part, the Soviet Union in both SALT I and II agreed not to interfere with NTM, which in effect has established the concept of "open skies" to a degree that could not have been envisioned when these proposals were first advanced in the midfifties.

The most difficult stage in the weapons cycle to inspect is that of research and development; and, for this reason, few arms control agreements explicitly limit activities in this area. Nowhere in any of the SALT agreements was there an explicit ban on weapons research although the ABM Treaty prohibits the *development* of sea-based, air-based, space-based, and mobile land-based ABM missiles as well as MIRVed ABMs. Article I of the SALT II Treaty provides that the parties "exercise restraint in the development of new types of strategic offensive arms." Weapons explicitly mentioned in the treaty as being prohibited in terms of development include rapid reload launchers, missiles fired from surface ships, and fractional orbital missiles. The testing and deployment of sea and ground-based cruise missiles were to be prohibited only during the protocol phase.

Despite the verification problems involved, detection of a weapons system prior to testing is still possible. Dr. William J. Perry, former undersecretary of defense for research and engineering, indicated on July 18, 1979, that "we monitor the activities of the [Soviet missile] design bureaus and production plants well enough that we have been able to predict every ICBM before it ever began its tests."[25]

As indicated above, detection of testing is one of the easier inspection problems, for ascertaining whether or not a given delivery system was tested apparently can be determined with a high degree of accuracy by national technical means. More difficult are efforts to determine the qualitative capabilities of a given weapons system by observing testing programs. The range of a delivery system, for example, can be purposefully restrained in a test so as not to communicate a weapon's true potential. A particular problem was posed in connection with the SALT II requirement that only air-launched cruise missiles with a range over 600 kilometers are to be counted in the ALCM ceilings. The Soviet decision not to place any limit on the maximum range of the air-launched cruise missile eliminated an equally difficult verification problem but at the cost of doing nothing to restrain a powerful weapons system that is easy to conceal. Additional verification problems may arise with respect to determining whether a cruise missile is ground-, sea-, or air-launched. Also, how does one determine whether the cruise missile is conventionally armed or nuclear armed? The latter would not present such a problem but for the fact that because of the relatively low cost of the cruise missile it would not be an economic absurdity to arm them with conventional weapons. The same cannot be said for most other long-range missiles.

The number of reentry vehicles involved in a given MIRV test may be difficult to determine since feints can be used without releasing a separate missile. What is observable may not be an accurate reflection of the degree of fractionism actually achieved. In order to alleviate U.S. concern on this issue, the Soviet Union agreed in May 1979 to place restrictions on such missile release simulations.

To facilitate the monitoring of testing activities, the ABM Treaty provided that all missile testing be conducted at pre-designated sites, easily observable from outside national boundaries. This principle was carried over into the SALT II Treaty for offensive missile testing. The SALT II Treaty in article XVI also requires that the other side be notified well in advance whenever an ICBM test is to be conducted, except for single ICBM test launches confined to the national territory of the state.

Ground radar stations located outside the country provide the major means for United States' monitoring of Soviet missile tests. Questions were raised about the ability of NTM to do an adequate job of verification following the loss of two U.S. radar monitoring sites as a result of the 1979 Iranian revolution. Although aerial flights close to Soviet borders could provide some of the necessary information, the United States was not reassured on this issue until a similar radar installation was established to monitor Soviet missile-testing programs from Chinese territory. For its part, the Soviet Union relies heavily upon monitoring equipment located on Soviet ships a short distance from the major U.S. testing sites of Cape Canaveral and Vandenberg Air Force Base.

During the SALT II negotiations the United States raised questions concerning the encoding or encrypting of the telemetry in the Soviet missile testing program. Such encoding consisted of efforts to conceal or disguise the electronic signals that were transmitted from the missile to ground stations. But in disguising such signals, which are necessary to determine a missile's performance, the Soviet Union was interfering with the ability of the United States to monitor Soviet missile developments. As long as concern is focused on the quantity of missiles as in SALT I, interference in the telemetry process presented no problem, but since SALT II provides for qualitative limits as well, the United States argued that such a practice interferes with national technical means of inspection. After considerable debate on the issue, the Soviet Union finally agreed to accept a ban on telemetry encryption whenever such encoding would impede verification.

Verifying that states are living up to the quantitative limits of an agreement presents special problems. To deal with one of those problems, the SALT agreements have limited numbers of launchers but not missiles, which are more difficult to verify. The silos in which ICBM launchers are emplaced take some two years to construct, providing ample time to monitor efforts to increase launcher capability. Counting numbers of missiles is more difficult since they may be placed underground or hidden in large buildings located close to existing silos. Because of their huge metallic size, ICBMs are detectable in many, but not all, instances by electronic devices on satellites. Despite possible verification problems, the SALT II Treaty provided that extra missiles may not be stored near launchers since such a practice would introduce the possibility of rapid reload—a particular problem in view of the cold-launch capability of the Soviet Union. This process enables the Soviets to raise the ICBM out of its silo, fire it with minimal damage to the silo, and therefore to use the silo for another launch. The ABM Treaty provided a similar proscription against developing rapid reload capabilities for ABM launchers.

If a launcher is allowed to become mobile, additional verification problems may arise. A conflict is created between the deterrent objective of developing an invulnerable retaliatory capability in which mobility would be a major asset and the arms control objective of adequate verification. This conflict in part explains the meandering position of the United States on the issue of mobile ICBMs. In the SALT I agreements, the United States appended a unilateral statement prohibiting the development of mobile ICBMs, largely because of concern about verifiability. The increasing vulnerability of the ICBM caused the United States subsequently to express more concern about protecting its ICBM capability, making missile mobility a more attractive option.

Verification considerations continued to plague U.S. decisions about a mobile ICBM basing-plan as more than thirty plans have been examined and found wanting for one reason or another. President Carter rejected the proposed multiple aim point (MAP), which would have involved a large shell game. Under this plan MX missiles would be moved from one silo to another so as to keep the Soviet Union uncertain about the exact location. Since silos provide the basis for counting launcher capability, the plan created serious verification problems.

The Carter administration finally decided in favor of a racetrack system making use of 200 MX missiles and 4,600 shelters located in Utah and Nevada. Each missile would move around a track containing 23 shelters, and presumably the Soviet Union would not know exactly in which shelter the MX was located. Verification would be possible since the missiles would be shown in open trenches from time to time.

For its part, the Soviet Union minimized verification problems related to mobile ICBMs when it agreed in SALT II to dispense with its SS-16 mobile ICBM. The West was concerned not only with the problems involved in counting the number of SS-16s in Soviet arsenals but also with the prospect that the Soviet Union might convert the intermediate-range mobile SS-20 into an intercontinental-range SS-16. The conversion requires only an addition of a third stage rocket since the SS-20 already provides the necessary first two stages.

Since the great strength of submarines is that they are highly mobile, it might seem that these weapons systems would create the most serious verification problems, but submarines must come to port from time to time. If the invulnerable retaliatory capability necessary for an effective deterrent is to be guaranteed, it is important that verification techniques not be so refined that they can spot all nuclear submarines at a given time. Capabilities for counting numbers of submarines and SLBMs positioned on them have generally been viewed as adequate without improving current technology.

A more serious verification problem related to both ICBMs and SLBMs is that of identifying the number of MIRVs positioned on each missile once it is deployed. Since inspection is restricted to national technical means, the main procedure used for verification is that of monitoring MIRV tests. Although the procedure allows a state utilizing national technical means to ascertain the potential MIRV capability of a missile, it does little to distinguish between a missile that is actually deployed in a MIRV mode and one which is not. An important breakthrough was made when the Soviet Union agreed to count any missile that has been tested with multiple independently targeted warheads against the 1,200 MIRV limit in SALT II even if the missile is deployed with a single warhead missile as was planned by the Soviets.

Although the Nixon administration linked on-site inspection to any acceptance of a MIRV ban, it is by no means clear that such inspection would solve the verification problem once the missiles are deployed. In a press briefing on December 3, 1974, Secretary of State Henry A. Kissinger noted that "you couldn't inspect every missile every day. With the time delays that would be involved until you get to the site, they could easily take off the MIRV warhead and put on a single warhead, have a MIRV storage, and when you leave put the MIRV back on the missile."[26]

As an aid to identifying SLBMs and ICBMs that have been MIRVed, SALT II required that externally observable design features be provided. A similar requirement was made with respect to the heavy bombers that will be carrying cruise missiles. In the parlance of arms control such efforts have been referred to as providing functionally related observable differences or FRODs.

As part of the verification procedure, SALT I established a bilateral Standing Consultive Commission (SCC) to deal with alleged treaty violations. The SCC has considered a number of allegations from both the Soviet Union and the United States, all of which until recently were satisfactorily resolved. According to a 1982 estimate, thirty-four complaints on the SALT I regime were made by both sides and all were settled "by the cessation of the objectionable activity or a satisfactory explanation of it."[27] For example, in the summer of 1973 the United States accused the Soviet Union of illegally constructing new silos which the Soviets argued were designed for command and control functions, not missile launchers. After discussion in the SCC, the United

States accepted the Soviet explanation. Subsequent accusations of Soviet testing of anti-aircraft radars in what might be considered an ABM mode in violation of the ABM Treaty led the Soviet Union to desist from the practice. The Soviet Union in March 1976 acknowledged a technical violation in its schedule for dismantling some fifty-one obsolete missiles as new weapons came on line. It was indicated that the delay was related to inclement weather, and the Soviet Union soon corrected the problem.

For its part, the Soviet Union accused the United States of interfering with NTM when the latter placed covers over missile silos under construction to protect workers from severe winter weather in Montana. After hearings before the SCC, the United States changed the practice. Other allegations were made with respect to U.S. radar programs and the status of Atlas and Titan ICBM launchers. Satisfactory explanations were provided in each instance.

The necessity for reliable verification increases with more extensive arms reductions. When armaments are reduced to a low level, the ability of a state to evade the provisions of a treaty can be more critical in upsetting the arms balance. Since the SALT agreements have been little more than cosmetic, the inability to detect minor violations will have little impact upon national security; remaining arsenals will continue to provide a sufficient deterrent.

Evaluating verification requirements should be related to the probabilities that a state will attempt to violate a disarmament agreement. Presumably the state favored the agreement or it would not have ratified it. Rather than take risks that would provide a legal justification for the other side to abrogate a treaty, a state will be interested in demonstrating compliance. A 100 percent guarantee of detection is unnecessary since a state may well be sufficiently deterred with a 50 percent probability of being caught. When placed in this perspective, the estimated 80 percent reliability in detecting mobile missiles, one of the more difficult inspection problems, becomes much more acceptable.[28]

WAS SALT WORTH ITS SALT?

Considerable optimism greeted the successful conclusion of SALT I in May 1972, as U.S. government officials suggested savings in strategic defense spending of $5 to $15 billion over the next five years. On July 9, 1979, Secretary of Defense Harold Brown told the Senate Committee on Foreign Relations that the just signed SALT II Treaty would save as much as $30 billion over the next decade.[29] Despite such optimistic assessments, the strategic arms budgets in the United States and the Soviet Union have risen considerably above levels established before the opening of the SALT Talks with the number of strategic nuclear weapons more than quadrupling since 1969. Even had SALT II been ratified, Secretary Brown's assessment may have been overly optimistic, for defense spending was beginning to rise even before the treaty was signed.

In reviewing what has been achieved in a decade of Strategic Arms Limitation Talks, there is reason to be pessimistic. Agreements reached both within and outside SALT have had little, if any, impact on the reduction of armaments. For example, the SALT I agreements contained no provisions for reducing existing weapon systems. Nor was there much constraint upon qualitative improvements as both sides were allowed to modernize and MIRV their missiles. Admittedly, the Anti-Ballistic Missile Treaty nipped in the bud what might have become a very costly ABM race, but whether such a race would have occurred, given the increasing skepticism about the effectiveness of such a system, is highly debatable. American scientific opinion was overwhelmingly united during the seventies in opposition to anti-ballistic missile systems, recognizing that there were just too many ways of countering any ABM system through such devices as MIRVs, decoy missiles, and penetration aids.

In order to evaluate the utility of partial measures such as those reached at SALT, one needs to examine the cost of reaching such agreements. These costs have included the concessions that have been necessary to placate domestic interests, the price paid for ''bargaining chips'' that have not been cashed, and the suspicion and distrust that have arisen owing to concern over treaty evasions.

Because it has sometimes been more difficult to work out a compromise with various interests within the United States and the Soviet Union than between the two governments, certain agreements have, in fact, accelerated the arms race. This was true in the case of the Limited Test Ban Treaty of 1963 and the Threshold Nuclear Test Ban Treaty signed in 1974 by the United States and the Soviet Union. In both instances, military interests asked for and received an accelerated nuclear-testing program compatible with the respective treaties.

Similar trade-offs to domestic forces have been apparent at several stages during the SALT talks. According to one reporter, the Joint Chiefs of Staff were reticent about even approving the negotiations as such unless the Nixon administration would support the deployment of MIRV.[30] John Newhouse, in his comprehensive chronicle of the SALT I negotiations, has indicated that the acceleration of the Trident program was Kissinger's quid pro quo to the Joint Chiefs for supporting the Soviet edge in missile capability provided in SALT I.[31]

The political cost to future agreements inherent in efforts to sell the SALT agreements to the U.S. Congress should also not be overlooked. Interest in obtaining Senate support for SALT I led the Nixon administration to support the Jackson amendment, which called for equality of arms levels in any future agreements. On the surface, such expectations would appear to be well taken; but, in the case of negotiations for strategic arms limitation, the amendment has made negotiation difficult because of disagreement on what constitutes essential equivalence, as noted above.

It would seem that the SALT agreements have actually worked to the advantage of certain groups involved in weapons procurement. The Interim Offensive Arms Agreement in particular may have benefited military interests. It gave the appearance of inequality, allowing those in favor of increased spending to exploit the issue. Since the public often does not understand the advantages that a state has in a number of other military areas to offset such inequalities, it tends to be susceptible to arguments for increasing armaments in areas not limited by treaty.

Concessions to generate support for the SALT II Treaty can also be found during the Carter period. The *New York Times* reported, for example, that the White House agreed to press for improved air defenses and a new medium-range bomber in an effort to induce the Joint Chiefs of Staff to accept the exclusion of the Soviet Backfire bomber from the treaty.[32] President Carter, perhaps motivated by the uphill battle to get Senate approval for the SALT II Treaty, made numerous concessions in 1979 to those favoring a stronger military establishment. These included agreement to increase the defense budget by $13 billion, the decision to go ahead both with MX and a longer-range Trident missile, the acceptance of a mobile basing system for MX, a stepped up civil defense program, and a draft registration. In addition, Carter decided to position intermediate-range ballistic and cruise missiles in Europe and to fire Paul Warnke as SALT negotiator and head of the Arms Control and Disarmament Agency, replacing him with the more conservative Lt. General George M. Seignious. It is important to remember that all of these moves were taken prior to the Soviet incursion into Afghanistan in December, leading President Carter to declare that he had misjudged Soviet intentions. It was after the Soviet invasion that the president asked that the SALT II Treaty be shelved although it was not clear at the time whether the treaty would have achieved the required two-thirds Senate vote approving ratification.

If these arguments for supporting arms control negotiations are not sufficiently persuasive to influence the military conservative, one need only look at yet another advantage provided by such negotiations—they can be, and have been, used to justify the production of "bargaining chips," in the form of new weapon systems as noted in chapter 3. The production of such chips creates pressures for the other side to develop its own bargaining chips, and the stimulation of an arms race rather than arms reduction is the inevitable outcome.

Throughout the SALT talks there was a constant search for a bargaining chip to enable one side or the other to prevail. The ABM became the first of many such chips as the Johnson administration, in its waning days, proposed to make the Sentinel ABM system a bargaining chip for the upcoming SALT negotiations. Earlier arguments for the system as a protection against a possible nuclear strike from China, as a device for countering an accidental missile launching, and as a protection against a first strike, had all been found wanting. The Nixon administration also used the bargaining chip argument in trying to sell its Safeguard ABM system. The U.S. SALT negotiator, Gerard Smith, went so far as to send an urgent telegram to members of the Senate in August 1970 suggesting that a vote in favor of limiting the Safeguard system to two sites, instead of the twelve proposed, would be detrimental to the outcome of SALT.[33] Without such an intervention, the restriction on Safeguard quite likely would have passed. As it was, the proposal failed by five votes.

The Nixon administration also sought to justify the MIRV system as a hedge against the Soviet ABM. MIRV was to have made it clear to the Soviet Union that it would never be able to provide an effective defense against a United States retaliatory strike. There was no discussion of stopping MIRV developments once agreement on the ABM was reached and, as indicated above, MIRVing continued at a rapid pace.

Perhaps the best illustration of how a military bargaining chip can force the development of unneeded weapons and, in turn, impede the prospects of arms control, is found in the development of the cruise missile. According to John W. Finney, it was Secretary of State Henry Kissinger who proposed that the Pentagon undertake development of long-range cruise missiles as a bargaining chip for the SALT II negotiations. Kissinger reportedly lamented in private conversations that he "didn't realize the Pentagon would fall in love with cruise missiles."[34] Similar second thoughts had been expressed by Secretary Kissinger about the MIRV system, which had earlier been sold as a bargaining chip but after production became a serious obstacle to reaching agreement because of the inspection problems it created. Kissinger is reported to have said that he wished he "had thought through the implications of the MIRVed world more fully in 1968–70."[35] The best time to stop an arms race involving any weapon system is before work begins on the weapon—at a time before vested interests become committed and before deployment complicates inspection.

Despite the recurring failure to derive any arms control benefits from bargaining chips, both sides have continued to use the bargaining chip argument in support of a number of weapons systems. Such arguments have been made by Pentagon and administration officials with respect to proposals for Trident, the B-1 bomber, NCA defense, the development of an advanced airborne command post, the maneuvering reentry vehicle, MX, the cruise missile, and Pershing II missile.

According to some authorities, the SS-9 represented an effort by the USSR to create its own bargaining chip. Also the rapidity with which the Soviet Union rushed into development of the SS-16 through SS–20 series was suggestive of a desire to increase its bargaining position during SALT II. The same can be said of the scheduling of a series of ICBM tests at the end of May 1972, just as SALT I was signed, and further tests conducted on the eve of the resumption of the SALT talks on February 20, 1974. The Soviet resumption of hunter-killer satellite tests in 1978, following a two-year moratorium, was also reported to have been scheduled to coincide with the SALT talks.

Bargaining chips tend to increase fear on the part of the adversary, and the traditional reaction is one of responding in kind. Soviet leader Yuri V. Andropov warned that if the United States went ahead with the MX, the Soviet Union would be forced to counter it with an analogous missile. He also noted that long-range cruise missiles would be built to meet the threat of U.S. cruise missiles.[36] If either side emphasizes bargaining chips it becomes all the more difficult for the moderates in the other country to plead for realistic arms restraint. Ammunition is merely provided for the more hawkish elements to press for higher defense budgets and to sabotage any effort towards arms reduction.

On the whole, bargaining chips have been costly, but if it could be shown that partial agreements such as those reached in SALT had stimulated more extensive reductions of armaments, they would be worth the price. Unfortunately, this does not seem to have been the case. Instead, the agreements to date have tended to generate increased suspicion and have actually slowed down the momentum toward more significant agreements.

Suspicion about possible evasions of an arms control agreement is likely to be pervasive in a world that is high in threat-perception and heavily armed. Indeed, a state may be trapped by public pressures into retaliating against an adversary's violation (or assumed violation) even if it is not in that state's interest to do so. There is something more compelling about the need to react to perceived increments of weapons controlled by a treaty than to buildups not so regulated. Such suspicion is likely to set back the cause of disarmament further, and even to accelerate the arms race. A number of accusations of alleged Soviet violations of the SALT I agreements have been noted, including assertions that the Soviet Union had tested a type of radar system that could be utilized in an ABM system, that it had replaced smaller ICBMs with missiles above the size-limitations agreed on, and that it had used decoys and camouflage to interfere with United States national technical means of verification. The Soviet Union in turn accused the United States of camouflaging some of its missiles. Ambiguities of this sort, as well as those arising over the unilateral interpretations that were publicized by the United States and the Soviet Union at the time of signing the SALT agreements, are likely to pose further difficulties in the future. Rather than serving as confidence-building measures as some have suggested, verification procedures are just as likely to increase mutual suspicion and distrust. This is certainly the direction that verification issues have taken during the Reagan period as will be pointed out in the next chapter.

WHO GAVE UP WHAT?

As the data in chapter 3 indicated, during the SALT negotiations both sides made numerous concessions—a prerequisite for successful negotiation. These moves can be evaluated from yet another perspective by examining which side was able to negotiate an agreement more to its liking. Such an assessment requires the comparing of preferences with final outcomes as has been done for the SALT II Treaty in table 6.1.

Since the positions of the United States and the Soviet Union changed over time, the preference shown reflects the position most vigorously pressed by each state before resolution. The preferred position might be viewed as the most favorable one considered realistically possible among a range of alternatives; obviously, in the strict sense, the preferred position would restrict only the weapons of the other side while leaving one's own options open.

In addition to setting forth the preferred positions of the two sides on the various provisions of the SALT II Treaty, the table indicates whose

Table 6.1 Results of SALT II Compared to Preferred Positions

SALT II Provisions	U.S. Preference	Soviet Preference
Equal aggregates (missiles-bombers)	*Equal aggregates (missiles-bombers)	Extend interim levels (bombers excluded)
Ceiling 2,250 (1982)	Ceiling 2,000 or less	Ceiling (2,400–2,500)
1,320 MIRV sublimit (cruise on bomber = one MIRV)	More MIRVs to compensate for Soviet throw-weight	*Proposed as low as 1,100. U.S. basically set 1,320 level
1,200 sublimit on MIRVed missiles	*Low number to allow at least 100 bombers with cruise missiles	Preferred 50 more to limit number of bombers with cruise
820 MIRV sublimit on ICBMs	*U.S. concern to limit MIRVed ICBMs although a lower number would have been preferred	A larger sublimit would be to Soviet advantage
300 + limit on Soviet heavy missiles; U.S. to have none	Limit Soviets to 150 heavy ICBMs; U.S. not interested, in heavy missiles for itself	*Not to reduce 300 + level achieved at SALT I
Limit fractionism of MIRV (10-ICBM; 14-SLBM)	*Limit fractionism to level Soviets already capable of according to U.S.	Claimed fractionism had not proceeded as far as U.S. claimed
If missile tested with MIRV all will be considered MIRVed	*Count if tested with MIRV	Wanted to deploy same ICBM in both single and MIRV mode
Test and deploy one new ICBM	Varied over time. Restrict after own tests and deployment and before those of other	Varied over time. Restrict after own tests and deployment and before those of other
Notify in advance of certain ICBM launches	Limit number of ICBM tests	*No limit to tests proposed
Allow mobile land- and air-launched ICBMs (light variety only)	Unilateral statement opposing in 1972. Reversed 1974–75	Refused to accept ban in 1972; later began to favor ban to stop MX

SALT II Provisions	U.S. Preference	Soviet Preference
Complete ban on SS-16 mobile missile	*Concerned about verification problems and mobile ICBM potential when combined with intermediate range SS-20	Wanted SS-16 for its ICBM potential when combined with SS-20 launchers
Extra missiles not to be stored near launchers	*Concerned about Soviet reload capabilities using same launcher	Appeared not to have raised the issue
Ceiling on throw-weight and launch weight of both heavy and light missiles	*Concerned about qualitative improvements of existing missiles; will impede somewhat	Appeared to be interested in keeping options open
Ban on ballistic missiles (600+ Km) not yet employed (e.g., FOBs and surface ships)	Interested in prohibiting FOBs, which Soviets have developed	Less interested than U.S. in emplacing missiles on ships
Forward-based systems not included in treaty	*Exclude; consider only at SALT II or MBFR	Want included, particularly if low ceilings on delivery systems are established
Statement agreeing not to increase production or capability of Backfire Bomber	Would have liked to have included in ceilings; settled for Soviet statement	*Backfire should be excluded entirely from ceilings
Not to circumvent treaty by providing technology and weapons to allies	No inclusion or compensation to USSR for NATO allies' strategic forces	Include allied strategic weapons in ceilings or compensate USSR
Air-launched cruise missile range not limited	*2,500+ kilometer range desired	ALCM to be limited to 600 kilometers in range

SALT II Provisions	U.S. Preference	Soviet Preference
Average of 28 cruise missiles per bomber	*Variable number: 35+ on some, less on others	Wanted a limit of 20 per bomber
ALCMs of 600+ Km range may be positioned only on heavy bombers	Had been interested in deploying ALCMs on FB-111s (Provision will prevent deployment on Backfire)	Didn't want to see ALCMs positioned on FB-111s
Exchange data regularly on own arsenals	*Wanted Soviets to be more forthcoming on force levels	Tradition of secrecy on military strength force levels
National means of verification	Would have liked to have seen on-site inspection	*Limit to national means of verification
Not to interfere with national means of inspection	*Concerned with evasion issue far more than Soviets	Tends not to admit such action as a possibility
Ban on any telemetry encryption impeding verification	*Highly concerned on this issue; Soviets accept U.S. draft language	Not concerned about establishing controls to prohibit the masking of missile tests
Protocol limits: testing and deployment of mobile ICBMs and ASBMs; ban on deployment of sea and ground based cruise	*Wants to keep option open on all noted systems; since none of activities are scheduled before 1982 restrictions are moot	Less interested in systems than U.S. Will want to extend restrictions if possible
Protocol to expire December 31, 1981	*Wanted specific expiration date (Ranged from Octber 1980-June 1981)	Protocol to expire three years after ratification
Treaty to expire in 1985	*Favored 10-year treaty to expire in 1985	Wanted permanent treaty

*Preference appears to be more compatible with final outcome.

position seemed to prevail in the final outcome. Asterisks indicate whose position was best reflected in the treaty's actual provisions.

Of the twenty-eight provisions, twenty-two are more consonant with the position of one side or the other. In most cases—seventeen of the twenty-two—the provision seems closer to the position of the United States. In six cases, both sides apparently compromised in roughly equal measure or varied their positions so substantially over time that their preferences were not clear.

Obviously, the provisions of the treaty are not equally important; no quantitative measure can provide a definitive picture of which side's concessions were more critical. The structure of the treaty appears to be more in keeping with the positions taken by the United States, despite the fact it refused to ratify SALT II. One objective not achieved was a lower ceiling on Soviet ICBMs to reduce the vulnerability of United States land-based missiles, and the final U.S. decision to accept only national means of verification represented a significant retreat from its original position.

It might be noted that the United States is viewed by some analysts as taking less extreme positions during negotiations than the Soviet Union. As a result, the Soviet Union may only appear to have made more concessions, while in truth it merely gravitated to the more equitable and realistic positions that the United States assumed from the beginning.[37] Such an interpretation is undoubtedly affected by one's own values, and Soviet leaders are likely to see the United States negotiating positions as extreme.

Of course, detractors might well argue that the give-and-take in the SALT negotiations has been largely irrelevant, because the agreements have been little more than cosmetic in their effect, allowing both sides to produce whatever weapons they seriously wanted. No weapons system that the United States has been highly interested in building was prohibited by the SALT II Treaty. Restrictions on land- and sea-based cruise missiles and the mobile MX missile were to be limited to the duration of the protocol, which was scheduled to expire at the end of 1981, thus leaving these options fully open. Although there were restrictions placed on the Soviet Union, including the requirement to dismantle some 250 missiles by 1982, the proscriptions were not severe. Since the Soviet Union has not been as prone to dismantle its missiles when more modern versions come on line, it has a number of relatively obsolete liquid-fueled missiles in its arsenal that it could easily afford to dismantle.

A similar analysis could be made for the SALT I agreements in which perhaps the payoffs to each side were more balanced in terms of preferences. During the talks on the anti-ballistic missile, the Soviet Union achieved its basic objective of limiting the development of the Safeguard ABM system. The United States could rest assured that it would not be forced to enter into a costly ABM race with the Soviet Union—a race that would threaten the stability of the nuclear deterrent system. At the same time options for research and development on the anti-ballistic missile remained open for both parties.

With respect to the Interim Offensive Arms Agreement, the United States was able to obtain a five-year freeze on the number of SLBMs and ICBMs. This freeze was especially important for the United States, which had no plans to add to its number of offensive missile systems during the five-year period. Both sides perhaps lost in the failure to freeze the qualitative arms race. This was particularly unfortunate since it allowed the development of MIRVed weapons, thereby increasing the number of strategically deliverable nuclear warheads severalfold during the course of the SALT negotiations. The period since the signing of SALT I has also witnessed the development of cruise missile technology, which complicates efforts to achieve verifiable arms control.

CONCLUSION

Little progress was made on controlling strategic nuclear weapons during the early postwar disarmament negotiations. As long as the United States had nuclear weapons and the Soviet Union had none, successful negotiation on nuclear arms control was impossible. It was only after the Soviet Union began to approach the United States in terms of strategic capability that serious strategic arms control negotiations became a reality.

The decade of the seventies proved to be the most productive of any in terms of reaching agreements on strategic arms. Among the agreements signed during the decade were the Anti-Ballistic Missile Treaty and the Interim Offensive Arms Agreement during SALT I, the SALT II Treaty, and a number of other agreements dealing with such issues as accidental war, the stationing of weapons on the seabed, and restrictions on biological and environmental warfare.

Despite the achievements, a number of complicating factors interfered with efforts to negotiate more significant limitations on strategic arms. Among these was the problem of what to do about forward-based systems in Europe. These systems were viewed, perhaps justifiably, as strategic weapons by the Soviets, given the ability of such weapons to reach targets within the Soviet Union. Determining which weapons systems were equivalent and how strategic power should be compared between the superpowers also presented difficulties as did concern about whether to establish qualitative and/or quantitative limits on strategic nuclear weapons. Finally, verification has presented a number of problems for arms control as the United States has traditionally been highly concerned about having adequate verification and the Soviet Union, with its more closed society, has feared too much intrusion. By the 1970s the development of verification procedures using satellite technology had progressed to the point that the United States found it possible to accept national technical means of inspection as an adequate verification system. For its part, the Soviet Union agreed not to interfere with national technical means.

Despite the seeming progress made on arms control during the decade, a number of questions remained as to whether the SALT agreements were in fact worth their salt. Rather than slowing the nuclear arms race, strategic arms increased substantially during the decade of SALT. At the same time, the costs of reaching what were essentially cosmetic agreements were exceedingly high as the SALT process added to U.S.-Soviet strategic arsenals as a result of the success achieved in arguing for the creation of military bargaining chips and the tendency to reward conservative domestic groups for their support for arms control by building additional weapons not covered by treaty restrictions. The suspicions aroused over the verification procedures also did little to improve the strategic or political relationship between the United States and the Soviet Union.

The SALT decade ended on an ominous note as the SALT II Treaty was withdrawn from Senate consideration, never to be ratified. In evaluating the SALT II Treaty, the evidence suggests that the United States, for the most part, obtained its generally preferred position more often than did the Soviet Union as seventeen of twenty-two provisions of the treaty were found to be more compatible with the position taken by the Carter administration than those assumed by the Soviet Union.

Among the many lessons about negotiating behavior that can be derived from the SALT experience is, first and foremost, the importance of rough military parity before agreement can be reached. Even then, it is often difficult to agree to anything other than a freeze upon weapons at the point of relative parity. If, as in the case of the United States, no ongoing strategic weapons are being built, expecting to gain anything beyond a freeze is quite unrealistic.

The international climate appears to have affected progress in SALT, showing that progress can be made on arms control when states are willing to make arms control agreements the centerpiece of a policy of détente. Tensions in distant areas can be used as a pretext for slowing progress on arms control as in the case of events taking place in Angola in 1975, in the horn of Africa in 1978, and the Soviet invasion of Afghanistan in 1979.

The negotiations of the seventies proved to be among the most businesslike of the entire postwar period. Part of this was undoubtedly due to the fact that the negotiations were conducted bilaterally and often informally. This reduced the temptation of turning the negotiations into propaganda forums.

Domestically, the decade of the seventies showed a more activist Congress in the field of arms control than previously. On the whole, Congress proved to be more of a restraint on arms control than a facilitator as illustrated by the 1972 Jackson amendment and the opposition to strategic arms control voiced by a strong minority during the Carter era. The decision to withdraw the treaty from Senate consideration probably had as much to do with concern as to whether the necessary two-thirds vote could be achieved as it did with the Soviet invasion of Afghanistan in 1979.

The fact that President Nixon was able to obtain overwhelming congressional support for the SALT I agreements underscores again the advantages that a more conservative president with proven anti-communist credentials has in selling agreements to Congress and the American public. Such credentials, however, may be less suited to the reaching of agreements with the Soviet Union as the case of President Ronald Reagan demonstrates—an issue to which we now turn our attention as we explore arms control negotiations in the 1980s.

7

Arms Control in the Eighties

As suggested in the preceding chapter, the 1970s proved to be one of the most successful decades in the postwar period in terms of the negotiation of a number of arms control agreements. Among these were the SALT I and SALT II treaties as well as agreements dealing with nuclear testing, biological weapons, the emplacement of nuclear weapons on the seabed, and measures designed to reduce the dangers of nuclear war. But the 1980s began on an ominous note with the decision of President Jimmy Carter to shelve the SALT II Treaty on the pretext of the Soviet invasion of Afghanistan in December 1979. The first year of the decade and Carter's last year as president was consequently a bleak year for arms control as several on-going bilateral negotiations on such topics as chemical arms, a comprehensive test ban, conventional arms transfers, and the militarization of the Indian Ocean were disrupted.

With the defeat of President Carter in the November election, a new administration came into power in which not a few of its members, beginning with President Ronald Reagan himself, were extremely hostile to the arms control effort. The general consensus among the president and his close advisors was that the Soviet Union had taken advantage of the arms control process during the seventies to engage in an unprecedented arms buildup. As a result, a "window of vulnerability" had been created as the Soviet Union neared a first strike capability that made the U.S. ICBM retaliatory capability vulnerable. Past arms control efforts were viewed by the new administration as fatally flawed, restricting primarily the U.S. arms efforts but not that of the Soviet Union. Furthermore, the Soviet Union was seen as having violated a number of the arms control agreements previously negotiated.

Believing as it did that the Soviet Union was in a militarily superior position, the Reagan administration felt it was necessary for the United

States to engage in a massive arms buildup before participating in any further arms control negotiations. Failure to do so would place the United States in an inferior bargaining position. As a result, priority was given to a planned $1.6 trillion arms buildup over a five-year period—a target that would more than double U.S. defense spending.

The emphasis upon a substantial arms buildup began to generate concern about the dangers of a revitalized arms race, resulting in a public outcry in favor of arms control. The movement, stimulated as it was by new studies pointing to the dangers of a "nuclear winter" that would destroy much of life as we know it on planet earth, led to demonstrations in favor of arms control throughout the United States. Resolutions in support of a freeze on nuclear weapons obtained considerable support not only on Capitol Hill but also in several state and local referenda on the subject.

Similar pressures favoring arms control negotiations were also mounting in Western Europe, primarily in reaction to the 1979 NATO decision to place U.S. cruise and Pershing II missiles on the territory of several European states. In fact, the ground swell in Europe was so extensive that it threatened to destroy the deployment effort entirely as European parliaments began to have second thoughts about the decision.

About the same time, the Soviet Union undertook a massive propaganda campaign in Western Europe designed to exploit the divisions over the issue among European allies. Several offers were made by the Soviets to freeze further emplacement of intermediate-range nuclear forces in return for restraint on the Western side.

As a result of these various pressures, the United States on November 30, 1981, reluctantly entered into bilateral negotiations with the Soviet Union on the issue of intermediate-range nuclear forces (INF). Progress has been slow with respect to negotiating controls on intermediate-range delivery systems, but the consensus is that prospects for controlling these weapons is brighter than it is for obtaining agreement on strategic arms or strategic defensive systems—subjects that will be discussed after the problems and tortuous course of the INF negotiations are examined.

INTERMEDIATE-RANGE NUCLEAR FORCE LIMITATIONS

Although the United States had been successful in keeping restrictions on intermediate- and short-range delivery systems out of the SALT agreements, the Joint Statement of Principles and Basic Guidelines for Subsequent Negotiations on the Limitation of Strategic Arms, which was signed along with the SALT II Treaty in 1979, provided that in subsequent SALT rounds either state may raise any issue relative to the further limitation of strategic arms. For the Soviet Union this meant the issue of U.S. forward-based systems, which the Soviets argued had strategic potential since such weapons were capable of hitting targets in the Soviet homeland. European states, given their concern about the extensive Soviet INF modernization program, were also placing increasing pressure upon the United States to begin negotiations. In fact, the December 1979 NATO decision to deploy 572 U.S. intermediate-range nuclear missiles on European soil required that a dual-track approach be used in which arms control negotiations would be undertaken in an effort to obtain reciprocal reductions in Soviet INF forces in return for agreement not to deploy the full contingent of 464 cruise and 108 Pershing II missiles. According to the plan, deployment would begin in December 1983 if agreement on restrictions were not reached before then.

Soviet efforts from the beginning have been designed to thwart the 1979 decision to place U.S. intermediate-range nuclear weapons on European soil. Before the two-track decision was even finalized, President Brezhnev in March and again in October and November 1979 warned NATO against deploying such weapons, promising to undertake immediate negotiations on the subject if NATO would refrain from deployment. Threats were made suggesting that deployment would ruin any chance of arms control for intermediate-range nuclear forces. After the NATO Council approved the decision in December, the Soviet Union rebuffed efforts to implement the second track calling for negotiations, saying that it would not negotiate as long as the deployment decision was upheld or the United States had not ratified the SALT II Treaty. By the summer of 1980, the Soviet Union had reconsidered its stance and agreed to enter negotiations without condition. Preliminary discussions were held with the Carter administration in the fall, but these were disrupted by the November elections in the United States that brought a new administration into power. It was over a year later before the Intermediate-range Nuclear Force Talks were begun.

The INF Negotiations

A major reason for the delay was the considerable bureaucratic in-fighting on the issue that occurred within the new Reagan administration. After several months of internal debate, agreement was finally reached on the so-called zero option, which required that both the United States and the Soviet Union eliminate all land-based, intermediate-range nuclear missiles. The obvious problem with such a proposal is that it was totally nonnegotiable. The United States at that time was asking the Soviet Union to destroy about 225 European-based SS-20s, and in return the United States would simply promise not to deploy comparable systems. The zero-option proposal would also have required that the Soviet Union dismantle 75 SS-20s in Asia that were targeted primarily against the Peoples Republic of China.

Adding to the inequity of the proposal from the Soviet perspective was the fact that no restrictions were imposed upon the deployment of cruise missiles on ships and submarines (SLCMs). Even if the United States were to forego its planned 464 ground-launched cruise missiles (GLCMs), unlimited cruise deployment could still proceed, albeit at sea, but potentially within sufficient range of the same Soviet targets. The acceleration of the U.S. production of these weapons during the early eighties did little to reassure the Soviet Union even though the United States was planning to arm a high proportion of the SLCMs with conventional rather than nuclear warheads.

Many military strategists within the United States government wanted not only to include the SS-20 in the proscribed weapons, but to extend the ban to cover Soviet SS-22s on the grounds that forward deployment of these systems, which have a range of less than 1,000 kilometers, threatens West European targets. Pressure from some within the U.S. government, as well as from European governments, resulted in the decision to exclude such systems in the proposed ban, for demanding the destruction of both SS-20s and SS-22s would appear far too one-sided. The inclusion of SS-22s in the ban might also lead the Soviet Union to make similar demands with respect to comparable shorter-range American nuclear systems stationed in Western Europe.[1]

The proposed zero option had the advantage of simplicity and appeared attractive on the surface, giving it considerable propaganda value. At the same time, it had been a proposal advanced earlier by German Chancellor Helmut Schmidt, albeit at a time before the Soviet Union had deployed so many of its SS-20s. By canceling an entire class of weapons, verification would also be considerably simplified. The discovery of a single vehicle would suffice to demonstrate evasion, whereas counting numbers is far more difficult, particularly when mobile systems like the SS-20 are involved.

Despite these advantages, dissatisfaction over the proposal within Western quarters began to increase as a result of the U.S. government's refusal to budge from what some regarded as only an initial bargaining ploy. The State Department, prior to the official tabling of the proposal, had actually favored what was called a zero-plus option in which the United States in its opening move would assert its preferences for zero but also indicate at the outset a willingness to consider a negotiated compromise higher than zero. The State Department was overruled on this issue as the negotiators were instructed to hold firm on the zero-only option. Indeed, the United States officially continued to do just that until President Reagan in March 1983 announced his willingness to accept an interim agreement establishing equal global levels of intermediate-range nuclear forces at the lowest mutually acceptable number.

The opening position taken by the Soviet Union in the INF talks proved to be just as nonnegotiable as that taken by the United States. The Soviet plan called for a 300 ceiling on intermediate-range nuclear missiles and aircraft for each side. The proposed reduction to 300 delivery systems was to be reached by 1990 with an interim stage of 600 in 1985. The problem with this proposal from the United States perspective was that it included not only aircraft and missiles but it would also count British and French nuclear forces in the ceiling. The United States would be allowed to retain less than 40 aircraft since French and British intermediate-range nuclear launchers stood at around 262 at the time. Under the plan the Soviet Union would be able to retain 300 triple-headed SS-20s in Europe as well as an unrestricted number of shorter-range nuclear-armed missiles and aircraft capable of striking targets in Western Europe from sites in Eastern Europe. Comparable shorter-range delivery systems located in Western Europe would be ineffective against the Soviet homeland.

As an alternative to the above proposal, the Soviet Union in the early stages of the negotiations suggested that all intermediate-range and tactical nuclear weapons be eliminated in Europe. This proposal would force all U.S. forward-based nuclear systems out of Europe as well as require the total elimination of French and British nuclear force capabilities. Although the Soviet Union would have to withdraw all of its intermediate-range nuclear missiles from the European part of the Soviet Union, Soviet strategic nuclear systems would remain as the only nuclear forces in Europe. Perhaps recognizing the total nonnegotiability of this proposal, the Soviet Union gave scant attention to the idea in subsequent rounds.

The United States and the Soviet Union disagreed intensely over what the actual European balance of forces was between East and West and exactly which forces should be affected. According to figures provided by the Soviet Union early in the negotiations, the two sides were about equally balanced in terms of intermediate-range nuclear forces with about 1,000 delivery systems on each side even prior to the introduction of the planned 572 Pershing II and cruise missiles. In its count, the Soviet Union included some 250 British and French systems, primarily composed of SLBMs, along with a number of U.S. tactical aircraft unable to reach Soviet territory from Western Europe. Since Soviet calculations sought to include all Western weapons systems capable of delivering nuclear weapons to Soviet territory, American aircraft on all six aircraft carriers in the U.S. Atlantic fleet were counted, despite the fact that only one or two were on patrol in European waters at any point in time. More extreme was the Soviet insistence upon including aircraft located in the United States simply because such aircraft could be transferred to the European theater. At the same time, the Soviet Backfire bombers located in Europe and elsewhere as well as Soviet SS-20s stationed in Asia were not counted. Soviet calculations included the Pershing I missile while exempting their own SS-12s and SS-22s which had comparable ranges. Prior to mid-1981, the Soviet Union was even counting Poseidon ballistic missiles aboard submarines that were assigned to NATO even though these weapons had already been covered by the SALT agreements.

For its part the United States objected strenuously to the inclusion of British and French forces, arguing that none of the latter's forces were committed to NATO. Although some British nuclear capabilities were designated for NATO's use, their primary function was to defend the United Kingdom. The United States also argued that it could not negotiate away the arms of another state. After all, the INF talks were bilateral, just as the Soviet Union had desired. The Soviet Union already enjoyed compensation for British and French nuclear forces, for, under the SALT agreements, it had been allowed to retain its heavy missiles as well as a considerably higher throw-weight capability. In return, the United States was allowed to keep its forward-based systems.

In the autumn of 1981, the United States presented quite a different picture with respect to the balance of intermediate-range nuclear forces between the two superpowers. Instead of equality, administration officials argued that the Soviet Union enjoyed a six to one advantage with some 3,825 weapons compared with 560 for the United States. Included in the U.S. numbers were some 2,700 Soviet fighter-bombers which the United States claimed to be slightly above the range of 1,000 kilometers but which the Soviet Union claimed to be below that threshold. The United States exempted both the Pershing I missile and F-4 Phantom fighters from its list on the grounds that they had a range of less than 1,000 kilometers—the range used to distinguish intermediate-range delivery systems from short-range ones. And so the game of numbers goes on, not so much in terms of disagreement over exactly how many weapons of a given variety each state has, but more over the issue of which systems should be counted as intermediate-range nuclear weapons.

Further complications in evaluating the military balance arose from the perspective of the qualitative aspects of weapons. Although the Soviet Union may have had more aircraft than the West, their quality was not as high. Similarly, the Soviet INF arsenal of SS-4s and SS-5s had become essentially obsolete, based as it was upon old liquid-fuelled missiles. It was concern about the obsolescence of these weapons that had led the Soviet Union to press for modernization with its SS-20 program in the first place. In fact, as the Soviet Union modernized, it dismantled some 650 of its SS-4s and SS-5s.

While the issue of equivalence was such a major stumbling block in the Strategic Arms Limitation Talks, it became just as difficult a problem in the Intermediate-range Nuclear Force Talks. In fact, the problems were perhaps even more complex in the latter because of the need to consider allied capabilities in addition to those of the United States and the Soviet Union.

In looking at the issue as to whether French and British forces should be taken into account in evaluating the balance of nuclear forces in Europe, it might be noted that the nuclear capabilities of these two states during the early eighties amounted to only about 4 percent of that of either the United States or the Soviet Union. However, both Britain and France are making rapid strides in a program of modernization that will eventually involve the replacement of all of their remaining single and clustered warheads with MIRVed SLBMs. The British, for example, plan to convert to the Trident II missile system, which represents the latest technological advance of the United States. It is estimated that by the 1990s the British will have an eightfold increase in target coverage.[2]

One complication in the INF talks, which was not a serious problem in the strategic arms talks, was the issue of the dual-capable quality of many aircraft and intermediate- and short-range missiles. Unlike the case for ICBMs, arming shorter-range missiles with conventional explosives can be cost effective. Indeed, Pershing I missiles as well as a number of cruise missiles have been armed both ways. It was the U.S. government's desire to protect the conventionally armed Pershing I missiles from being traded away that precluded a trade-off for Soviet SS-22s—a move that was favored by U.S. negotiator Paul Nitze. Negotiations over the cruise missile have also been difficult given the interest in using these vehicles for both conventional and nuclear missions.

The problem of negotiating controls on intermediate- and short-range missiles was complicated as the United States considered development of delivery systems that could be transformed with the insertion of a "clip-in" warhead, allowing either a nuclear or a conventional warhead to be inserted just prior to launch.[3] The new designs required for this flexibility would have destroyed any remaining distinguishing differences between nuclear and conventional missiles, making the problem of verification difficult at best, particularly for an agreement allowing a conventionally armed but not a nuclear-armed delivery system.

It was largely because of the dual capability of aircraft that the United States, especially its military, was hesitant to include such weapons in the negotiations. By calling the talks the Intermediate-range Nuclear Force Talks rather than using the more traditional term of Theater Nuclear Forces, the United States hoped to exclude short-range aircraft and tactical nuclear weapons from the discussion. According to Strobe Talbott, keeping aircraft out of the INF negotiations was such an obsession with the Joint Chiefs of Staff that the Assistant Secretary of Defense, Richard Perle, exploited that interest in order to obtain military support for the zero-only option.[4] Although the Joint Chiefs were predisposed to the zero-plus option, which would have allowed a limited number of INF missiles on both sides and was favored by the Department of State, Perle made it clear that such a stance would reopen the debate to include aircraft in the opening U.S. position. The threat of raising the issue was sufficient to convince the Chiefs to reconsider their position, and the end result was that aircraft were to be discussed only in some vague second phase of the negotiations, if at all.

In presenting the U.S. position in Geneva, Ambassador Paul Nitze noted several differences between aircraft and missiles that justified their separate treatment. Aircraft are designed to play a dual role, have a slower flight time, are more vulnerable to air defenses, and, unlike missiles, they are manned. Some of these distinctions are blurred when it comes to the cruise missile, which, as pointed out, can be made dual capable at a reasonable cost. The cruise missile, which is essentially a pilotless, jet-fuelled plane, also has a speed more comparable with that of aircraft as it flies about 600 miles per hour. Despite its slow speed, the cruise missile is far less vulnerable to air defenses than are manned aircraft. Its ability to fly low and to follow the terrain with highly sophisticated computer maps, makes the cruise missile relatively invulnerable to air defenses.

Complications also arose over the issue of what to do about intermediate-range nuclear forces deployed in Asia. According to the initial Soviet proposals, there would be no restrictions placed upon the number of INF forces deployed in that region. Therefore, if an agreement required the removal of such forces from Europe, they could simply be redeployed in Asia. Such a possibility created a highly sensitive issue for both U.S. allies in the region and China, as might be expected. Western European countries were also concerned because of the fact that, given the mobility of the SS-20, any such weapons reduced by agreement in Europe could simply be returned at a later date should circumstances merit such a move. For these reasons the United States has always insisted that global rather than regional ceilings on intermediate-range missiles be established.

Just as the Strategic Arms Limitation Talks allowed the SS-20 and the Backfire bomber to slip into the so-called gray area of noncoverage, so too have many INF proposals allowed weapons capable of carrying out the same European missions to escape control. For example, the Soviet short-range SS-21, SS-22, and SS-23 missiles can all strike Western European targets, particularly if deployed in Eastern Europe as was done in response to the U.S. deployment of cruise and Pershing II missiles in Western Europe beginning in November 1983. To the extent that the proposals have focused on intermediate-range missiles only, thousands of aircraft have been left uncovered. The narrow focus on restricting ground-launched cruise missiles overlooked the equally capable sea-launched cruise missile, which can be deployed on ships and submarines. Indeed, the United States has dramatically increased deployment of the latter, illustrating once again the balloon effect of arms control negotiations. Attempts to squeeze off one weapons system simply produces pressure for expansion elsewhere.

Although most attention in the INF talks was given to the Pershing II and cruise missiles on the American side and to the SS-20 for the Soviet Union, many other nuclear systems exist in the European theater and from time to time were discussed in the INF talks. When these talks opened in November 1981, the United States had 6,000 tactical nuclear warheads in Europe. Some 1,000 nuclear warheads had been removed the year before as part of the NATO two-track decision. In 1982 NATO agreed to reduce the number by a further 1,400 warheads, leaving only 4,600 theater nuclear warheads.

The primary reason for these reductions was related to the fact that they were becoming somewhat obsolete. Moreover, it was felt that by withdrawing more short-range battlefield nuclear weapons, the danger of escalating to a nuclear level during a future crisis or war would be reduced. Whatever the motivation, the fact remains that far more nuclear warheads were removed from European soil than were to be introduced under the two-track proposal calling for 572 new warheads. The critical difference in the old warheads and the new ones is that the latter are more threatening to the Soviet homeland, particularly the Pershing II missile, which is capable of striking targets in the Soviet Union in a matter of twelve minutes with a circular error probability (CEP) of less than 100 feet. The majority of the nuclear warheads already in Europe were for tactical use in the battlefield with a range below 100 kilometers.

The Soviet Union was reticent about negotiating limits on short-range delivery systems in Europe, for several of its own systems, such as its SS-12s, SS-22s, and SS-23s as well as various aircraft, would have been affected. The Soviets proposed that these systems be dealt with only after the central issue of intermediate-range nuclear missiles was settled. At the same time, the Soviet Union sought to control U.S. short-range delivery systems such as the Pershing I missile and F-4 fighters by suggesting incorrectly that their range surpassed 1,000 kilometers.

As a result of the many differences between the superpowers, progress during the early months of the INF negotiations was negligible. The United States was asking the Soviet Union to dismantle all of its intermediate-range missiles in return for a United States promise that it would not build any such weapons. The Soviet Union with its 300 ceiling was proposing substantial reductions in U.S. forward-based systems with virtually no constraints upon itself other than having to dismantle a number of obsolete SS-4s and SS-5s, which it had planned to do anyway. The complete nonnegotiability of the positions taken was readily recognized by the negotiators themselves, leading to the so-called walk in the woods proposal in the summer of 1982. Ambassador Paul Nitze suggested to his Soviet counterpart, Yuli Kvitsinsky, that the two meet together informally to try to work out a formula to overcome the negotiating impasse. The tentative agreement reached called for a ceiling on intermediate-range missiles of 75 launchers each. By restricting the count to launchers rather than missiles, the plan would have allowed the United States to deploy some 300 cruise missiles since each launcher was comprised of four cruise missiles. No Pershing II missiles, which seemed to frighten the Soviet Union most, would have been deployed. In turn, the Soviet Union would have been allowed only 225 intermediate-range missile warheads west of the Urals since each SS-20 has three warheads. The Soviets would also be allowed 90 SS-20s in Asia. The plan included some rather high ceilings on intermediate-range bombers as well as some limitations on shorter-range missiles, but no mention was made of French and British forces, and global equality in numbers was not required.

The plan ran into problems in both Washington and Moscow. Many officials in the United States government believed Nitze had exceeded his instructions. Of perhaps greatest concern was the required trade-off involving the nondeployment of the Pershing II missile, which President Reagan referred to as a "fast-flier" in contrast to the slow-flying cruise missile. Many officials were also concerned about backing off the requirement for equal global limits.

A number of commentators have argued that the United States was the first to reject the "walk in the woods" compromise as President Reagan on September 13, 1982, decided to stick with the zero-option proposal.[5] When Ambassador Nitze returned to Geneva at the end of the month, he was informed of the Soviet rejection of the compromise. Whether this rejection came as a response to the earlier U.S. decision cannot be certain. At any rate, Soviet negotiator Yuli Kvitsinsky was rebuked on continuing the informal process unless he could assure Washington's approval in advance of any tentative agreement.

Knowledgeable observers have suggested that it is quite unlikely that Kvitsinsky would have made the sorts of concessions he did in order to reach agreement without instructions from Moscow. Accordingly, it is reasoned that the Soviet Union must have approved of the general thrust and backed off because of Washington's rejection of the proposal. Ambassador Nitze, however, argues that the Soviet Union rejected the agreement first and that aspects of it were quite acceptable to the United States government.[6] Whatever the correct interpretation, the compromise did not work, and the INF negotiations stalled for several months.

During 1982–83, the Soviet Union undertook a number of initiatives in an effort to stop the imminent deployment of U.S. cruise and Pershing II missiles in Europe scheduled for late 1983. On March 16, 1982, President Leonid Brezhnev announced a unilateral quantitative and qualitative freeze on intermediate-range missiles in Europe, offering even to reduce a certain number of missiles if conditions were right. The moratorium was to last as long as negotiations on INF continued or until the United States began to deploy intermediate-range nuclear missiles on European soil. If the Soviet Union could have obtained U.S. compliance with the moratorium, it would have had no incentive to negotiate, for its objective would have been achieved.

There is some dispute as to whether or not the Soviet Union lived up to its announced unilateral moratorium. Of particular concern was whether the Soviet Union intended to include in the moratorium those sites that were under construction at the time of the announcement. According to Soviet arms expert David Holloway, the Soviet Union appears to have abided by its unilateral moratorium, except for completing work on two sites involving some 18 SS-20 missiles.[7] This view has also been supported by Raymond L. Garthoff, who believed that those sites under construction were not included just as similar sites were not included in the Interim Offensive Arms Agreement in SALT I.[8] Richard Perle, in a letter to the *Washington Post*, disputed the Garthoff assessment, arguing that the Soviet Union's own announcement referred to "termination of preparation for the deployment of missiles . . . including an end to the construction of launching positions for such missiles."[9] The latter phrase Mr. Perle took to mean an end to all construction, including that already begun. He was also disturbed that the Soviet moratorium in practice did not seem to apply to SS-20s located in Asia, which he regarded as capable of reaching West European soil. Whatever the correct interpretation, the Soviet moratorium impressed many Europeans and other advocates of restraint, leading to second thoughts about the proposed U.S. deployment.

In addition to promises of restraint on further INF deployments in return for similar U.S. restraint, the Soviet Union threatened military expansion if the United States proceeded with its planned deployment. On March 19, 1982, for example, Soviet leaders indicated that they would develop sea-based cruise missiles to counter the U.S. INF threat. The Soviet Union also began in the summer of 1982 to deploy short-range delivery systems such as SS-21s and Fencer fighter bombers on East German soil to counter the threatened NATO deployment.

Having backed away from the "walk in the woods" compromise and under increasing domestic and allied pressure to do something about the problem of nuclear weapons, President Reagan in a January 1983 letter to the European people offered to meet Yuri Andropov at the summit to sign an agreement encompassing the zero option. In making this proposal, the president knew that it would be rejected just as Gorbachev realized that his 1986 proposal for a quick, one-issue summit to sign a comprehensive test ban would not be received positively by the United States. The promise of a summit, which the adversary appeared to prize more highly in each instance, seemed not to have been a sufficient reward to compel what was perceived as a bad agreement.

Pressure for at least appearing to talk seriously about arms control continued to build, reaching a peak in the United States with the showing of the film *The Day After* in January 1983 and huge peace rallies throughout the United States. Further momentum for the peace movement resulted from President Reagan's March 8 speech before an evangelical conference in which he labeled the Soviet Union the "focus of evil" in the world. Given an increasingly bad press on the peace issue, the Reagan administration on March 29, the last day of the fourth round of the INF talks, tabled its so-called interim INF proposal. This plan represented the first significant official modification in the U.S. position on INF since the zero option was first introduced in 1981, although hints had been made prior to that time that the United States would accept something less than zero. Nevertheless, the United States continued to insist that the proposal was only an interim one and that it still preferred zero INF forces for both superpowers.

In many respects, the interim compromise was more in keeping with the initial December 1979 NATO decision that set the number of missiles higher than was thought necessary for the particular mission that NATO planners had in mind. The primary reason for introducing the missiles in the first place was not so much to match the SS-20 on a warhead per warhead basis but rather to bolster the credibility of extended deterrence. It was assumed that some of the 572 planned missiles would be traded away in negotiations with the Soviet Union. Europeans have always seemed insecure about the willingness of the United States to use its nuclear might to defend Europe against a massive conventional strike. Since it was felt that NATO's conventional forces were inferior to Soviet conventional forces, even with some 300,000 U.S. troops on European soil, European leaders have been concerned to couple the U.S. nuclear deterrent system with the defense of Europe. Given the predictable consequences of nuclear war, it was feared that the United States, in the event of a Soviet strike in Europe, would have a high incentive to remain on the sidelines or at least to limit the war, whether conventional or nuclear, to European soil. Comments made by President Reagan in October 1981 about the possibility of limiting nuclear war to the European region had hardly been reassuring to U.S. NATO allies.[10]

In presenting the interim proposal, Ambassador Nitze suggested that an acceptable range of equal levels of intermediate-range nuclear missiles for the two superpowers might be anywhere from 50 to 420 nuclear warheads each. The Soviet Union rejected all levels that would involve any U.S. deployment. It also objected to the inclusion of Asian INF forces in the global balance and the exclusion of British and French nuclear forces.

Despite Soviet rejection of the interim proposal, a number of formal concessions were made by the Soviet Union during the months leading to the scheduled U.S. deployment of cruise and Pershing II missiles. In the third round of the INF talks in the fall of 1982, the Soviet Union went so far as to suggest that some cooperative verification measures could be added to national technical means—a position it was unwilling to accept during the SALT negotiations. Several more concessions were made in January 1983 as the Soviet Union proposed reducing the level of inter-mediate-range nuclear forces to the number of nuclear weapons found in the French and British arsenals. At the time this was estimated to be 162 delivery systems, comprised largely of submarine-launched ballistic missiles. The Soviet Union for the first time also agreed to negotiate its shorter-range SS-21, SS-22, and SS-23 missiles. As pointed out earlier, these systems were capable of striking West European territory when deployed in Eastern Europe. Both concessions, however, remained con-tingent upon the United States' foregoing its deployment of intermedi-ate-range missiles on European soil.

In May the Soviet Union indicated a willingness to consider warheads in the count as well as missiles. Counting warheads instead of missiles would be beneficial to the West if one were balancing U.S. and Soviet intermediate-range nuclear forces alone since the United States cruise and Pershing II missiles are single warhead weapons, while the SS-20 has three warheads. As long as French and British forces were not fully MIRVed, such a proposal could still benefit the West. In fact, according to Soviet calculations, 140 rather than 162 SS-20s would be all that would be required to offset French and British nuclear forces. As these two NATO states modernize their forces, particularly as more SLBMs are MIRVed, a count based upon warheads would begin to favor the Soviet Union. A single MIRVed SLBM, armed with 14 warheads as permitted in the SALT II Treaty, would allow the Soviet Union to deploy almost five SS-20s with three warheads each. But even if agreement could be reached on counting warheads rather than missiles, it was obvious that disputes about the count would remain as the United States and the Soviet Union disagreed on how many warheads France and the United Kingdom had at the time. The Soviets claimed the two states had a total of 440 warheads, and the United States argued it was only about 300.

In August the Soviet Union reassured the NATO allies somewhat by making it clear that any reduction of existing SS-20s would result in the destruction of the weapons rather than redeployment in Asia. China and U.S. Asian allies could therefore breathe easier. In a proposal made on October 26, the Soviet Union offered several small concessions to the West. Included among these were less severe restrictions on convention-ally armed NATO aircraft and a freeze on the number of SS-20s in Asia, leaving that number at 108 missiles. On the eve of deployment itself, the Soviet Union offered unilaterally to scrap all of its SS-4 intermediate-range nuclear missiles in return for a U.S. deferral decision on the installation of its European missiles. It was probable that the Soviet Union would have dismantled them anyway, but it should be noted that with the reduction of both the SS-4s and SS-5s, the Soviet Union had reduced considerably more deliverable nuclear megatonnage than it had created with its deployment of SS-20s. The latter missile, however, is more accurate, albeit not nearly as accurate as the Pershing II and the cruise missile. It has been estimated, for example, that the Pershing II's kill probability against hardened targets is six times greater than that of the SS-20.[11]

A feeler was floated by Kvitsinsky on November 12 which suggested that British and French INF forces might be compensated for elsewhere, presumably in the START negotiations, thus allowing more U.S. aircraft into the ultimate INF ceilings proposed by the Soviet Union. But this offer was subsequently denied by the Soviet press agency TASS. It was also hinted that the Soviet Union would reduce its SS-20s to 120, but, as usual, the Soviet concessions required that no deployment of U.S. Pershing II and cruise missiles be permitted. Even if the Soviets were willing to go as low as 120 SS-20s, it should be noted that a better deal could have been obtained by the United States prior to the fateful December 1979 decision. At that time the Soviet Union was offering to freeze its buildup of SS-20s, which then stood at around 100 missiles, in return for a U.S. pledge not to deploy intermediate-range missiles in Europe.

In yet another effort to stall the planned deployment, the Soviet Union sought to influence European opinion by making a number of concessions in 1983 that would be particularly appealing to Western Europe. In January, for example, it offered NATO a nonaggression pact that would cover both conventional and nuclear weapons. The Soviet Union also agreed to remove all chemical weapons from Europe and, in another attempt to generate goodwill, it reacted positively to the Swedish proposal for a 300-kilometer nuclear-free zone in Central Europe. In fact, the Soviets did the Swedes one step better by proposing that the size of the zone be increased to 500-600 kilometers.

INF Deployment and Its Aftermath

With the delivery of the first nine Pershing II missiles to the Federal Republic of Germany on November 23, 1983, the Soviet Union, as it had threatened for months, broke off the INF talks, refusing to set a date for their resumption. The Soviet Union also made good on its threat to leave the START talks two weeks later. Thus 1984 became the first year in over fifteen in which bilateral strategic arms control negotiations between the United States and the Soviet Union were not held. Some bilateral negotiations did take place as the two met in June to discuss the verification requirements for a treaty banning chemical weapons. The Standing Consultative Commission established under the SALT I agreements to resolve conflicts over verification in the SALT process also met on two different occasions during the year. But all in all the year was a bleak one for arms control. Progress on arms control in 1984 seemed to be even less than that of the previous year—a year which the Arms Control Association had called the worst year for arms control since 1962.

In response to the U.S. deployment, the Soviet Union began to increase its own intermediate-range nuclear force. In the year following its walkout from the INF talks, the Soviet Union started construction on ten new SS-20 bases, which amounted to the most in any year since the SS-20 was first deployed in 1977.[12] A number of SS-22 missiles were shipped to East Germany, and on October 13, 1984, the Soviet Union announced that it had begun deployment of long-range cruise missiles aboard aircraft and submarines, many of which would be positioned close to U.S. territory.

With the Soviet Union's boycott of the arms control process, it was time for the United States to take the initiative in an effort to gain a reputation as peacemaker. Besides, 1984 was a presidential election year, and public opinion polls continued to show the public to be at odds with the president on arms control policy. Pressure for a more conciliatory position on the part of the Reagan administration was being exerted by several European allies that were having second thoughts about the two-track decision. In early May 1984 Prime Minister Bettino Craxi of Italy proposed suspending the deployment of further intermediate-range missiles if the Soviet Union would resume negotiations, and the following month, the Netherlands government announced that it would cancel deployment plans on Dutch soil if the Soviet Union would freeze further SS-20 development.[13]

On January 16, 1984, President Reagan delivered a highly conciliatory speech in which he noted that ''1984 finds the United States in the strongest position in years to establish a constructive and realistic working relationship with the Soviet Union.''[14] But it was perhaps Reagan's comments made almost a year earlier calling for a strategic defense system that set in motion the forces that ultimately brought the Soviet Union back to the negotiating table. As U.S. plans for the Strategic Defense

Initiative (SDI) gathered momentum, the Soviet Union began to express increased interest in negotiating controls on space systems. In June 1984 Soviet leader Konstantin Chernenko proposed immediate negotiations on banning anti-satellite and other space weapons. The United States agreed, but only on condition that the talks also encompass offensive weapons. Having recently made a point of walking out of the offensive missile talks, the Soviet Union rejected the condition. It was November before the Soviet Union was willing to swallow its pride and agree to the resumption of arms control negotiations that would cover both offensive and defensive weapons systems.

The Soviet Union, placed in the embarrassing position of returning to the arms control negotiations in January 1985 without obtaining satisfaction on the issue that caused its walkout in the first place, seemed determined to salvage its bargaining reputation by taking a hard stance in the resumed negotiations. Shortly after the first round of the Geneva talks ended, Paul Nitze cited a number of retractions from earlier Soviet positions.[15] In 1983, for example, the Soviet Union was willing to allow some longer-range air-launched cruise missiles, but in 1985 the Soviets were demanding that none exceed 600 kilometers. The Soviet 1985 proposals included no constraints on the deployment of SS-20s in Asia while in 1983 the Soviet Union had agreed to a limit of 108. It also seemed to have shown greater flexibility on the issue of allowable U.S. aircraft in the earlier talks. So much for the argument that building bargaining chips makes an adversary more conciliatory. The Strategic Defense Initiative may have increased Soviet incentive to return to the bargaining table, but it did not necessarily make the Soviet Union more conciliatory.

Having increased its intermediate-range nuclear force capability during 1984, the Soviet Union in April and again in October 1985 proposed a moratorium on further INF buildup. Soviet willingness to accept a moratorium on the deployment of intermediate-range delivery systems at that time was probably related to the fact that it had just begun flight testing the SS-28, which was to be the replacement missile for the eighteen year-old SS-20. The Soviet Union went a step further in November by actually reducing the number of SS-20s deployed in Europe from just under 300 to 243. But in making the reduction, it did so in a way that would permit quick reactivation.

During the November 1985 summit, President Reagan and Mikhail Gorbachev called for accelerated progress toward an "interim" INF agreement. Gorbachev for the first time also hinted that some American INF systems might remain in Europe and that a treaty restricting intermediate-range delivery systems might even be possible without agreement on strategic nuclear weapons and space defenses.[16]

As part of a renewed arms control offensive, Gorbachev visited Paris in the fall of 1985 during which he made proposals with particular appeal for West Europeans, perhaps in hopes of dividing the alliance. He promised President Francois Mitterand that the Soviet Union would accept an agreement on European missiles "outside of direct connection with the problem of space and strategic arms."[17] He also called for direct talks with France and Britain on the topic of nuclear weapons.

Continuing the conciliatory position assumed in the fall of 1985, Gorbachev on January 15, 1986, officially announced that he was no longer demanding that the Soviet Union be compensated for French and British nuclear forces. Instead, he proposed that only the United States and the Soviet Union be required to eliminate their European-based INF missiles over a 5- to 8-year period and that France and Britain pledge to freeze their respective nuclear systems. In effect, the Soviet Union was accepting the proposed U.S. zero option except for the failure to include Asian-based INF missiles in the ban. Under the plan, the United States would also have to agree not to transfer intermediate-range nuclear missiles or Trident II SLBMs to either Britain or France. Even this requirement may have been relaxed somewhat when Soviet Foreign Minister Eduard Shevardnadze, in a visit to London in July 1986, informed his hosts that the freeze does not affect French and British plans to "modernize their nuclear arsenals."[18] Important concessions were also made regarding verification as Gorbachev agreed to the on-site monitoring of the destruction of missiles.

The United States response to the various Soviet initiatives came in its February 24, 1986, proposal, which spelled out in detailed stages what the United States had suggested in more general terms in its 1983 interim proposal. According to the U.S. plan, intermediate-range missiles would be reduced during the first stage to 140 in Europe for each side along with a proportionate reduction in Asia. In the second stage those levels were to be reduced by an additional 50 percent, and in the third stage, scheduled to end in 1999, there were to be no INF missiles. Collateral limits would be made on short-range missiles, but no constraints were to be placed upon French and British nuclear forces.

As a result of the conciliatory behavior shown by the Soviet Union on the subject of intermediate-range nuclear forces during 1985–86, American officials noted that in preparing for the round of Geneva talks, which began in May 1986, they were able to identify 12 to 16 areas where U.S. and Soviet positions had converged.[19] This represented a substantial improvement over Ambassador Paul Nitze's 1982 analysis in which he found the two states to be divided on 33 issues related to controlling intermediate-range delivery systems.[20]

At the Reykjavik Conference in October 1986, agreement was reached that would have allowed each side to retain one hundred intermediate-range nuclear warheads as long as they were deployed out of range of European soil. Disagreement continued on how far to the east the Soviet Union would have to deploy its 33 allowable SS-20s and whether the United States could position its 100 Pershing II missiles in Alaska or would be confined to the continental United States. A possible solution was provided by Gorbachev in May 1987 when he offered to scrap all intermediate-range nuclear missiles on a global basis. The price, however, would be high since he made the offer contingent upon U.S. agreement to withdraw its nuclear arsenals deployed in Japan, South Korea, and the Philippines, and to restrict the movement of aircraft carriers in the region.

Also complicating the issue of controlling intermediate-range nuclear forces was the problem of what to do about short-range nuclear missiles. After the United States raised this issue, demanding that it be able to match Soviet short-range nuclear capabilities which stood at about 1,000 missiles, Gorbachev agreed to include the issue in the INF talks. During Secretary of State George Shultz's visit to Moscow in April 1987 Gorbachev offered to eliminate all shorter-range missiles with a range of 500 to 1,000 kilometers which the Soviets had deployed in Europe. The proposal was essentially a unilateral offer since the United States did not deploy any such weapons at the time.

The Soviet proposal to eliminate this category of weapons created a furor in both the United States and Europe as the Europeans feared that it would mean the beginning of the decoupling of the U.S. nuclear deterrent. But such a concern would appear not to be valid if one recalls that the United States would still retain some 4,500 nuclear devices on European soil capable of delivery by the remaining bombers and missiles stationed in Europe. The Federal Republic of Germany objected to the plan since it might force Germany to dismantle the 72 Pershing IA missiles under its control and only reluctantly agreed after the United States exerted considerable political pressure. Military interests in the United States opposed the idea since it would prevent them from deploying a shorter-range version of the Pershing II missile which would be achieved by eliminating one stage of the Pershing.

With the Soviet Union's removal of the linkage between an INF agreement and SDI in February 1987 and its decision to allow on-site inspection of factories and launch sites, considerable progress has been made—so much so that the two sides were able to agree upon a joint-working treaty proposal in early June. If agreement is reached on this issue as now seems quite likely, President Reagan will have achieved the zero option which he advocated in 1981—a proposal which was non-negotiable at the time, but with changed circumstances and a different Soviet leadership now appears achievable.

Although the United States and the Soviet Union may be successful in negotiating a ban on intermediate and short-range nuclear missiles, the meaningfulness of the agreement remains in doubt as a result of the probable exclusion of sea-based cruise missiles from the agreements. The United States is in the process of producing several thousand such weapons that can be armed with either conventional or nuclear war-heads. Since the Reagan administration, unlike its predecessor, made no effort to establish functionally related observational differences between conventional and nuclear armed SLCMs, the verification problem is a virtual nightmare. Without reasonable prospects of verification, the United States, as is perhaps appropriate, will continue to reject any effort to control the weapon system. The Soviet Union, having success-fully tested its own sea-launched cruise missile, proposed in July 1987 to limit the number to 400 nuclear-tipped SLCMs on each side.

The utility of any agreement on intermediate-range nuclear forces is likely to be undermined if similar constraints are not placed upon strate-gic weapons. With separate proposals being made in strategic and inter-mediate-range arms talks, it was possible for the United States and the Soviet Union to make a concession in one set of negotiations and take it away in the other. For example, the Soviet 1986 concession on allowing SLCMs to be deployed on submarines was undermined by the Soviet inclusion of SLCMs in their overall strategic ceiling levels. Even with agreement on limiting INF weapons, the Soviet Union can still use stra-tegic weapons against Europe as indeed a number of SS-11s and SS-19s have been so targeted, and retargeting them against the United States would be difficult.

The existence of two sets of negotiations has allowed considerable gamesmanship on the part of both sides. The Soviet Union excluded the Backfire bomber from its classification of intermediate-range systems, but continued to deny that the Backfire had intercontinental-range capa-bility. The United States has also been involved in a shell game in which it has argued that British and French forces should not be considered in START, for they are intermediate-range delivery systems and must not be considered in INF because they are strategic.[21] What all of this underscores is that any student of European regional arms control must also be aware of what is happening in concurrent strategic arms control, and it is to this topic that we now turn our attention.

STRATEGIC ARMS REDUCTION

In attempting to develop a position on the issue of strategic arms control, the Reagan administration first had to decide how to handle the issue of the unratified SALT II Treaty. While campaigning for the presidency, Reagan had declared the SALT II Treaty to be fatally flawed, particularly because of problems of verification and the failure of the treaty to do much about the huge Soviet military machine. Amending the treaty to meet the many objections appeared impossible, leading to recommendations for a fresh beginning. In an effort to separate his administration from past arms control policies, President Reagan insisted upon renaming the strategic arms talks, which finally got underway on June 29, 1982, the Strategic Arms Reduction Talks (START). This did not, however, resolve the issue of what to do about the SALT II Treaty, which the Soviet Union wanted to see ratified.

Complying with SALT

Despite the fact that a large number of senators from both parties favored the submission of the SALT II Treaty for a vote on ratification, several administration spokespersons argued that SALT II was no longer viable. Secretary of the Navy John Lehman declared in March 1981 that the United States should no longer consider itself bound by the treaty, and in testimony before the Senate Foreign Relations Committee on May 11, 1982, Secretary of State Alexander Haig declared that "we consider SALT II to be dead. We have so informed the Soviet Union."[22]

It was not long before new life was given to a treaty that had been pronounced dead as a number of bureaucratic forces pressed hard for continued U.S. adherence to the SALT agreements. Among these were the influential Joint Chiefs of Staff who felt that the SALT I and SALT II agreements placed important restrictions on further Soviet military buildup. At the same time, the SALT ceilings did not currently restrict any U.S. force modernization that had been planned under the ambitious military buildup of the Reagan administration. As a result, President Reagan on May 19, 1982, declared that the United States would not undercut the Interim Offensive Arms Agreement of SALT I or the SALT II Treaty so long as the Soviet Union did likewise. As part of this prom-

ise, the administration rescinded the planned deployment of fifty
MIRVed Minuteman III missiles that would have surpassed the SALT II
nuclear warhead limits and would have required an increase in silo size
beyond the 5 percent allowed. The administration also agreed in accordance with the SALT II Treaty to place functionally related observation
devices (FRODs) on the B-52 bombers that were to be used to carry
cruise missiles.

As weapons modernization continued during subsequent years, a
decision had to be made on whether or not to remain in compliance with
the SALT obligations. Although debate was intense on the subject
within the U.S. administration, the forces favoring support for the SALT
limits prevailed for several years. Additional Poseidons were dismantled
as new Trident submarines came on line. The Soviet Union likewise met
its obligation to stay within the SALT limits by destroying some 540
missiles and a number of Yankee-class submarines.

Continued adherence to the treaty was threatened in 1982 when the
Reagan administration chose a new basing-system for the MX missile.
The plan, referred to as Dense Pack, would have involved the placement of a hundred MX missiles in close proximity to each other so that
in-coming Soviet missiles, forced to concentrate on a compact target,
would destroy each other in a process called ''fratricide.'' It was
believed that a sufficient number of MXs would survive, allowing the
United States to strike a retaliatory blow. Former SALT negotiator
Paul Warnke has argued that Dense Pack would have violated obligations in both the Interim Offensive Arms Agreement and the SALT II
Treaty ''not to start construction of additional fixed ICBM launchers.''[23] Ultimately the administration backed off from the plan, not so
much over any concern about violating the SALT agreements but
rather as a result of scientific, public, and congressional objections to
Dense Pack.

As December 31, 1985, approached—the date on which the SALT II
Treaty would have terminated had it been ratified—a number of voices
within the U.S. military urged that the administration seek an extension
of some of the provisions of the unratified treaty.[24] On June 10, 1985,
President Reagan surprised many people by announcing that despite
charges of Soviet noncompliance, he would ''go the extra mile'' for
arms control by dismantling yet another Poseidon nuclear submarine to
accommodate deployment of a planned Trident submarine and thus
remain within the SALT ceilings.[25] The policy of not undercutting
SALT was reaffirmed by Reagan just a week before the scheduled 1985
expiration date, but the president was unwilling to commit the United

States to a full-year extension as had been proposed by General Secretary Mikhail Gorbachev.

The policy of compliance with SALT continued for several months thereafter, despite vigorous campaigning by Caspar Weinberger and others who argued that because of continuing Soviet violations of SALT and other arms control agreements, the United States should take compensatory action by exceeding the SALT limits. The campaign was not initially successful, for on April 21, 1986, it was reported that the United States had decided to dismantle yet two more Poseidon submarines and thus remain in compliance with SALT as the seventh Trident submarine was brought on line.[26] Given this decision, it was quite unexpected when the president announced on May 27, 1986, that the United States would no longer make its strategic planning decisions on the basis of the SALT restrictions and that the United States would in all probability exceed those limits when it deployed its 131st bomber loaded with air-launched cruise missiles later in the year. It was also indicated that the administration would continue with its planned Poseidon dismantlement, not because of concern about complying with SALT, but rather because it made economic sense to do so. Six years into the Reagan administration it appeared that conservative forces had finally destroyed a hated symbol of U.S.-Soviet détente. The SALT II Treaty, which had been declared dead several years earlier, seemed to have finally met that fate on November 28, 1986, with the threatened cruise missile deployment. The Soviet Union, while noting that the U.S. action freed it from its SALT commitments, indicated that it would continue to adhere to the SALT II Treaty for the time being.

Perhaps the major factor leading to the decision to scuttle SALT in 1986 was the fact that the Joint Chiefs of Staff had taken a neutral stance on the subject, declaring continued compliance to be a political question not a military one. As long as it would restrain Soviet military programs without appreciably affecting the U.S. strategic buildup, as the Chiefs continued to believe it might, SALT adherence was beneficial to U.S. military interests.

A number of arguments have been made over the years by opponents of the SALT agreements to justify their opposition to continued compliance. In the first place it was argued that the Soviet Union had violated the SALT agreements on numerous occasions and that the United States should therefore take action to assure that it is not placed at a disadvantage. The two most serious violations, according to the administration as it sought to justify the May 1986 decision, were the Soviet construction of the mobile SS-25 intercontinental-range ballistic missile and the continued efforts by the Soviet Union to encrypt the telemetry of its missile tests in violation of the prohibition on interference with the national technical means of verification used by the other side.

As will be recalled, the SALT II Treaty allowed only one new intercontinental-range ballistic missile, and this the Soviet Union declared to be the SS-24, which was first tested in the fall of 1982. In December 1982 the Soviet Union tested the SS-25, which it began to deploy three years later. The Soviet Union claimed that the latter missile was only a modernized version of the SS-13 while the United States declared that the new missile went beyond the 5 percent SALT II allowance on the size of a new missile as measured by its length, largest diameter, launchweight, and throw-weight. ACDA Director Kenneth L. Adelman has argued that the SS-25 is not just "slightly" larger than the SS-13 but is roughly twice its size.[27] According to another analysis, intelligence community experts believe that the SS-25 exceeded the 5 percent limit only with respect to throw-weight, and even that is ambiguous since estimates have been so inconsistent that the variation might still be within the 5 percent range.[28] The Soviet Union has asserted that assessments of the throw-weight of the SS-25 have been overestimated by the United States because of the inclusion of a heavy package of test instruments.

Second, in declaring itself no longer bound by SALT, the United States argued that it was necessary to negotiate a new treaty that would provide substantial reductions in strategic arsenals. According to U.S. officials, SALT did little to cap Soviet strategic growth as the Soviet Union was able to increase the number of its strategic nuclear warheads from 5,000 to 9,200 while adhering to the SALT II limits.[29] Of course, in doing so it was only catching up to the United States, which had an appreciable lead in warheads over the Soviet Union when SALT II was signed.

Third, it was suggested that even if the SALT agreement had some restraining effects on Soviet strategic growth, it was unlikely that the Soviet Union would markedly increase its strategic power even if U.S. rejection of the treaty would allow it to do so. Economic restrictions and security interests would probably dictate little change in Soviet strategic spending whether the United States continued to comply with SALT or not. It is interesting to note in this regard that some of the very same people in the administration who were saying earlier that SALT II should not be ratified since it would allow the Soviet Union to "break out" of the arms constraints by developing a first-strike capability were arguing in 1986 that even without SALT constraints the Soviet Union was unlikely to add appreciably to its missile capability.

Fourth, it was noted that since the SALT II Treaty had expired several months before, there was little need to continue to adhere to its restrictions. The treaty limits could have been followed until a replacement treaty was negotiated, and there was precedence for such an approach. Both sides continued to honor the Interim Offensive Arms Agreement long beyond its 1977 expiration date. It could be argued that had the expiration date of the SALT II Treaty been a major consideration for the administration, it would have ended its involvement with SALT on December 31, 1985, rather than almost five months later.

Fifth, some administration officials perhaps saw rejection of the SALT II Treaty as the first step toward a possible renegotiation or even a U.S. abrogation of the 1972 ABM Treaty that was a part of the SALT I agreements. The ABM Treaty had become a particular target for those favoring the Strategic Defense Initiative, popularly referred to as "Star Wars," since SDI would probably violate portions of the ABM Treaty.

Finally, some administration advisors favored strong presidential action on the SALT II Treaty as a way of enhancing the president's bargaining strength in arms control negotiations. By no longer adhering to the SALT limitations, the United States was implicitly communicating that it might engage in an unlimited arms race that by all accounts the Soviet Union cannot afford at this time as Mikhail Gorbachev has been attempting to change Soviet priorities by paying more attention to domestic economic development.

In making the decision to end adherence to the SALT II Treaty, the administration considerably misjudged the reaction of both the United States Congress and its NATO allies. On June 19, 1986, the House of Representatives overwhelmingly approved a nonbinding resolution by a vote of 256 to 145, urging the president to remain in compliance with SALT. Threats were also made by Congress to restrict spending on any weapons system that would exceed the SALT limits.

During a NATO meeting held in Nova Scotia within days of the U.S. announcement, the foreign ministers present unanimously criticized the decision.[30] Even Prime Minister Margaret Thatcher of Britain, Reagan's closest NATO ally on strategic matters, was highly critical of the president's move. The fact of the matter is that Europe has become more interested in arms control while the United States has become less interested. The pattern was essentially the opposite of that of the seventies.

Even though the United States was clearly justified from the standpoint of international law in making the decision to consider itself no longer bound by the SALT II Treaty, the question remains as to whether or not it was a wise decision politically and militarily. By rejecting the continuance of the SALT obligations, the United States lost the opportunity to call attention to alleged Soviet violations of the treaty. No longer would it be able to raise such issues and perhaps be able to resolve some of them as it had during various meetings of the Standing Consultative Commission in the past.

Second, since the Soviet Union was in a better position than the United States to increase its offensive arsenal rapidly, taking away the SALT ceilings would be to the American disadvantage. The Soviet SS-18, which had so preoccupied U.S. military planners in the past, could easily be MIRVed to 20 or 30 warheads rather than limited to the ten allowed under SALT II. The Soviet Union also has an advantage over the United States in the number of existing plants for constructing additional missiles. Congressman Les Aspin has estimated that because of production-line disparity alone, Soviet forces could grow 65 percent by 1989 compared to 45 percent growth for the United States.[31] A June 1985 CIA study estimated that the Soviet Union could rapidly expand its strategic forces to nineteen thousand warheads from the current ten thousand if released from SALT II restrictions.[32] Congressional and budgetary restraints within the United States would make it difficult for the U.S. to follow suit.

Third, removal of the limitations on numbers of strategic weapons would allow the Soviet Union to modernize further without destroying existing weapons. Although Assistant Secretary of Defense Richard Perle has argued that it makes little difference whether the Soviets dismantle their SS-11s and SS-13s in view of the relative obsolescence of these missiles,[33] the fact of the matter is that the additional numbers of missiles would increase pressures to add to the U.S. strategic forces to guarantee ICBM survivability. Concern about the huge Soviet military offensive capability, which would only grow larger without the SALT dismantling requirements, was the major reason that the Reagan administration rejected the SALT II Treaty in the first place.

Fourth, the rejection of the SALT II Treaty would allow the Soviet Union to engage in unrestricted missile testing. Under the treaty all multiple ICBM tests and individual tests directed outwardly from the country were to be announced well in advance. This provision was designed to lessen the danger of misconstruing a test with an actual attack, but it has the additional advantage of allowing the adversary to monitor a testing program more closely. This is important, particularly if one wants to ascertain if the other side is testing multiple missile launchings. Such tests would be essential for any state planning a first strike since, to be successful, such a strike would require the coordinated launching of hundreds of missiles.

Finally, the verification opportunities provided by the treaty would be lost if SALT were overthrown without a replacement. Under such conditions, the Soviet Union would have little difficulty concealing its strategic weapons tests and deployments. Without the SALT verification requirements, silos could be covered and mobile missiles hidden. It would also no longer be illegal to interfere with the national technical means of verification of the other side. Although the Soviet Union may not have adhered fully to the restrictions on the encryption of its missile tests, it has still allowed the United States to collect considerable information about Soviet missile capability—information that may well be lost without SALT.

Regardless of one's views about continued compliance with SALT, one might legitimately ask why the administration chose to make the announcement in May 1986 that it would no longer adhere to the SALT limits after having lived up to them for several years. After all, the decision had already been made in April to dismantle two Poseidon submarines, thus keeping the United States under the SALT limit for several more months. The proposed deployment of cruise missiles on the 131st B-52 bomber that threatened to exceed the SALT ceiling was more than six months off, and the United States even then could have stayed within the SALT II limits by destroying a few additional delivery systems. In fact, the Navy itself had planned to dismantle the *Alexander Hamilton*, but the *Hamilton* was given a reprieve at the last minute as the United States substituted another Poseidon submarine that had been damaged by running aground. With minimal destruction of existing systems, the United States could have remained under the SALT II ceiling until 1988 when the seventh Trident was scheduled to be commissioned.

There are both economic and military reasons justifying the dismantlement of Poseidon submarines, and these were used by the administration in arguing for the spring 1986 destruction of the two Poseidons. The nuclear reactors in both had reached their useful life, and the submarines were in desperate need of refurbishing. It was estimated that keeping them in commission would have cost $300 million each, diverting scarce military resources from areas that were viewed as more important.[34]

The reason for the decision no longer to adhere to the SALT limitations was probably due largely to bureaucratic compromise. With a divided administration, the decision allowed those who opposed arms control agreements and the entire SALT process to claim a victory. At the same time, those elements within the administration favoring continued adherence to the SALT limitations had some breathing space since the anticipated violation of the SALT agreements regarding the size of missile forces was still some months away. Supporting the position of the arms controllers, the decision provided that the two submarines would be dismantled rather than merely mothballed as the Pentagon had preferred.

Confusion surrounded the decision to back away from the no-undercut policy because of the varying interpretations presented by President Reagan. But when the conflicting statements were sorted out, it was clear that the United States regarded the SALT agreements dead and would no longer make its strategic planning contingent upon SALT restrictions. The final nail was driven into the SALT coffin during a special July 1986 meeting of the Standing Consultative Commission (SCC) called to review the U.S. decision rejecting continued compliance with SALT. At this time, the United States informed the Soviet Union that the 1972 Interim Offensive Arms Agreement and the SALT II Treaty would no longer be "fitting subjects in the SCC."[35]

In some respects the decision was very similar to President Eisenhower's announcement on December 29, 1959, that the United States no longer felt itself bound by the unilateral moratorium on nuclear testing, despite the fact that it had no immediate intention to resume testing. The Eisenhower statement may have unfortunately helped minimize the world outrage against the Soviet Union when the latter eventually broke the moratorium in September 1961 and began engaging in the most extensive series of nuclear tests in history. After all, it was the United States which had first declared itself to be free to resume nuclear testing. The Soviet Union may likewise use this latest United States announcement regarding SALT as an excuse for engaging in even more blatant and excessive violations of the SALT agreements. Unless there is an immediate military need and willingness to reverse an arms control restraint, a nation might do well to think about the implications of making premature announcements of this sort.

A New Start with START?

As has been indicated, the Reagan administration came into power with a number of reservations about arms control, and only after considerable domestic and international pressure did it agree to participate in negotiations on the subject. Since so much energy had been spent criticizing SALT, it was necessary to present proposals that diverged from past U.S. positions. A major consideration in opposing SALT had been that the agreements failed to reduce strategic arms to any appreciable degree. It was therefore to be expected that the United States would present more sweeping proposals calling for substantial cuts in existing strategic arms.

The opening proposals for strategic arms reduction presented by the Reagan administration were doomed to failure from the beginning, focused as they were upon deep reductions in Soviet ICBM capability, which represents the major part of the Soviet nuclear deterrent. Under the American plan, introduced by President Reagan in his May 1982 Eureka College speech, both sides would have been required during the first phase to reduce the total number of individual missile warheads by about a third to a level of 5,000 each, positioned on no more than 850 land or sea-based missiles. Only half of the 5,000 warheads could be placed on land-based missiles, which are the most accurate and threatening to the United States. What the administration seemed to have in mind in making the proposal was a complete restructuring of the Soviet strategic arsenal so that less reliance would be placed on Soviet ICBM capability and more on its SLBM forces.

From the standpoint of a credible deterrent posture it might appear highly desirable to force the Soviet Union to place a higher percentage of its strategic power into SLBM capability, but the proposal was a threat to Soviet strategic interests. The Soviet Union was being asked to install half of its strategic capability on SLBMs, thus placing it at a distinct disadvantage since the bulk of Soviet SLBMs are of the older liquid-fueled variety. Furthermore, the Soviet Union is forced to operate from far fewer overseas naval bases than the United States, making it impossible for the Soviets to have as high a percentage of submarines on active duty as the United States. Equal numbers under these conditions would mean unequal capabilities.

Since the Soviet Union has about 75 percent of its strategic nuclear power on land-based missiles compared to 25 percent for the United States, the proposal would have required that the Soviet Union reduce its ICBM force by 1,500 missiles compared to 850 for the United States. The "collateral constraints" also included in the U.S. proposals would have forced the Soviet Union to reduce substantial numbers of its medium and heavy ICBMs that form the bulwark of Soviet nuclear capability. Only 210 such missiles would be allowed, down from the existing 788. Within these limits the Soviet Union would have been required to reduce its largest and best missile, the SS-18, by two-thirds from its current number of 308 to 110. At the same time, the United States would have been allowed to build both the highly accurate and destructive MX and Trident II missile systems.

While concentrating upon reducing the most powerful of the Soviet strategic forces during the first phase, the initial U.S. START proposal would have deferred action aimed at controlling those weapons in which the United States had a considerable advantage—the cruise missile and the heavy bomber—until the second phase. Further restrictions upon Soviet nuclear capability would also have been required in the latter phase as the Soviet Union would have to reduce its total nuclear throw-weight to levels compatible with those of the United States. Some objective observers believed, however, that the USSR was justified in maintaining the extra throw-weight given its less accurate missiles and inability to have as many submarines on station at any given time.

The extremity of the United States position in its initial START proposals was recognized by Alexander Haig, who was secretary of state at the time the proposals were made. Haig writes in his memoirs that the proposed limits on ICBM warheads "would require such drastic reductions in the Soviet inventory as to suggest they were unnegotiable."[36] Although a case can be made for beginning a round of negotiations with extreme positions, as suggested in chapter 3, effective negotiation requires at least the promise of some benefits for the other side.

The Soviet response to the Reagan strategic arms control proposal was presented initially in July 1982 and confirmed publicly in December by Yuri V. Andropov shortly after he had succeeded Leonid Brezhnev as head of the Communist party. The Soviet plan provided for a reduction in strategic delivery vehicles, including both missiles and bombers, to 1800. To meet such levels, the Soviet Union would have to reduce the number of its strategic delivery systems more than 25 percent compared to about 10 percent for the United States. These reductions were close to those proposed by President Carter in March 1977 but fell far short of the 850 missile limit in the Reagan plan. In contrast to American proposals, the Soviet plan did not specify a sublimit on the number of ICBM warheads, and the number of bombers would be restricted from the beginning instead of waiting until the second phase.

Although one can argue that the initial U.S. START proposal was nonnegotiable, the Soviet plan included various provisions that made it totally unacceptable to the United States. Chief among these was the requirement that the United States dismantle its forward-based systems. The pattern had become well established as virtually all new strategic arms negotiations have begun with similar demands. The Soviet argument for insisting upon a ban on forward-based systems is that such weapons can strike Soviet territory and thus must be regarded as strategic. After it is clear that no progress can be made so long as such a pro-

posal is on the table, the Soviet Union has usually dropped the
requirement, asking the United States to respond to the Soviet gesture
with concessions of its own. In the case of the START talks, the appro-
priateness of including forward-based systems in the Soviet proposals
was questionable since such systems were more relevant to the ongoing
INF talks.

Just as the United States attempted to limit Soviet areas of strength,
the Soviet Union in its proposals sought to reduce U.S. advantages, particularly with respect to intercontinental-range bombers and air-
launched cruise missiles. Limits on bombers were made an integral part
of the Soviet ceilings on delivery systems, albeit with the Soviet Backfire bomber exempted as before. More serious was the seeming Soviet
retraction on air-launched cruise missiles that were limited to a range of
600 kilometers. Previously the Soviet Union had agreed to an unlimited
range for such missiles as long as they were not deployed on more than
120 bombers with an average limit of 28 missiles per bomber. It was not
until July 1983 that the Soviet Union returned to its SALT II position by
dropping the 600 kilometer restriction.

In July 1983 the Soviet Union added explicit sublimits to its overall
proposed ceiling of 1,800 delivery systems. Under the modified plan
each side would be restricted to a sublimit of 1,200 MIRVed delivery
systems, consisting of ICBMs, SLBMs, and bombers loaded with cruise
missiles. Such a sublimit represents a reduction of 120 delivery systems
from the SALT II levels. MIRVed ICBMs and SLBMs would be limited
to 1,080 of which 680 could be ICBMs. Of particular concern to the
United States was the fact that the Soviet plan would allow the Soviet
Union to retain all of its SS-18 and SS-19 missiles.

Both the United States and the Soviet Union held rigidly to these
proposals for a number of months as little progress was made in the
START negotiations. When the United States finally modified its
START position in 1983, the change was primarily due to domestic
pressures rather than a reaction to any moves made by the Soviet
Union. For example, its June 1983 plan calling for a relaxation in the
850 ceiling for land- and sea-based missiles was proposed in an effort
to accommodate the development and deployment of the Midgetman
missile as proposed by the President's Commission on Strategic
Forces. This blue-ribbon commission, commonly referred to as the
Scowcroft Commission, had been appointed by President Reagan to
develop an acceptable plan for basing the MX missile. Over thirty previous basing-modes had been proposed—all of which failed for various political, economic, or strategic reasons. In recommending that

some 100 MX missiles be placed in existing silos on an interim basis, the Scowcroft Commission recognized that the problem of ICBM vulnerability would not be solved. Consequently, it went on to recommend that the United States should in the future attempt to place less reliance on stationary MIRVed ICBMs and instead develop a smaller mobile ICBM, which was dubbed the Midgetman. It was believed that the Midgetman missile would help stabilize the nuclear deterrent system, because it would be less threatening and a less inviting target than current multiple-warhead missiles. Since each Midgetman would have only one warhead, the 850 limit on ICBMs and SLBMs would be unduly restrictive, leading the United States to suggest that 1,100–1,200 missiles would be a more appropriate ceiling. Although the U.S. willingness to increase the number of allowable missiles represented movement toward the Soviet position, the limit of 2,500 warheads on land-based missiles would remain, making the proposal just as objectionable from the Soviet perspective. At that time a 2,500 warhead ceiling would have meant a cut of more than half in the Soviet warheads on intercontinental missiles while permitting a slight increase in comparable American warheads.[37]

Similarly, the administration's decision in October to incorporate the idea of build-down into the U.S. START proposal was not a direct reaction to any Soviet initiative but was rather a response to congressional pressure. Forty-five senators had cosponsored a resolution supporting the build-down proposal, making it clear that their support of the MX missile would be dependent upon the administration's accepting the idea of build-down. In its simplest terms build-down required that each superpower remove more than one nuclear warhead for each new one deployed. The plan, as incorporated into the United States proposal, would attempt to encourage the Soviet Union to place more of its strategic capability into less vulnerable mobile systems by requiring that more warheads be destroyed if a nation deploys fixed, land-based missiles than if it deploys sea-based or mobile land-based missiles. Accordingly, two old warheads would have to be destroyed for every new fixed ICBM warhead; three warheads, for every two new SLBM warheads. Only mobile land-based missile warheads could be replaced on a one-to-one basis. In order to assure that reductions would actually occur, the American plan also required an annual build-down of at least 5 percent, regardless of whether or not modernization occurred.

As might be expected, U.S. governmental interests were hardly unanimous in their support for the plan. The Arms Control and Disarmament Agency strongly opposed build-down until overruled by the president.[38] The Joint Chiefs of Staff were unenthusiastic, but ultimately acquiesced, surmising correctly that the Soviet Union would reject the plan anyway. The civilian chiefs in the Defense Department opposed the build-down plan; the National Security Council was cool to the idea; and the State Department remained neutral. The primary support came from the president's political advisors, who were concerned primarily about congressional and public criticism of the president's record on arms control.

In the short term, the build-down proposal could be quite destabilizing, particularly as long as the United States and the Soviet Union continued to rely upon fixed multiple-warhead ICBMs. U.S. plans for deploying 100 MX missiles with ten warheads each would require the dismantlement of 2,000 nuclear warheads. As many as 550 Minuteman IIIs with three warheads each and 350 Minuteman IIs and Titans, each armed with one warhead, would have to be reduced. From a relatively secure 1,050 launchers, the United States would have to deter the Soviet Union with only 250 land-based missiles. A very attractive target for a Soviet preemptive attack would consequently be provided. The required reductions would also make the Soviet Union, particularly to the extent that it wanted to continue relying upon its powerful SS-18, far more vulnerable to a U.S. preemptive strike, leading to even greater pressures upon the Soviet leaders to initiate a nuclear attack.[39]

Concessions made by the United States with respect to heavy bombers and ALCMs, areas in which it enjoyed the advantage, were more meaningful, but perhaps not as significant as might appear at first blush. The U.S. spring 1983 proposal to establish a ceiling of 400 heavy bombers was of little interest to the Soviet Union since the Soviet Backfire bomber would be counted in the totals. As pointed out in the last chapter, whether or not to include the Backfire as a strategic weapon was a controversial issue since that bomber does not have intercontinental-range capability to fly to and from the United States without refueling.

The October proposal to collapse the two phases of the U.S. START plan into a single one may have been potentially more important, but since the specific restrictions proposed for the second phase held little interest for the Soviet Union, other than the fact that bombers and air-launched cruise missiles would be regulated, the significance of the move is questionable. The Soviet Union obviously could not be pleased with that part of the plan that moved the ceilings on nuclear throw-weight, where the Soviets enjoyed a considerable superiority, into the first phase. Although the United States showed some flexibility in indicating that the total throw-weight need not be reduced as low as current

American levels, the proposal remained unacceptable to the Soviet Union since it was also made clear that the United States would have the right to increase its own throw-weight to whatever level was agreed upon.

In a similar vein, the meaningfulness of the flexibility shown by the United States on the issue of air-launched cruise missiles may have been more apparent than real. Although the June 1983 American proposal called for limits on ALCMs that would be lower than the 28 average per bomber agreed upon in SALT II, the United States was already adhering to a unilateral pledge, made at the time of signing the SALT II Treaty, not to place more than twenty ALCMs on each B-52 bomber. In fact, it was only installing twelve per bomber. In deploying air-launched cruise missiles on the B-1 bomber, the Reagan administration planned to position only twenty-two per bomber, somewhat below the average allowed. To agree to lower numbers in effect was doing no more than continuing existing U.S. policy.

Prior to Mikhail Gorbachev's rise to power in March 1985 about the only strategic arms concessions offered by the Soviet Union, aside from returning to positions it had already agreed upon in SALT II, were those spelling out sublimits on the number of MIRV missiles that would be allowed to each side. There are several plausible explanations for the rigidity shown by the Soviet Union in the START talks. Perhaps the main reason for its lack of flexibility was related to its belief that a SALT II Treaty had already been negotiated and it was the responsibility of the United States to ratify an agreement that the U.S. had already signed. Second, strategic arms issues did not lend themselves as readily to the Soviet objective of dividing the Western alliance system as did the issue of intermediate-range missiles. As a result, greater Soviet flexibility was shown with respect to the latter negotiations. Third, the Soviet Union had threatened to end all talks on strategic arms control as well as the INF talks if the United States deployed Pershing II and cruise missiles in Europe, and it made good on its threat within two weeks of the initial deployment. Finally, the lack of Soviet initiatives and flexibility on strategic arms was undoubtedly related to the fact that within a period of only three years after the Soviet Union tabled its initial START proposal it had four different leaders—Leonid Brezhnev, Yuri Andropov, Konstantin Chernenko, and Mikhail Gorbachev. Under such conditions a state must necessarily be more preoccupied with internal matters rather than foreign affairs. The rapidity of the changes hardly provided adequate time for a new Soviet administration to develop its own arms control policy.

The Gorbachev Initiatives

With the resumption of arms control negotiations under the rubric of the Geneva umbrella talks, which began in March 1985 and consisted of separate negotiations on strategic arms, intermediate-range nuclear forces, and strategic defensive systems, there was renewed hope for some progress on offensive arms control. Soon after the Geneva talks got underway, Konstantin Chernenko died, leaving the reins of power to his successor, Mikhail S. Gorbachev. Although the succession may have slowed the new government somewhat, by mid-1985 the Soviet Union began offering more arms control initiatives than it had at any time in the postwar period. These included a number of unilateral initiatives that have already been noted, such as a freeze on further deployment of INF forces in April 1985 and extended in October. The Soviet Union also instituted a unilateral ban on nuclear testing on August 6, 1985, extending it several times despite the fact that the United States failed to follow suit.

A number of concessions involving verification measures were also made during the early Gorbachev period. These included agreement to open Soviet space laboratories to outside inspection; acceptance of monitoring posts to verify Soviet and American troop reductions in central Europe; proposals to allow on-site inspection of Soviet nuclear tests (in return for U.S. acceptance of a test ban moratorium); agreement to allow on-site verification of INF missile destruction;[40] procedures for monitoring long-range missiles as they leave the factory; restrictions on mobile missiles that would confine them to specified areas in order to facilitate detection; and agreement to make trains carrying SS-24 mobile ICBMs look different from ordinary rail cars.[41] When these moves are added to the Soviet January 1985 proposal for on-site verification of chemical weapon production centers and its February agreement with the International Atomic Energy Agency to provide inspection of Soviet peaceful nuclear energy facilities, it is clear that the Soviet Union had come a long way in terms of agreeing to more onerous inspection requirements.

In a dramatic reversal of its strategic arms proposals that until that time had called for only minimal reductions below the SALT II levels, the Soviet Union in late September 1985 introduced a plan calling for a 50 percent reduction in offensive delivery systems, contingent on the cessation of U.S. efforts to develop its proposed strategic defense system. In a compromise with the United States position, the Soviet plan also called for sublimits on a given weapons system to be placed at 60 percent of the total. Although this was 10 percent higher than what the

United States wanted, it was a considerable improvement over existing Soviet force structures in which land-based missiles represented 75 percent of the total.

Although on the surface the Soviet Union finally seemed to be accepting the Reagan administration's proposals for extensive cuts in strategic delivery systems, the proposed Soviet reductions would affect both U.S. intermediate-range and intercontinental-range delivery systems while exempting comparable Soviet INF forces. The rationale was that American intermediate-range nuclear forces could reach Soviet territory but Soviet INF forces could not strike American territory. For good measure, the Soviet Union also included all of the U.S. nuclear forward-based delivery systems in the proposed cuts and a ban on modernization that threatened the U.S. Trident II D-5 missile, the Stealth bomber, and the Midgetman missile while allowing the Soviet Union to deploy its new SS-23, SS-24, and SS-25 missiles as well as a new bomber.[42] The result was that the Soviet proposal was a complete nonstarter. What the Soviet Union was asking was an across-the-board 50 percent reduction of all U.S. systems—short-range, intermediate-range, and intercontinental-range—while allowing only its intercontinental-range systems to be included in the reductions. Fifty percent clearly did not mean 50 percent for the Soviet Union. Nevertheless, the Soviet Union was able to capitalize upon world headlines showing it to be in favor of substantial arms reductions. Clearly the Soviet Union had assumed the upper hand in the arms control propaganda war.

During the next several months a virtual blizzard of arms control proposals came from Soviet sources. In almost all cases the proposals were presented publicly in major speeches and were often published in paid advertisements in Western newspapers. While continuing to support its proposal for a 50 percent reduction in those weapons that the Soviet Union labeled as strategic, the Soviet Union in October called for a quick 200–300 reduction in ICBMs on both sides to show good faith. The next month it offered to reduce its heavy ICBMs in return for U.S. limits on the planned Strategic Defense Initiative.

The Soviet Union's most radical disarmament measures were proposed by General Secretary Gorbachev in January 1986 when he presented a fifteen-year plan calling for complete nuclear disarmament in which all nuclear weapon states were expected to participate.[43] The proposal for the first time placed an explicit deadline for the initial 50 percent reduction that was to be reached over the next five to eight years. Also starting in 1990, other countries must freeze their nuclear arms and agree not to deploy them outside their own borders.

Like so many general and complete disarmament proposals of the past, perhaps it is only the first phase that should be taken seriously. As indicated previously, the 50 percent reduction required in this phase was unacceptable to the United States as long as the Soviet Union insisted upon including American forward-based systems in the proposal. An important concession was made in this regard in late May 1986 when the Soviet Union tabled a plan that dropped the demand that U.S. nuclear-capable fighter planes and carrier aircraft within range of the Soviet Union be counted as strategic weapons. The Soviet Union also no longer insisted that submarine-launched long-range cruise missiles be banned. In presenting these important concessions, the Soviet Union at the same time took a step backward when it modified its strategic reduction requirements by calling for a one-third reduction rather than a 50 percent reduction as previously proposed. This change meant a new ceiling for each side of 8,000 strategic nuclear charges (warheads and bombs). With a 60 percent limit on nuclear warheads based on land-based missiles, some 4,800 ICBM warheads would be allowed under the new plan. The earlier ceilings, placed at 6,000 and 3,600 warheads, respectively, were actually somewhat more acceptable to the United States than were the new limits.

United States concessions to the various Gorbachev initiatives were relatively slow in coming, partially as a result of serious divisions within the Reagan administration itself. In early November 1985 Secretary of State George Shultz met Gorbachev in Moscow where he presented the American response to the Soviet September proposal for a 50 percent reduction in strategic arms. The U.S. plan, which represented the first new U.S. strategic arms proposal in two years, accepted the notion of a 50 percent reduction but made explicit recommendations on how those reductions might be applied. According to the proposal, reentry vehicles on ICBMs and SLBMs would be limited to 4,500 warheads, 500 less than provided in President Reagan's Eureka proposal. A subceiling of 3,000 warheads on ICBMs would be allowed, roughly halfway between the earlier U.S. proposal of 2,500 and the proposed Soviet limit of 3,600. The American proposal also called for a 1,500 ceiling on the number of air-launched cruise missiles and a 350 limit on heavy bombers. A 50 percent reduction in ballistic missile throw-weight would be required of the Soviet Union, but Soviet throw-weight would still be left at a figure slightly higher than that of the United States. In essence, these proposals changed previous U.S. strategic arms control proposals very little other than providing adjustments for slightly deeper cuts to match the Soviet-proposed 50 percent reduction. Even the build-down concept was retained as the suggested means for implementing the agreed reductions. Two weeks after Shultz's visit to Moscow Mikhail Gorbachev and Ronald Reagan met at the Geneva summit where they confirmed that one of their primary goals was to obtain a 50 percent reduction in strategic arms.

Perhaps the most controversial aspect of the U.S. November 1985 plan was its proposed ban upon the deployment of mobile, land-based intercontinental ballistic missiles. Not only would adherence to such a provision be strongly resisted by the Soviet Union, which was in the process of deploying the mobile SS-24 and SS-25 ballistic missiles; but many U.S. military strategists, beginning with members of the Scowcroft Commission, felt that American security could be enhanced by producing the mobile Midgetman missile in order to assure an invulnerable ICBM capability.

Some have suggested that the U.S. inclusion of a ban on mobile ICBMs, at that time, was merely a bargaining ploy to be relinquished as soon as the United States perfected the Midgetman, which was not expected to be operational until the early 1990s. Others would have been just as pleased if such a missile did not enter the U.S. arsenal, and for them the proposal was supported as a way of obtaining their procurement preferences. Although mobile missiles can help stabilize nuclear deterrence by making land-based missiles less vulnerable, their effect on arms control can be devastating since verifying such weapons, particularly in the absence of a complete ban upon them, is difficult at best.

A number of military experts opposed production of the Midgetman because it would compete with other preferred weapons systems for funds. Despite its relatively small size, the Midgetman was not an inexpensive weapons system. In fact, according to a 1985 Air Force estimate, each warhead on the Midgetman, in view of the missile's mobility and need for an operating team, would cost four times as much as each one on the MX.[44] To make the missile cost-effective, some Pentagon officials began suggesting that the Midgetman be increased in size and carry additional warheads, defeating the purpose of the missile in the first place. Indicative of the general lack of support for the Midgetman in the Pentagon was Secretary of Defense Caspar Weinberger's blunt acknowledgement in the fall of 1985 that "the Midgetman is a missile that is designed by Congress . . . and we are working on it because that's our direction."[45]

Apparently the administration has not been serious about its proposed ban on mobile missiles, for in its FY-1988 budget it asked for an additional 50 MX missiles that would be placed on railroad cars to make them less vulnerable to enemy attack. Although requests were also made at the same time for continued development of the Midgetman, many in the Pentagon believed that budgetary pressures would dictate against the latter, allowing further concentration upon the preferred MX mobile missle system.[46]

At the Reykjavik summit in October 1986, Gorbachev and Reagan apparently agreed to the ultimate destruction of all ICBMs, which would have made the issue of mobile missiles moot. As the meetings have now been reconstructed, it appears that the two reaffirmed the 1985 Geneva Summit goal for a 50 percent reduction in strategic arms to be achieved over a five-year period.[47] In the final sessions at Reykjavik, President Reagan proposed the elimination of all ballistic missiles over a period of ten years. Such a plan would have deprived the Soviets of their most formidable weapons while allowing the United States to capitalize on cruise missiles and bombers where it had a decided advantage. Consequently, Gorbachev countered by proposing the elimination of all nuclear weapons as he had been suggesting since January. Unexpectedly, the president's response was one of agreement.

Subsequently, controversy has raged over the issue both as to whether President Reagan agreed to the elimination of all nuclear arms in ten years as Gorbachev claims or just ballistic missiles as the president now says. Regardless of which position was taken, it is clear that the issue of the follow-on to the first-phase 50 percent reduction had not been settled in Washington or with the NATO allies prior to Reykjavik. A barrage of criticism erupted on both sides of the Atlantic as many defense analysts expressed concern about the need for continued Western reliance upon nuclear weapons, including ballistic missiles, to deter superior Soviet conventional forces. Many military experts within and outside the administration breathed a collective sigh of relief that the wide-ranging tentative agreement on the abolition of strategic nuclear arms ultimately failed as a result of President Reagan's rejection of the Soviet insistence that agreement on strategic weapons be linked to the restrictive Soviet interpretation of the ABM Treaty that would have limited testing of the strategic defense system to the laboratory.

The United States has retreated somewhat from the strategic arms position it assumed at Reykjavik. In April 1987 the Reagan administration decided to extend the time required for the 50 percent reduction in strategic forces from five years to seven years. Moreover, the countdown for this reduction was not to begin until the treaty is signed. The delay apparently was motivated by the Joint Chiefs of Staff's desire to deploy additional weapons, particularly sea- and air-launched cruise missiles. In effect, the proposed 50 percent reduction would represent somewhat less than 50 percent of strategic offensive capability if measured by stockpiles now existing. The administration plan presented in Geneva in May also included no provision for further negotiations aimed at the eventual elimination of all strategic offensive weapons as proposed at Reykjavik.

It is interesting to note that for all of the rhetoric expended by the Reagan administration accusing the Soviet Union of noncompliance with past arms control agreements, little attention has been given to issues of verification in the U.S. START proposals. As a result, numbers rather than specific debate on verification requirements have been the most frequently raised issues in the strategic arms talks. Nevertheless, it is clear that the Reagan administration's proposals will demand far more onerous verification requirements than those introduced by the United States during the SALT era. For example, the insistence upon counting missiles rather than launchers and upon measuring comparable throw-weight will require considerable on-site inspection. This, coupled with the administration's insistence that something more than adequate verification be required, does not augur well for the prospects of reaching agreement on strategic arms reduction.

THE STRATEGIC DEFENSE INITIATIVE

On March 23, 1983, President Ronald Reagan presented a vision to the American people in which the world would no longer need to live under the threat of nuclear retaliation but rather could rely on a system capable of defending against a nuclear attack. Few experts took the plan seriously at the time, particularly as it might apply to population defense. Nevertheless, some saw the proposal as a way to build a limited system to reduce the vulnerability of ICBMs in order to provide a more credible deterrent—in effect a return to an anti-ballistic missile system which had been strictly limited by the ABM Treaty in 1972. Yet the image of a shield against nuclear weapons gradually captured the popular imagination. The stage had been partially set by the anti-nuclear movement, which had painted such a horrible picture of the dangers of nuclear war that many Americans had an intense need to believe that there might be a defense against such weapons of mass destruction.

As indicated in the last chapter, during the sixties and seventies military experts had concluded that an ABM system might not be effective and would in fact tend to destabilize the nuclear deterrent system. Scientific developments in the eighties led some to reevaluate this assessment.

Scientists began to see potential in such new technologies as laser and high-energy particle beams as a way of defending against a missile attack. These new assessments caught the attention of the president, resulting in a proposed $26 billion research effort over a period of five years to determine the feasibility of developing such a system.

The proposed system was called the Strategic Defense Initiative or more popularly "Star Wars." The initial concept called for a three-tiered system in which missile interception would focus first upon the missile's boost phase during which satellites would warn of missile launchings within seconds. Response at the boost phase would have to be virtually automatic since there would be less than five minutes to intercept. In the second phase there would be an attempt to intercept the remaining missiles during the twenty-minute flight phase. The terminal phase, lasting about two minutes, would seek to destroy any remaining warheads as they re-entered the atmosphere.

It was believed that if each layer of the three-tiered system could be made 90 percent effective, only eight out of 8,000 RVs would be able to arrive on target, thus providing a nearly perfect defense.[48] Many technical questions were raised about the proposed system, leading many scientists to question its efficacy. There are just too many actions that an adversary can take to counter a system designed to intercept ballistic missiles, even in the case of the latest technological advances using lasers and particle beams. For example, the adversary may develop fast-burn boosters; it may insulate its offensive missile boosters to absorb the beam's energy; it can make the missile spin or shift its trajectory so that a laser beam cannot focus long enough to penetrate the target; a liquid film can be secreted, making penetration of the target difficult; thousands of decoys such as balloons or other chaff can be launched, making it impossible for the defender to determine which objects contain nuclear warheads; space mines may be placed in the path of American space weapons; or an ICBM attack can be concentrated and the number of warheads substantially increased to overwhelm any conceivable strategic defensive system. Additional counter measures might include the use of offensive systems that are less vulnerable than ICBMs to anti-ballistic missile systems, such as cruise missiles and SLBMs that fly at a lower trajectory. Even bombers loaded with stand-off missiles and gravity bombs can be expected to deliver some of their payloads. Finally, an aggressor might attack the communications and computer systems of the defender, neutralizing the defender's ability to detect and respond to a launch.

For a missile defense system to be a desirable option, the cost of building that system ought to be less than the cost of countering the system offensively. Esimates of the cost of SDI have been placed at $500 billion to $1 trillion (or 20-50 percent of what the United States spent on strategic nuclear weapons between 1945 and 1985).[49] The engineering requirements of building such a system are likewise enormous as it has been noted that anywhere from 2,750 to 5,000 launchings of shuttle or shuttle-sized rockets would be required to place all of the needed hardware into space.[50] In view of the delay and problems encountered as a result of the Challenger space shuttle explosion, the prospects for such a feat appear difficult at best.

Given the many ways of countering a strategic defense system and the numerous technological complexities involved, it is little wonder that an overwhelming number of the 451 members of the prestigious National Academy of Sciences responding to a written questionnaire believed that it was most unlikely that a survivable and cost-effective system could be built within the next twenty-five years. This survey, which was limited to those scientists from relevant fields such as physics and mathematics, revealed that 78 percent of the respondents felt that the prospects were "extremely poor" or "poor." Only 4 percent said the odds of success were better than even.[51]

Another problem confronting the Strategic Defense Initiative has been the generally negative reaction given the proposal by American allies.[52] After so much energy had been expended in attempting to couple the U.S. deterrent system with that of Europe through the deployment of INF forces on European soil, the United States threatened to undo the whole process by pressing the allies to support the Star Wars proposals. SDI, rather than reassuring European leaders, raised doubts about whether the United States would come to the aid of the allies in the case of a Soviet attack, particularly if the U.S. felt secure with its defensive shield. They feared that an effective strategic defense system could lead the United States to ignore Europe, while concentrating upon a strategy of "Fortress America." Others refuted this notion, suggesting that the additional security provided the United States would make the U.S. feel more secure about going to the defense of Europe, recognizing that it would not be decimated in the process. Secretary of Defense Caspar Weinberger sought to reassure European doubts by suggesting that SDI would be "equally effective against SS-20s and other intermediate-range Soviet weapons."[53]

Transferring ABM components to Western Europe would not only violate article 9 of the ABM Treaty, but it is also questionable whether a sufficiently effective nuclear shield could be developed against shorter-range delivery systems with their lower trajectories. At minimum, from the allied perspective, SDI would force the Soviet Union to develop comparable defensive systems—systems that may not be effective against the overwhelming offensive might of the United States but would be sufficient to neutralize the much smaller French and British nuclear deterrent systems.

The United States seemed out of step with much of the rest of the world as well on the issue of space-based weapons. It was the only state to abstain on a 1984 General Assembly resolution calling for peaceful uses of outer space. Some 150 United Nations members voted in favor of the resolution.[54]

The effectiveness of the Strategic Defense Initiative is also dependent upon a restrained Soviet reaction to the U.S.'s building such a system. The danger is that a defensive shield is likely to accelerate an offensive arms race. Although part of the brief of the Reagan administration in support of SDI suggested that the Soviet Union would be more likely to accept an agreement on offensive arms control if it recognizes that such weapons would not be effective against such a shield, it is just as likely that the opposite might occur. Scientists at the Lawrence Livermore National Laboratory, a federal nuclear design lab, suggested that if both superpowers build missile defenses, the United States might have to compensate by building heavier and more powerful nuclear warheads.[55]Caspar Weinberger noted on the eve of the 1985 Reagan-Gorbachev summit that even a probable Soviet defense would require that the United States increase its offensive forces.[56]

An illustration of the fact that the Soviet Union also thinks in offensive terms when trying to cope with the defensive systems of the other side can be found in its June 1986 arms control proposal. According to the proposal, the United States would be able to engage in SDI research, but in return the Soviet Union asked for an increase from 6,000 to 8,000 in the number of strategic offensive warheads that would be allowed each side. The dilemma is that without meaningful restraints on offensive arms, which a state is reluctant to accept since it needs a hedge against defensive systems, no missile defense system can be totally effective. According to Richard D. DeLauer, the undersecretary of defense for research and development during Reagan's first term and a strong supporter of SDI, ''this is why we need arms control.''[57]

Rather than simply accelerating an offensive arms race, efforts to build a defensive shield against nuclear weapons may induce a preemptive strike on the part of the adversary. If the Soviet Union, for example, believes that the United States is nearing a highly effective defensive shield against a nuclear strike, incentives will be high to initiate a strike before the system is completely in place. With the installation of what is perceived as an effective U.S. defensive shield, the Soviet Union would realize that it would no longer have a deterrent against the United States.

Perhaps in partial recognition of the provocative aspects of building SDI, the Reagan administration sought to reassure the Soviet Union by offering in November 1985 to sell missile defenses to the Soviet Union at cost. Given the high level of distrust between the two superpowers, it is hardly likely that the Soviet Union would accept such an offer, much less that the American public would allow it to be put into effect. Considerable dismay arose among the American public when President Reagan first broached the topic of sharing defensive systems with the Soviet Union during a 1984 campaign debate with Walter Mondale.

Criticism was also leveled against the Strategic Defense Initiative since its full development would violate a number of arms control agreements. These include first and foremost the 1972 Anti-Ballistic Missile Treaty. Among provisions of the ABM Treaty which would be violated if the Strategic Defense Initiative were developed are article I, which says in part that each party "undertakes not to deploy ABM systems for a defense of the territory of its country" and article V, which requires that the parties undertake "not to develop, test, or deploy ABM systems or components which are sea-based, air-based, space-based, or mobile land-based." Agreed Statement D requires the parties to discuss ABM systems and components that might be created in the future and demands that such systems be in accord with other articles of the treaty.

The debate on the compatibility of SDI with the ABM Treaty revolved largely around the question of whether or not research on ABM systems would be allowed and what constituted research. The ABM Treaty did not ban research, recognizing that it would be difficult, if not impossible, to verify such a ban. That the Soviet Union also accepted such an interpretation when the ABM Treaty was signed is suggested by a statement made in support of ratification of the treaty by A. A. Grechko before the Presidium of the Supreme Soviet on September 29, 1972. In this speech Grechko indicated that the treaty "places no limitations whatsoever on the conducting of research and experimental work directed toward solving the problem of defending the country from nuclear missile strikes."[58]

The Reagan administration has gone to great lengths in an attempt to justify tests that many experts, including those who were involved in the negotiations themselves, believe would violate the ABM Treaty. In April 1985, the Defense Department released a report listing fifteen SDI experiments to be conducted in the next five to ten years that it asserted would not violate the treaty.[59] In making such a claim, it appeared to be engaging in considerable subterfuge. For example, the Department of Defense argued that since the proposed target was a satellite rather than a missile, two of the tests would not violate the treaty. Yet it was clear what the ultimate target for these systems would be, particularly since the United States was in the process of developing the F-15 anti-satellite killer system, which had already proven itself effective. By testing the SDI laser "below the power level and beam quality required for a ground-based laser ABM weapon," the Pentagon rationalized that its proposed laser tests would remain in compliance with the ABM Treaty. Missile boost-phase and midcourse tracking surveillance systems would be tested, according to the report, but these tests would not violate the treaty since the experimental system involved "would not be provided with the capability necessary to achieve ABM performance levels."

In the fall of 1985 lawyers for the Defense Department and the legal advisor for the Department of State, following a quick review of the negotiating record, concluded that the ABM Treaty prohibited only the military deployment of new space-based systems. Their argument was that the record revealed that the United States had failed to convince the Soviet Union that "exotic" ABM systems should be banned. The United States should therefore take a similar position, treaty language notwithstanding. The Defense Department study concluded that the negotiating record justified both testing and deployment of exotic ABM systems such as lasers and directed energy beams, whereas the legal advisor to the State Department indicated that it allowed only testing.[60] The fact that virtually all of the principal negotiators of the ABM Treaty disagreed with both of these views did not seem to bother the advocates of these revisionist interpretations.

The United States has also used alleged Soviet violations of the ABM Treaty as a potential justification for no longer adhering to the treaty. The primary Soviet violation cited in this connection is the Soviet construction of the Krasnoyarsk radar system, which the United States claims, given the geographical location of the system in Siberia, is designed for tracking ballistic missiles rather than providing early warning of a nuclear attack. According to former SALT negotiator Paul C. Warnke, if one used the reasoning of the Pentagon's 1985 report noted above, the Soviet Union would not be in violation of the ABM Treaty until some time in 1988, when the Krasnoyarsk facility is expected to be activated.[61]

The criticism directed against the Soviet's Krasnoyarsk and other radar installations would seem to have less legal and moral standing since the United States itself is pressing ahead with plans to construct two new large phased-array radars in Greenland and Britain. The compatibility of these radars with article VI of the ABM Treaty and Agreed Statement F has been raised by a number of authorities. Agreed Statement F holds that large phased array radars may be deployed only at ABM sites or on the periphery of each side's territory. Article VI prohibits future radars "except at locations along the periphery of its national territory and oriented outward." The Reagan administration claims that it is not building any new radars but merely modernizing existing ones. According to some authorities, an earlier classified U.S. statement made it clear that the United States would not be allowed to replace such radars with large phased array radars.[62]

Despite laying the groundwork for justifying a possible U.S. abrogation of the ABM Treaty, the Reagan administration, largely in response to an outcry against such a move on the part of Congress and several NATO allies, initially announced that it would continue to live within the more restrictive definition of what is allowed with respect to research on the Strategic Defense Initiative. In an effort to bargain with Congress, rather than the Soviet Union, the administration threatened in the spring of 1986 to reconsider its decision to abide by the ABM Treaty if Congress went ahead with its plans to reduce the budget of the SDI program.[63]

In addition to violating the ABM Treaty, the Strategic Defense Initiative would be incompatible with the 1967 Outer Space Treaty, which prohibits the deployment of nuclear weapons in space. Those parts of the program that utilize only conventional explosives, such as the F-15 anti-satellite system, would not be affected since the Outer Space Treaty applies only to nuclear weapons and weapons of mass destruction. Space-based weapons such as the X-ray laser, which uses large mirrors positioned in space to reflect beams capable of destroying missiles, would constitute a violation since nuclear explosions are used to produce the laser beam. This particular weapon would also violate the Limited Test Ban Treaty, which disallows nuclear explosions in all environments except underground.

In 1981 the Soviet Union sought to close the gap in the coverage of the Outer Space Treaty by proposing that all weapons, not just nuclear ones, be banned from deployment in outer space. The Soviet Union's August 1983 proposal went a step further by proposing a ban upon the testing and use of all weapons in outer space. The latter proposal also included a ban on manned spacecraft used for military purposes, which many U.S. officials thought the Soviet Union would attempt to apply to the U.S.

shuttle program. A ban on the testing of anti-satellite systems was also included in the draft treaty as well as the requirement that all existing systems be destroyed.

Regardless of the desirability or the legality of the Strategic Defense Initiative, there is no question but that the plan caught the attention of the Soviet Union. SDI was clearly responsible for inducing the Soviet Union to return to the negotiating table, which it had left in November 1983 as a result of the U.S. deployment of the Pershing II and cruise missiles in Europe. The Soviet Union's arms control position since that time has been largely directed toward restricting the development of the Strategic Defense Initiative, probably due in large measure to a recognition that it could not compete effectively with the United States in a technological space race of the magnitude envisioned in the Reagan plan. The Soviet position has been that no research, testing, development, or deployment of such systems should be allowed. A hint of greater flexibility on the issue was suggested by a September 1985 *Time* magazine interview with Mikhail Gorbachev in which Gorbachev suggested that some research on SDI would be allowed.[64] Subsequent discussion, however, had made it clear that the Soviet Union is unwilling to accept anything more than basic laboratory testing of space-based systems.

The Soviet Union, in an effort to get the United States to agree to its proposed ban on space-based weapons, offered to link such a ban to substantial reductions of offensive missiles. After getting nowhere with this proposal, because of President Reagan's insistence that the strategic defense initiative was nonnegotiable, the Soviet Union initiated a new approach in which it sought to at least delay American deployment of its proposed space-based defensive system. The Soviets proposed that the two superpowers agree not to withdraw from the ABM Treaty for a period of fifteen to twenty years and that they work to tighten the language on allowable research, development, and testing of new missile defense systems. The Soviet Union seemed particularly interested in closing the loophole in the ABM Treaty that allows a state to withdraw with six months notice.

Prospects for a renegotiated ABM Treaty improved somewhat in July 1986 when President Reagan sent a letter to Gorbachev in which he indicated a willingness to discuss the disputed issues related to the ABM Treaty. The letter was viewed by some within the administration as a way of signaling that the United States was willing to bargain with the Soviet Union on space-based defenses.[65] In this way the president could save face on his position on SDI, which he had continued to argue was not negotiable.

Although the United States was unwilling to commit itself to the Soviet's proposed 15-20 year guarantee of the ABM Treaty, the president indicated that a seven-and-a-half year delay in the deployment of space-based defense systems would be acceptable if the Soviet Union would agree to accept U.S. proposals for an expanded definition of research to include the development and testing of ABM components rather than just laboratory research.[66] In agreeing to such a delay the United States would not be conceding much since the director of the Strategic Defense Initiative, Lieutenant General James A. Abrahamson, announced about the same time that deployment could not begin for another decade even if the research proved SDI to be a desirable option.[67] The administration in effect gave Moscow a choice: either adhere to the ABM Treaty with its right of withdrawal after six months or agree to a new treaty that would allow actual deployment of SDI weapons after 1993.

At the 1986 Reykjavik summit both sides apparently agreed to the notion of a ten-year guaranteed adherence to the ABM Treaty. At the same time, the United States made it clear that it disagreed with the Soviet insistence that the treaty permitted only laboratory research. The U.S. position was that the ABM Treaty allowed not only research but the right to develop and test certain ABM components. It was basically over this issue that the summit failed as the Soviets continued to insist that its interpretation was proper and, more importantly, that agreement on INF and strategic force reductions was contingent upon that interpretation.

In February 1987, in a move led largely by Secretary of Defense Caspar Weinberger, the Reagan administration declared that it would follow the broad interpretation of the ABM Treaty that would allow testing of exotic ABM systems. Because of concern that the SDI might not continue as a viable program beyond the Reagan era, there was great interest in conservative circles for beginning deployment of a first-stage space defense system, utilizing kinetic heat-seeking missiles to intercept Soviet ICBMs. Even though such weapons would be obsolete by the midnineties when lasers and high particle beam weapons are expected to be ready for possible deployment, it was believed by some that the beginnings of a space system would be necessary in order to keep the SDI program alive beyond the current administration. It has already been shown on many occasions that if a substantial investment can be made in a given weapons system many groups will have a vested interest in keeping the system alive. Besides, continuing a system will be the only way to justify the billions already spent. But according to former Secretary of Defense Harold Brown, the kinetic-kill missile proposed by the administration for early deployment would clearly violate the ABM Treaty even when using the broad interpretation of the treaty since such technologies were clearly available when the treaty was negotiated.[68] There is some reason to believe that the primary objective of the Reagan administration for advocating accelerated testing and partial deployment of ABM components was more related to the desire to scuttle the ABM Treaty itself. Such a move would obviously be an open invitation to the Soviet Union to ignore its obligations under the treaty.

Additional evidence of the administration's hostility to the ABM Treaty is provided by President Reagan's April 1987 decision to reduce the time-span for adhering to the treaty from the ten years agreed at Reykjavik to five years. In contrast with earlier U.S. policy, the U.S. arms control negotiators in Geneva have also been ordered not to discuss the issue of treaty interpretation in the negotiations.

The prospects for an agreement on limiting the Star Wars program remains relatively remote, particularly as long as the Reagan administration continues to believe so strongly in the potential of the system. Even though some within and outside the administration might favor a temporary agreement prohibiting the testing and deployment of various SDI weapons systems while allowing research to continue, there is concern that any such restrictions might lead Congress to reject funding for the research program. After all, if eventual testing and deployment cannot be guaranteed, why waste billions of dollars for research on a system that may never be deployed?

ANTI-SATELLITE WEAPONS

Efforts to guarantee the peaceful uses of space have also been complicated by the development of anti-satellite weapons. With the successful test of Sputnik in 1957, the United States became increasingly concerned about the dangers of the use of space for military purposes and the possibility that the Soviet Union would attempt to build anti-satellite weapons of its own. As a result, research was begun on the development of an anti-satellite system (ASAT) under the so-called Satellite Inspection Technique or SAINT program. Under this plan the United States in 1963–64 developed two operational ASAT systems—one deployed at Kwajalein Atoll and the other at Johnston Island. The Kwajalein Atoll ASAT system remained operational until 1967, and the Johnston Island system until 1975.

The Soviet Union tested its first ASAT system five years after the United States. Between 1968 and 1982, U.S. officials detected some 20 tests of a Soviet ground-launched anti-satellite weapons system. Only 45 percent of the tests were believed to have been successful though.[69] The Soviet tests were based primarily upon a technology that the United States had developed in the sixties and subsequently abandoned. The United States ASAT system now utilizes an F-15 airplane that is capable of launching an eighteen-foot missile with such deadly accuracy that only a conventional homing-device is needed rather than an nuclear warhead.

Little attempt was made in formal disarmament negotiations to control ASAT weapons during the sixties and early seventies. Instead, what evolved were tacit understandings on space systems and ASAT weapons.[70] The Soviet Union informally accepted the launching of U.S. Reconnaissance satellites beginning in 1960, despite dire predictions that the Soviet Union would attempt to destroy them. Over time, with the United States tacitly accepting the launching of Soviet space systems, it became established that neither would interfere with the reconnaissance satellites of the other. By 1963 the Soviet Union had dropped its demand for a ban on reconnaissance satellites from its formal arms control proposals. This approach was ultimtely formalized in the SALT I agreements in which the United States and the Soviet Union agreed not to interfere with the national technical means of the other side—means that relied heavily upon satellite surveillance.

The importance of unilateral constraint for arms control can also be seen in the American decision to cancel the SAINT program in 1963. General Bernard Schriever and Eugene Zuckert, the secretary of the Air Force at the time, have noted that the primary reason for the cancellation of the program was fear of escalating the arms race.[71] In addition to cancelling the SAINT program, Secretary of Defense Robert McNamara tacitly communicated a U.S. downgrading of space weapons by using annual military posture statements and testimony before Congress to communicate that the United States believed that there was no military requirement for such systems. The fact that the United States and the Soviet Union agreed in 1963 to renounce the orbiting of weapons of mass destruction weakened one of the prime reasons for developing ASAT weapons. This renunciation was formalized in the 1967 Outer Space Treaty. The Soviet Union also showed restraint when it suspended all ASAT tests from December 1971 to February 1976.

The resumption of Soviet ASAT testing in 1976 placed pressure upon the United States to resume its own tests. Some felt it important tht the United States remain active in the ASAT race in order to deter the Soviet use of such weapons by being able to threathen a comparable retaliatory response. In 1977 the Carter administration proposed bilateral talks on the subject of anti-satellite systems, and these were begun the following year. Little was accomplished during the two years of these negotiations because of the Soviet insistence that the U.S. space shuttle be included among the prohibited systems.

In an effort to provide some inducement to the Soviet Union to engage in serious negotiation, the Carter administration budgeted funds for ASAT testing and development. Under the original plan the system was to be operational by 1985. The first ASAT test in the program, however, did not occur until 1985, delaying the program until at least 1987.

The Reagan administration refused to resume the ASAT talks, largely on the grounds that it felt that such an agreement could not be verified. The administration demanded that a verification system would have to be virtually foolproof, particularly since the United States had relatively few military satellites and their loss could be disabling. Verification of ASAT weapons is exceedingly difficult since one is dealing with easily concealable weapons as well as weapons that are used for conventional and other purposes. Even satellites can be employed as anti-satellite weapons by maneuvering them into the path of another satellite. Effective verification would require at minimum on-site inspection of numerous launches.

Another factor in the Reagan administration's rejection of engaging in talks on the subject of anti-satellite weapons related to the administration's commitment to the Strategic Defense Initiative. To the extent that the United States was determined to develop a comprehensive anti-ballistic missile system, it was impossible to support an ASAT ban. After all, the very same weapons, whether based upon more traditional BMD systems or upon more exotic laser and directed particle beams, can be used in attacking satellites. The technical problems of overwhelming satellite systems are much simpler than attacking incoming missiles since satellites are fewer in number, are more detectable, and move in more predictable ways. By the same reasoning, it might be argued that the continued existence of ASAT testing and deployment makes a ban on satellite missile defense systems an impossible task, for ASAT weapons, with some upgrading, could threaten ballistic missiles as well. According to a Pentagon official involved in space policy, the overlap between anti-satellite technology and "Star Wars" is so great that if the United States is forced to stop testing ASAT weapons, "it would slow down certain parts of S.D.I. today and probably prevent the completion of the research program."[72]

Recognizing this problem, Kenneth Adelman on the eve of the resumption of U.S. ASAT testing in September 1985 virtually ruled out any agreement on such weapons even if some of the troublesome verification problems could be solved. In issuing his blanket condemnation of a ban on ASAT, Adelman noted that the administration had concluded that "it could not foresee any possible agreement to limit anti-satellite weapons that would be in the national interest."[73]

Congress did not share such a view as the House of Representatives amended the FY 1985 defense authorization bill by banning U.S. tests against objects in space unless the Soviets resume their own tests of anti-satellite weapons. The Soviet Union had unilaterally suspended such tests in 1983. The following year the Republican-controlled Senate voted 61 to 28 to allow full-scale testing of anti-satellite weapons only if the president certifies that he is willing to negotiate limits on such weapons with the Soviet Union.

Part of the congressional opposition to the U.S. ASAT program has to do with weaknesses in the program itself. Congressman George Brown, citing a General Accounting Office study, concluded that the study "shows that the ASAT program is way over budget, way behind schedule and unable to meet its mission requirements. If Congress gives this program the go-ahead, we'll end up with a multi-billion dollar boondoggle that's obsolete the day its employed."[74] Recognizing some of these problems, the Pentagon has cut the number of F-15 ASAT missile bases from two to one and reduced the number of missiles it planned to buy by two-thirds.[75] At the same time, it threatened to escalate the ASAT arms race by focusing on the more promising anti-satellite technology under development in the SDI, such as lasers and particle beams.

A persuasive argument can be made that the United States may actually benefit more from restrictions on ASAT testing and deployment than would the USSR. The United States is far more dependent upon military satellites for communication, command, control and intelligence-gathering (C^3I). Some 70 to 80 percent of all U.S. long-haul military C^3 is transmitted by satellite relay. Satellites are vital to American intelligence operations as well since the United States does not have the information-gathering advantages of dealing with an open society that the Soviet Union does. Consequently, anything that will protect U.S. military satellites will benefit U.S. interests. A ban on the testing of ASAT would also lock in the technological superiority in anti-satellite systems that the United States now enjoys. Finally, a ban at this time would preclude the development of a Soviet ASAT system that could threaten the security of high-orbiting space systems that are now largely immune to existing Soviet ASAT systems. Both states, of course, would stand to benefit economically from restrictions on ASAT testing and deployment, for such systems are not inexpensive. The price of the U.S. ASAT program was pegged at $3.6 billion, which perhaps could be better used to buy a Nimitz-class carrier or 200 F-16 fighter aircraft.[76] Savings could also be gained if the need for building defensive and evasive capabilities into satellites were eliminated.

The time would seem to be ripe for negotiating an ASAT agreement as the Soviet Union continues to adhere to its moratorium on ASAT testing. The price of such an agreement would probably have to include a willingness to forego U.S. plans to test and deploy the Star Wars system. As long as the United States insists upon deploying space-based weapons systems, the Soviet Union will find it necessary to develop a capability to neutralize those weapons. It was perhaps in recognition that the Reagan administration was unlikely to bargain away its planned defensive shield that the Soviet Union dropped its demand for a ban on the testing and deployment of ASAT in 1985. A glimmer of hope for separate negotiations on ASAT weapons arose the following year when the Soviet Union indicated a willingness to negotiate on any one of three space-based systems—ASAT weapons, anti-ballistic missile systems, or weapons able to attack targets on earth and in the earth's atmosphere. At the same time, the Soviets indicated that they would prefer a ban on all three systems.

CONCLUSION

The Reagan administration came into power with a generally hostile attitude toward arms control, believing that past negotiations on the subject and the agreements that had been reached primarily benefitted the Soviet Union. It was also argued by the administration that the Soviets had exploited those agreements by violating a number of their provisions.

The importance of executive leadership for successful arms control negotiations was evident as the Soviet Union was virtually paralyzed on arms control policy during the first Reagan term as it had three different leaders. Similarly, President Reagan failed to exert strong leadership in the arms control area as shown by his inability to generate a consensus on the U.S. negotiating position from the strongly conflicting views shown by various bureaucratic interests. The result was that negotiations often took place without any clear instructions as to what the United States position was.

Given the paralysis within the Reagan administration on arms control, Congress became a more active participant in the process by making specific proposals for negotiating positions, sending representatives to monitor the negotiations, and threatening various administration defense programs that might undercut the interests of arms control.

Both internal and external public opinion also became a greater force to contend with than in previous decades. Considerable pressure was exerted by the nuclear freeze movement in the United States as well as European publics concerned about the emplacement of intermediate-range nuclear weapons on European soil. It was partially because of such activities that a reluctant American administration finally agreed to negotiate.

Public pressure, as well as a recognition that the SALT agreements had some restraining effects upon the arms policies of the Soviet Union, led the administration to announce a no-undercut policy with respect to the SALT agreements as long as the Soviet Union did likewise. It adhered to this policy until May 1986 and then continued to remain in technical compliance with SALT for some time thereafter.

Both the United States and the Soviet Union legitimately can be accused of presenting nonnegotiable positions with respect to intermediate-range nuclear forces, strategic arms, and space-based systems that formed the three major topics of discussion during the Reagan period. Their behavior raises questions about whether either state was serious about arms control. The rhetoric surrounding the talks during the Reagan era was perhaps the most vituperative since the 1950s. Nevertheless, the strategic arms buildup engaged in by the United States appears to have increased Soviet incentive to negotiate on arms control matters. President Reagan's initiation of an extensive research program on strategic defense systems was similarly instrumental in getting the Soviet Union to return in 1985 to the arms talks that it had broken off almost a year and a half earlier. These pressures, however, were not sufficient for obtaining negotiated agreements, and the eighties so far have to be written off as the least productive for arms control since the early postwar years.

A considerable part of the blame for the lack of progress on arms control during the Reagan years can be placed upon the administration itself. Former SALT negotiator Gerard Smith put the issue very well when he wrote *New York Times* columnist James Reston, asking rhetorically what we Americans would think if the Soviets had:

- Failed to ratify the three latest arms control agreements that their premier had signed;
- Walked away from negotiations for a comprehensive test ban and for limitations on anti-satellite systems;

- Announced that that treaty's correct interpretation permitted the development and testing of systems that the treaty by its very terms prohibited;
- Refrained from starting negotiations about strategic arms for many months, and then made offers that their former minister of foreign affairs had acknowledged to be nonnegotiable and "absurd";
- While claiming violations, had refrained from making effective use of the Standing Consultative Commission to resolve disputes or was reported to have denied permission for its delegates to raise the issues;
- Announced that it was breaking out of an agreement setting ceilings on missiles and bombers because of the bad behavior of the other party.[77]

Since these actions accurately describe what the United States had done in its arms control policy in recent years, can there be any question as to why the Soviet Union harbors such suspicion about U.S. negotiating behavior on arms control?

8

Toward a More Secure World

The search for national security through arms control and disarmament has been a disappinting one. Agreements, particularly those involving reductions of armaments, have been few and far between. Whether, on balance, the arms control effort has contributed to increased propects for peace and security in the world is essentially a toss-up. On the one hand, positive outcomes have been achieved, such as the restraints placed upon the spread of nuclear weapons, the adoption of procedures designed to reduce the prospects of nuclear war by accident and miscalculation, and a few agreements imposing ceilings on weapons, all of which have added a certain predictability to military planning. On the negative side, disarmament negotiations may have actually contributed to the heavy burden of arms now seen in the world. The belief that one must negotiate from strength, the need to make payoffs in the form of additional hardware to obtain the support of the military and other conservative groups for a given disarmament policy, and the fear and suspicion evoked by concern that the other party might violate any agreement reached have all tended to accelerate rather than reduce reliance on weapons.

NEGOTIABLE WEAPONS SYSTEMS

An analysis of the postwar disarmament negotiations provides a number of lessons as to which weapons systems are negotiable and why. Such an analysis also underscores why so little has been achieved in some forty years of effort, involving thousands of meetings and hundreds of proposals. Several reasons can be identified that help explain why the United States might prefer to focus negotiations on one weapons system while the Soviet Union prefers to address another. Since the nature of the arms

245

race is always changing as new strategies and weapon refinements are developed, these preferences never remain static. Each party reacts to the strategic situation of the moment. For this reason, arms control negotiations have often had a musical-chairs quality, with one side gravitating to the position of the other just as the latter moves on. This pattern was evident in the decisions on whether to stress limits on defensive arms, offensive arms, or both. When the two sides began exploring the prospects of strategic arms limitations in 1966–67, the United States preferred to address only anti-ballistic missiles while the Soviets wanted to place the emphasis on offensive weapons; by the time SALT I opened, however, the positions were completely reversed.

Several factors influence the kinds of weapons systems that a state would like to see regulated. First, a state is likely to propose testing restrictions on systems that it has already successfully tested in an effort to prevent the adversary from following suit. For example, during the nuclear test ban negotiations, proposals for an immediate test ban usually followed each U.S. or Soviet test series. After its successful round of ICBM tests in 1972, the Soviet Union proposed a freeze on all new strategic programs. The intent was to keep the United States from developing the Trident and the B-1 bomber while allowing the Soviet Union to retain its four new ICBM systems—SS-16 through SS-19. Similarly, the United States sought to prevent the Soviet Union from testing MIRVs by proposing in April 1970 a ban on MIRV testing and deployment. This proposal would have allowed the United States to continue producing MIRVed weapons, first successfully tested in August 1968, some five years before Soviet tests began.

Second, a state will rarely negotiate with regard to a weapons system that it has not yet achieved but which the other side possesses. The Soviet Union rejected the Baruch Plan in 1946 despite the fact that the United States seemed willing to relinquish its monopoly on nuclear weapons to an international control force. Also, the Soviet Union, not yet having tested its first MIRV system, was reluctant even to discuss MIRV controls during SALT I. When a state does not share in a prohibited weapon technology, it may consider itself at the mercy of its adversary, precariously relying on the latter's promises not to produce the prohibited weapons secretly nor to maintain existing but undetected stockpiles ready for use.

Third, proposals to freeze a weapons system at a particular quantitative level will generally be made by the state with a numerical edge. The United States preferred a freeze of strategic delivery systems at existing levels during the late 1960s, and the Soviet Union pushed similar proposals during the 1970s after the numerical balance had tipped in its favor. The Soviet Union deferred the destruction of strategic missiles to the last stage of its general and complete disarmament proposals when it thought it was ahead in 1959, but it moved that matter to the fore a year or so later when it became clear that the United States was in the superior strategic position. President Reagan's opposition to a freeze in the 1980s was related to the perception that the United States was behind in the arms race, whereas the Soviet Union embraced the freeze movement whole-heartedly.

Fourth, given the concern about developing bargaining chips, states will have to be in a position near equality before a given weapons system is negotiable. The fact that there have been no naval arms control negotiations designed to limit the size of U.S. and Soviet surface fleets since 1945 is related to the fact that only recently has the Soviet surface navy become anywhere comparable to that of the United States.[1]

Fifth, a state may choose to negotiate with regard to a particular weapons system if it believes itself falling behind, qualitatively or quantitatively, and sees little chance of reversing its inferior position. The Soviet Union became more willing to negotiate restrictions on the ABM after 1967 when it realized that its Galosh system around Moscow was not likely to be effective. The subsequent U.S. decision to proceed with its own ABM system, which was likely to be a superior system to that of the Sovit Union, probably accounted for the high priority that the Soviets gave to the conclusion of an ABM treaty during SALT I. The Soviet Union, in attempting to negotiate a ban on the testing and deployment of a strategic defense system, recognized that it would have difficulty competing with the United States in the highly sophisticated "Star Wars" technology.

Sixth, if the opposition shows no interest in building a given weapons system, a state will have little incentive for introducing controls on that system in its own proposals. The Soviet Union felt little pressure for negotiating an offensive missile agreement during SALT I since the United States was not adding to its offensive capability, at least in terms of numbers of missiles. The recognition of limited Soviet incentives in the SALT talks led the United States to press for funding new weapons systems that could be used for bargaining chips.

Seventh, a state is likely to try to regulate areas of weapons development in which the adversary would probably be a clear winner in an all-out arms race. For example, some authorities have warned of the danger of allowing unlimited production of sea-based cruise missiles, arguing that the Soviet Union has a great advantage in that realm because it has far more conventional submarines with usable torpedo slots and because it enjoys a superior air defense system capable of intercepting cruise missiles.[2]

Eighth, a strategic arms proposal might originate with the desire to destroy obsolete weapons. U.S. proposals for bomber burnings in the 1960s appear to have been so motivated. Soviet plans to dismantle its SS-4s, SS-5s, and SS-11s were related to the fact that these weapons had come to the end of their useful life.

Ninth, a weapons system may also prove to be negotiable simply because a state is not interested in it, views the weapon as technologically infeasible, or considers it not worth the cost. It was cost-effectiveness calculations that induced the United States and the Soviet Union to ban nuclear weapons in outer space and on the seabed floor. Cost and effectiveness considerations also entered into the willingness to limit the ABM in 1972. As exotic ABM systems appear to be more feasible, particularly those based on laser technology, they have again become non-negotiable weapons systems as far as many within the Reagan administration are concerned.

Tenth, even though a state may hesitate to forego a given weapons system completely, it may be willing to accept temporary limitations. For example, since the United States had neither the ability nor the desire to test or develop the mobile MX missile before 1982, accepting the protocol to SALT II did nothing to change U.S. planning with regard to MX. The same can be said of the restrictions on the deployment of ground- and sea-based cruise missiles—both of which could still be tested during the three-year span of the protocol. The Reagan administration's willingness in 1986 to delay deployment of SDI weapons for a period of seven-and-a-half years was related to the fact that the system was not expected to be ready for deployment for at least a decade.

Eleventh, a proposal to regulate a weapons system might be motivated not so much for its inherent arms control value but rather as a political weapon to exploit divisions within the opposition, whether within the adversary's government or within the opposing alliance system. Moscow's decision to move the destruction of missile systems in its early general and complete disarmament schemes from the third stage to the first seemed partially designed to exploit French interests in a ban on missiles. Other issues raised have included forward-based systems, the neutron bomb, and ground- and sea-launched cruise missiles—all involving serious differences of opinion among the NATO allies. Since the prospect of developing almost any new weapon finds both supporters and opponents in Moscow and Washington, opportunities exist for dividing domestic constituencies simply by raising an issue.

Finally, to be negotiable, a weapons system must be verifiable. Although the United States has been more concerned about verifiability than the Soviet Union, both sides were in agreement that laboratory research on strategic defense systems could continue since there was no way to verify compliance with respect to restrictions on such activities. As the perception of the verifiability of MIRV improved, the Joint Chiefs of Staff reversed their position during the SALT negotiations and agreed to make MIRV a negotiable weapons system.

Obstacles to Disarmament

Our examination of the postwar nuclear disarmament negotiations has revealed a number of obstacles confronting disarmament. Perhaps chief among these obstacles is that of verification as the United States has regarded inspection procedures that would be acceptable to the Soviet Union as being insufficient; and the Soviet Union, for its part, has viewed the verification demands of the United States as too intrusive. While the development of space satellites and a number of other verification technologies has made national technical means of inspection an effective and less intrusive procedure for ascertaining compliance with arms control agreements, the Reagan administration issued a litany of charges that the Soviet Union had violated a number of arms control agreements. Such alleged violations, combined with the demands by the Reagan administration for yet more intrusive verification procedures, made significant arms control measures a virtual impossibility.

The Soviet Union over the years has shown an increased willingness to accept more extensive verification techniques, including on-site inspection to monitor nuclear test bans and to observe restrictions on the production and dismantlement of both long and short range missiles. It has agreed to allow inspectors at chemical production plants and at peaceful nuclear facilities as well as inspectors to observe troop movements and conventional arms reductions. Even if these more intrusive verification procedures are implemented, assessments may still vary as to whether the other side is living up to the letter of an agreement, particularly with regard to those agreements that deal with the qualitative aspects of weapons as opposed to numbers of weapons.

A second obstacle to disarmament has been the problem of asymmetry in weapons systems between the United States and the Soviet Union as well as differing geopolitical requirements for security. How does one ascertain equivalence when states, given different geopolitical situations and technologies, emphasize different weapons systems? Further questions arise about the equivalence of allied forces and the implications of unequal threat situations confronting the Soviet Union and the United States as the former is concerned about a threat from China as well as the nuclear capabilities of U.S. NATO allies. Under such conditions, imaginative arms control proposals and trade-offs will be necessary if one expects to obtain mutually satisfactory arms control agreements. Of one thing we can be certain and that is that attempts to use arms control to force the other side to make dramatic changes in its force structures, as in the case of the Reagan administration proposals that would place severe restrictions on the ratio of ICBMs that the Soviet Union would be allowed, are doomed to failure.

In the third place, although technology might benefit the arms control regime by providing improved verification techniques, technological change is often an impediment to successful negotiation. The belief that one might develop the ultimate weapon or the ultimate defensive system leads decision makers to reject restraints upon military research and development. This, coupled with the fear that the opposition may succeed in breaking out of any arms control restraints established, leads to conservatism in arms control policy as decision makers seek to keep their options open. Moreover, that technology that may contribute to both peaceful activities as well as military purposes makes negotiation on arms control exceedingly difficult as experience with attempts to control nuclear energy make abundantly clear.

A fourth major obstacle confronting arms control and disarmament is that of distrust and tension in the world. The United States, in particular, has insisted over the years that disarmament is contingent upon the peaceful resolution of a number of political disputes. Admittedly, a high level of distrust generated by political differences is hardly conducive to creating the sort of environment necessary to reach a consensus on disarmament issues, but low levels of tension reduce the incentives for doing anything about the arms problem. Indeed, it is because there is tension and an imminent danger of war that arms control becomes all the more important. Perhaps what is needed is a recognition that although arms control agreements entail a certain level of risk so does nuclear deterrence. Neither system is foolproof, and it is perhaps foolhardy to ask so much more of disarmament than we ask of deterrence. Nevertheless, the problem of distrust must be addressed, and any disarmament agreement must include adequate verification procedures. This will not guarantee that an arms agreement may not break down, but adequate guarantees must be provided so that neither side will seriously be disadvantaged by such a failure.

Finally, progress on arms control is complicated by the fact that positions taken on disarmament issues are often dictated by the domestic political situation. The observation that the most difficult negotiations on arms control have generally occurred within governments rather than between governments has become commonplace. The Reagan administration, in particular, was confronted with deep divisions between the State Department and the Defense Department on various issues of arms control. According to one authority, "bureaucratic factors and pressures from labor and industry are of such critical importance to weapons development and procurement decisions that little can be done to control the arms race by negotiation at the international level."[3]Additional complicating factors arise because of the role played by Congress—a role that became a limiting force with respect to the SALT II Treaty and a driving force favoring more serious negotiations during the Reagan period. The positions taken by Congress have in turn been influenced by what has often been a fickle American public on the issues of arms control and disarmament.

Although the Soviet leadership is considerably less constrained by parliamentary and public opinion in formulating its arms control policy than is the United States leadership, deep divisions, dating back to the years of Khrushchev, have existed among various bureaucratic interests. Brezhnev was forced to pay considerable attention to the wishes of the military in formulating his arms control policies. Gorbachev also was subjected to considerable criticism from the military for his nineteen month unilateral test ban moratorium in 1985–87, but nevertheless persisted in the policy.

When it comes to disarmament policy, it has generally been the naysayers who have had the last word. It is always easier to persuade others of possible risks in a new approach to peace than to convince them of the utility of pursuing a different strategy. The military, in particular, has had considerable leverage in this regard because of its expertise on national security matters.

TOWARD MORE EFFECTIVE BARGAINING ON ARMS CONTROL

To the extent that one believes that arms control and disarmament offers a useful approach to improved security, what lessons can be learned from the past to increase the prospects for verifiable and effective arms control in the future? The evidence from several sets of arms control negotiations underscores the importance of reciprocity of concessions, as significant correlations were found in U.S.-Soviet scores during the early postwar disarmament negotiations, the test ban negotiations, and the SALT talks. At the same time, there was some evidence of approach-avoidance behavior, especially in the test ban negotiations, as retractive behavior became evident at the point the two sides were nearing agreement. Such findings raise questions about measuring the meaningfulness of concessions, particularly with respect to long-range and more comprehensive disarmament schemes. Were reciprocation strategies followed in such cases because there was little chance for an agreement on significant reductions being reached, thus making the concessions cheap, or do such concessions represent a serious attempt to reach agreement? It may be that the recent Gorbachev initiatives have been taken largely with the expectation that the United States would never reciprocate, enabling the Soviet Union to assume the moral high ground with respect to the issues of disarmament by making concessions that are never expected to become part of an agreement. Perhaps one should not denigrate the seriousness with which the Soviet Union has approached the issue of arms control in recent years. There appears to be a very real concern about the sluggish Soviet economy. Operating as it is with half the gross national product of the United States, the Soviet Union is forced to devote twice the percentage of its GNP to the military effort just to stay even with the United States.

This is not to suggest, as some officials within the Reagan administration appear to believe, that the Soviet Union will make the preponderant number of concessions on arms control for the sake of agreement. Nor does it mean that the United States can engage the Soviets in an arms race that will bleed the Soviet Union into submission or result in the overthrow of its government because of domestic discontent. Given its ability to demand greater sacrifice on the part of its public, the Soviet Union may find itself better able than the United States to compete in an all-out arms race. It has already demonstrated its ability to compete and even to prevail in the quantitative arms race.

Obviously, if differences on disarmament issues are to be narrowed, concessions will have to be made. Care should be taken in the way such concessions are presented. The United States, for example, might attempt to stagger its concessions more effectively than it has in the past, for it has introduced most of its concessions early in the negotiations. Such behavior tends to raise the aspiration level of the Soviet Union, making agreement more difficult to achieve. There is even some evi-

dence that the assumption of a harder line in the previous round of negotiations results in a more forthcoming Soviet response in the subsequent
round. Our analysis of evolving U.S.-Soviet positions on arms control
during the Reagan period suggests that perhaps the United States has
gone too far in the other direction, begrudgingly changing positions only
after considerable pressure has been exerted by Congress, the American
public, and U.S. allies to be more compromising in its bargaining
position.

With time running out on the Reagan presidency and with some
administration officials concerned about the president's place in history
and interested in diverting attention from the Iran arms sales controversy, pressure for a more conciliatory U.S. position continues to be
exerted. This pressure, coupled with Mikhail Gorbachev's interest in
diverting scarce resources from the Soviet military buildup in an effort to
stimulate the sluggish Soviet economy, may eventually produce the first
nuclear arms control agreement of the Reagan presidency. Past experience as well as current discussion, however, suggests that such an agreement is likely to be a limited one, confined at most to an agreement to
remove intermediate-range and short-range nuclear missiles from European soil. Prospects for such an agreement rose considerably as a result
of Gorbachev's February 1987 decision to separate agreement on INF
from U.S. acceptance of the Soviet position on the Strategic Defense
Initiative.

It has been largely because of the failure of arms control negotiations
to produce anything more than largely cosmetic agreements that a
number of authorities, led by Kenneth L. Adelman, the director of the
Arms Control and Disarmament Agency, have suggested that unilateral
approaches to arms restraint may actually be preferable to negotiated
arms control agreements.[4] Abram Chayes has noted a number of reasons
why formal negotiations tend to exacerbate rather than alleviate the arms
race. These include the belief that one needs to build bargaining chips in
order to negotiate effectively; the tendency in formal negotiations to
assume a hostile stance for negotiating purposes; and the pressures generated to build to treaty limits or to intensify efforts in areas not covered
by the treaty.[5] One might add to this list the suspicions that are generated
by the fear that the other side is evading a negotiated agreement. There is
something more compelling about taking action against an adversary if
there is a real or imagined violation of a formal agreement than if one is
dealing with a tacit understanding. The resulting acrimony in many
cases is likely to be a more serious problem for continued security interests and good relations than is the alleged violation itself. Since the

negotiating process focuses upon asymmetries in weapon systems, the political decision maker may find it difficult to reject a given weapon system even if that system is not in the nation's particular security interest. The fact that the other side has the weapon and that the weapon is publicized as a result of the negotiating process may create pressures to follow suit. One wonders just how many weapons have been built simply because the other side has them rather than for any intrinsic need for the weapon.

It may be more useful to pursue unilateral approaches to arms control during periods of high tension, particularly since such tension tends to turn formal disarmament negotiations into propagandistic and vituperative sessions that do little to improve relations between the superpowers or to improve the prospects of agreement. Informal and tacit understandings on arms control issues might usefully be pursued when bureaucratic divisions are sharp and public opinion is seriously divided on national security issues; otherwise arms control negotiations become only another political football in the domestic political arena. When a state feels unsure of its bargaining position and is highly concerned about changing that position for fear of losing its bargaining reputation or credibility, it might be useful to pursue tacit dealings rather than formal negotiation.

In utilizing unilateral approaches to enchance national security interests, what is perhaps most important is that the state take actions that will not undermine existing or potential arms control agreements. One might think twice about producing weapons that complicate arms control, such as sea-launched cruise missiles with their inherent verification difficulties. In designing weapons systems, it would seem preferable, to the extent possible, to pay attention to functionally related observable differences (FRODs) in order that distinctions can be made between those systems designed to carry conventional warheads rather than nuclear ones. Nuclear weapons can also be designed in such a way as to reduce the need for reliability testing. In short, what is required is to pay more attention to the arms control implications of new weapons systems— something that the congressionally-mandated Arms Impact Statements were supposed to do. Unfortunately, the consensus is that such statements have generally failed in keeping destabilizing weapons systems and those that threaten the prospects for arms control off the production line.

Perhaps more than anything, arms control and disarmament as an approach to peace require political will—a will to take slight risks and to reject the notion that more arms means more security. It requires a belief that deterrence can work just as successfully at lower levels of armament and that there is no need to match the adversary arm for arm in order to be secure. Disarmament as an approach to peace will also require a willingness to stand up to strong political forces in both the United States and the Soviet Union that have vested interests in an ever larger military component.

Notes

Chapter 1

1. Jonathan Schell, *The Fate of the Earth* (New York: Avon Books, 1982).

2. Carl Sagan, "Nuclear War and Climatic Catastrophe: Some Policy Implications," *Foreign Affairs* 62 (Winter 1983/84): 257–92. For a more recent and less pessimistic review of the research on nuclear winter, see Starley L. Thompson and Stephen H. Schneider, "Nuclear Winter Reappraised," *Foreign Affairs* 64 (Summer 1986): 981–1005.

3. Hannes Adomeit, "Soviet Risk-Taking and Crisis Behavior: From Confrontation to Coexistence," *Adelphi Papers*, no. 101 (Fall 1973).

4. Stephen S. Kaplan, *Diplomacy of Power: Soviet Armed Forces as a Political Instrument* (Washington, D.C.: Brookings Institution, 1981), p. 53.

5. Barry M. Blechman and Stephen S. Kaplan, *Force Without War: U.S. Forces as a Political Instrument* (Washington, D.C.: Brookings Institution, 1978), pp. 128-29. A favorable outcome was defined as one in which two-thirds of the American objectives were obtained.

6. Ruth Sivard, *World Military and Social Expenditures, 1983* (Washington: World Priorities, 1983).

7. Tom Wicker, "War by Accident," *New York Times*, November 21, 1982.

8. John Steinbrunner, "Nuclear Decapitation," *Foreign Policy* 45 (Winter 1981–82): 18.

9. George C. Wilson and Walter Pincus, "Missile Survival Questioned," *Washington Post,* May 19, 1983.

10. Lisa D. Shaw, "Nuclear Arms Limitation Policy," in Paul R. Viotti (ed.), *Conflict and Arms Control* (Boulder, Colo.: Westview Press, 1986), p. 51.

11. Lloyd Jensen, *"The Postwar Disarmament Negotiations: A Study in U.S.-Soviet Bargaining Behavior"* (Ann Arbor: University of Michigan, Ph.D. dissertation, 1963, pp. 234–47.

Chapter 2

1. Edward Luttwak, *Strategy and Politics* (New Brunswick, N.J.: Transaction Books, 1985), p. 129.

2. U. Alexis Johnson, *The Right Hand of Power* (Englewood Cliffs, N.J.: Prentice-Hall, 1984), p. 585.

3. Ibid., p. 586.

4. I. William Zartman and Maureen R. Berman, *The Practical Negotiator* (New Haven, Conn.: Yale University Press, 1982), p. 157.

5. U.S. Arms Control and Disarmament Agency, *Annual Report, 1983* (Washington: Government Printing Office, 1984), p. 31.

6. "Ten 'Commandments' for Negotiating with the Soviet Union," *New York Times,* January 12, 1986.

7. Ibid.

8. Hannes Adomeit, "Soviet Risk-Taking and Crisis Behavior: From Confrontation to Coexistence," *Adelphi Papers,* no. 101 (1973).

9. Falk Bomsdorf, "Arms Control as a Process of Self Constraint," in Uwe Nerlich (ed.), *Soviet Power and Western Negotiating Policies* (Cambridge, Mass.: Ballinger Press, 1983), vol. 2, p. 85.

10. Fred Iklé, *How Nations Negotiate* (New York: Harper and Row, 1964), p. 149.

11. Alexander Haig, *Caveat* (New York: Macmillan, 1984), pp. 223 and 229.

12. Henry A. Kissinger, *Nuclear Weapons and Foreign Policy* (New York: Harper and Row, 1957), p. 425.

13. Cited in Zartman and Berman, *The Practical Negotiator,* p. 208.

14. William Hyland, "The USSR and Nuclear War," in Barry M. Blechman (ed.), *Rethinking the U.S. Strategic Posture* (Cambridge, Mass.: Ballinger, 1982), p. 50.

15. Samuel B. Payne, *The Soviet Union and SALT* (Boulder, Colo.: Westview Publishing Co., 1981), p. 105.

16. Strobe Talbott, *Deadly Gambits* (New York: Alfred A. Knopf, 1984), p. 159.

17. Dusko Doder, "Chernenko's Tenure: A Political Statement," *Washington Post,* July 29, 1985.

18. Ole R. Holsti, "The Belief System and National Images," *Journal of Conflict Resolution* 6 (September 1962); 608–17.

19. Michael Krepon, *Strategic Stalemate: Nuclear Weapons and Arms Control in American Politics* (New York: St. Martin's Press, 1984), p. 65.

20. Glenn T. Seaborg, *Kennedy, Khrushchev, and the Test Ban* (Berkeley: University of California Press, 1981), p. 297.

21. Ibid., p. 297.

22. Raymond Garthoff, "Banning the Bomb in Outer Space," *International Security* 5 (Winter 1980–81): 26.

23. Ted Greenwood, *Making the MIRV* (Cambridge, Mass.: Ballinger, 1975), p. 127.

24. Harvey Starr, "The Kissinger Years," *International Studies Quarterly* 24 (December 1980): 489.

25. Talbott, *Deadly Gambits,* pp. 237, 250, and 263.

26. Lou Cannon, "Fresh Tests Awaiting Negotiator-in-Chief," *Washington Post,* March 26, 1983.

27. Paul Francis Walker, *"The United States Arms Control and Disarmament Agency: Policy Making in Strategic Arms Limitation"* (Cambridge, Mass.: Massachusetts Institute of Technology, Ph.D. Dissertation, 1978), p. 159.

28. Earl H. Voss, *Nuclear Ambush: The Test Ban Trap* (Chicago: Henry Regnery Co., 1963), p. 315.

29. Henry A. Kissinger, *Years of Upheaval* (Boston: Little, Brown and Co., 1982), p. 271.

30. Johnson, *The Right Hand of Power,* p. 604.

31. Duncan L. Clarke, *Politics of Arms Control* (New York: Free Press, 1979), p. 105.

32. Talbott, *Deadly Gambits,* p. 229.

33. For a fascinating discussion of these bureaucratic struggles, see ibid.

34. Johnson, *The Right Hand of Power,* p. 587.

35. Duncan L. Clarke, "Nixon Installs a Peace Cabinet—But Where is the Peace Agency?" *War/Peace Report*, (January-February 1973), p. 28.

36. Thomas W. Wolfe, "Soviet Approaches to SALT," *Problems of Communism* 19 (September-October 1970): 8.

37. Paul Nitze, "The Strategic Balance Between Hope and Skepticism," *Foreign Policy* (Winter 1974–75), p. 143.

38. Igor S. Glagolev, "The Soviet Decision Making Process in Arms Control Negotiations," *Orbis* 21 (Winter 1978): 772.

39. Colin S. Gray, *The MX ICBM and National Security* (New York: Praeger, 1981), p. 9.

40. Newhouse, *Cold Dawn*, p. 192.

41. Johnson, *The Right Hand of Power*, p. 586.

42. Nikita Khrushchev, *Khrushchev Remembers: The Last Testament*, trans. by Strobe Talbott (Boston: Little, Brown, 1974), pp. 32–33.

43. Richard Burt, "Arms Control and Soviet Strategic Forces," in John Erickson and E. J. Feuchtwanger (eds.), *Soviet Military Power and Performance* (London: Macmillian and Co., 1979), p. 160.

44. Abraham S. Becker, "Sustaining the Burden of Soviet Defense," in Nerlich (ed.), *Soviet Power and Western Negotiating Policies*, vol. 1, p. 250.

45. Arkady N. Shevchenko, *Breaking With Moscow* (New York: Alfred A. Knopf, 1985), p. 203.

46. Paul C. Warnke, "Improving the SALT Process," in William Epstein and Bernard T. Feld (eds.), *New Directions in Disarmament* (New York: Praeger Publishers, 1981), p. 32.

47. Cited in Raymond Garthoff, "The Military and SALT," in Jiri Valenta and William C. Potter (eds.), *Soviet Decisionmaking for National Security* (London: George Allen and Unwin, 1984), p. 146.

48. Payne, *The Soviet Union and SALT*, p. 64.

49. Kissinger, *Years of Upheaval*, p. 269.

50. Raymond Garthoff, *Soviet Strategy in the Nuclear Age* (New York: Praeger, 1958), p. 223.

51. Talbott, *Deadly Gambits*, p. 94.

52. Rose E. Gottemoeller, "Soviet Arms Control Decision Making Since Brezhnev," in Roman Kolkowicz and Ellen Propper Mickiewicz (eds.), *The Soviet Calculus of Power* (Lexington, Mass.: D.C. Heath, 1986) p. 90.

53. Garthoff, "The Military and SALT," p. 143.

54. Stephen J. Flanagan, "Congress, the White House, and SALT," *Bulletin of the Atomic Scientists* 34 (November 1978): 36.

55. Talbott, *Deadly Gambits*, p. 168.

56. Robert Lyle Butterworth, "The Arms Control Impact Statements," in Robert Harkavy and Edward Kolodziej (eds.), *American Security and Policy Making* (Lexington, Mass.: D. C. Heath, 1980), p. 150.

57. Duncan L. Clarke, "Integrating Arms Control, Defense and Foreign Policy in the Executive Branch of the U.S. Government," in Hans Guenter Brauch and Duncan L. Clarke (eds.), *Decisionmaking for Arms Limitation* (Cambridge, Mass.: Ballinger Publishing Co., 1983), p. 13.

58. Bernard Gwertzman, "Reagan Approves New Arms Offer for Geneva Talks," *New York Times*, October 4, 1983.

59. Lou Cannon, "Reagan Sends Team Back to Arms Talks with New Proposals," *Washington Post*, October 5, 1983.

60. Talbott, *Deadly Gambits*, p. 341.

61. Kissinger, *Years of Upheaval*, p. 1150.

62.Clarke, *Politics of Arms Control*, p. 51.

63. Talbott, *Deadly Gambits*, p. 244.

64. Charles Bohlen, *Witness to History* (New York: Norton, 1973), p. 197.

65. Canada, as participant in the Manhattan project in which the first atomic bomb was built, was also made a member of the Atomic Energy Commission although Canada was not a member of the Security Council at the time.

66. France was allocated a seat on the Eighteen Nation Disarmament Conference but refused to occupy it due to President Charles DeGaulle's independent stance on foreign policy issues.

67. For a description of the procedures used, see Lloyd Jensen, "Soviet-American Bargaining Behavior in the Postwar Disarmament Negotiations" (Ann Arbor: University of Michigan, Ph.D. Disseration, 1963), Appendix A.

68. Arthur Lall, *Negotiating Disarmament* (Ithaca, N.Y.: Cornell University Center for International Studies, 1964), pp. 22-23.

69. Don Oberdorfer, "Six Nonaligned Countries Offer to Monitor a Nuclear Test Ban," *Washington Post,* October 29, 1985.

70. Iklé, *How Nations Negotiate*, p. 205.

71. Smith, *Doubletalk*, p. 94.

72. Talbott, *Deadly Gambits*, p. 172.

73.Haig, *Caveat*, p. 118.

74. Talbott, *Deadly Gambits*, p. 194.

75. Zartman and Berman, *The Practical Negotiator*, p. 19.

76. Smith, *Doubletalk*, pp. 151–52.

77. Cited in Joseph G. Whelan, *Soviet Diplomacy and Negotiating Behavior* (Boulder, Colo.: Westview Press, 1983), p. 487.

78. Thomas Wolfe, *The SALT Experience* (Cambridge, Mass.: Ballinger Publishing Co., 1979), p. 156.

79. Seaborg, *Kennedy, Khrushchev, and the Test Ban*, p. 180.

80. Wolfe, *The SALT Experience*, p. 70.

81. Smith, *Doubletalk*, p. 65.

82. Ibid., p. 59.

83. Ibid., p. 467.

84. Daniel Druckman, "Human Factors in International Negotiations: Social-Psychological Aspects of International Conflict," *Sage Professional Paper in International Studies 02-020* (Beverly Hills: Sage Publications, 1973), p. 50.

Chapter 3

1. John Newhouse, *Cold Dawn* (New York: Holt, Rinehart and Winston, 1973); Gerard Smith, *Doubletalk: The Story of SALT I* (Garden City, N.Y.: Doubleday, 1980); Mason Willrich and John Rhinelander, *SALT: The Moscow Agreements and Beyond* (New York: Free Press, 1974); Henry A. Kissinger, *White House Years* and *Years of Upheaval* (Boston: Little, Brown, 1979 and 1982); Strobe Talbott, *Endgame: The Inside Story of SALT II (New York: Harper and Row, 1979);* Thomas W. Wolfe, *The SALT Experience* (Cambridge, Mass.: Ballinger Publishing Co., 1979); Zbigniew Brzezinski, *Power and Principle* (New York: Farrar, Straus, and Giroux, 1983); Cyrus Vance, *Hard Choices: Critical Years in America's Foreign Policy* (New York: Simon and Schuster, 1983); Arms Control and Disarmament Agency, *Documents on Disarmament* (Washington:

Government Printing Office, 1969–79), plus other scattered sources and newspaper and journal articles.

2. A test for intercoder reliability for the weighting of concessions in both the early postwar disarmament and the test ban negotiations was found to be significant at the .001 level. In the case of the SALT negotiations an independent coder agreed with the author's assessment in 37% of the cases and 85% of the weighted codings revealed either agreement or a difference of only one point.

3. Joseph Nogee and John Spanier, *The Politics of Disarmament* (New York: Praeger, 1962).

4. Bernard Berelson and Gary A. Steiner, *Human Behavior* (New York: Harcourt, Brace and World, 1964), p. 272.

5. Arthur Lall, *Negotiating Disarmament* (Ithaca, N.Y.: Cornell University Center for International Studies, 1964), pp. 22–23.

6. Unlike earlier disarmament talks it was not always easy to identify the beginning and end of a bargaining round. For SALT I (1969–72) formal breaks in the talks, whether held in Helsinki, Vienna, or Geneva, were used. During SALT II (1972–79) the end of a foreign ministers meeting was often used since most of the critical moves tended to be made at such sessions rather than in the Geneva talks, which had become the permanent site for the SALT negotiations.

7. Daniel Druckman, "Social Psychology and International Negotiation: Processes and Influences," in R. F. Kidd and M. J. Saks (eds.) *Advances in Applied Social Psychology,* Vol. 2, (Hillsdale, N.J.: Lawrence Erlbaum Associates, 1983), p. 72.

8. Richard J. Stoll and William McAndrew, "Negotiating Strategic Arms Control, 1969–1979: Modelling the Bargaining Process," *Journal of Conflict Resolution* 30 (June 1986): 315–26.

9. Sidney Siegel and L. Fouraker, *Bargaining and Group Decision Making* (New York: McGraw-Hill, 1960), pp. 93–95.

10. Other negotiation bodies during the period were excluded from this analysis because they usually did not extend over a long enough period to justify breaking concessions into the time units in which they occurred or they were interrupted by debates on other topics.

11. Gerard Smith *Doubletalk: The Story of SALT I* (Garden City, N.Y.: Doubleday, 1980), p. 333.

12. Henry A. Kissinger, *Years of Upheaval* (Boston: Little, Brown, 1982), p. 1007.

13. John G. Cross, *The Economics of Bargaining* (New York: Basic Books, 1969), p. 51.

14. Daniel Druckman, "Dogmatism, Prenegotiation Experience, and Simulated Group Representation as Determinants of Dyadic Behavior in a Bargaining Situation." *Journal of Personality and Social Psychology* 6 (1967): 279–90.

15. Smith, *Doubletalk,* p. 465.

16. Philip E. Mosely, "Techniques of Negotiation," in Raymond Dennett and Joseph Johnson (eds.), *Negotiating with the Russians* (Boston: World Peace Foundation, 1951), p. 299.

17. Henry A. Kissinger, *White House Years* (Boston: Little, Brown, 1979), p. 752.

18. Lloyd Jensen, "SALT on the Shelf: Problems and Prospects," *Parameters: Journal of the U.S. Army War College* 10 (December 1980); 58–59.

19. Smith, *Doubletalk,* p. 195.

20. I. William Zartman, "Negotiation as a Joint Decision-Making Process," in I. William Zartman (ed.) *The Negotiation Process: Theories and Applications* (Beverly Hills, Calif.: Sage Publications, 1978), pp. 67–81.

21. Gilbert R. Winham, "Complexity in International Negotiation," in Daniel Druckman (ed.) *Negotiations: A Social-Psychological Perspective* (Beverly Hills, Calif.: Sage Publications, 1977), pp. 347–66.

22. Smith, *Doubletalk*, p. 194.

23. Inis L. Claude, Jr., *Swords Into Plowshares* (New York: Random House, 4th ed., 1971), p. 289.

24. J. David Singer, *Deterrence, Arms Control, and Disarmament (Columbus: Ohio State University Press, 1962), p. 180.*

25. *Subcommittee on Disarmament, Senate Foreign Relations Committee, Hearings Before . . .* (Washington: Government Printing Office, Part 11, January 10, 1957, p. 1902.

26. Samuel P. Huntington, "Arms Races: Prerequisites and Results," in C. J. Friedrich and S. E. Harris (eds.), *Public Policy*, 1958 (Cambridge, Mass.: Harvard University Press, 1958), p. 81.

27. Lloyd Jensen, "The Postwar Disarmament Negotiations: A Study in American Soviet Bargaining Behavior" (Ann Arbor: University of Michigan, Ph.D. dissertation), p. 155.

28. Samuel B. Payne, *The Soviet Union and SALT* (Boulder, Colo.: Westview Publishing Co., 1981), p. 15.

29. Walter C. Clemens, Jr., *The Superpowers and Arms Control* (Lexington, Mass.: D. C. Heath, 1973), p. 81.

30. Jackson Diehl, "Gorbachev Says U.S. Act Hurt Ties, But Offers New 'Initiatives' on Forces," *Washington Post,* April 19, 1986.

31. Raymond L. Garthoff, *Detente and Confrontation: American-Soviet Relations from Nixon to Reagan* (Washington: Brookings Institution, 1985), p. 592.

32. Brzezinski, *Power and Principle*, p. 349.

33. Institute for Defense and Disarmament Studies, *Arms Control Reporter*, October 18, 1984.

34. Lloyd Jensen, "Military Capabilities and Bargaining Behavior," *Journal of Conflict Resolution* 9 (June 1965): 161–63.

35. U.S.-Soviet conflict data are reported in Daniel Frei and Deiter Ruloff, "Detente on Record," in Daniel Frei (ed.), *Definitions and Measurement of Detente* Cambridge, Mass.: Oelgeschlager, Gunn, and Hain, 1981), p. 80.

36. Bruce Russett and Donald R. DeLuca, " 'Don't Tread on Me': American Opinion on Foreign Policy in the Eighties," *Political Science Quarterly* 96 (1981): 383. Poll results were averaged on an annual basis in making the calculations since most years included more than one poll.

37. P. Terrence Hopmann, "Internal and External Influences on Bargaining in Arms Control Negotiations," in Bruce M. Russett (ed.), *Peace, War, and Numbers* (Beverly Hills, Calif.: Sage Publications, 1972), pp. 313-17.

38. David E. Lilienthal, *Change, Hope, and the Bomb* (Princeton, N.J.: Princeton University Press, 1963), p. 49.

39. Robin Ranger, *Arms and Politics, 1958–1978* (Toronto: Macmillan of Canada, 1979), p. 68.

40. Smith, *Doubletalk,* p. 226.

41. Barry M. Blechman, "Do Negotiated Arms Limitations Have a Future," *Foreign Affairs* 59 (Fall 1980): 107.

42. Robert J. Einhorn, *Negotiating From Strength: Leverage in U.S.-Soviet Arms Control Negotiations* (New York: Praeger, 1985).

43. Jensen, 'Military Capabilities and Bargaining Behavior," pp. 155–63.

44. Leonard Silk, "Soviet and U.S. Military Costs," *New York Times*, January 23, 1985.

45. Einhorn, *Negotiating from Strength*, pp. 19–20.

46. Ibid., p. 95.

47. R. James Woolsey, "Chipping Away at the Bargains," *Daedalus* 104 (Summer 1975): 180.

Chapter 4

1. Earl H. Voss, *Nuclear Ambush: The Test Ban Trap* (Chicago: Henry Regnery Co., 1963), p. xvi.

2. Robert A. Devine, *Blowing on the Wind: The Nuclear Test Ban Debate, 1954–1960* (New York: Oxford University Press, 1978), p. 149.

3. Henry A. Kissinger, "Nuclear Testing and the Problem of Peace," *Foreign Affairs*, 37 (October 1958): pp. 1–18.

4. Voss, *Nuclear Ambush*, p. 159.

5. Glenn T. Seaborg, *Kennedy, Khrushchev, and the Test Ban Treaty* (Berkeley: University of California Press, 1981), p. 17.

6. Harold K. Jacobson and Eric Stein, *Diplomats, Scientists, and Politicians: The United States and the Nuclear Test Ban Negotiations* (Ann Arbor: University of Michigan Press, 1966), p. 246.

7. Voss, *Nuclear Ambush*, p. 338.

8. Alva Myrdal, *The Game of Disarmament* (New York: Pantheon Books, 1982), p. 92.

9. Sir Edward Bullard, "The Detection of Underground Explosions," in Herbert F. York (ed.), *Arms Control* (San Francisco: W. H. Freeman and Co., 1973), pp. 140–50.

10. Arthur T. Hadley, *The Nation's Safety and Arms Control* (New York: Viking, 1961), p. 50.

11. Jacobson and Stein, *Diplomats, Scientists, and Politicians*, p. 386.

12. Ibid., p. 497.

13. Department of State, *Documents on Disarmament, 1945–1959*, (Washington: Government Printing Office, 1960), Vol 2, pp, 1427–36.

14. Eighteen Nation Disarmament Committee, *Official Records*, PV 19, p. 38.

15. Robert S. Jastrow, "Politics of the Afrikaner Bomb," *Orbis* 27 (Winter 1984): 832.

16. Department of State, *Documents on Disarmament, 1945–1959*, Vol. 2 p. 1591.

17. Michael Wright, *Disarm and Verify* (New York: Praeger, 1964), p. 126.

18. Eisenhower letter to Gordon Gray, June 14, 1961. *The Declassified Documents Quarterly Catalog* (Washington: Research Publications, 1980), p. 216.

19. Seaborg, *Kennedy, Khrushchev, and the Test Ban Treaty*, p. 139.

20. United States Arms Control and Disarmament Agency, *Documents on Disarmament, 1962* (Washington: Government Printing Office, 1963), p. 74.

21. Ibid., 1963, p. 220.

22. Joseph G. Whelan, *Soviet Diplomacy and Negotiating Behavior* (Boulder: Westview Press, 1983), p. 374.

23. Center for Defense Information, *The Defense Monitor*, Vol. 14, No. 8 (1985).

24. Jacobson and Stein, *Diplomats, Scientists, and Politicians*, p. 246.

25. Bernard J. Firestone, *The Quest for Nuclear Stability* (Westport, Conn.: Greenwood Press, 1982), pp. 102-3.

26. Devine, *Blowing on the Wind*, p. 273.

27. Seaborg, *Kennedy, Khrushchev, and the Test Ban Treaty*, p. 222.

28. Stephen Hilgartner, Richard C. Bell, and Rory O'Connor, *Nukespeak: The Selling of Nuclear Technology in America* (San Francisco: Sierra Club Books, 1982), p. 166.

29. Henry A. Kissinger, *Years of Upheaval* (Boston: Little, Brown, 1982), p. 1167.

30. Theo Ginsberg, *The Question of Peaceful Explosions for the Benefit of Non-Nuclear Weapon States,* UN Document, A/Conf. 35/Doc. 2 (July 3, 1968).

31. William B. Bader, *The United States and the Spread of Nuclear Weapons* (New York: Pegasus, 1968), p. 54.

32. Kennedy letter to Senators Mansfield and Dirksen dated September 11, 1963. ACDA, *Documents on Disarmament, 1963,* pp. 490–91.

33. Geneva Conference on the Discontinuance of Nuclear Weapon Tests, GEN/DNT/PV 141, December 1, 1959.

34. Swedish Delegation, "Nuclear Explosives, 1945-83," *Conference on Disarmament,* CD/430, February 7, 1984.

35. Thomas O'Toole, "Talks by U.S.-Soviets on A-Test Curbs Falter," *Washington Post,* January 18, 1975.

36. Zbigniew Brzezinski, *Power and Principle* (New York: Farrar, Straus, Giroux, 1983), p. 172.

37. Seaborg, *Kennedy, Khrushchev, and the Test Ban Treaty,* pp. 296–97.

38. "Soviet Noncompliance with Arms Control Agreements," reprint of President Reagan's Message to Congress in Paul R. Viotti (ed.), *Conflict and Arms Control* (Boulder, Colo.: Westview Press, 1986), p. 170.

39. Walter Pincus, "U.S. Secretly Protested Radiation Leaks from Soviet Arms Tests, Perle Says," *Washington Post,* May 9, 1986.

40. Walter Pincus, "U.S. Seeks A-Test Talks with Soviets," *Washington Post,* March 13, 1983.

41. Walter Pincus, "U.S. Drops Soviet Talks to Continue A-Arms Testing," *Washington Post,* September 8, 1983.

42. Garcia Robles, Conference on Disarmament (CD/PV 297, March 7, 1985), p. 21.

43. Leslie Gelb, "U.S.-Summit Stance: Nuclear Testing Will Go On," *New York Times,* October 4, 1985.

44. Lynn R. Sykes and Jack F. Evernden, "The Verification of a Comprehensive Nuclear Test Ban," *Scientific American* 247 (October 1982): 54.

45. Don Oberdorfer, "Six Nonaligned Countries Offer to Monitor a Nuclear Test Ban," *Washington Post,* October 29, 1985, p. A14.

46. Michael R. Gordon, "New Measures Seen for Soviet A-Test," *New York Times,* November 4, 1985.

47. Don Oberdorfer, "New CIA Calculations Cast Doubt on Test Ban Violations by Soviets," *Washington Post,* April 4, 1986.

48. Gelb, "U.S.-Soviet Stance: Nuclear Testing Will Go On."

49. Dan Caldwell, "Comprehensive Test Ban: An Effective SALT Substitute," *Bulletin of Atomic Scientists* 36 (December 1980): 32.

50. Walter Pincus, "U.S. Reveals Nuclear Arms Suffer Reliability Problems," *Washington Post,* March 12, 1986.

51. See Hugh E. Dewitt and Gerald E. Marsh, "Stockpile Reliability and Nuclear Testing," *Bulletin of Atomic Scientists* 40 (April 1984), pp. 40–41.

52. Donald Kerr, "Nuclear Weapon Test Bans," in Warren Heckrotte and George C. Smith (eds), *Arms Control in Transition* (Boulder, Colo.: Westview Press, 1983), pp. 81–82.

53. Cited in Flora Lewis, "Chicken or Egg?" *New York Times,* February 23, 1986.

54. Bruce Russett and Fred Chernoff, *Arms Control and the Arms Race* (New York: W. H. Freeman and Company, 1985), p. 95.

55. Flora Lewis, "Chicken or Egg."

56. Cristine Russell, "Underground Test Called Crucial for SDI," *Washington Post*, February 15, 1987.

57. R. Jeffrey Smith, "Soviets Agree to Broad Seismic Test," Science 233 (August 1, 1986): 511.

Chapter 5

1. William Sweet, *The Nuclear Age* (Washington: *Congressional Quarterly*, 1984), p. 97.

2. Joseph S. Nye, "Prospects for Nonproliferation," in Rodney W. Jones (ed.), *The Nuclear Suppliers and Nonproliferation* (Lexington, Mass.: D. C. Heath, 1983), p. 219.

3. Anthony C. Ross and Peter King, *Australia and Nuclear Weapons* (Sydney, Australia: Sydney University Press, 1966), p. 15.

4. See Kenneth N. Waltz, "Toward Nuclear Peace," in Dagobert L. Brito, et al., *Strategies for Managing Nuclear Proliferation* (Lexington, Mass.: D. C. Heath, 1983), pp. 118-33.

5. Arnold Kramish, *The Peaceful Atom* (New York: Harper and Row, 1963), p. 18.

6. Duncan L. Clarke, *Politics and Arms Control* (New York: Free Press, 1979), pp. 15–16.

7. Cited by Ellen Collier in U.S. Senate Foreign Relations Committee, *Nonproliferation Treaty* (Hearings, February 18 and 19, 1969), p. 463.

8. Bernard J. Firestone, *The Quest for Nuclear Stability* (Westport, Conn.: Greenwood Press, 1982), p. 110.

9. UN Document, A/5976 (September 24, 1965).

10. Eighteen Nation Disarmament Committee (ENDC), PV 268 (June 28, 1966).

11. U.S. Arms Control and Disarmament Agency, *Documents on Disarmament, 1965* (Washington: Government Printing Office, 1966), pp. 347–49.

12. Lloyd Jensen, *Return from the Nuclear Brink: National Interest and the Nuclear Nonproliferation Treaty* (Lexington, Mass.: D. C. Heath, 1974), p. 2.

13. John Simpson, "Diagnosis and Treatment," in John Simpson and Anthony McGraw (eds.), *The International Nonproliferation System* (London: Macmillan, 1984), p. 169.

14. Roger Richter, "Testimony," *Bulletin of Atomic Scientists,* 37 (October 1981): 29–31.

15. "International Atomic Energy Agency Says it Had Inspection Problems in '81," *New York Times*, July 6, 1981.

16. Sweet, *The Nuclear Age*, p. 151.

17. Cited in Robert L. Beckman, *Nuclear Non-Proliferation: Congress and the Control of Peaceful Nuclear Activities* (Boulder, Colo.: Westview Press, 1985), pp. 290–91.

18, ENDC/PV 223 (August 12, 1965), p. 19.

19. For a discussion of the IAEA safeguards system, see Lawrence Scheinman, *The Nonproliferation Role of the International Atomic Energy Agency* (Washington: Resources for the Future, 1985) and International Atomic Energy Agency, *IAEA Safeguards: An Introduction* (Vienna: IAEA, 1981).

20. U.S. Arms Control and Disarmament Agency, *Documents on Disarmament, 1982*, p. 350.

21. *Louisville Courier-Journal*, March 12, 1969.

22. Robert Scheer, *With Enough Shovels: Reagan, Bush and Nuclear War* (New York: Random House, 1982), p. 6.

23. UN Document, A/C.1/PV 1570 (May 17, 1968), p. 2.

24. Jensen, *Return from the Nuclear Brink* p. 79.

25. Ibid., p. 52.

26. Glenn T. Seaborg, *Kennedy, Khrushchev, and the Test Ban Treaty* (Berkeley: University of California Press, 1981), p. 248.

27. Thomas O'Toole, "Talks by U.S.-Soviets on A-Test Curbs Falter," *Washington Post*, January 1, 1975.

28. John Simpson, "Diagnosis and Treatment," p. 172.

29. Michel Eyraud, "La France face a un eventuel traite de non-dissemination des armes nucleaires," *Politique Etrangere*, no. 4–5 (1967): 477.

30. "Reflections on the Quarter," *Orbis* 11 (Spring 1967): 8.

31. *Facts on File*, July 16-22, 1970, p. 509.

32. George W. Ball, "We Are Playing a Dangerous Game with Japan," *New York Times Magazine*, June 25, 1972, pp. 35–36.

33. Lewis A. Dunn, *Controlling the Bomb: Nuclear Proliferation in the 1980s* (New Haven: Yale University Press, 1982), p. 44.

34. *Washington Post*, July 16, 1980.

35. Sweet, *The Nuclear Age*, p. 116.

36. George H. Quester, "Nuclear Proliferation," in Bernard Brodie, et al., *National Security and International Stability* (Cambridge, Mass.: Oelgeshlager, Gunn and Hain, 1983), p. 232.

37. Walter C. Clemens, Jr., "National Security and U.S.-Soviet Relations," in Burns H. Weston (ed.), *Toward Nuclear Disarmament and Global Security* (Boulder, Colo.: Westview Press, 1984), p. 353.

38. William C. Potter, "U.S.-Soviet Cooperative Measures for Nonproliferation," in Jones et al., *The Nuclear Suppliers and Nonproliferation*, (Lexington, Mass.: D. C. Heath, 1985), p. 11.

39. Raymond L. Garthoff, *Detente and Confrontation* (Washington: Brookings Institution, 1985), p. 763.

40. J. B. Devine, "The USA's Nuclear Non-Proliferation Policy," in Simpson and McGraw, (eds.), *The International Nuclear Non-Proliferation System*, p. 112.

41. M. J. Wilmhurst, "The Development of Current Non-Proliferation Policies," in Ibid., p. 44.

42. Richard Kennedy, "Nuclear Trade: Reliable Supply and Mutual Obligation" in Jones et al., *The Nuclear Suppliers and Nonproliferation*, p. 30.

43. Dunn, *Controlling the Bomb*, p. 105.

44. Institute for Defense and Disarmament Studies, *Arms Control Reporter*, April 8, 1985.

45. David Ignautius, "U.S. Pressuring Pakistan to Abandon Controversial Nuclear Arms Program," *Wall Street Journal*, October 25, 1985.

46. Bob Woodward, "Pakistan Reported Near Atom Arms Production," *Washington Post*, November, 1986.

Chapter 6

1. J. David Singer, *Deterrence, Arms Control, and Disarmament* (Columbus: Ohio State University Press, 1962), p. 216.

2. Richard J. Barnet, *Who Wants Disarmament?* (Boston: Beacon Press, 1960), p. 86.

3. Lewis A. Dunn, *Controlling the Bomb* (New Haven: Yale University Press, 1976), p. 28.

4. Edmund Beard, *Developing the ICBM* (New York: Columbia University Press, 1976), p. 121.

5. Ibid., p. 218.

6. U.S. Department of State, *Documents on Disarmament, 1945–59* (Washington: Government Printing Office, 1960), p. 687.

7. "Bulganin Letter to Eisenhower," *New York Times*, February 4, 1958.

8. U.S. Department of State, *Documents on Disarmament, 1945-59*, pp. 973–77.

9. Ibid., pp. 1460–74.

10. U.S. Arms Control and Disarmament Agency, *Documents on Disarmament, 1961*, pp. 439–42.

11. Ibid., 1965, pp. 75–76.

12. *Washington Post*, May 21, 1965.

13. Duncan L. Clarke, "Nixon Installs a 'Peace Cabinet'—But Where Is the Peace Agency?" *War/Peace Report* (January–February, 1973), p. 28.

14. Ted Greenwood, *Making the MIRV: A Study of Defense Decisionmaking* (Cambridge: Ballinger, 1975), p. 116.

15. Raymond L. Garthoff, "SALT and the Soviet Military," *Problems of Communism* 24 (January-February 1975): 29.

16. John Newhouse, *Cold Dawn: The Story of SALT* (New York: Holt, Rinehart and Winston, 1973), p. 107.

17. Gerard Smith, *Doubletalk: The Story of SALT I* (Garden City, N.Y.: Doubleday, 1980), p. 360.

18. Thomas Wolfe, *The SALT Experience* (Cambridge: Ballinger 1979), p. 124.

19. Mark M. Lowenthal, "The START Proposal: Verification Issues" (Washington: Congressional Research Service, June 25, 1982), p. 1.

20. U.S. Department of Defense, *Annual Report of the Secretary of Defense* (Washington: Government Printing Office, 1980).

21. *Defense Monitor*, August 1974, p. 3.

22. U.S. Senate, Committee on Foreign Relations, *The SALT II Treaty, Hearings*, 96th Cong., 1st Sess., Part II, July 16–19, 1979, pp. 242–43 and 258.

23. Roger P. Labrie, *SALT Handbook: Key Documents and Issues, 1972–1979* (Washington: American Enterprise Institute, 1979), p. 291.

24. *New York Times*, May 3, 1974, p. 3.

25. *Defense Monitor*, XI, No. 7 (1982).

26. Labrie, *SALT Handbook*, p. 303.

27. William H. Kincade, "Challenges to Verification: Old and New," *Arms Control* 3 (December 1982): 23.

28. Clarence A. Robinson "SALT Proposals Facing Hurdles," *Aviation Week and Space Technology*, December 9, 1974, p. 13.

29. U.S. Senate, Committee on Foreign Relations, *The SALT II Treaty, Hearings*, Pt. 1, p. 110.

30. Cited by Milton Leitenberg in Committee on Foreign Relations, U.S. Senate, *Detente Hearings*, 93rd Congress, second session, 1974, p. 475.

31. Newhouse, *Cold Dawn*, p. 246.

32. *New York Times*, July 14, 1978.

33. "ABM: Boondoggle or Bargaining Chip," *Nature* 227 (August 22, 1970): 770.

34. John W. Finney, "Cruise Missiles Provoke Conflict with the Military as Well as with Soviets," *New York Times*, January 21, 1976.

35. Roger P. Labrie, *SALT Handbook* (Washington: American Enterprise Institute, 1979), p. 298.

36. "Excerpts from Speech by Andropov on Medium-Range Nuclear Missiles," *New York Times,* December 22, 1982, p. A14.

37. For a discussion of this tendency in United States negotiating tactics and Soviet efforts to exploit it, see Roy O. Kohler, *SALT II: How not to Negotiate with the Russians* (Coral Gables: Advanced International Studies Institute, University of Miami, 1979).

Chapter 7

1. Lawrence Freedman, "Negotiations on Nuclear Forces in Europe, 1969-83," in Hans-Henrick Holm and Nikolaj Petersen (eds.), *The European Missile Crises* (London: Francis Pinter, 1983), p. 136.

2. Eric J. Grove, "Allied Nuclear Forces Complicate Negotiations," *Bulletin of the Atomic Scientists* 42 (June/July 1986): 21.

3. Fred Hiatt and Rick Atkinson, "Insertable Nuclear Warheads Could Convert Arms," *Washington Post,* June 15, 1986.

4. Strobe Talbott, *Deadly Gambits,* (New York: Alfred A. Knopf, 1984), pp. 66–68.

5. Talbott, *Deadly Gambits,* pp. 144–47 and Ir Faurby, Hans-Henrick Holm, and Nikolaj Petersen, "Introduction," in Holm and Petersen (eds.), *The European Missile Crisis,* p. 21.

6. Paul Nitze, Speech delivered to the American Association for the Advancement of Science Convention, New York City, May 26, 1984.

7. David Holloway, "The INF Policy of the Soviet Union," in Holm and Petersen (eds.), *The European Missile Crisis,* p. 106.

8. Raymond L. Garthoff, "The SS-20 Moratorium: Who Is Telling the Truth," *Washington Post,* April 26, 1983.

9. Richard Perle, "Letters to the Editor," *Washington Post,* May 12, 1983.

10. Robert Scheer, *With Enough Shovels: Reagan, Bush and Nuclear War* (New York: Random House, 1982), p. 6.

11. Carl G. Jacobsen, *The President's Arms Posture: Sins of Omission* (Miami: University of Miami Center for Advanced International Studies, n.d.), p. 2.

12. U.S. Arms Control and Disarmament Agency, *1984 Annual Report* (Washington: Government Pri..ting Office, 1985), p. 20.

13. John Borawski, "The Future of INF," *Parameters* 15 (Summer 1985), p. 39.

14. "Transcript of Reagan's Speech on Soviet-American Relations," *New York Times,* January 17, 1984, p. A8.

15. Institute for Defense and Disarmament Studies, *Arms Control Reporter,* May 1, 1985.

16. Walter Pincus, "Soviets Offer INF Draft Pact," *Washington Post,* May 16, 1986.

17. Richard Bernsten, "Gorbachev Urges Arms Agreement with Europeans," *New York Times,* October 5, 1985.

18. Karen De Young, "Soviets Modify Stance on British, French Arms," *Washington Post,* July 17, 1986.

19. Walter Pincus, "Soviets Offer INF Draft Pact."

20. Paul Nitze, Speech delivered to the American Association for the Advancement of Science Convention, New York City, May 26, 1984.

21. Raymond L. Garthoff, "Postmortem on INF Talks," *Bulletin of the Atomic Scientists* 40 (December 1984): 9.

22. Cited in Leo Sartori, "Will SALT II Survive?" *International Security* 10 (Winter 1985–86): 151, and A. A. Tinajero, *President Reagan's START Proposal* (Washington: Congressional Research Service, Library of Congress, June 9, 1982).

23. Judith Miller, "Anti-Arms Groups Relent Plan for MX," *New York Times*, November 24, 1982.

24. Walter Pincus, "Administration Urged to Seek Extension of Some SALT II Curbs," *Washington Post*, March 5, 1985.

25. "Reagan Statement on Arms Accord," *New York Times*, June 11, 1985, p. A10.

26. Walter Pincus and Don Oberdorfer, "Two Subs to be Dismantled," *Washington Post*, April 22, 1986.

27. Kenneth L. Adelman, "Why Mr. Reagan Is Right about SALT," *New York Times*, June 15, 1986.

28. Institute for Defense and Disarmament Studies, *Arms Control Reporter*, 1985.

29. Adelman, "Why Mr. Reagan Is Right about SALT."

30. Bernard Gwertzman, "NATO Faults U.S. on Intent to Drop 1979 Arms Treaty," *New York Times*, May 30, 1986.

31. David Ignautius, "Without SALT the Race is On," *Washington Post*, June 8, 1986.

32. Cited in Don Oberdorfer, "Last Minute Conservative Pleas Influenced Reagan's Decision," *Washington Post*, June 1, 1986.

33. David Hoffman, "Reagan Calls SALT II Dead," *Washington Post*, June 6, 1986.

34. Michael R. Gordon, "Administration Split on Arms Treaty Compliance," *New York Times*, March 27, 1986.

35. Walter Pincus, "U.S. to End SALT II Discussions with Soviet Union Later this Year," *Washington Post*, July 25, 1986.

36. Alexander Haig, *Caveat: Realism, Reagan, and Foreign Policy* (New York: Macmillan and Co., 1984), p. 223.

37. Raymond L. Garthoff, "An Arms Nonoffer," *Washington Post*, June 12, 1983.

38. Gerard Smith, "The Arms Control and Disarmament Agency: An Unfinished History," *Bulletin of the Atomic Scientist* 40 (April 1984): 13.

39. Herbert Scoville, "Build-Down (-Doom?), *New York Times*, October 11, 1983.

40. Stephen S. Rosenfeld, "Signal from Gorbachev," *Washington Post*, January 31, 1986.

41. Michael R. Gordon, "Moscow Said to Signal Willingness to Work on Arms Pact Verification," *New York Times*, June 22, 1986.

42. Paul H. Nitze, "Arms Control," in Joseph Kruzel (ed.), *American Defense Annual, 1986-1987* (Lexington, Mass.: D. C. Heath, 1986), p. 180.

43. "Nuclear Disarmament by the Year 2000," *New York Times*, February 5, 1986, p. A13.

44. Bill Keller, "Doubts Increase over Future of U.S. Land-Based Missiles," *New York Times*, June 17, 1985.

45. R. Jeffrey Smith, "Midgetman Missile Plans Generate Political Debate," *Science* 232 (June 6, 1986): 1186.

46. Richard Halloran, "White House Seeks Funds for Basing MX on Train Car," *New York Times*, December 20, 1986.

47. Michael Mandelbaum and Strobe Talbott, *Reagan and Gorbachev* (New York: Vintage Books, 1987), pp. 171–81.

48. Sidney D. Drell, Philip J. Farley, and David Holloway, "Preserving the ABM Treaty," *International Security* 9 (Fall 1984): 68.

49. Colin S. Gray, "Strategic Forces," in Kruzel (ed.), *American Defense Annual, 1986–1987*, p. 82.

50. Thomas Karas, *The New High Ground: Systems and Weapons of Space Age War* (New York: Simon and Schuster, 1983), p. 181 and William J. Broad, "Reverberations of the Space Crisis," *New York Times*, June 15, 1986.

51. "Doubt Cast on Missile Shield," *New York Times*, October 31, 1986.

52. Peter Osnos, "ABM Plan Spurs European Concern Over Timing, Defense Implications," *Washington Post*, March 30, 1983.

53. *The Arms Control Reporter*, February 10, 1985, p. 575 B. 9.

54. United Nations General Assembly, Resolution 39/59 (1984).

55. Fred Hiatt and Rich Atkinson, "SDI Seen Spurring Warhead Growth," *Washington Post*, June 2, 1986.

56. Ralph Earle, Speech delivered to the American Association for the Advancement of Science Convention, Philadelphia, Pa., May 28, 1986.

57. Charles L. Gellner, "The Reagan Administration," in Paul R. Viotti (ed.), *Conflict and Arms Control* (Boulder, Colo.: Westview Publishers, 1986), p. 34.

58. Alan B. Sherr, "The Languages of Arms Control," *Bulletin of Atomic Scientists* 41 (November 1985): 26.

59. Walter Pincus, "Space Defense Tests to Avoid Treaty Breach," *Washington Post*, April 21, 1985.

60. Don Oberdorfer, "ABM Reinterpretation: A Quick Study," *Washington Post*, October 22, 1985.

61. Walter Pincus, "Space Defense Tests to Avoid Treaty Breach," *Washington Post*, April 21, 1985.

62. Michael R. Gordon, "U.S. Pursues Plan for New Radars Despite Fears of Treaty Violation," *New York Times*, December 12, 1986.

63. Michael R. Gordon, "ABM Pact Tied to Fund Pledge for Star Wars," *New York Times*, May 19, 1986.

64. "Moscow's Vigorous Leader," *Time Magazine*, September 9, 1985.

65. Leslie H. Gelb, "Reagan is Termed Ready to Discuss ABM Pact Change," *New York Times*, July 22, 1986.

66. Leslie H. Gelb, "Reagan Reported to Stay Insistent on 'Star War' Test," *New York Times*, July 24, 1986.

67. Walter Pincus, "Star Wars Chief Says Deployment, if Feasible, Would Take at Least Decade," *Washington Post*, July 24, 1986.

68. R. Jeffrey Smith and Joanne Omang, "Forms of ABM Consultation Not Settled, Shultz Says," *Washington Post*, February 12, 1987.

69. Charles Mohr, "Space Arms: Debate Over the Value of a Treaty," *New York Times*, July 10, 1984.

70. For an intriguing analysis of the tacit bargaining involved in the consensus that evolved on satellite reconnaissance and ASAT systems see Gerald Steinberg, *Satellite Reconnaissance: Informal Bargaining* (New York: Praeger Publishers, 1983).

71. Ibid., p. 84.

72. Bill Keller, "Entwined with 'Star Wars', Anti-Satellite Debate Grows," *New York Times*, August 26, 1985.

73. Charles Mohr, "Official Defends Space-Weapon Test," *New York Times*, September 12, 1985.

74. R. Jeffrey Smith, "Pentagon Plans New Antisatellite Tests," *Science* 233 (July 25, 1986): 409.

75. Walter Pincus, "Pentagon May Discard ASAT System," *Washington Post*, July 22, 1986.

76. Donald L. Hafner, "Approaches to the Control of Antisatellite Weapons," in William J. Durch (ed.), *National Interests and the Military Use of Space* (Cambridge, Mass.: Ballinger Publishing Co., 1984), p. 250.

77. James Reston, "Now the Silly Season," *New York Times*, July 6, 1986.

Chapter 8

1. Philip Towle, "Unilateralism or Disarmament by Example," *Arms Control* 2 (May 1981): 116.

2. Henry S. Bradsher, "Soviets Seek Ban on New U.S. Missile," *Washington Star*, June 26, 1975.

3. George W. Rathjens, "Changing Perspectives on Arms Control," *Daedalus* 104 (Summer 1975): 205.

4. Kenneth L. Adelman, "Arms Control Without Agreements," *Foreign Affairs* 63 (Winter 1984–85): 240–63.

5. Abram Chayes, "Nuclear Arms Control After the Cold War," *Daedalus* 104 (Summer 1975): 16.

Appendix

Table A.1 USSR Concessions (1946–60)

USSR Concessions and Retractions	Date	Mag.
Drops insistence on national legislation as main inspection device.	11-29-46	5
Agrees to policy of submitting information on own armed forces at home as well as in foreign countries	11-29-46	2
Day-to-day decisions of control agency to be made by majority	12-4-46	5
Agrees to periodic inspection	2-18-47	4
Ban on possession doesn't include destruction in 3 months	2-18-47	3
Agrees to ''inspection, supervision, and *management*'' of all atomic plants	2-18-47	2
Delete word *management* (retraction)	3-5-47	− 2
Inspection system to include mining facilities	6-11-47	2
Inspection personnel selected on an international basis	6-11-47	3
International Control Commission to conduct peaceful atomic research	6-11-47	2
Special investigation permitted in cases of suspicious events	6-11-47	3
Simultaneous conclusion of prohibition and control treaties	10-2-48	4
Continuous inspection	6-3-49	5
3-month limit to destroy atomic weapons (retraction).	10-25-49	−3
Drops reference to 3-month limit for destroying atomic bombs	10-23-50	3

272

USSR Concessions and Retractions	Date	Mag.
First proposal envisaging one control organ for both nuclear and conventional weapons	12-11-51	3
Agrees to control provisions and atomic disarmament in same resolution	12-12-51	4
Agrees to use Anglo-French proposal of June 11, 1954, as basis for discussion	9-30-54	1
First time for stages	9-30-54	5
Agrees to continuous inspection but without reference to domestic jurisdiction	9-30-54	3
Reduction of armed forces without specifying 1/3 reductions—hint of acceptance of fixed ceilings	9-30-54	2
50% reduction of agreed conventional force reduction before nuclear prohibition	9-30-54	3
Instructs Disarmament Commission to study proposal of U.K. and France banning the use of atomic weapons but with the right to use them in self-defense against aggression	9-30-54	1
Separate control organs for conventional and nuclear arms—former to be temporary (retraction).	9-30-54	−3
Calls for immediate agreement on destruction of nuclear weapons (retraction).	3-1-55	−3
Returns to proposing 1/3 reduction for conventional weapons and armed forces (retraction)	3-22-55	−2
Signed convention providing for use ban no longer a precondition for disarmament	3-30-55	3
Nuclear possession ban after 75% of the conventional reductions complete	5-10-55	3
Agrees to force level of 1-1.5 million for U.S.-USSR-China.	5-10-55	3
Stresses need for political settlement	5-10-55	2
Nuclear production ban begins before possession ban, i.e., at very beginning of second stage	5-10-55	3
Ground inspection control posts	5-10-55	5
Access to budgetary records	5-10-55	2
No longer insists upon separate control organs for nuclear and conventional weapons	5-10-55	3
Admits difficulties of preventing clandestine production and detecting hidden nuclear stockpiles	5-10-55	2

USSR Concessions and Retractions	Date	Mag.
Nuclear weapons may be used for defensive purposes with permission of Security Council	7-21-55	3
Will consider aerial inspection for final stage	9-19-55	1
Agrees to establishment of control system pending the initiation of arms reduction	3-27-56	4
Accepts 2.5 million and 750,000 level for first-stage forces (non-Big Five limited to 150-200,000 men).	7-12-56	2
Officially accepts aerial inspection: 800 kilometers each side of line dividing East and West	11-17-56	4
Agrees to unilateral obligations not to use nuclear weapons (no convention needed)	3-18-57	3
Drops insistence on 200,000 level for forces of lesser powers	4-30-57	3
Aerial inspection extended to include eastern Siberia for Alaska and western U.S.; also a little beyond 800 kilometers to the east of European line	4-30-57	2
Control posts at airfield only in second stage, along with nuclear disarmament (retraction)	4-30-57	−2
Accepts 2.5-2.1-1.7 million armed force levels (but with no conditions such as political settlement)	7-19-57	3
Indicated acceptance of idea of international disarmament depots for the storage of arms	Summer 57	2
Five-year nuclear weapons use ban pending agreement (retraction)	9-20-57	−3
Agrees to reduce armaments according to mutual lists	9-20-57	2
Fails to stress ban on foreign bases, would discuss possibility of *limiting*	9-20-57	1
Aerial inspection of all of USSR after abolition of atomic weapons and substantial conventional reductions	5-5-58	2
Aerial inspection to include Turkey, Iran, Japan in addition to territories of 4-30-57 (also back to 800-kilometer extensions—retraction).	11-28-58	−1
First commitment on numbers of control posts: Warsaw, 28; West, 54 (inludes 6 each for U.S. and USSR)	11-28-58	2
NATO and Warsaw aerial inspection groups to photograph own side, but must include representatives of the other side (retraction)	12-12-58	−2

USSR Concessions and Retractions	Date	Mag.
Equal representation of sides in the International Supervisory Body and the Control Posts (retraction)	12-12-58	−2
If West doesn't agree to comprehensive measures, may accept partial measures, including those suggested 5-10-55	9-19-59	2
Four-year time limit for GCD (retraction)	9-19-59	−3
Extensive conventional disarmament in first stage, i.e., 1.7 million level (retraction)	9-19-59	−2
Aerial inspection relegated to third stage (retraction)	9-19-59	−3
Cut-off in nuclear production in second stage instead of third	6-2-60	3
More flexible on four-year timetable but limit must be specified	6-2-60	3
Place militia at disposal of Security Council where necessary	6-2-60	3
Moves production-possession ban on delivery systems from third to first stage	6-2-60	0
Moves ban on foreign bases from second to first stage (retraction)	6-2-60	−3
Permanent control teams at some plants	6-2-60	3
On-site inspection over disbanding of troops and destruction of armaments	6-2-60	3
1.7 million level moved to second stage	6-2-60	2
Period between signature and ratification should be used for taking practical steps to establish control organ	6-14-60	3
Khrushchev: "As for control over the destruction of armaments and disarmament, let the United States propose a system of such control. We shall accept whatever proposals the U.S. will make . . ."	9-9-60	3
1.7 million level moved back to first stage (retraction)	9-23-60	−2
Proposes troika for U.N. secretariat and Security Council. The agents of enforcement in Soviet plans (retraction).	10-13-60	−3

Table A.2 U.S. Concessions (1946–60)

U.S. Concessions and Retractions	Date	Mag.
International control system may operate in framework of Security Council. Unless otherwise specified, no sanctions without agreement of permanent members	12-14-46	4
Ownership and management of large-scale mining and industrial operations *re* thorium and uranium unnecessary	12-31-46	4
Quotas *re* ownership of nuclear materials will be put into treaty rather than left to discretion of International Agency	9-11-47	4
Production of nuclear fuels to be restricted to that required for plants actually entering into construction	9-11-47	3
Controls limiting powers of the agency, e.g., procedure for warrants, restrictions on inspector's behavior, etc.	9-11-47	2
Less emphasis upon punishment of violators and more upon establishing effective warning system in case of violations	9-11-47	2
Security Council to be primarily responsible for sanctions involving violation of conventional arms agreement	5-18-50	3
Disclosure in each stage of both nuclear and conventional weapons	4-5-52	2
Staging made more specific, making clearer how it would lead to atomic disarmament	4-5-52	2
Not as adamant about U.N. Plan—will support only until better plan devised (or as good)	4-5-52	2
Softens meaning of "ownership," suggesting several restraints on ownership powers	5-14-52	3
Commits self on reduction levels, e.g., 1-1.5 million, 700 to 800 thousand for U.K. and France (conditional on political settlement, e.g., Korea)	5-28-52	2
Accepts veto with regard to conventional and atomic reductions—physical sanctions only in accordance with chapter VII of Charter	5-17-54	5
Abandoned procedure of getting General Assembly approval of Western resolutions—worked out compromise with Soviets—first unanimous disarmament resolution since 1946	11-4-54	3

U.S. Concessions and Retractions	Date	Mag.
Nuclear *possession* ban may begin before conventional arms reduced (i.e., after 75% of agreed conventional reductions)	4-19-55	3
Eisenhower's departure from disarmament to open skies (retraction)	7-21-55	-5
Reservation placed on all past United States proposals (retraction)	9-6-55	-5
Opposes nuclear-production-possession ban unless better inspection techniques can be developed (clearly didn't expect much in this regard—retraction)	10-7-55	-4
Agrees to production ban if satisfactory progress on effective inspection system	3-19-56	3
Calls for limited inspection zones, demonstration test area	3-21-56	2
Devises plan for first phase of a comprehensive plan: forces 2.5 million and 750 thousand	4-3-56	1
Proposes limits on nuclear possession by transferring to peaceful uses	4-3-56	2
10% expenditure reduction in first stage. 15% for second stage	4-8-57	1
Proposes second stage reductions of 2.1 million level for armed forces	6-20-57	2
Third stage force reduction—1.7 million level (conditional on poliltical settlement).	6-25-57	2
Will transfer 53% of nuclear materials to peaceful uses compared to Soviet's 47%	7-5-57	1
Package proposal made inseparable (retraction)	8-29-57	-3
Alternative aerial inspection zones:	8-29-57	2
(1) All U.S.-Canada for USSR		
(2) Arctic inspection zone		
(3) Linked with one of the above would be an all-European and significant amount of western Russia		
First GCD plan	3-16-60	4
First unequivocal statement on possession on ban since 1955 reservation	4-26-60	3
Agrees to reduce forces as low as 1.7 million for second stage—third stage to internal security level	6-27-60	3

Table A.3 USSR Concessions: Test Ban Negotiations

USSR Concessions and Retractions	Date	Mag.
Agrees to reciprocal control posts for policing test ban (2 or 3 year moratorium)	6-14-57	5
One convention for both control and cessation measures	11-29-57	3
Proposes Commission of 3 Founder States. Will accept 7 providing the 3 have a veto	12-8-58	2
Agrees to a single administrator	12-12-58	4
Headquarters staffing: East-West parity in key positions	1-30-59	2
4 or 5 out of 10 or 11 specialists at control posts to be foreigners (Total at each post to be 30)	2-2-59	3
Control Commission: 3 Soviet, 3 West, and 1 neutral	2-11-59	1
Responsible duties for foreigners at control posts (not to be just observers)	2-20-59	3
Agrees to peaceful detonations (if able to see internal design)	2-23-59	4
Proposes amendment article requiring 2/3 rather than unanimity (but must be ratified by the three)	3-19-59	2
Agrees to U.S. duration article allowing withdrawal under specified circumstances	3-19-59	3
Agrees to U.S. proposal for periodic review of the inspection system	3-19-59	2
Accepts concept of quota for on-site inspection	4-23-59	4
No veto for on-site inspection if within bounds of quota	4-27-59	3
Agrees to technical discussion of methods for detecting high-altitude tests	5-14-59	2
Agrees to consider creation of a permanent corps of inspectors at headquarters	6-9-59	2
Veto not to be used in regard to on-site inspection at any stage	6-11-59	3
Raises foreign inspectors at control post to 6 or 7	6-22-59	2
Drops veto re treaty violations	6-30-59	4
Will drop veto on staffing when agreement is reached on that subject	6-30-59	2
Drops item veto on budget	6-30-59	2

USSR Concessions and Retractions	Date	Mag.
Will delete veto on control posts and aircraft routes if these matters will be defined in advance with the host country (host country would have right to propose alternative routes)	7-16-59	3
Proposes that 10 of 30 specialists at each control post be foreign	7-24-59	2
Agrees to technical study re Berkner findings	11-24-59	2
Administrator may recommend inspection sites, patterns for air sampling flights and equipment	12-3-59	2
Will accept control posts of thirds (last third divided again into thirds) if West agrees to 3-3-1 commission.	12-14-59	1
If 3-3-1 proposal accepted, Soviets will allow 2/3 vote on budget: Each state's share must be inserted in treaty	12-14-59	1
Parity between two sides of observers on air flights	2-4-60	2
Accepts British idea for criteria for inspection of suspicious events (e.g., localization in 200 sq. kilometers, etc.)	2-16-60	2
Joint research could begin immediately after signature, but need use only chemical explosives	2-17-60	1
Agrees to a ban above 4.75 magnitude with a *moratorium* below that level	3-19-60	4
Agrees to unilateral moratorium on tests below threshold (to last 4-5 years)	5-3-60	2
Will allow limited number of underground tests to verify detection effectiveness, but no decoupling experiments	5-3-60	2
No research on Soviet territory; USSR to have a veto over U.S. research (retraction)	6-3-60	-3
Proposes 3 deputy administrators including one neutral who would succeed administrator if latter unable to fulfill functions	6-21-60	2
Soviets accept 5 deputies, but object to administrator appointing 4	7-5-60	2
Proposes 3 on-site inspections annually, including events both above and below 4.75 magnitude (retraction)	7-26-60	-2
It will take four years to construct the control system, and on-site inspection is to be postponed for that long (retraction).	8-11-60	-1

USSR Concessions and Retractions	*Date*	*Mag.*
Soviet demand for troika in administrative office (retraction)	3-21-61	−5
Soviets insist on linking test ban with disarmament (retraction)	6-4-61	−5
Not to be any controls for test ban "while the arms race and intensified military preparations continue . . . " (retraction)	8-28-61	−5
Soviets resume testing (retraction)	9-1-61	−3
Proposes treaty with national systems of detection for atmospheric explosions and a moratorium on underground tests while adequate internal detection procedures are devised	12-5-61	1
Accepts neutral nation suggestion that nation allow visits to "suspicious and significant events upon invitation"	4-24-62	2
Suggests creation of an international scientific organ to examine the data of national observation posts	4-24-62	2
Accepts notion of automatic seismological instruments (black box)	12-3-62	4
Proposes three automatic seismic stations with international teams to remove recording device	12-10-62	1
Accepts notion of two or three on-site inspections	12-19-62	2
Agrees to relocate proposed automatic seismic stations if U.S. desires	1-7-63	1
Khrushchev proposes ban on tests in atmosphere, outer space, and underwater without control; not to include underground tests	7-2-63	5

Table A.4 U.S. Concessions: Test Ban Negotiations

U.S. Concessions and Retractions	*Date*	*Mag.*
Offers not only limitation of tests but ultimate elimination (linked to nuclear production cut-off)	1-12-57	3
Agrees to place nuclear test ban in first stage of disarmament program	7-5-57	3
Dulles proposes 10-month test suspension	7-22-57	2

U.S. Concessions and Retractions	Date	Mag.
Agrees to 12-month suspension and 12-month extension if satisfactory progress toward nuclear production cut-off	8-21-57	2
Hardtack data presented. Desires Commission to discuss (retraction)	1-5-59	−2
Drops link between test ban and disarmament	1-19-59	5
Control post staff in USSR: one-half Anglo-American, one-half "International," and no nationals in key positions	1-26-59	1
Accepts qualified veto re revision of treaty, new detection methods, air routes, budgets	2-5-59	3
Control Commission: 3 permanent, 1 Soviet, 1 West, and 2 neutrals (if Soviets drop veto)	3-2-59	2
Staff Headquarters: one-third each side; top positions parity	3-5-59	3
Agrees to unanimity in selecting administrator	3-4-59	3
Treaty to remain indefinitely, subject to inherent right to withdrawal in case of violation or inadequate control	3-10-59	2
Eisenhower calls for atmospheric and underwater test ban instead of comprehensive one (retraction)	4-13-59	−4
Accepts Soviet proposal as modified by U.K. on amendments that would require ratification by all three	4-14-59	2
Agrees to quota for on-site inspections but with no veto	5-5-59	4
Agrees to concept of a limited number of nationals having technical functions at control posts	5-8-59	3
Specified the number of 4 or 5 nationals for control posts	6-22-59	1
Staffing of control posts by thirds (administrator and 10 technical personnel may come from host country)	7-20-59	3
The deputy administrator or some other individual chosen by the Control Commission will be acting administrator in case of no agreement on successor	1-29-60	2
Phased comprehensive treaty: 4.75 level but no moratorium below	2-11-60	1
Qualified acceptance of Soviet criteria for suspicious events. Regards localization in 200 sq. kilometers as too small	3-2-60	2

U.S. Concessions and Retractions	Date	Mag.
A representative of the host national may accompany international observers on aerial flights	3-14-60	2
Proposes *unilaterally* declared moratorium for tests below 4.75 (contingent on treaty signature and research provisions)	3-29-60	4
Proposes to stagger terms of administrator and deputy (to minimize succession problem)	4-8-60	1
Agrees to permanent flight routes if Soviet Union accepts proposal for selection of 2 technical observers for each flight by the administrator	4-13-60	2
Third-third of control staff to be proportioned so as not to prejudice the legitimate interests of both sides	5-9-60	2
Agrees to localization of 200 sq. kilom. except where insufficient control posts around event—in such a case area would be 500 sq. kilom	5-12-60	2
Proposes two assistant adminstrators just below deputy adminstrator	6-28-60	1
Agrees to British proposal for 5 deputy administrators (East-West parity plus 1)	7-6-60	2
Pool old nuclear weapons for research purposes (if Soviets agree U.S. will get Congress to OK showing of internal design of these old weapons)	7-12-60	3
Finally specified length of underground test moratorium (2 years or as long as research progresses plus 3 months to evaluate)	9-27-60	2
Five deputies-appointed by administrator and confirmed by the commission	10-20-60	2
Agrees to 3-year moratorium for underground tests	3-21-61	2
Agrees to *total* ban on high altitude tests	3-21-61	3
Agrees to accept Soviet safeguards for nuclear devices used in research	3-21-61	1
Will reduce control posts in USSR from 21 to 19 (Reduce one in U.S.)	3-21-61	1
Will allow Soviets to have twice as many annual inspections of opponent's territory	3-21-61	2
Proposes parity for Control Commission (4 West, 4 Soviet, and 3 neutrals).	3-21-61	4
Right to veto budget as whole, but not an item veto	3-21-61	3

U.S. Concessions and Retractions	Date	Mag.
Makes it mandatory that third-third (control posts) be divided equally between East, West, and neutrals.	3-28-61	3
Proposes sliding scale on inspections—12 to 20 annually	5-29-61	2
With more manned or unmanned control posts, U.S. will agree to reduce or even abolish threshold	8-28-61	3
Control Commission by majority vote may recommend control system to be used for reduced threshold 6 months before moratorium on underground tests ends.	8-28-61	2
On-site inspection teams may consist of 50% from nonaligned countries.	8-30-61	2
Atmospheric test ban with no controls	9-3-61	3
Refuses test moratorium during procedural talks (retraction)	12-5-61	−1
Expressed acceptance of nationally owned and operated detection networks	2-12-62	3
Proposes to shorten time before beginning of inspection process (retraction)	2-12-62	−2
Agrees to allocate limited number of inspections to areas of low seismic activity	3-15-62	1
Reduces seismic threshold to 0	3-15-62	2
Accepts eight-nation plan if it is read to mean nations "must" accept the control commissions inspection parties	5-29-62	1
Will reduce number of on-site inspections subject to acceptance of recognition procedures for international control of seismic events	8-6-62	2
Hints reduction if in-country permanent stations subject to international control of their technical adequacy	8-6-62	2
Uninspected treaty to be extended to all but underground tests	8-31-62	2
Proposed that the number of automatic seismic stations be in three figures	12-11-62	0
Suggests 8-10 on-site inspections per year	12-28-62	2
7-10 automatic seismic stations on Soviet territory	2-12-62	2
Lowers on-site inspection to six annually	5-22-63	1

Table A.5 USSR Concessions in the Salt Talks

USSR Concessions and Retractions	Date	Mag.
Open ocean sanctuaries where anti-submarine warfare would be prohibited	12-69	3
Accepts U.S. ABM proposal for NCA	4-70	3
Unverifiable MIRV ban on production and deployment but not testing	5-70	2
Indicated no serious opposition to a prohibition on SAM upgrading	7-70	2
U.S. foreign-based systems would be allowed in return for higher ceilings for Soviets in ICBMs and SLBMs	8-70	3
Agrees to U.S. proposal to prohibit intercontinental sea and land-based cruise missiles.	11-70	2
Agrees to a standing commission to consider ambiguities in the implementation of the agreement	12-70	3
Agrees not to count U.S. medium-range bombers in the ceiling	12-70	3
Will count SS-11s directed toward Europe	12-70	3
Agrees to ban on inland water missile launchers	12-70	2
Agrees to noninterference with national means of inspection	12-70	4
Will count SLBMs on diesel-powered subs (previously only those on nuclear subs were to be counted)	12-70	3
Prefers NCA but will settle for something else	2-71	2
Kissinger and Dobrynin agree upon offensive weapons freeze with provision for modernization	3-71	2
Returns to rigid insistence on NCA only (retraction)	3-71	− 2
Georgi Arbatov informs U.S. that SS-9 slowdown is indicative of willingness to negotiate on heavy missiles	4-71	2
Willing to consider limits on ABM radar installations	4-71	2
U.S. can have one ABM site around Washington and *one* at an ICBM site while USSR could have one around Moscow and *two* around ICBM fields.	4-71	2
Hints U.S. could have both its ABM sites around ICBM field	5-71	3
Decision supporting Interim Offensive Agreement plus ABM implied Soviets have dropped demand on limiting forward-based systems.	5-71	3

USSR Concessions and Retractions	Date	Mag.
Will stop ICBM construction when an ABM agreement is reached	5-71	2
Offers to join MBFR talks matching a long-standing NATO proposal	5-71	2
Proposes ban on development and testing of ABM warheads as well as actual deployment (U.S. rejected; concerned about verification)	8-71	3
Accepts U.S. position for ban on deployment of future exotic ABM systems	8-71	3
Will not give early warning radars ABM capability; will not test in ABM mode or deploy them except at locations on periphery and directed outward	8-71	2
Proposes ABM around each capital plus one at ICBM site	9-71	2
Agreements signed on improving hot line and avoidance of nuclear war	9-71	2
Preliminary understanding on measures to prevent incidents between warships on the high seas; idea pressed by Nixon	10-71	1
Accepts ban on ABM systems for defense of country or an individual region (indicative of Soviet acceptance of mutual assured destruction)	11-71	2
Agrees not to convert from light to heavy missiles	12-71	4
Accepts U.S. proposal that offensive missile freeze can be reflected in a formal agreement	1-72	2
Agrees not to relocate ICBM silos	1-72	2
Agrees in principle to a sublimit on SS-9	1-72	3
Agrees to SLBM freeze	4-72	4
Agrees to ban on all large ABM type radars, subject to certain defined exceptions	4-72	2
Accepts U.S. demand for a 5-year Interim Offensive Arms Treaty	4-72	2
While still refusing to define a heavy missile, accepts limit on increase in size of silos by 10-15%	5-72	3
Tacitly accepts U.S. estimate of 41-42 existing subs, which would require the Soviet Union to retire a higher number of conventional sub to stay within its 62 limit	5-72	3

USSR Concessions and Retractions	Date	Mag.
Accepts 1,500 kilometer distance between ABM sites as proposed by U.S.	5-72	1
Agreed interpretation that there shall be no significant increase in number of ICBM or SLBM tests	5-72	3
Modifies nuclear no-use pledge proposal by indicating that it would not affect obligations to third parties or the right of collective self defense	7-72	3
Expresses a general interest in setting limits on MIRV	11-72	3
Concedes principle of qualitative limitations	6-73	4
Agreement on Prevention of Nuclear War	6-73	2
To conclude permanent treaty on offensive weapons by end of 1974	6-73	3
Asks for an extra 60 launchers to compensate for FBS and China threat (retraction)	7-73	−2
Outrageous Soviet draft; called the 21 Soviet demands; emphasis on withdrawal of nuclear forces abroad and halting of B-1 and Trident (retraction)	9-73	−4
Proposes limit on number of nuclear tests	2-74	3
Hints that Soviets might drop insistence on counting FBS at very end of process after all other issues are resolved	2-74	3
Agrees to reveal test sites, supply information on geological formations, and permit U.S. to calibrate inspection equipment (Threshold Test Ban Treaty)	3-74	3
Offers U.S. a 10% edge in MIRVed missiles: 1,000 for USSR and 1,100 for U.S.	3-74	3
Agrees to a ten-year offensive missile agreement	4-74	2
Willing to consider on-site inspection re chemical warfare treaty	5-74	4
Signs Threshold Test Ban Treaty	7-74	2
Agreement to reduce to one ABM site each	7-74	2
Accepts equal aggregates on offensive weapons	10-74	3
Drops insistence on including forward-based systems	11-74	4
Accepts 2,400 level (100 lower than desired)	11-74	2
Agrees to heavy missile freeze	11-74	3
Ban on new silo construction	11-74	3

USSR Concessions and Retractions	Date	Mag.
Drops proposed ban on air launched missiles in return for U.S. dropping proposed ban on land mobile missiles	11-74	3
Reintroduces demand for compensation for FBS (retraction)	1-75	-4
Agrees to group MIRVed and single SS-18s separately, along with display of special MIRV handling equipment	5-75	3
Ban on manufacture of new weapons (had in mind B-1, Trident, cruise missiles, and neutron bomb)	6-75	1
Warsaw Pact force level data provided for the first time	6-75	2
Limit both cruise and Backfire	7-75	3
Soviets proposed for the first time during CTB talks to permit on-site inspection of underground nuclear tests	7-75	5
Accepts ban on storing missiles and re-launch equipment near launch sites	9-75	3
Accepts 7,000 pound limit on light missiles and 15,000 on heavy missiles	9-75	2
If a system (including SS-18) has been tested in MIRV mode, all will count as MIRVed	9-75	3
Gromyko accepts cruise bomber proposal but cruised B-1 counts as 3 MIRVed systems and B-52 as one MIRVed	1-76	2
Indicates willingness to reduce aggregate to 2,200	1-76	3
Signs an agreement on modernization or replacement of the one ABM site allowed	9-76	1
Signs an agreement for enhancing communication over the hot line	9-76	1
Agrees not to deploy SS-16 in a mobile mode	3-77	3
U.S. would be allowed to continue development of ALCMs, but must accept a three-year moratorium on ground- and sea-launched versions	5-77	1
Accepts three-tier formula: Vladivostok formula (until 1985); 3-year protocol; joint statement on follow-up negotiations	5-77	3
Wants tests for one new single warhead missile to allow SS-11 but stop MX (retraction)	5-77	−3

USSR Concessions and Retractions	Date	Mag.
Agrees to count only ALCMs › 2,500 kilometers in the MIRV limits	10-77	3
Agrees not to produce, test, or deploy the mobile SS-16	10-77	4
Allow 25-30% on ALCM distance to account for zigzag	11-77	3
May test and develop long-range sea and land cruise missiles even during the protocol if they are not MIRVed	11-77	2
Agrees to make any single warhead ICBM distinguishable from MIRVed launchers to aid in identification	1-78	3
Agrees to total ban on mobile missiles	1-78	3
Agrees to hazy noncircumvention rule that U.S. says will not hamper its ability to cooperate with NATO	3-78	1
Agrees to 1,200 (instead of 1,250) for MIRVed missiles (will allow U.S. 120 ALCMs)	4-78	1
Allow one new MIRV missile (had been trying to stop MX)	4-78	3
Gave up ban on wide-bodied ALCM carriers (747s)	4-78	1
Brezhnev announces in response to Carter decision to defer neutron bomb that the Soviets will not begin production of such bombs unless the U.S. does	4-78	1
Gromyko agrees to 5% limit on increasing or decreasing the physical dimensions of a missile	5-78	3
Total ban on new missiles for entire period (Soviets willing to forego new SS-11 replacement if U.S. would stop MX)	5-78	3
Gromyko indicates acceptance of follow-up missile (either MIRVed or unMIRVed) if U.S. would accede to certain unspecified issues still dividing them	7-78	2
Agrees to fractionism of 4 for SS-17 and 6 for SS-19 if ALCM limit of 20 is not accepted by U.S.	7-78	2
Agrees not to increase Backfire production or payload	9-78	3
Gromyko accepts notion of average number of cruise per bomber provided the number is agreed upon	9-78	2
Withdraws insistence upon a ban on new SLBMs	9-78	3

USSR Concessions and Retractions	*Date*	*Mag.*
Agrees to eliminate range restrictions on ALCMs if U.S. agrees to extend 600-kilometer range limits of ground- and sea-launched cruise missiles into the main treaty	9-78	2
Will give up exemption on encryption if U.S will give up conventionally armed cruise	10-78	1
Accepts ban on heavy mobile missiles	10-78	3
Accepts 10 and 14 fractionism limits respectively for ICBMs and SLBMs	10-78	3
Agrees to give advance notification of all extraterritorial launches and all tests involving more than one ICBM in the air at a time	10-78	2
U.S. may continue to test ground- and sea-launched cruise during whole treaty period	10-78	3
Average ALCM per bomber raised from 20 to 25	10-78	1
Reversed position on downsizing from 5% preferred by U.S. to 20% (retraction)	12-78	− 3
Agrees to ban encryption when it impedes verification (drops 10-78 condition)	12-78	3
If in force by March 31, 1979, protocol would expire March 31, 1981	12-78	1
Agrees to provide disclosures about numbers of own arsenal	12-78	2
Average ALCMs per bomber raised to 27	12-78	1
Will allow 10 seismic monitoring devices on Soviet territory to monitor comprehensive test ban treaty	1-79	2
Accepts 28 average for ALCMs but U.S. must make a statement indicating it does not plan to deploy more than 20 per carrier	1-79	1
Reduces proposed limit on downsizing of missiles from 20% to 10%	2-79	1
Brezhnev to produce letter indicating a limit of Backfire production to no more than 30 per year and USSR will not upgrade it to perform missions of heavy bombers	3-79	2
Agrees to 28 average for cruise missiles on bombers	3-79	1
Accepts 5% limit on downsizing re length, diameter, and throw-weight of missiles	4-79	3
Accepts December 31, 1981, end to protocol	5-79	1

USSR Concessions and Retractions	Date	Mag.
Accepts restriction on missile release simulations (bus stop feints)	5-79	2
Drops concern about distinguishing Minutemen IIs and IIIs which were placed in the same field in Malmstrom.	5-79	1
Accepts U.S. demand for a more precise definition placing restrictions only on ALCMs not sea- and ground-launched cruise missiles which may be deployed after 1981.	6-79	1
Agrees to dismantle all fractional-orbiting ballistic missile systems and their launchers	−79	3

Table A.6 United States Concessions in the SALT Talks

U.S. Concessions and Retractions	Date	Mag.
Nixon announces he will resubmit Geneva protocol to Senate; also announces unilateral renunciation of bacteriological methods of warfare and a no-first-use of lethal or incapacitating chemicals	11-69	3
Proposed 100 ABM launchers each around Washington and Moscow	3-70	3
MIRV ban on testing and deployment, but not on production (inspection required)	3-70	2
Freedom to mix delivery systems within an overall ceiling	7-70	3
Will exclude Soviet MRBMs, IRBMs, and cruise missiles from numerical limits	8-70	3
Offers to limit Safeguard in return for Soviet limit of 250 heavy missiles	8-70	2
Abandons efforts for MIRV control, reduction, and comprehensive offensive arms limitation	8-70	1
Nixon wrote Brezhnev suggesting U.S. might help Soviets modernize if Soviets soften their position on political issues like SALT	1-71	2
Drops demand for equality in numbers of offensive weapons	1-71	4
Kissinger indicates that SLBMs could either be included or excluded	2-71	3

U.S. Concessions and Retractions	Date	Mag.
Kissinger suggests 18-month to 2-year interim offensive missile freeze	2-71	1
Rise in aggregate to 2,000 offensive launchers with no sublimit for missiles	2-71	2
Modernization and replacement of offensive launchers would be allowed	3-71	3
Moscow could keep Galosh and U.S. could complete four Safeguard sites (retraction)	3-71	−4
Each side could have one NCA or three ABM sites at ICBM fields	3-71	1
Freeze only selected systems (mentioned only ICBMs with no reference to a sub-limit on heavy missiles)	5-71	2
Revives insistence on including SLBMs (retraction)	8-71	−3
Freeze on ICBMs as of December 31, 1971	8-71	1
Two ABM sites for U.S. at ICBM sites and one for the Soviets to protect Moscow	8-71	1
Agreements signed on improving hot line and avoidance of accidental war	9-71	2
Agrees that ABM limits can be in the form of a treaty	1-72	2
Proposes equality re ABM (2 + 2) *provided* Soviets agree to include SLBMs (otherwise 2 to 1).	3-72	2
If Soviets would include SLBM, U.S. would allow Soviet offensive numerical advantage, subject to their scrapping SS-7 and SS-8 plus a certain number of H-class submarines.	4-72	3
Nixon assures Brezhnev that U.S. will stop at 656 SLBMs rather than go to the 710 allowed in SALT I	5-72	2
Nixon commits U.S. not to dismantle and replace the Titan ICBM in exchange for the right to deploy the Trident submarine	5-72	2
Withdraws proposal that Interim agreement explicitly ban mobile land-based ICBMs (used a unilateral statement instead)	5-72	2
Offers to halt deployments of Minuteman combined with a ban on flight tests of new MIRVs (Soviets reject because of the latter provision)	11-72	1

U.S. Concessions and Retractions	*Date*	*Mag.*
Kissinger hints to Dobrynin that U.S. would not develop ALCMs over 3,000 kilometers in range if Soviets would not MIRV heavy missiles	5-73	3
Agreement on Prevention of Nuclear War	6-73	2
Accepts provision that surveillance of qualitative limits would be conducted by national means of detection	6-73	5
To conclude a permanent treaty on offensive weapons by the end of 1974	6-73	2
Proposes throw-weight limit on MIRV in return for 2-3 year extension of Interim Offensive Missile agreement	3-74	2
No limits on payloads of long-range bombers or missiles without MIRVs	3-74	3
Agrees to a ten-year offensive missile agreement	4-74	2
U.S. could have more MIRVs and Soviets more throw-weight	4-74	2
Moscow could MIRV 700 ICBMs; Washington 550 MIRVed Minutemen plus 500 MIRVed SLBMs	6-74	2
Signs Threshold Test Ban Treaty	7-74	2
No throw-weight limit on MIRV	7-74	3
Agreement to reduce to one ABM site each	7-74	2
Proposes equal MIRV limit of 1,000	10-74	3
Gives green light to mobile ICBMs (long favored by USSR)	11-74	3
Accepts 2,400 level (300 higher than wanted)	11-74	2
Accepts 1,320 MIRV limit (preferred 1,000)	11-74	2
Agrees not to emplace MX on seagoing ships, ocean floor, or air-launched vehicles.	11-74	2
Allows Soviets to keep all their heavy missiles	11-74	3
Won't count Backfire bomber in the 2,400 aggregate	11-74	4
Air-launched missiles in excess of 600 kilometers are to be limited (later claims proposal does not refer to cruise missiles)	11-74	3
Accepts SS-18 in both MIRV and single modes with verification by national technical means if Soviets will group in kind and display MIRV handling equipment	5-75	3

U.S. Concessions and Retractions	Date	Mag.
Would allow 200-400 Backfire bombers above the Vladivostok ceiling in return for corresponding number of U.S. cruise missile carriers	9-75	2
Kissinger offers 120 free allowance in Backfire bomber	1-76	2
Proposes limit of 275 Backfire bombers for 5 years during which U.S. could place cruise missiles on surface ships	1-76	2
Heavy bombers with cruise missiles would count against 1,320 MIRV ceiling	1-76	3
Proposes reducing SALT ceiling from 2,400 to 2,200 (retraction)	1-76	−1
Ford administration decides not to accept Kissinger-Gromyko Backfire-cruise solution reached in January. Asks instead that these issues be set aside temporarily for three years while ratifying Vladivostok ceilings (retraction)	2-76	−2
Signs Treaty on Underground Nuclear Explosions for Peaceful Purposes (includes on-site inspection)	5-76	2
Signs an agreement on modernization or replacement of the one ABM site allowed	9-76	1
Signs an agreement for enhancing communication over the hot line	9-76	1
Prohibition on construction of new ICBM launchers (Stop MX as well as new Soviet ICBMs)	3-77	3
Limit heavy missiles to 150 (retraction)	3-77	−2
Proposal for deep and unequal cuts (retraction)	3-77	−4
Ban on development, testing, and deployment of all nuclear and conventional cruise missiles of less than intercontinental range	3-77	3
Two- to three-year executive agreement limiting cruise missiles (rejected; not as strong as a treaty)	5-77	2
Allow 190 heavy missiles to be MIRVed	5-77	1
Carter accepts moratorium on testing and developing sea and land cruise missiles with a range over 600 kilometers	5-77	3
Carter publicly accedes to Soviet demand that Vladivostok be the basis for discussion	7-77	3

U.S. Concessions and Retractions	Date	Mag.
Offers 220 and subsequently 250 heavy missiles to the USSR	7-77	1
Won't count Backfire as a strategic weapon if Soviets formally agree to restrictions on refuelling and basing	9-77	3
U.S. will continue to honor Interim Agreement after its October 1977 expiration date	9-77	2
Gave up on insistence of reducing Soviet heavy missile force; allows them to keep all 308	9-77	2
Proposes 120 ALCM allowance within the 1,320 MIRV limit; U.S. may buy extra ALCM carries by paying a price in MIRVed missiles but Soviet could not do same (modified version of January 1976 proposal which U.S. had backed off).	9-77	2
Won't count Backfire if limited to current rate of 25 per year	11-77	3
Heavy bombers with cruise missiles will not count as part of MIRV sublimits	3-78	2
Offers to modify aircraft armed with cruise missiles to distinguish them from civilian transports	4-78	2
Offers two alternatives: 1. Ban on new missile types during protocol period. 2. Ban with one exception (MIRVed or unMIRVed) for treaty duration	4-78	2
Accepts 2,250 overall ceiling (had proposed 2,160)	4-78	1
Agrees to December 31, 1981, expiration date of protocol	4-78	1
Carter suggests U.S. might compromise on number of ALCMs per plane if Soviets will allow 10 warheads on MX	9-78	1
Changes position by proposing a ban on the testing of depressed-projectory missiles (retraction)	9-78	−2
Withdraws proposed exemption for conventionally armed cruise missiles on aircraft other than heavy bomber	11-78	3
Agrees to reduce average number of ALCMs allowed on bomber from 35 to 30	11-78	1
Accepts Soviet proposal banning multiple warheads on cruise missiles	12-78	3

U.S. Concessions and Retractions	Date	Mag.
Withdraws depressed-projectory missile proposal after Soviets link acceptance of proposal to limits on anti-submarine warfare	12-78	2
U.S. would no longer insist on rigid timetable for reduction to 2,250 level by end of 1981 as long as there was a steady reduction during year	2-79	1
If Moscow would accept 5% limit on downsizing of missiles, Washington would agree to multiple warhead ban on cruise	2-79	1
Agrees to 28 average for cruise missiles on bombers	3-79	1
Accepts joint statement promising not to place more than 20 ALCMs on their current heavy bombers	3-79	2
Vance agrees to provide a formal statement indicating Minuteman would not be MIRVed beyond three warheads	5-79	3
Will provide numerical breakdown on Minuteman IIs and IIIs as well as formal notification if Minuteman IIIs are ever put into Minuteman II silos	5-79	2

Glossary

Air-launched cruise missile (ALCM). Unmanned jet-propelled missile launched from a flying vehicle.

Anti-ballistic missile (ABM) system. Weapon designed to intercept and destroy ballistic missiles.

Anti-satellite (ASAT) system. Weapon system for destroying or damaging artificial earth satellites.

Ballistic missile defense (BMD). Defensive system designed to protect one's own offensive missiles.

Biological weapons (BW). Living organisms or infective material designed to cause death or disease.

CBM. Confidence-building measures designed to reduce anxiety about the other side's intentions.

Chemical weapons (CW). Chemical substances that have direct toxic effects.

Circular error probability. A measure of delivery accuracy based on a 50 percent probability of falling within a given circle.

C^3I. Refers to command, control, communications, and intelligence functions.

Counterforce. Targeting adversary's force capabilities.

Countervalue strategy. Targeting forces against civilian targets.

Encryption. Encoding communications for the purpose of concealing information.

Fission. Process whereby heavy atoms split into lighter nuclei, releasing considerable energy.

Forward-based systems (FBS). Military bases and launching sites close to the territory of the adversary.

Fractional orbital bombardment system (FOBS). A missile that achieves partial orbit, but then is fired back to earth.

Fractionation. The division of the payload of a missile into several warheads.

Functionally related observable differences (FRODs). Requirement that delivery systems with different missions be designed differently.

Fusion. Process in which lighter atoms, especially those of the isotopes of hydrogen, combine to form a heavy atom and in the process release substantial energy.

296

Ground-launched cruise missiles (GLCM). Unmanned jet-propelled missile launched from the ground.

Intercontinental ballistic missile (ICBM). A ballistic missile with a range in excess of 5,500 kilometers.

Interim Offensive Arms Agreement. Part of SALT I agreements that froze ICBMs and SLBMs at existing levels for five years.

Intermediate-range nuclear forces (INF). Nuclear weapons with a range of less than 5,500 kilometers. Sometimes called medium-range if over 1,000 kilometers.

International Atomic Energy Agency (IAEA). A U.N.-related agency that monitors compliance with NPT and safeguards agreements as well as promotes the peaceful uses of nuclear energy.

JCS. Joint Chiefs of Staff.

Kiloton. Measure of explosive yield of a nuclear weapon equivalent to 1,000 tons of TNT.

Limited Test Ban Treaty (LTBT). Treaty signed in 1963 that prohibits nuclear testing in the atmosphere, in outer space, and underwater.

Maneuverable reentry vehicle (MARV). Reentry vehicle whose flight can be adjusted to evade ballistic missile defenses and gain increased accuracy.

Megaton. Measure of explosive yield of a thermonuclear weapon equivalent to one million tons of TNT.

Multiple independently targetable reentry vehicle (MIRV). Reentry vehicles, carried by one missile, which can be directed toward independent targets.

Multiple reentry vehicles (MRV). Multiple warheads that cannot be independently targeted.

National Command Authority (NCA). Top national security decision makers in Washington and Moscow.

National Technical Means of Verification (NTM). Assets such as reconnaissance satellites and radars that are under national control and are used to monitor the other sides' compliance with arms agreements.

Neutron weapon. Nuclear device designed to maximize radiation effects and reduce blast and thermal effects.

Nuclear fuel cycle. Refers to steps from mining fissionable materials to enriching and fabricating fuel elements, reprocessing spent fuel, and disposing of waste.

Nuclear Nonproliferation Treaty (NPT). Treaty negotiated in 1968 to prevent the spread of nuclear weapons to additional states.

Payload. Weapons and penetration aids carried by a delivery vehicle.

Peaceful Nuclear Explosives (PNEs). Explosions designed for civilian purposes such as digging canals. United States and Soviets signed a treaty on the subject in 1976.

Plutonium (Pu). A fissionable material that can be used in nuclear weapons.

Rapid reload. Capability of a launcher firing a second missile within a short period of time.

Reentry vehicle (RV). That part of a strategic ballistic missile that carries a nuclear warhead to its target.

Sea-launched cruise missile (SLCM). Unmanned jet-propelled missile launched from a ship or submarine.

Standing Consultative Commission (SCC). A permanent U.S.-Soviet commission established by SALT I to review issues of treaty implementation and verification.

Strategic Arms Limitation Talks (SALT). Talks on strategic weapons involving the United States and the Soviet Union that lasted from 1969 to 1979.

Strategic Arms Reduction Talks (START). U.S.-Soviet strategic arms talks that began in 1982 and were adjourned *sine die* in December 1983.

Strategic Defense Initiative (SDI). The so-called Star Wars system proposed by President Reagan in March 1983 to provide a national defense against nuclear attack.

Strategic nuclear forces. ICBMs, SLBMs, and bombers capable of intercontinental range.

Submarine-launched ballistic missile (SLBM). A ballistic missile carried in and launched from a submarine.

Telemetry. Data transmitted by radio that convey information about a weapons test.

Thermonuclear weapon. Nuclear weapon in which the main explosive is based upon fusion reactions (also referred to as a hydrogen weapon).

Threshold Test Ban Treaty (TTBT). Treaty signed in 1974 placing a 150-kiloton limit on underground nuclear tests.

Throw-weight. The total weight that can be carried by a missile to target.

TRIAD. Refers to the three components of the U.S. strategic force: ICBMs, SLBMs, and intercontintental-range bombers.

Uranium enrichment. The process of increasing the content of uranium 235 above that found in natural uranium for use in reactors and nucleaer explosives.

Weapon-grade material. Enriched uranium or plutonium suitable for a nuclear weapon.

Yield. Released nuclear explosive energy measured in terms of TNT equivalent. See kiloton and megaton.

Index